ASCENT®

CENTER FOR TECHNICAL KNOWLEDGE

CW01574802

AutoCAD® Civil 3D® 2016 Review for Certification

Official Certification Preparation

Revision 2.0

May 2016

AUTODESK.
Authorized Author

ASCENT - Center for Technical Knowledge®
AutoCAD® Civil 3D® 2016
Review for Certification
Revision 2.0

Prepared and produced by:

ASCENT Center for Technical Knowledge
630 Peter Jefferson Parkway, Suite 175
Charlottesville, VA 22911

866-527-2368
www.ASCENTed.com

Lead Contributor: Michelle Rasmussen

ASCENT - Center for Technical Knowledge is a division of Rand Worldwide, Inc., providing custom developed knowledge products and services for leading engineering software applications. ASCENT is focused on specializing in the creation of education programs that incorporate the best of classroom learning and technology-based training offerings.

We welcome any comments you may have regarding this student guide, or any of our products. To contact us please email: feedback@ASCENTed.com.

AS-CV16RFC-20-SG

Contents

Preface

AutoCAD® Civil 3D® 2016: Review for Certification is a comprehensive review guide to assist in preparing for the AutoCAD Civil 3D 2016 Certified Professional exam. It enables experienced users to review learning content from ASCENT that is related to the exam objectives.

New users of AutoCAD Civil 3D should refer to the Autodesk Official Training Guides (AOTG) from ASCENT, such as:

- *AutoCAD® Civil 3D® 2016 Fundamentals*
- *AutoCAD® Civil 3D® 2016 for Surveyors*

Exam Topic	Exam Objectives	Chapter(s)
Styles	Create and use object styles	• Ch. 1
	Create and use label styles	
Lines and Curves	Use the line and curve commands	• Ch. 2
	Use the Transparent commands	
Points	Create points using the Point Creation commands	• Ch. 3
	Create points by importing point data	
	Use point groups to control the display of point	
Surfaces	Identify key characteristics of surfaces	• Ch. 4
	Create and edit surfaces	
	Use styles and settings to display surface information	
	Create a surface by assembling fundamental data	
	Use styles to analyze surface display results	
	Annotate surfaces	
Parcels	Design a parcel layout	• Ch. 5
	Select parcel styles to change the display of parcels	
	Select styles to annotate parcels	

Exam Topic	Exam Objectives	Chapter(s)
Alignments	Design a geometric layout	• Ch. 6
	Create alignments	
Profiles & Profile Views	Create a surface profile	• Ch. 7
	Design a profile	
	Create a profile view style	
	Create a profile view	
Corridors	Design and create a corridor	• Ch. 8
	Derive information and data from a corridor	
	Design and create an intersection	
Sections and Section Views	Create and analyze sections and section views	• Ch. 9
Pipe Networks	Design and create a pipe network	• Ch. 10
Grading	Design and create a grading model	• Ch. 11
	Create a grading model feature line	
Managing and Sharing Data	Create a data sharing setup	• Ch. 12
Plan Production	Create a sheet set	• Ch. 13
	Use view frames	
Survey	Identify key characteristics of survey data	• Ch. 14
	Use description keys to control the display of points created from survey data	
	Create a boundary drawing from field data	

Note on Software Setup

This review guide assumes a standard installation of the software using the default preferences during installation. Lectures and practices use the standard software templates and default options for the Content Libraries.

Students and Educators can Access Free Autodesk Software and Resources

Autodesk challenges you to get started with free educational licenses for professional software and creativity apps used by millions of architects, engineers, designers, and hobbyists today. Bring Autodesk software into your classroom, studio, or workshop to learn, teach, and explore real-world design challenges the way professionals do.

Get started today - register at the Autodesk Education Community and download one of the many Autodesk software applications available.

Visit www.autodesk.com/joinedu/

Note: Free products are subject to the terms and conditions of the end-user license and services agreement that accompanies the software. The software is for personal use for education purposes and is not intended for classroom or lab use.

Lead Contributor: Michelle Rasmussen

Specializing in the civil engineering industry, Michelle authors training guides and provides instruction, support, and implementation on all Autodesk infrastructure solutions, in addition to general AutoCAD.

Michelle began her career in the Air Force working in the Civil Engineering unit as a surveyor, designer, and construction manager. She has also worked for municipalities and consulting engineering firms as an engineering/GIS technician. Michelle holds a Bachelor's of Science degree from the University of Utah along with a Master's of Business Administration from Kaplan University.

Michelle is an Autodesk Certified Instructor (ACI) as well as an Autodesk Certified Evaluator, teaching and evaluating other Autodesk Instructors for the ACI program. In addition, she holds the Autodesk Certified Professional certification for Civil 3D and is trained in Instructional Design.

As a skilled communicator, Michelle effectively leads classes, webcasts and consults with clients to achieve their business objectives.

Michelle Rasmussen has been the Lead Contributor for *AutoCAD Civil 3D Review for Certification* since its initial release in 2013.

In this Guide

The following images highlight some of the features that can be found in this Student Guide.

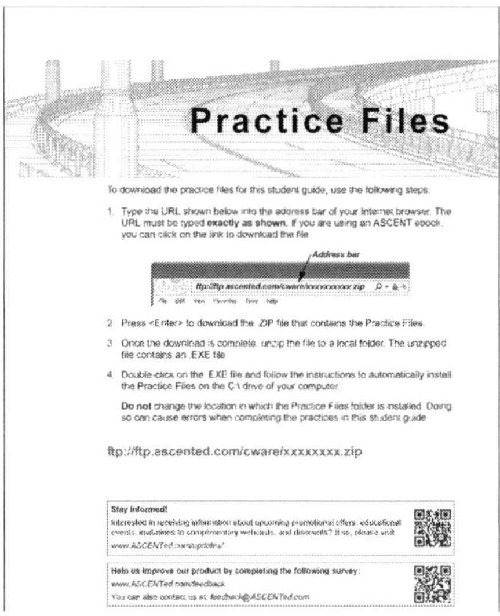

Practice Files

To download the practice files for this student guide, use the following steps.

1. Type the URL shown below into the address bar of your Internet browser. The URL must be typed **exactly as shown**. If you are using an ASCENT ebook, you can click on the link to download the file.

2. Press <Enter> to download the .ZIP file that contains the Practice Files.
3. Once the download is complete, unzip the file to a local folder. The unzipped file contains an .EXE file.
4. Double-click on the .EXE file and follow the instructions to automatically install the Practice Files on the C:\ drive of your computer.

   Do not change the location in which the Practice Files folder is installed. Doing so can cause errors when completing the practices in this student guide.

ftp://ftp.ascented.com/cware/xxxxxxx.zip

Stay Informed!
Interested in receiving information about upcoming promotional offers, educational events, invitations to complementary webcasts, and discounts? If so, please visit *www.ASCENTed.com/updates/*

Help us improve our product by completing the following survey:
www.ASCENTed.com/feedback
You can also contact us at: *feedback@ASCENTed.com*

FTP link for practice files

Practice Files

The Practice Files page tells you how to download and install the practice files that are provided with this student guide.

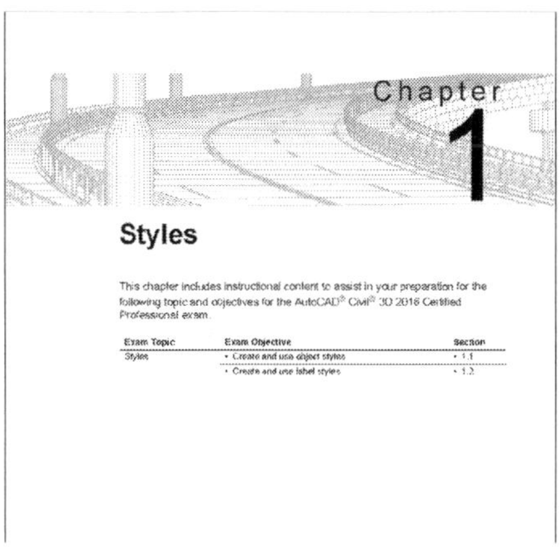

Chapter 1

Styles

This chapter includes instructional content to assist in your preparation for the following topic and objectives for the AutoCAD® Civil® 3D 2016 Certified Professional exam.

Exam Topic	Exam Objective	Section
Styles	• Create and use object styles	• 1.1
	• Create and use label styles	• 1.2

Exam Topics and Objectives in the chapter

Chapters

Each chapter begins with a list of the exam topics and objectives covered in the chapter.

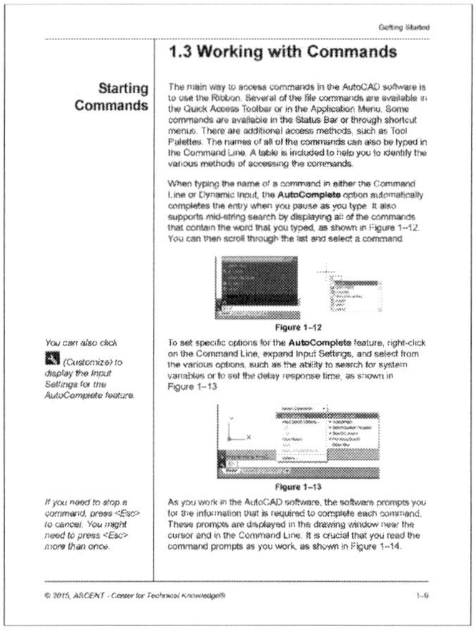

Getting Started

1.3 Working with Commands

Starting Commands

Figure 1–12

Figure 1–13

Side notes

Side notes are hints or additional information for the current topic.

Instructional Content

Each chapter is split into a series of sections of instructional content on specific topics. These lectures include the descriptions, step-by-step procedures, figures, hints, and information you need to achieve the chapter's Learning Objectives.

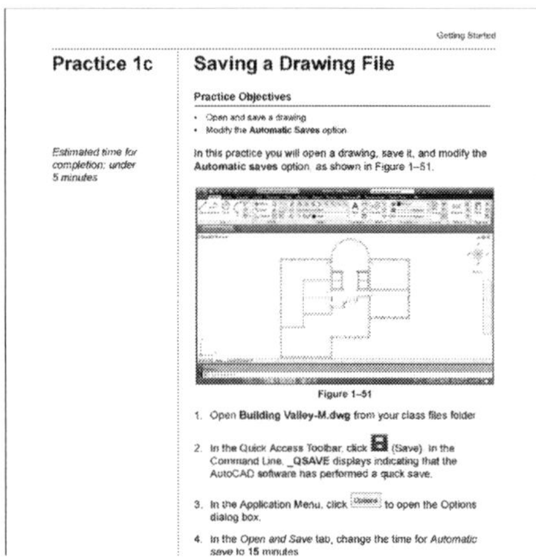

Getting Started

Practice 1c

Saving a Drawing File

Practice Objectives

Figure 1–51

Practice Objectives

Practices

Practices enable you to use the software to perform a hands-on review of a topic.

Some practices require you to use prepared practice files, which can be downloaded from the link found on the Practice Files page.

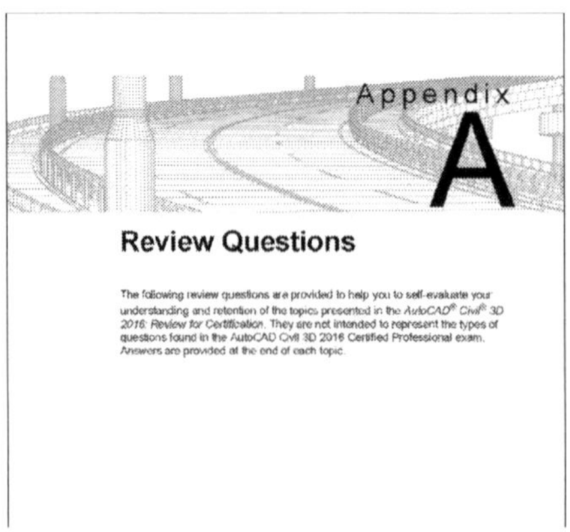

Appendix A

Review Questions

Review Questions

Review questions, located at the end of this guide, enable you to self-evaluate your understanding of the key topics and objectives in this guide.

Practice Files

To download the practice files for this student guide, use the following steps:

1. Type the URL shown below into the address bar of your Internet browser. The URL must be typed **exactly as shown**. If you are using an ASCENT ebook, you can click on the link to download the file.

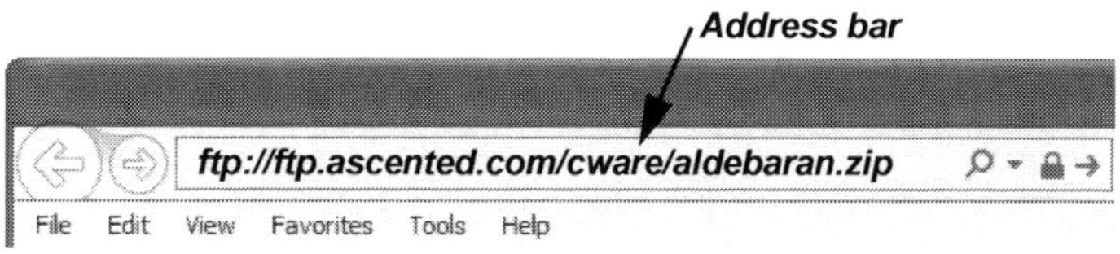

2. Press <Enter> to download the .ZIP file that contains the Practice Files.

3. Once the download is complete, unzip the file to a local folder. The unzipped file contains an .EXE file.

4. Double-click on the .EXE file and follow the instructions to automatically install the Practice Files on the C:\ drive of your computer.

   Do not change the location in which the Practice Files folder is installed. Doing so can cause errors when completing the practices in this student guide.

ftp://ftp.ascented.com/cware/aldebaran.zip

Stay Informed!

Interested in receiving information about upcoming promotional offers, educational events, invitations to complimentary webcasts, and discounts? If so, please visit:

www.ASCENTed.com/updates/

Help us improve our product by completing the following survey:

www.ASCENTed.com/feedback

You can also contact us at: *feedback@ASCENTed.com*

Chapter 1

Styles

This chapter includes instructional content to assist in your preparation for the following topic and objectives for the AutoCAD® Civil® 3D 2016 Certified Professional exam.

Autodesk Certification Exam Objectives in this Chapter

Exam Topic	Exam Objective	Section
Styles	• Create and use object styles	• 1.1
	• Create and use label styles	• 1.2

1.1 Create and Use Object Styles

A drawing template (.DWT extension) contains all blocks, Paper Space title sheets, settings, and layers for a new drawing. As with the AutoCAD software, a template (.DWT) file in the AutoCAD Civil 3D software is the source file from which new drawings acquire their settings, units, layers, blocks, text styles, etc., and therefore, enforces standardization. With the AutoCAD Civil 3D software, in addition to the AutoCAD components noted, the drawing template is also the source for specific AutoCAD Civil 3D styles and settings. As you learn, AutoCAD Civil 3D styles and settings (Feature and Command) have a profound impact on the appearance of objects, labels, and tables. These styles and settings also act as the primary mechanism that controls the behavior and default actions. Selecting the correct template for your intended design and standards needs is a significant component of fully using the benefits that the AutoCAD Civil 3D software offers. Therefore, it is highly recommended that all styles and setting be set up in the template file before you use the AutoCAD Civil 3D software in a project.

To use the AutoCAD Civil 3D software efficiently and effectively, you need to configure styles and settings to control the object display. All of these styles and settings affect the final delivered product and enable you to deliver a product with consistent quality.

To create a template file, use the **Save As** command and in the Save As dialog box, change the *File of Type* to **DWT**.

Drawing Settings in Detail

The values in Drawing Settings influence every aspect of the drafting environment. Each tab has values affecting a specific drawing area. For example, layer naming properties, coordinate systems, default precisions, input and output conventions, abbreviations for alignment, volume units, etc. After implementing the AutoCAD Civil 3D software, you only need to access the first two tabs.

To access Drawing Settings, in the *Settings* tab in Toolspace, select and right-click on the drawing name (at the top), and select **Edit Drawing Settings**.

Units and Zone

In the Drawing Settings dialog box, the *Units and Zone* tab (as shown in Figure 1–1), sets the Model Space plotting scale and coordinate zone for the drawing. The scale can be a custom value or selected from a drop-down list. A zone is selected from a drop-down list of worldwide categories and coordinate systems.

A drawing which has been assigned a coordinate system enables points to report their grid coordinates and/or their longitude and latitude. Conversely, when assigning a coordinate system, grid coordinates and Longitude and Latitude data can create points in a drawing.

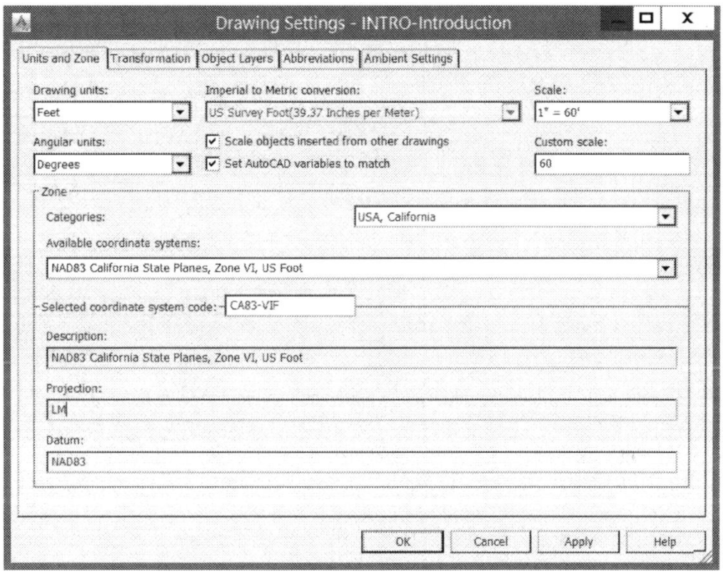

Figure 1–1

When plotting from the *Model* tab, the drawing scale in the upper right corner is the scale at which you would prefer the drawing to be printed. When in the *Model* tab, changing this scale automatically updates all AutoCAD Civil 3D annotations that are scale-dependent. (AutoCAD Civil 3D annotations are automatically resized for correct plotting in each viewport that displays them based on that viewport's scale.)

Changing the drawing scale does not automatically change the **Itscale** variable, since it assumes that you most often prefer to leave it at **Itscale = 1**. If this is not the case, you need to assign this variable manually. Refer to the AutoCAD User Guide if you need more information on variables, such as **Itscale**.

You can also set the drawing scale by assigning a different annotation scale in the Status Bar, as shown in Figure 1–2. In layouts you can change either the VP Scale or Annotation Scale and have both update.

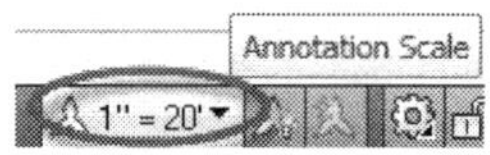

Figure 1–2

Transformation

During the life of a project, there can be reasons to change local point coordinates to a coordinate system. The values in the *Transformation* tab (as shown in Figure 1–3), transform local coordinates to a State Plan Coordinate system, UTM system, or other defined planar system.

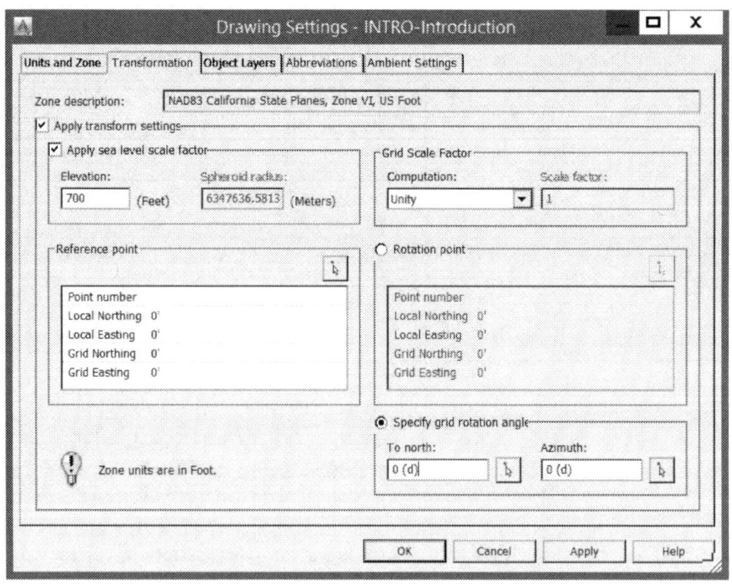

Figure 1–3

Object Layers

The *Object Layers* tab (shown in Figure 1–4), assigns layer names to AutoCAD Civil 3D objects. A modifier, which can be a prefix or a suffix, is associated with each layer's name. The value of the modifier can be anything that is typed into its *Value* field. Traditionally, the value is an * (asterisk) with a separator (a dash or underscore). The AutoCAD Civil 3D software replaces the asterisk with the name of the object of the same type. For example, the base surface layer name is **C-TOPO** with a suffix modifier of -* (a dash followed by an asterisk). When a surface named **Existing** is created, it is placed on the layer **C-TOPO-EXISTING**, and when a surface named **Base** is created it is placed on the layer **C-TOPO-BASE**.

The last column of the *Object Layers* tab enables you to lock the values. When a value is locked at this level, the AutoCAD Civil 3D software does not permit it to be changed by any lower style or setting.

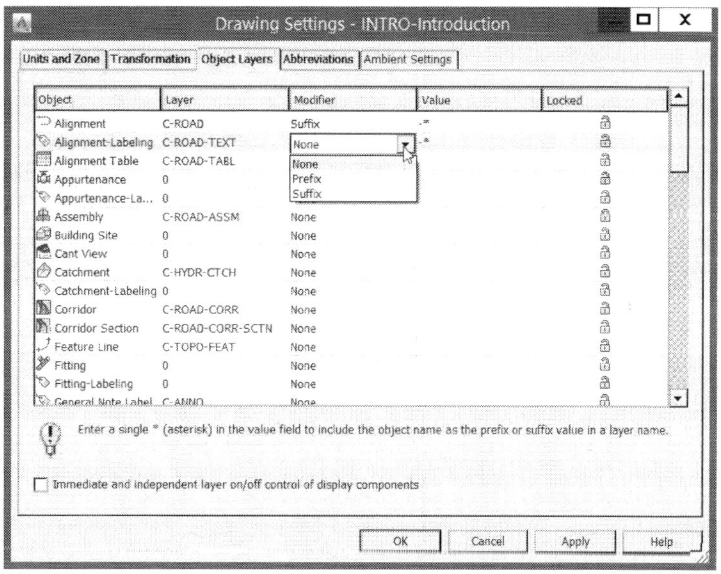

Figure 1–4

To change the listed object layers, double-click on a layer name. In the Layer Selection dialog box (shown in Figure 1–5), select the layer from the list. If the layer does not exist, click **New** in the Layer Selection dialog box. This opens a second dialog box, in which you can define a new layer for the object type.

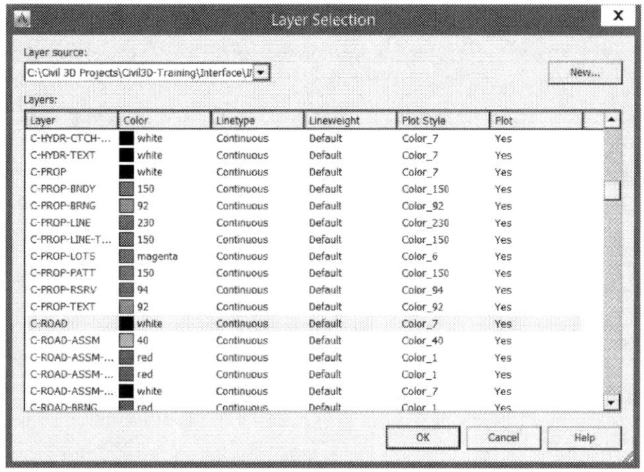

Figure 1–5

Abbreviations

The *Abbreviations* tab (shown in Figure 1–6), sets standard values for reports referencing alignment or profile data. Some entries in this panel have text format strings that define how the values associated with the abbreviation display in a label.

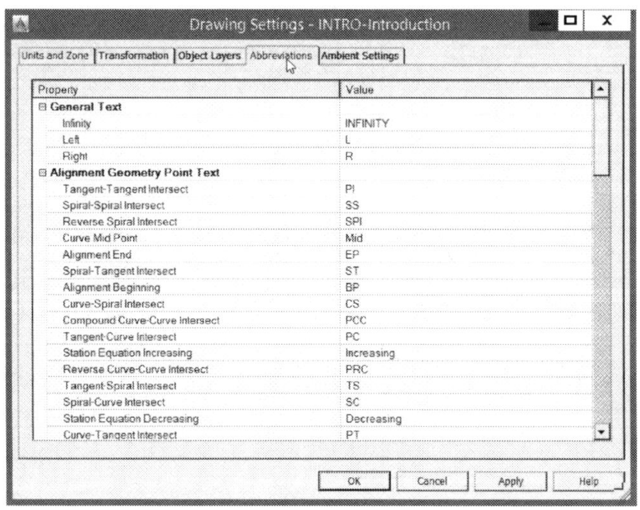

Figure 1–6

Ambient Settings

In the *Ambient Settings* tab (shown in Figure 1–7), the values influence prompting and reports. For example, the *Direction* area affects the prompting for direction input: **Decimal Degrees**, **Degrees Minutes and Seconds** (with or without spaces), or **Decimal Degrees Minutes and Seconds**. Any value set at this level affects everything (labels and commands) in the drawing.

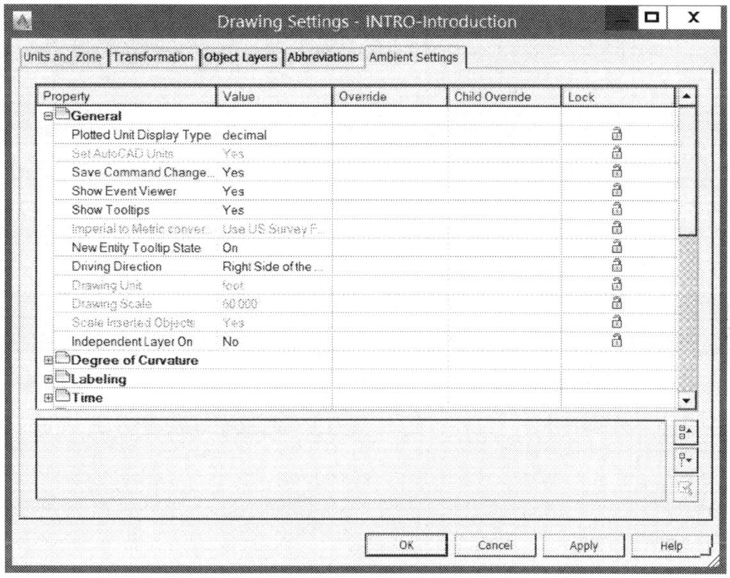

Figure 1–7

Edit Label Style Defaults

The values assigned in the Edit Label Style Defaults dialog box (shown in Figure 1–8), control text style, plan orientation, and the basic behavior of label styles. Similar to Feature Settings, this dialog box is available at the drawing level and at the individual objects level. Editing Label Style defaults at the drawing level affects all label styles in the drawing. Editing them at the object level (such as surfaces) only affects that object's labels.

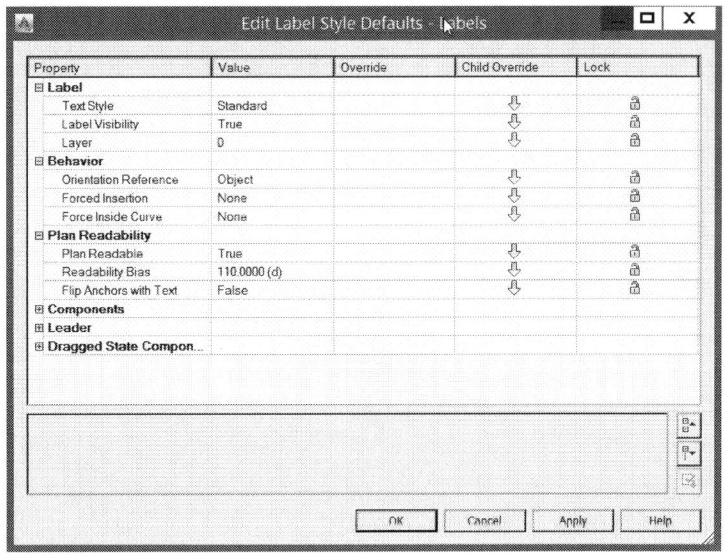

Figure 1–8

In the *Label, Behavior,* and *Plan Readability* areas, the values affect the overall visibility of labels, their default text style, label orientation, and the rotation angle that affects plan readability.

The values in the *Components, Leader,* and *Dragged State Components* areas affect the default text height for the label, colors for the text, leader, surrounding box, and type of leader. There are also several settings defining what happens to a label when you drag it from its original position.

Edit Autodesk LandXML Settings

The LandXML Settings dialog box (shown in Figure 1–9), provides settings that control how Autodesk LandXML data is imported and exported from the AutoCAD Civil 3D software. Autodesk LandXML is a universal format for storing Surveying and Civil Engineering data that enables you to transfer points, terrain models, alignments, etc., between different software platforms. For more information, see *www.landxml.org* and the AutoCAD Civil 3D Help system. The dialog box can be opened by right-clicking on Drawing Name in the *Settings* tab and selecting **Edit LandXMLSettings**.

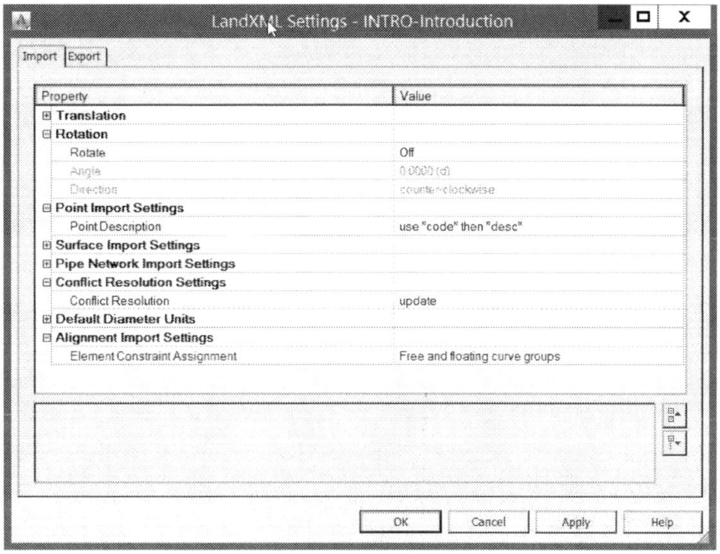

Figure 1–9

Feature Settings

In Settings, each object type collection has an Edit Feature Settings dialog box, as shown for Surface in Figure 1–10. Its main function is to assign default naming values, initial Object and Label styles, and overriding the default values found in Edit Drawing Settings for that object type. You can access the feature settings by right-clicking on the object tree in the *Settings* tab and selecting **Edit Feature Settings**.

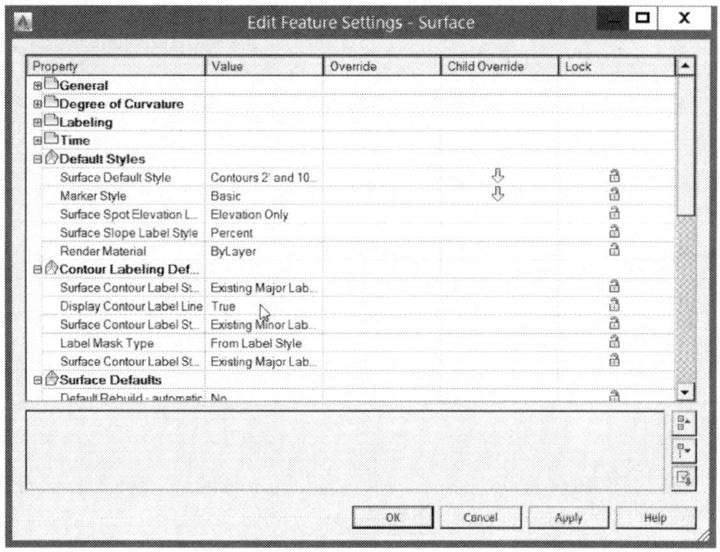

Figure 1–10

Command Settings

Similar to feature settings, in the Edit Command Settings dialog box (shown in Figure 1–11), you can set the default object and label styles used when creating objects with a specific command. Each object type contains a unique set of commands. Typical values in these dialog boxes include the name format (surface 1, parcel 1, etc.), design criteria (minimum area, frontage, length of vertical curve, and minimum horizontal curve), etc. To open the dialog box, expand a collection in Settings until the commands are displayed. Right-click on the command to which you want to assign default settings and select **Edit Command Settings**.

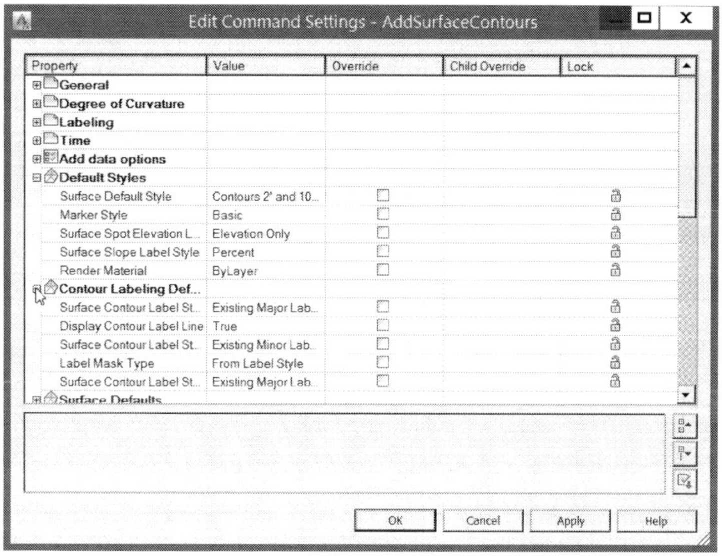

Figure 1–11

Hint: Style and Setting Overrides

In the Edit Label Style Defaults, Feature Settings and similar dialog boxes, a downward pointing arrow in the Child Override column indicates that a setting or style lower in the settings tree has a different value than the one displayed. Selecting the arrow (which creates a red **x** over the icon) and clicking **OK** removes the variant settings and makes all lower settings and styles match those assigned in the dialog box. This can be a quick way of standardizing multiple settings dialog boxes and styles at the same time.

For example, in the Surface Label Style defaults window (shown in Figure 1–12), some surface label styles are assigned a layer other than 0 and a visibility of false, because an arrow is present in the *Child Override* column. Since an arrow is not shown for the Text Style property, all surface label styles are using a text style of **Standard**.

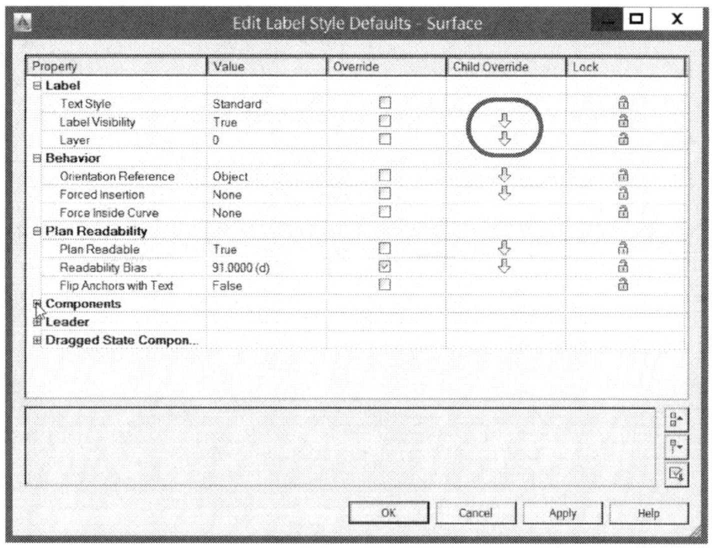

Figure 1–12

The *Override* column indicates whether a value in this window is overriding a higher settings dialog box. Clicking the **Lock** icon prevents you from changing that value in a lower setting's dialog box or style

Styles

Styles are preconfigured groups of settings specific to an individual object type or label that make the objects print the way you want them to print. For example, in the list of surface styles shown in Figure 1–13, each surface style is configured differently to display different features, such as contours at different intervals and on the correct layers. The display of a terrain model could be changed by swapping one surface style for another. Styles enable an organization to standardize the look of their graphics by providing preconfigured groupings of display settings.

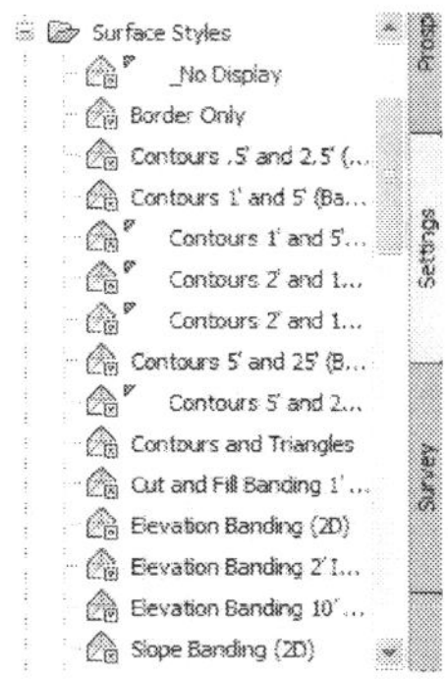

Figure 1–13

The two categories of styles you work with most often are Object Styles and Label Styles. Some objects have table styles as well. Object styles control how AutoCAD Civil 3D objects (points, surfaces, alignments, etc.) display, what combination of components the object displays, which layers they display on, and many other settings. Label Styles are similar except that they control the text and other annotations associated with the objects.

For example, an alignment object style specifies many settings including the layers on which to draw tangents and curve segments (which might be different) and which symbols to add at certain points as required (such as a triangle at the PI point). Alignment label styles include major and minor station labels, the display of station equations, design speeds, and similar annotation. By separating object and label styles, you can mix and match the right combination for a specific object.

Styles are the lowest items in the Settings tree and are typically dependent on other settings above them. If a style is given a unique setting, different from feature settings or label style defaults (such as a different text height), then that style is considered to have an override.

Styles in Depth

Styles are central to the AutoCAD Civil 3D software. Their flexibility enables an Office or Company to create a unique *look* for their drawings. By changing the assigned style, you can change the composition of a profile view as shown in Figure 1–14.

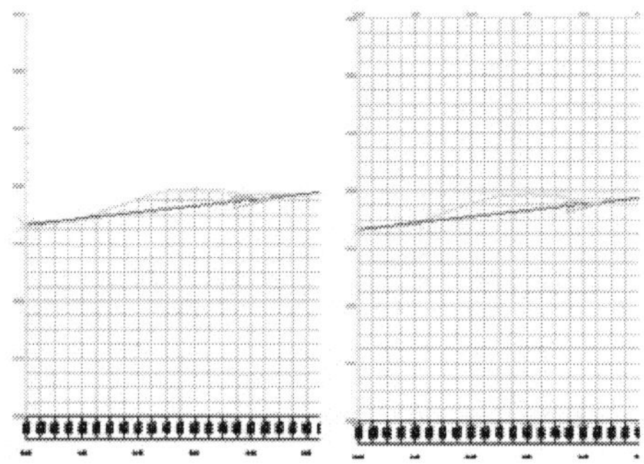

Figure 1–14

In the *Settings* tab in Toolspace, an object type branch identifies each style type and lists its styles below each heading. An example is shown in Figure 1–15.

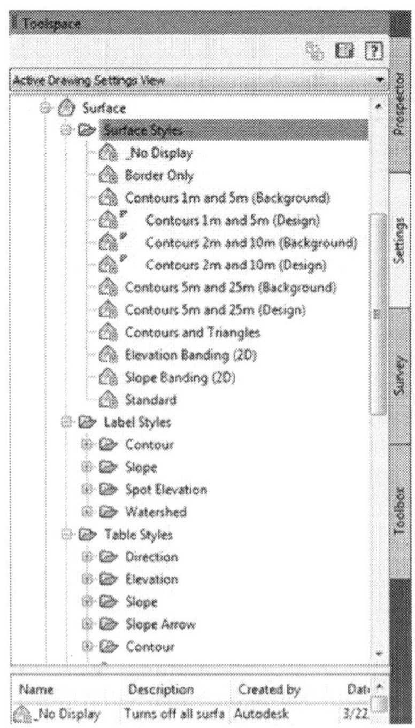

Figure 1–15

Object Styles

Object Styles stylize an object's data for display. To edit a style, in the *Settings* tab, right-click on the style and select **Edit**. Most of the work for all object styles is done in the *Display* tab. For certain objects, other tabs might need to be modified.

For example, in the Surface Style dialog box, the *Display* tab enables you to toggle on or off triangles, borders, contours, and other items as well as define the layer, color, linetype, etc. that are assigned to them, as shown in Figure 1–16. The *Contours* tab sets the contour interval, smoothing, and other settings, as shown in Figure 1–17.

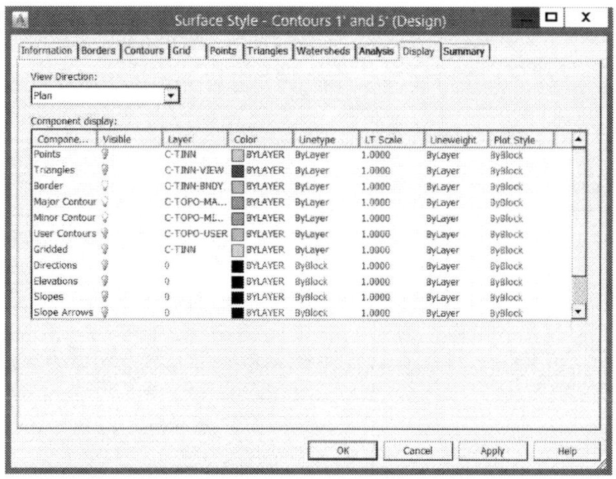

Figure 1–16

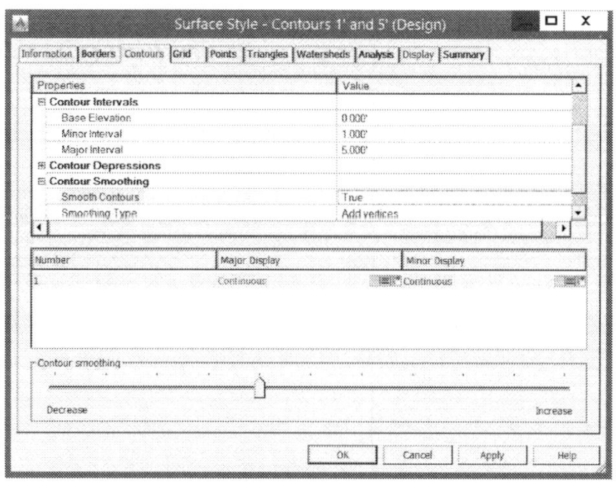

Figure 1–17

From the default AutoCAD Civil 3D template, the respective Parcel Style dialog box for Open Space, Road, or Single Family, (as shown in Figure 1–18), define how each displays their segments and hatching by assigning different layers for the components. The other tabs are rarely used for the Parcel styles.

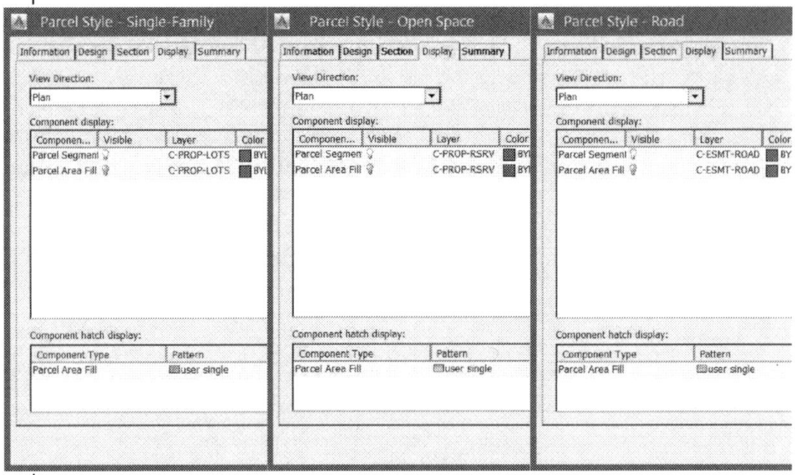

Figure 1–18

An object style represents a specific task, view, type, or stage in a process. For example, a surface style for developing a surface, reviewing surface properties, or documenting surface elevations as contours for a submission. For Parcels, styles represent a type such as open space, commercial, easement, single family, etc. One style can cause an object to look different in various views. For instance, you might want to display both the point and the label in the plan view but only the point marker in a model (3D view). As shown in Figure 1–19, there are four view directions to consider when creating an object style.

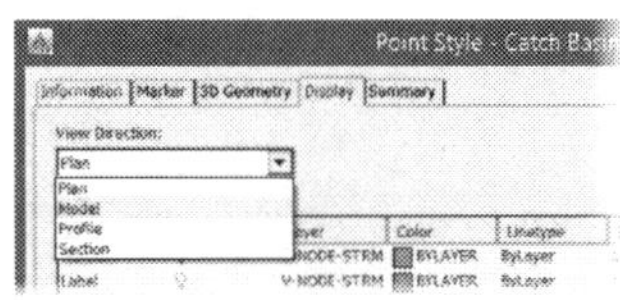

Figure 1–19

Survey Figures

Survey figures consist of linework generated by coding and placed in a file that is imported into the Survey Database. A figure represents linear features (edge-of-pavement, toe-of-slopes, etc.)

A figure has many functions, which include:

- Acting as linework in a drawing.
- Acting as breaklines for a surface definition.
- Acting as parcel lines.
- Acting as a pipe run.
- Acting as targets for *Width* or *Offset Targets* in a Corridor.
- Acting as targets for *Slope* or *Elevation Targets* in a Corridor (e.g., limits of construction for a road rehab project might be to the face of walk, which exists in the drawing as a Survey Figure, hence a target).

The Figure Prefix database should be set up before importing any survey data to obtain the required entities in a drawing. As point and label styles and the Description Key Set need to exist before importing points, figure styles and entries in the Figure Prefix database need to exist before importing survey data.

Figure Styles

Figure styles (found in the *Settings* tab of the Toolspace under General>Multipurpose Styles) affect how the survey linework displays in a drawing. They should be part of your template file. These styles are not critical. However, to make figures work more efficiently, you should define the layers they use in the drawing.

- Figure styles are tied to the Figure Prefix database. The Figure Prefix database assigns a figure style to a figure that is imported into a drawing.
- A figure style includes the layers for its linework and markers.
- A marker is a symbol placed on the figure's segment midpoints and end points. They call attention to the figure's geometry. Although a figure style includes marker definitions, they do not need to display.
- In the Figure Line Style dialog box, the *Information* tab assigns a name to a style. The *Profile*, and *Section* tabs define how the marker displays in various views.

- The *Display* tab defines which figure's components display and which layers they use for plan, model, profile, and section views, as shown in Figure 1–20.

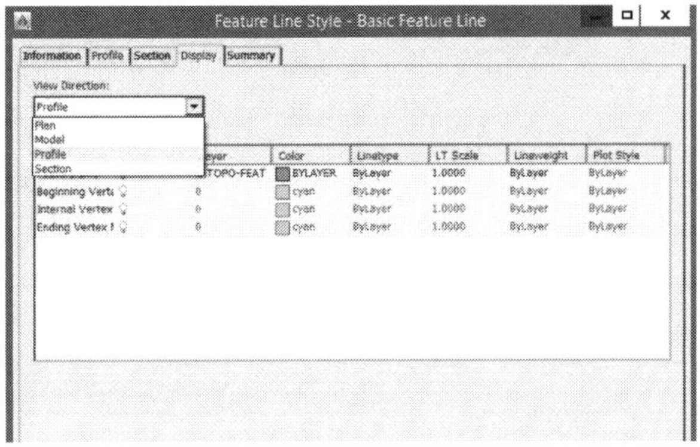

Figure 1–20

Points

Points are often most heavily used at the beginning and end of a project. Surveyors collect data about existing site conditions (elevations, utilities, ownership, etc.) and set out the points for those who are going to build the design. Their world is coordinates, which are represented by points. Each point has a unique number (or name) and a label containing additional information (usually the elevation at the coordinate and a short coded description).

There are no national standards for point descriptions in the Surveying industry. Each company or survey crew needs to work out its own conventions. There are no standards for symbols either. Each firm can have its own set of symbols. The symbols used in a submission set can be specified by the firm contracting the services.

AutoCAD Civil 3D cogo points are a single object with two elements: a point style and a point label style. A cogo point definition is shown in Figure 1–21.

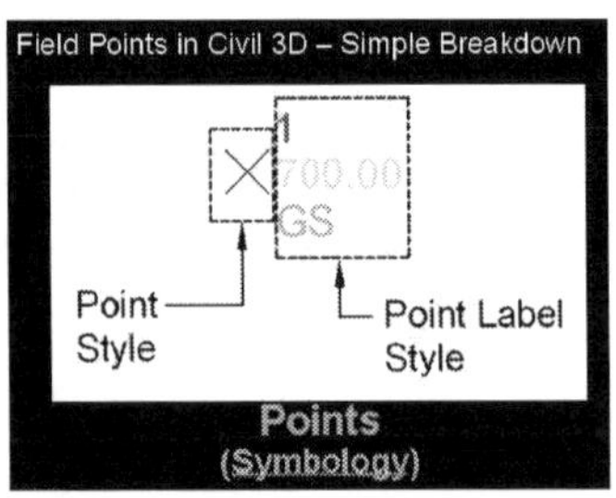

Figure 1–21

The following is important cogo point information:

- A point style (no matter what it displays), an AutoCAD node, a custom marker, or a block is selectable with an AutoCAD **Node** object snap.

A point label is not limited to the point's number, elevation, and description. A point label can contain lines, blocks, and other point properties. For example, point labels might only display an elevation or description. This text can be manually overridden (as shown in Figure 1–22) or it can consist of intelligent variables that represent point characteristics (such as its convergence angle).

In U.S. state plane coordinate systems, the convergence angle is the difference between a geodetic azimuth and the projection of that azimuth onto a grid (grid azimuth) of a given point.

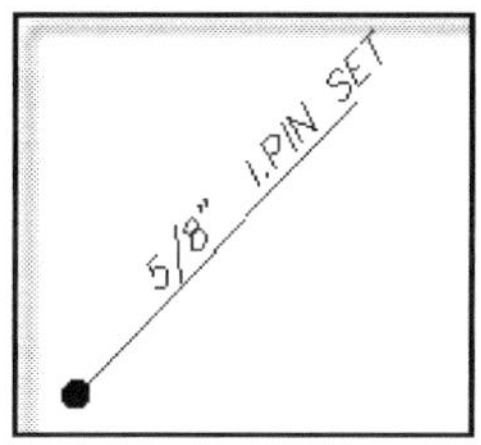

Figure 1–22

Point Marker Styles

A surveyor interacts with points daily. To easily use AutoCAD Civil 3D points, you need to have a basic understanding of them and their related styles.

The AutoCAD Civil 3D software provides metric and imperial template files that contain several point styles: AutoCAD Civil 3D Imperial (NCS) and AutoCAD Civil 3D Metric (NCS). These two templates use the National CAD standards for their layers and provide examples of styles that you can use in a project. To customize these styles, you need to modify and expand the list of point styles. When installing the AutoCAD Civil 3D software, the first thing you should do is set one of these two templates as your default template. Alternatively, you can develop your styles and use your template.

A point style defines a point's display, its 3D elevation, and its coordinate marker size. In the example shown in Figure 1–23, the point style is an X for a ground shot.

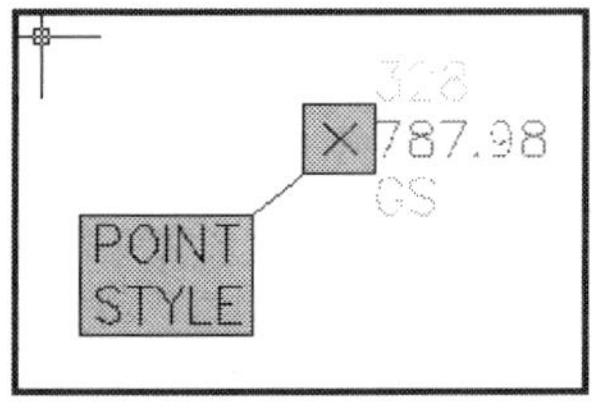

Figure 1–23

The Point Style dialog box has five tabs: *Information*, *Marker*, *3D Geometry*, *Display*, and *Summary*.

The *Information* tab sets the point style's name and description, as shown in Figure 1–24.

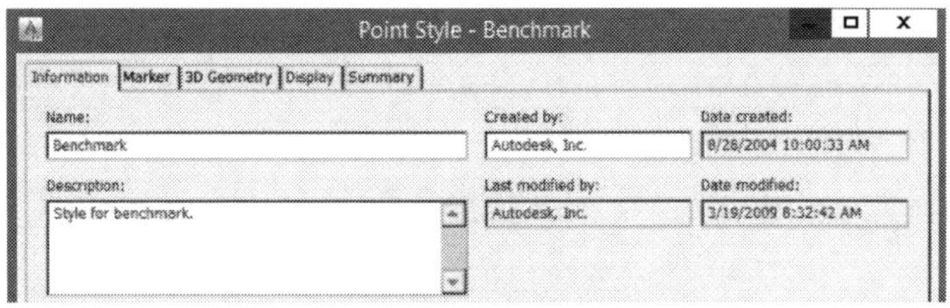

Figure 1–24

The *Marker* tab supports three marker definition methods, as shown in Figure 1–25.

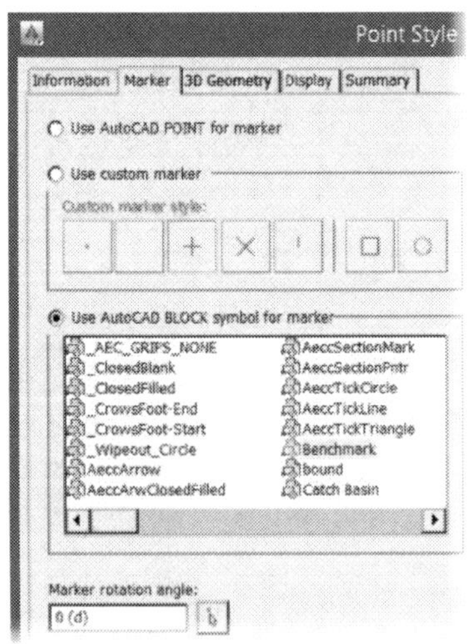

Figure 1–25

- **Use AutoCAD POINT [node] for marker:** All points in the drawing follow AutoCAD's **PDMODE** and **PDSIZE** system variables. You do not have independent control over points using this option.

- **Use custom marker:** This option creates markers similar to an AutoCAD point (node). However, the marker is under the AutoCAD Civil 3D software's control, and each point style can display a different combination of marker styles. When using this option, select the components of the style from the list of Custom marker style shapes. A custom marker can have shapes from the left and right sides. The first comes from one of the five icons on the style's left side, and you can optionally add none, one, or both shapes from the right.

- **Use AutoCAD BLOCK symbol for marker:** This option defines the marker using a block (symbol). The blocks listed represent definitions in the drawing. When the cursor is in this area and you right-click, you can browse to a location containing drawings that you want to include as point markers.

Options for scaling the marker are displayed in the marker panel's top right corner. The most common option is **Use drawing scale** (as shown in Figure 1–26), which takes the marker size (0.100) and multiplies it by the current drawing's annotation scale, resulting in the final marker size. When the annotation scale changes, the AutoCAD Civil 3D software automatically resizes the markers and their labels to be the appropriate size for the scale.

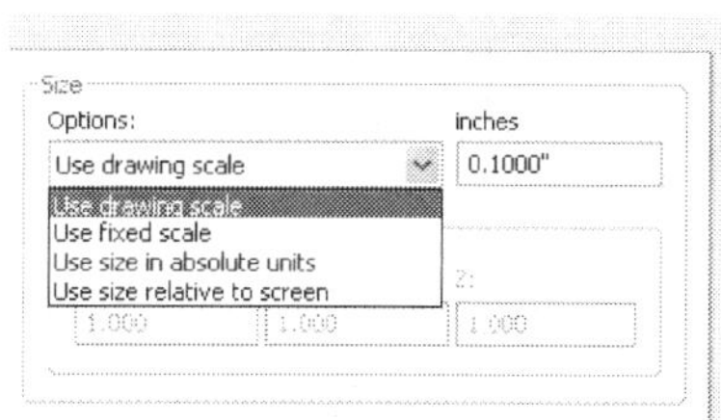

Figure 1–26

The other options are described as follows:

Use fixed scale	Specifies user-defined X, Y, and Z scale values.
Use size in absolute units	Specifies a user-defined size.
Use size relative to screen	Specifies a user-defined percentage of the screen.

The *3D Geometry* tab affects the point's elevation. The default option is **Use Point Elevation** (as shown in Figure 1–27), which displays the point at its actual elevation value.

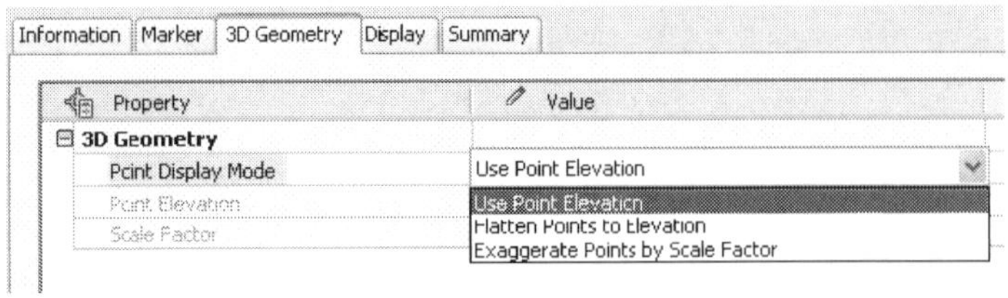

Figure 1–27

The other options are described as follows:

Flatten Points to Elevation	Specifies the elevation to which the point is projected (flattened). The Point Elevation cell highlights if this option is selected and is 0 elevation by default. When using an AutoCAD object snap to select a marker using this option, the resulting entity's elevation is the default elevation of 0. If selecting by point number or point object, the resulting entity is the point's actual elevation.
Exaggerate Points by Scale Factor	Exaggerates the point's elevation by a specified scale factor. When selecting this option, the Scale Factor cell highlights.

The *Display* tab assigns the marker and label layers, and sets their visibility and properties. Setting the property to **ByLayer** uses the layer's properties. Alternatively, you can override the original layer properties by setting a specific color, linetype, or lineweight.

A style's view direction value affects how the point and label components display in the plan, model, profile, and section views, as shown in Figure 1–28.

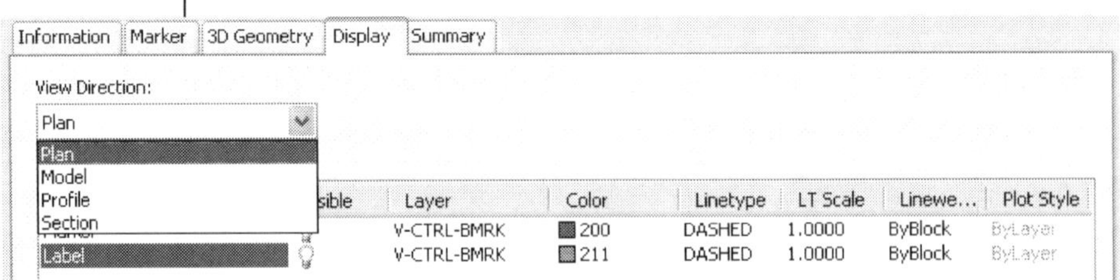

Figure 1–28

The *Summary* tab is a report of all of the style's settings. Controlling a leader arrow from a label in the dragged state, points to the boundary of the marker (yes) or the center of the marker (no). It is also changed under **Marker>Leader** and stops at marker. You can also edit style variables in this tab.

Templates

A drawing template (.DWT extension) contains all blocks, Paper Space title sheets, settings, layers, AutoCAD Civil 3D styles, and content-specific settings for a new drawing.

Creating Template Files

To use the AutoCAD Civil 3D software efficiently and effectively, you need to configure styles and settings to control the object display. All of these styles and settings affect the final delivered product and enable you to deliver a product with consistent CAD standards. Once all of the styles required for a set of drawings have been created, saving the file as a template enables you to use the same styles over and over in various projects. To create a template file, use the **Save As** command and in the Save As dialog box, change the *File of Type* to **DWT**. After giving it a name, the Template Options dialog box opens as shown in Figure 1–29. It enables you to enter a description, set the measurement units, and save new layers as reconciled or unreconciled.

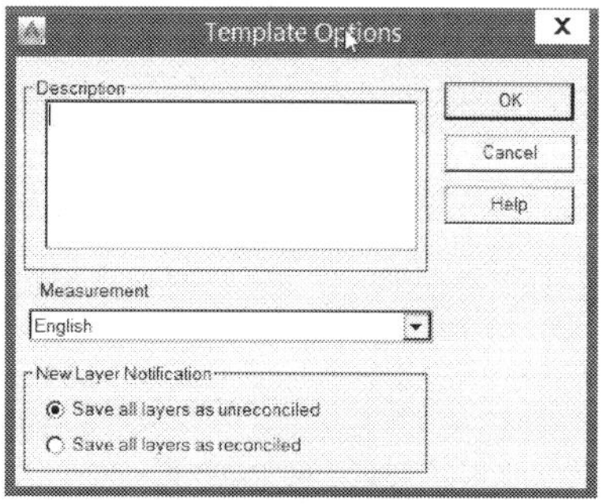

Figure 1–29

Once an AutoCAD Civil 3D style has been created, it can be transferred between drawings and templates by selecting the style and dragging it to the required file. When dragging a style to a drawing, any associated style layers also transfer.

The method of transferring styles is to use the Styles commands located in the *Manage* tab>Styles panel. There are two commands: **Import** and **Purge**, as shown in Figure 1–30.

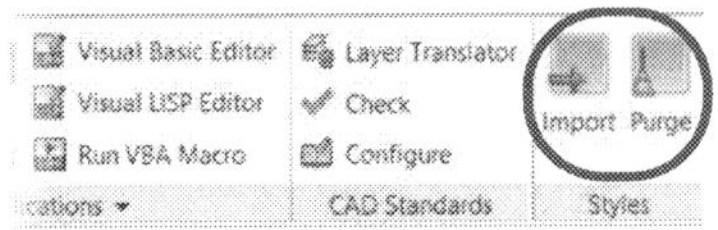

Figure 1–30

Import Styles

The **Import** styles command prompts you for a source drawing from which to import the styles into the current drawing. The Import Civil 3D Styles dialog box opens as shown in Figure 1–31. It lists the styles that are available for import and also displays the style differences between the source and the current drawing. Each style collection lists three subcategories, styles to be added, styles to be deleted, and styles to be updated.

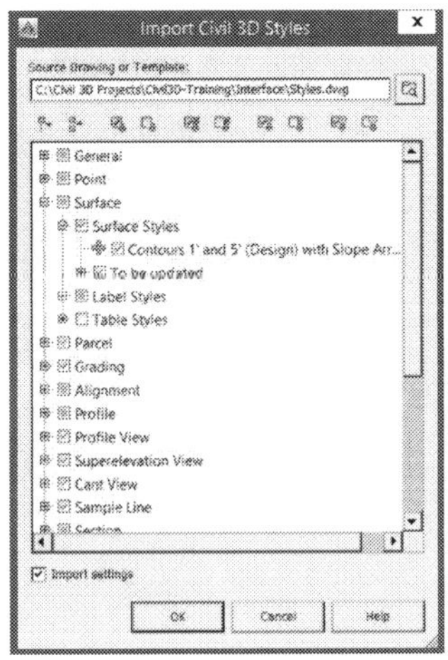

Figure 1–31

Purge Styles

The Purge styles command enables you to purge all of the selected unused styles in a drawing. However, you might need to run this command more than once as there might be some styles that are used as parents to other styles. The purging information is displayed in the Style Purge Confirmation dialog box, as shown in Figure 1–32. The Command Line prompts you when there are no unused styles in the drawing.

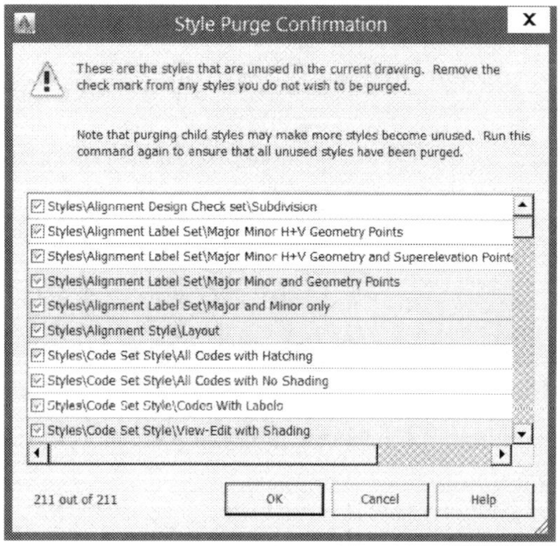

Figure 1–32

1.2 Create and Use Label Styles

Label Styles

Label styles produce annotation of critical values from existing conditions or a design solution. A label annotates a contour's elevations, a parcel's number and area, an horizontal geometry point's station on an alignment, etc.

A label style can have text, vectors, AutoCAD blocks, and reference text. The content of a label depends on the selected object's components or properties. For instance, a Line label can annotate bearing, distance, and coordinates, and use a direction arrow. A Parcel Area label can contain a parcel's area, perimeter, address, and other pertinent values. A surface label can include a spot elevation and reference for an alignment's station and offset.

- To access the values of a label style, in *Settings*, select the style, right-click on its name, and select **Edit**.
- A style's initial values come from Edit Label Style Defaults and the style's definition.
- All labels use the same interface.
- The object properties available for each label vary by object type.

Each label style uses the same tabbed dialog box. The Information tab describes the style and who defined and last modified its contents. The values of the *General* tab affect all occurrences of the label in a drawing. For example, if Visibility is set to False, all labels of this style are hidden in the drawing. Other settings affect the label's text style, initial orientation, and reaction to a rotated view.

The *Layout* tab lists all of a label's components. A label component can be text, line, block, or tick. The Component name drop-down list (shown in Figure 1–33), contains all of the defined components for the style. When selecting a component name in the drop-down list, the panel displays information about the component's anchoring, justification, format, and border.

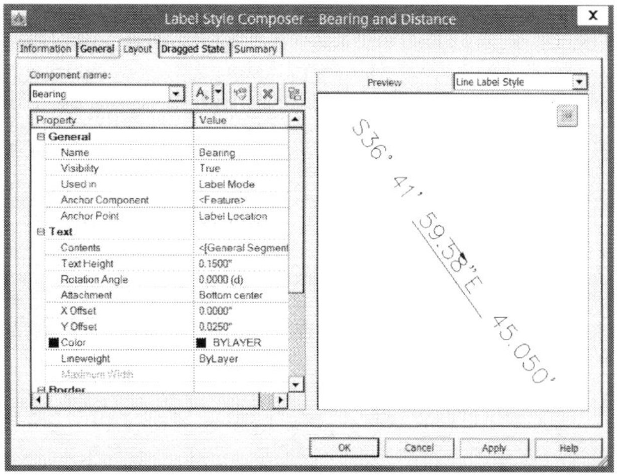

Figure 1–33

When defining a new text component, you assign it an object property by clicking (Browse) for Contents. This opens the Text Component Editor dialog box, as shown in Figure 1–34. The Properties drop-down list displays the available object properties. The number and types of properties varies by object type. For example, a parcel area label has more and different properties than a line label does. Once a property has been selected, units, precision, and other settings can be set to display the property correctly in the label. Click next to Properties to place the property in the label layout area to the right.

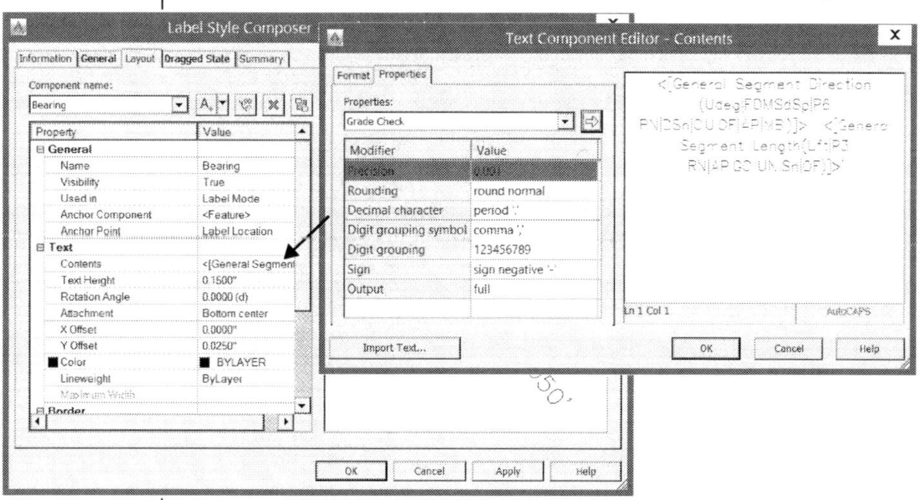

Figure 1–34

The values in the *Dragged State* tab define a label's behavior when it is dragged to a new location in the drawing.

The key to having the label display correctly when it is not in the dragged state, is to line up the Anchor Point of the component with the **Attachment** option for the text. Each has nine options from which to select. The options are shown in Figure 1–35.

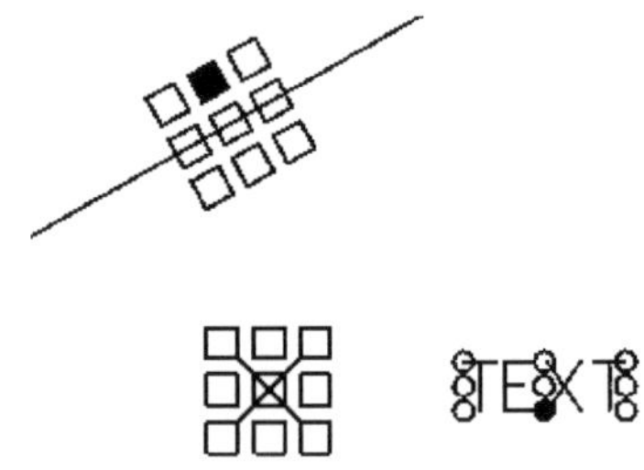

Figure 1–35

Lining up the square hatched Anchor Point with the circular hatched attachment option results in the text centered above the object similar to the bearing distance label shown in Figure 1–36.

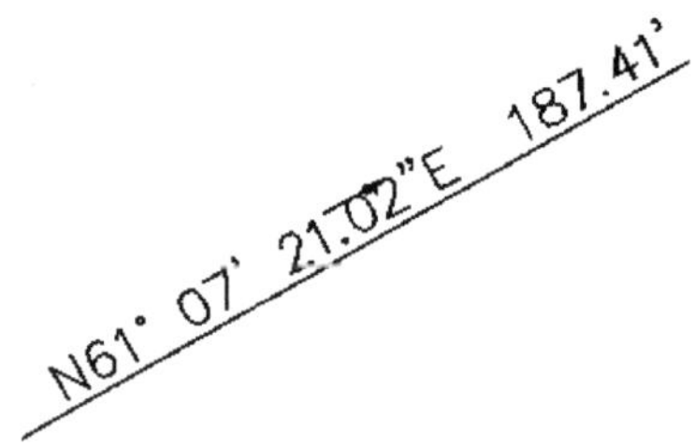

Figure 1–36

Point Label Style

The AutoCAD Civil 3D point label style annotates point properties beyond the typical point number, elevation and description. A typical point label style is shown in Figure 1–37.

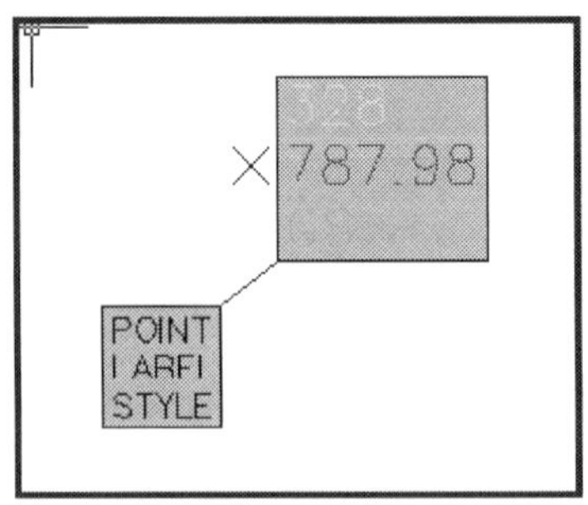

Figure 1–37

All AutoCAD Civil 3D label style dialog boxes are the same. The basic behaviors for a label are in the settings in the Edit Label Style Defaults dialog box. The values in this dialog box define the label layer, text style, orientation, plan readability, size, dragged state behaviors, etc.

In the *Settings* tab, the drawing name and object collections control these values for the entire drawing (at the drawing name level) or for the selected collection (*Surface*, *Alignment*, *Point*, etc.) To open the Edit Label Style Defaults dialog box, select the drawing name or a heading, right-click, and select **Edit Label Style Defaults...**, as shown in Figure 1–38.

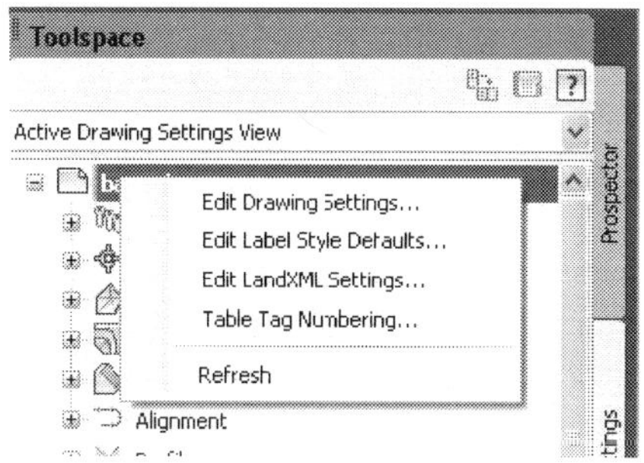

Figure 1–38

The Label Style Composer dialog box contains five tabs, each defining specific label behaviors: *Information*, *General*, *Layout*, *Dragged State*, and *Summary*.

The *Information* tab names the style, as shown in Figure 1–39.

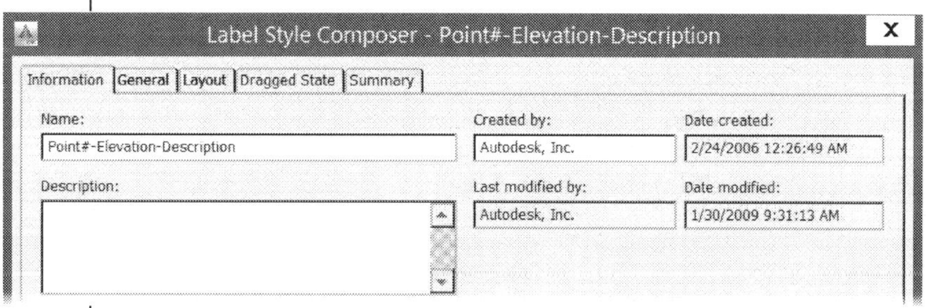

Figure 1–39

The *General* tab contains three properties: *Label* (text style and layer), *Behavior* (orientation), and *Plan Readability* (amount of view rotation before flipping text to read from the bottom or the right side of the sheet), as shown in Figure 1–40.

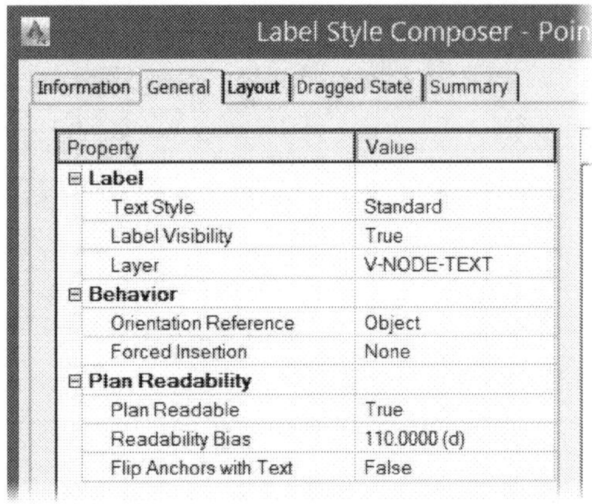

Figure 1–40

The *Label* property sets the *Text Style*, *Label Visibility*, *Layer*. Select the *Value* cell next to the *Text Style* and *Layer* to open browsers and change their values. Selecting the *Label Visibility* cell displays a drop-down list containing the options **true** and **false**.

The *Behavior* property sets two variables that control the label's location. The *Orientation Reference* variable contains the three label orientation options.

Object	Rotates labels relative to the object's zero direction. The object's zero direction is based on its start to end vector. If the vector changes at the label's anchor point, the orientation updates automatically. This is the default setting.
View	Forces labels to realign relative to a screen-view orientation in both model and layout views. This method assumes that the zero angle is horizontal, regardless of the UCS or Dview twist. If the view changes, the label orientation updates as well.
World Coordinate System	Labels read left to right using the WCS X-axis. Changing the view or current UCS does not affect label rotation. The label always references the world coordinate system.

Under the *Behavior* property, the **Forced Insertion** variable has three optional values that specify the label's position relative to an object. This setting only applies when the *Orientation Reference* is set to **Object** and the objects are lines, arcs, or spline segments.

None	Maintains label position as composed relative to the object.
Top	Adjusts label position to be above an object.
Bottom	Adjusts label position to be below an object.

- Note: If you select **Top** or **Bottom**, the value of *Plan Readable* should set to **True**.

The *Plan Readability* property has three variables that affect how text flips when rotating a drawing view.

Under the *Plan Readability* property, the *Plan Readable* variable has two options.

True	Enables text to rotate to maintain left to right readability from the bottom or right side of the drawing.
False	Does not permit text to flip. The resulting text might be upside down or read from right to left.

The *Readability Bias* variable is the amount of rotation required to flip a label to become left to right readable. The angle is measured counter-clockwise from the WCS 0 (zero) direction.

The *Flip Anchors with Text* variable has two options:

True	If the text flips, the text anchor point also flips.
False	The label flips, but maintains the original anchor point. The behavior is similar to mirroring the original text.

The *Layout* tab defines the label contents, as shown in Figure 1–41. A label component is an object property that it labels. Point properties include northing, easting, raw description, etc. A label might have one component with several properties or several components each containing an object property.

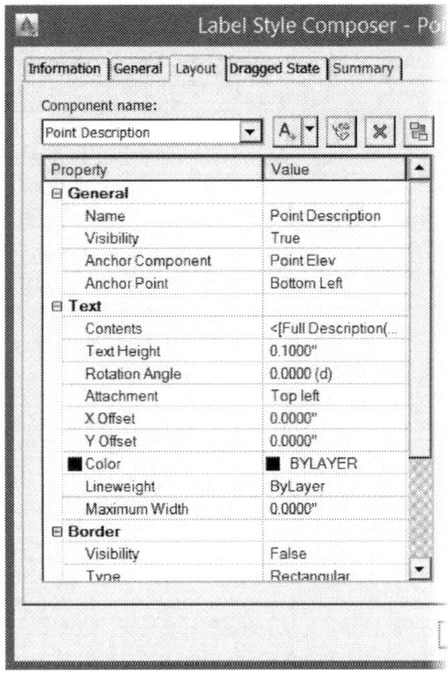

Figure 1–41

A point style label component can be text, lines, or blocks. Other object type label styles can include additional components, such as reference text, tics, directional arrows, etc. To add a component, expand the drop-down list (as shown in Figure 1–42) and select the component type.

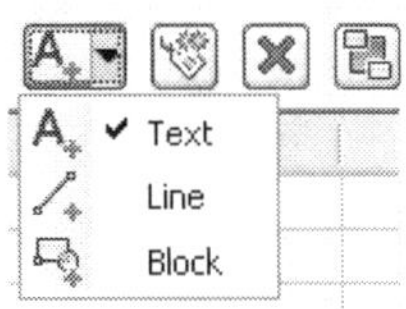

Figure 1–42

The remaining icons in the *Layout* tab are described as follows:

	Copies the current component and its properties.
	Deletes the current component.
	Changes the display order of a label's components. For example, use this icon to change the draw order of the label's components (such as text above a mask).

Depending on the label component type, it might have any combination of three areas: *General*, *Text*, and *Border*. *General* defines how the label attaches to the object or other label components, its visibility, and its anchor point.

If the label component is text, the *Text* property values affect how it displays its object property. To set or modify a label's text value, select the cell next to *Contents* to display ... (shown in Figure 1–43). Click ... to open the Text Component Editor dialog box.

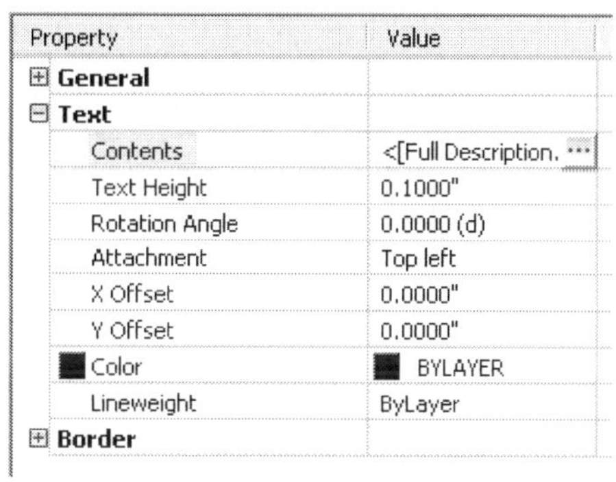

Figure 1–43

The Text Component Editor dialog box (shown in Figure 1–44), defines the properties that the label annotates. When creating a label component, double-click on the text in the right pane to highlight it. In the left pane, select the property that you want to add, set the property's format values, and then click to add the new property to the label component.

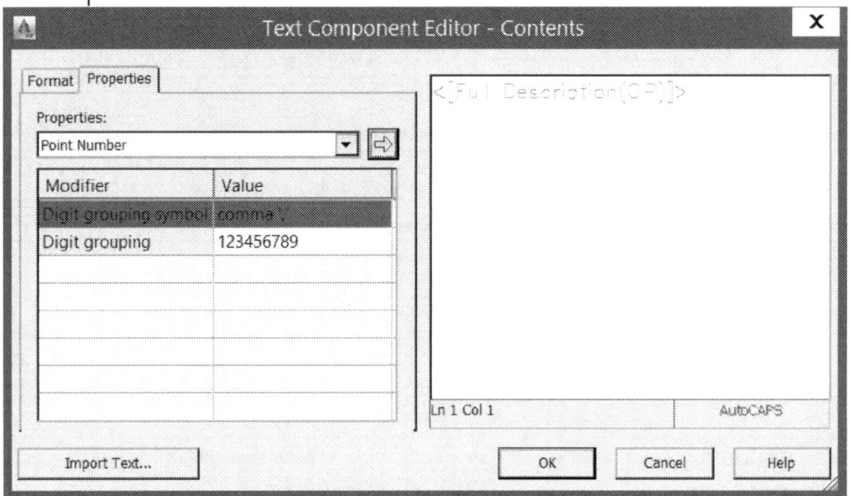

Figure 1–44

It is important to maintain the process order and to remember that the text on the right in brackets needs to be highlighted before you can revise its format values on the left.

The *Dragged State* tab has two properties: *Leader* and *Dragged State Components*. This tab defines how a label behaves when you are dragging a label from its original insertion point.

The *Leader* property defines whether a leader displays and what properties it displays. You can use the label's layer properties in the *General* tab (**ByLayer**) or override them by specifying a color, as shown in Figure 1–45.

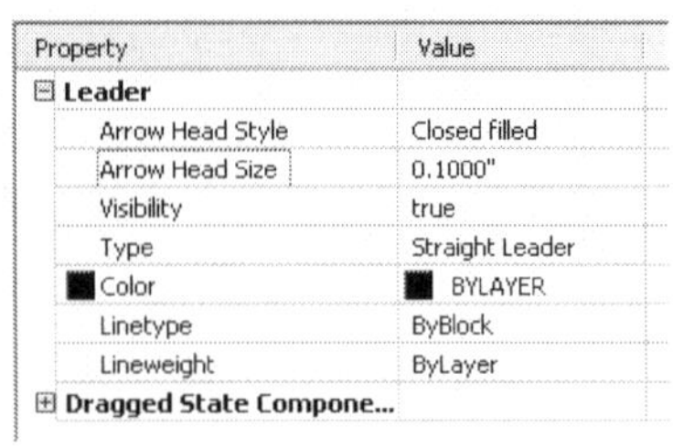

Figure 1–45

The *Dragged State Components* property defines the label component's display after it has been dragged from its original position. Select the cell next to *Display* to view the two display options, as shown in Figure 1–46.

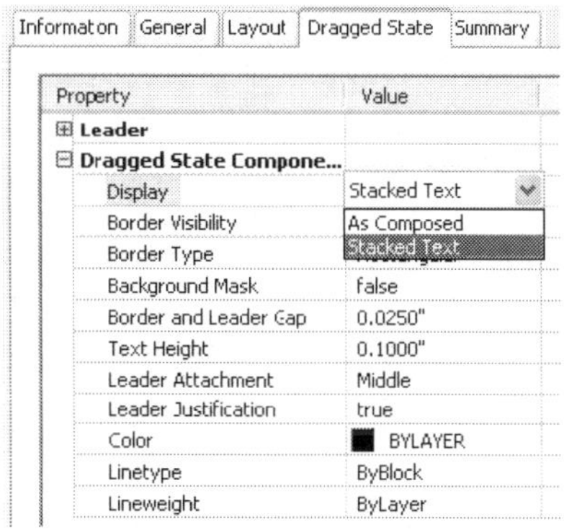

Figure 1–46

As Composed	The label maintains its original definition and orientation from the settings in the Layout panel. When you select **As Composed**, all of the other values become unavailable for editing.
Stacked Text	The label text becomes left justified and label components are stacked in the order listed in Layout's Component Name list. When you select **Stacked Text**, all of the blocks, lines, ticks, and direction arrows are removed.

The *Summary* tab lists the label component, general, and dragged state values for the label style. The label components are listed numerically in the order in which they were defined and report all of the current values.

Practice 1a AutoCAD Civil 3D Styles

Practice Objectives

- Create an object and label style to be used in the drawing.
- Import object and label styles to be used in the drawing and purge any styles not being used.

Estimated time for completion: 10 minutes

In this practice you will create AutoCAD Civil 3D styles, import styles, and purge styles for both objects and labels.

Task 1 - Create an object style.

1. Open **INTRO-Introduction.dwg** from the *C:\Civil 3D Projects\Civil3D-Training\Interface* folder.

The tabs are listed vertically along the right side of the Toolspace.

2. Select the *Settings* tab to make it active.
3. Click the **+** sign next to Parcel, and then click the **+** sign next to Parcel Styles. Five parcel styles are already in the drawing, but a new one needs to be created to designate blocks.
4. Right-click on Parcel Styles and select **New**. In the *Information* tab, type **Blocks** in the *Name* field.
5. In the *Display* tab, highlight both the Parcel Segment and Parcel Area Fill (press <Shift> to select both), click **0** under the *Layer* column. Create a new layer named **C-PROP-BLOCK** and set its *color* to **blue**, as shown in Figure 1–47.

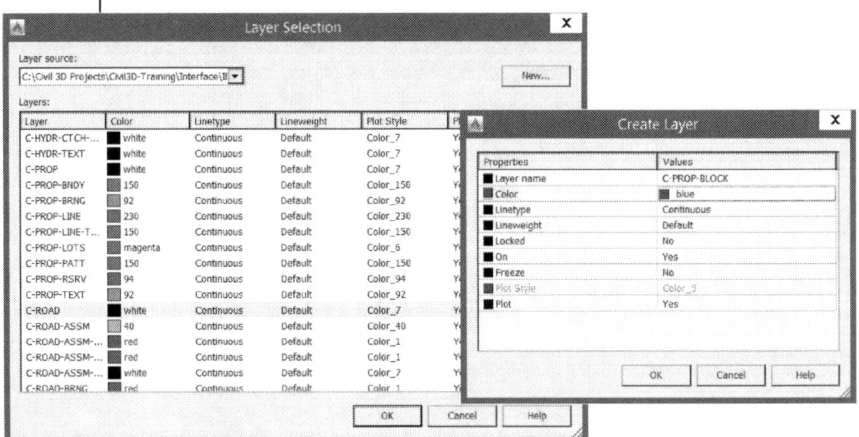

Figure 1–47

6. Click **OK** to exit the Create Layer dialog box. Click **OK** to exit the Layer Selection dialog box.

7. Verify that the light bulb is on for the Parcel Segment visibility and off for the Parcel Area Fill visibility, as shown in Figure 1–48.

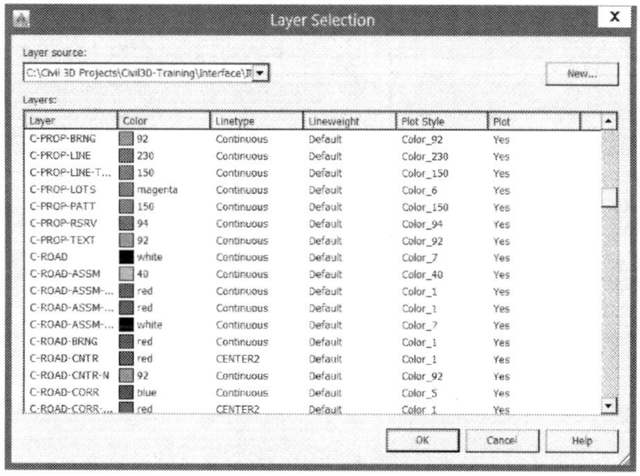

Figure 1–48

8. Click **OK** to exit the Parcel Style dialog box.

9. Save the drawing.

Task 2 - Work with a label style.

1. Verify that the *Settings* tab is still active.

2. View the label style default. In the *View* tab>Views panel, expand the Named Views drop-down list and select **Contour label**. It will zoom to a preset view of the contour labels, as shown in Figure 1–49.

Figure 1–49

Note that the labels are not rotated to the correct drafting standards. The contour label style being used is rotating the text so that it remains plan readable (so they do not display upside down). The highlighted labels are rotated more than 90 degrees from horizontal. This is caused by the *Readability Bias* setting being larger than 90 degrees. This setting controls the viewing angle at which the contour text should be flipped.

3. If needed, you can change the setting in this specific contour label style only. To assign this new value to all of the surface label styles, right-click on the *Surface* collection in the *Settings* tab and select **Edit Label Style Defaults**.

4. Under the Plan Readability property, set the *Readability Bias* to **110º**, as shown in Figure 1–50, and click **OK**.

Property	Value	Override	Child Override	Lock
⊞ **Label**				
⊞ **Behavior**				
⊟ **Plan Readability**				
Plan Readable	True			
Readability Bias	91.0000 (d)			
Flip Anchors with Text	False			
⊞ **Components**				
⊞ **Leader**				
⊞ **Dragged State Compone...**				

Figure 1–50

5. Click **+** next to Surface, and then click **+** next to Label Styles and Contour. Right-click on Existing Major Labels and select **Edit**.

6. In the *Layout* tab, click (Browse) next to Contents to open the Text Component Editor. Delete all of the information in the content area to the right.

7. In the Properties drop-down list, select **Surface Elevation**, change the *Precision* to **1**, and click to place it in the content area, as shown in Figure 1–51.

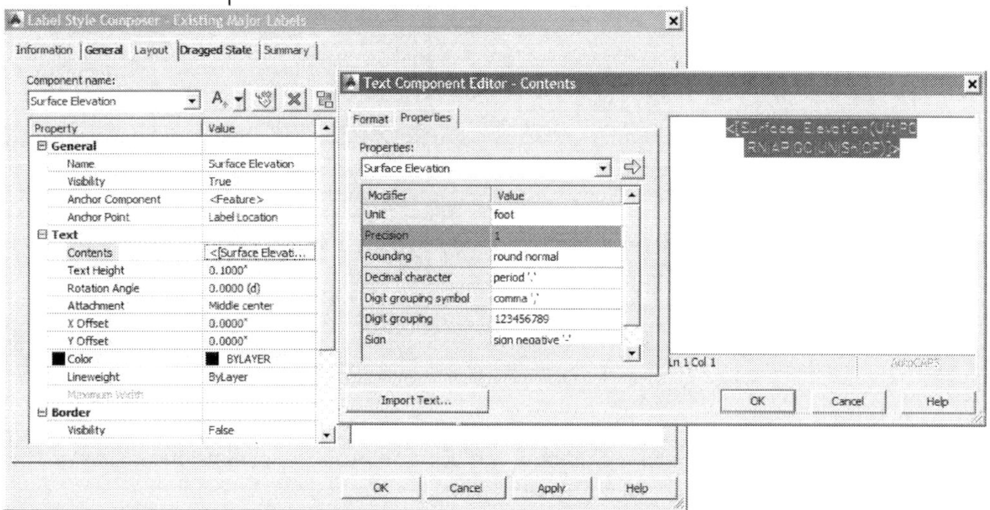

Figure 1–51

8. Click **OK** to exit the Text Component Editor dialog box. Click **OK** again to exit the Label Style Composer dialog box.

9. Repeat Steps 5 to 8 to change the **Existing Minor Labels** style in the same way.

10. Save the drawing.

Task 3 - Import and purge styles.

1. In the *Manage* tab>Styles panel, click (Import).

2. Select and open the **Styles.dwg** file from the *C:\Civil 3D Projects\Civil3D-Training\Interface* folder.

3. Expand *Surface Styles* and verify that **Contours 1' and 5' (Design) with Slope Arrows** is selected, as shown in Figure 1–52.

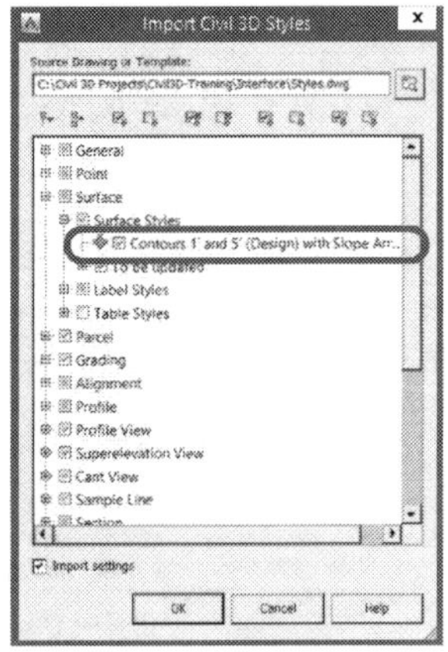

Figure 1–52

4. Click **OK** in the Warning dialog box regarding overwriting duplicate styles. Click **OK** in the Message dialog box.

5. Change the surface style to the newly imported style by changing the surface properties. Note the slope arrows shown in Figure 1–53.

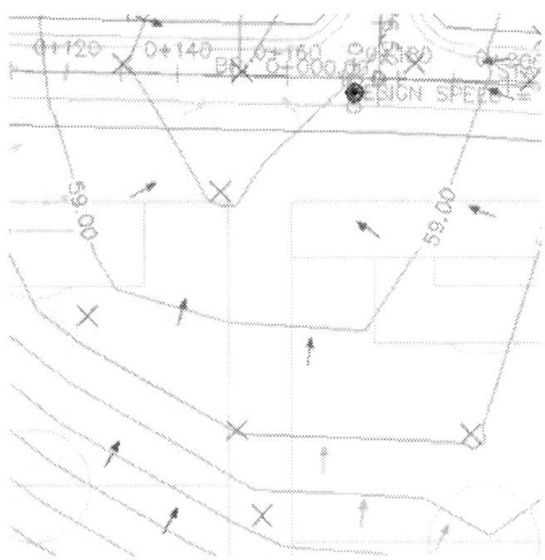

Figure 1–53

6. In the *Manage* tab>Styles panel, click (Purge).

7. Clear any styles that you do not want to purge and click **OK**.

8. Save and close the drawing.

Practice 1b — Point Marker Styles

Practice Objective

- Create a point marker and label style to ensure that the correct symbol is assigned to specific points.

Estimated time for completion: 35 minutes

In this practice you will create a new point style and apply it to an existing group of points.

Task 1 - Add a Block Symbol.

1. Open **SUV1-B1-Survey-.dwg** from the *C:\Civil 3D Projects\Civil3D-Training\Survey* folder.

The aerial images used in this chapter was attached using the AutoCAD® Map 3D FDO connection.

2. To toggle off the aerial images: In the *Home* tab>Palettes panel, click (Map Task Pane) and when prompted, select **ON**. In the Task pane>*Display Manager* tab, clear the **MainSite Imperial** option, as shown in Figure 1–54. Close the map Task pane.

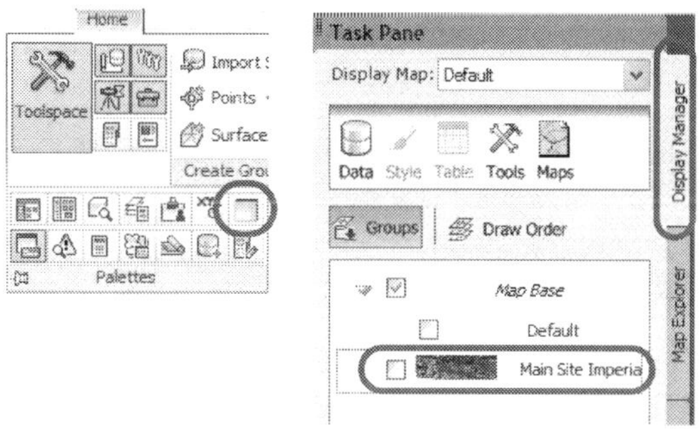

Figure 1–54

3. In the Toolspace>*Settings* tab, expand the *Point* collection until *Point Styles* is displayed. Expand the *Point Styles* collection.

Review the Point Styles list and note that there is no light pole style.

4. In the *Point Styles* list, select the **Guy pole** style, right-click, and select **Copy...**

5. In the *Information* tab, change the point style's name to **Light Pole.**

6. Select the *Marker* tab. Select the **Use AutoCAD BLOCK symbol for marker** option. In the block list, scroll across as required and select the AutoCAD block **ST-Light**, as shown in Figure 1–55.

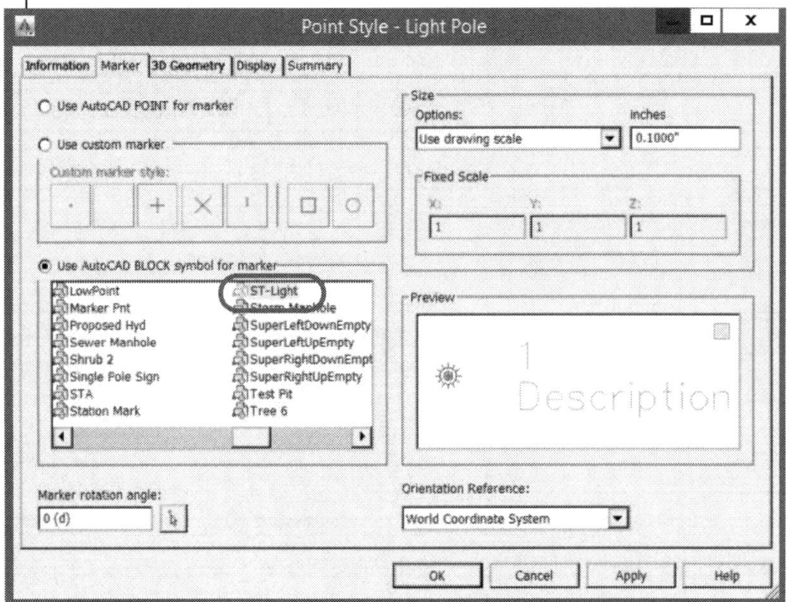

Figure 1–55

7. Select the *Display* tab and note that the layer settings are from the Guy Pole point style.

8. You can reassign the marker and/or label layer by selecting the layer name. Select the layer name to display the drawing layer list.

9. Click **New** in the top right corner of the Layer Selection dialog box. The Create Layer dialog box opens (as shown in Figure 1–56), enabling you to create new layers without having to use the Layer Manager.

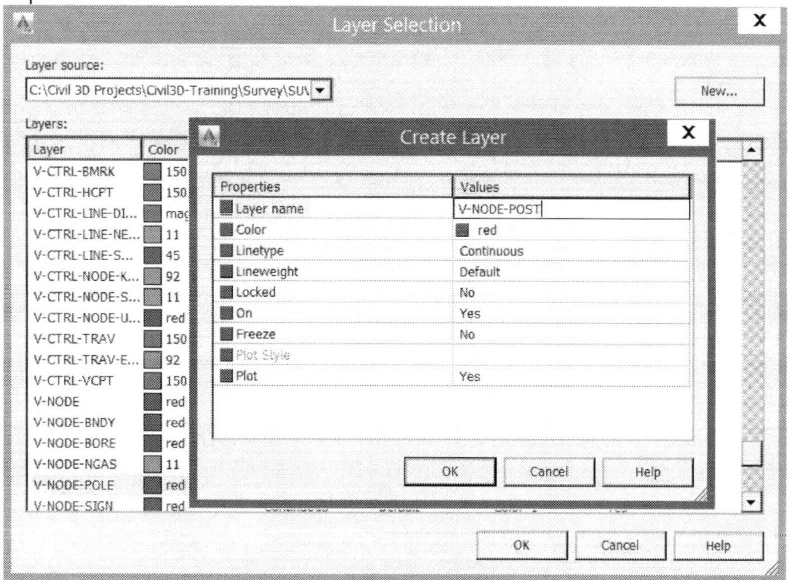

Figure 1–56

10. Click **Cancel** to exit the Create Layer dialog box. Click **Cancel** to exit the Layer Selection dialog box.

11. Click **OK** to create the point style.

12. Review the *Point Styles* list and note that Light Pole is now a point style, as shown in Figure 1–57.

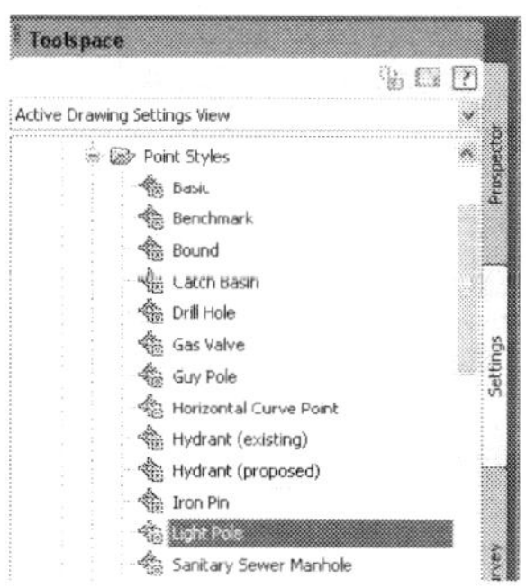

Figure 1–57

13. Save the drawing.

Task 2 - Create a Point Label Style's Components.

1. Continue working with the drawing from the previous task, or open **SUV1-B2-Survey.dwg**.

2. In the Toolspace>*Settings* tab, expand the *Point* collection until the *Point Label Styles* list displays.

3. From the list of point label styles, select **Point#-Elevation-Description**, right-click, and select **Copy**.

4. In the *Information* tab, change the name to **Point#-Description-N-E**.

5. Select the *Layout* tab and do the following (shown in Figure 1–58):

   - Select **Point Number** in the *Component name* drop-down list.
   - Set the *Anchor Component* to **<Feature>**.
   - Set the *Anchor Point* to **Top Right**.
   - Set the *Attachment* to **Bottom left**.

These settings attach the bottom left of the label to the top right of the point object.

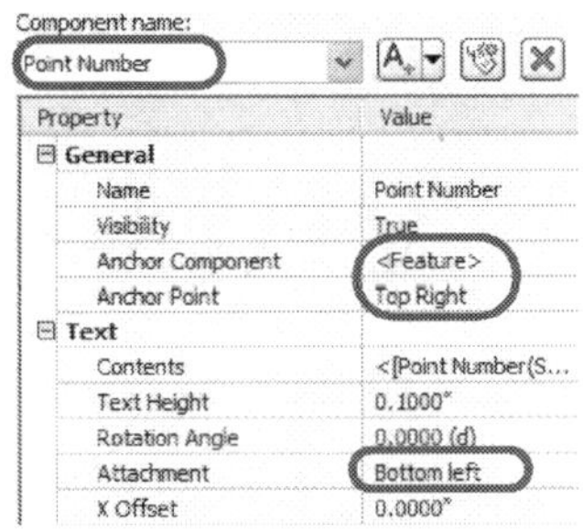

Figure 1–58

Since the elevation label is not needed, you can delete it.

6. Select **Point Elev** in the Component name drop-down list and click , as shown in Figure 1–59. At the *Do you want to delete it?* prompt, click **Yes**.

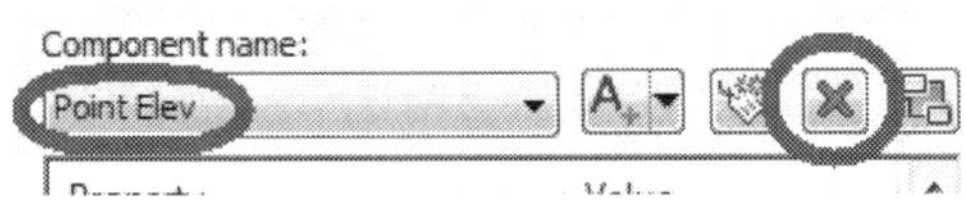

Figure 1–59

7. Select **Point Description** in the Component name drop-down list and do the following (shown in Figure 1–60):
   - Set the *Anchor Component* to **Point Number**.
   - Set the *Anchor Point* to **Bottom Left**.
   - Set the *Attachment* to **Top Left**.

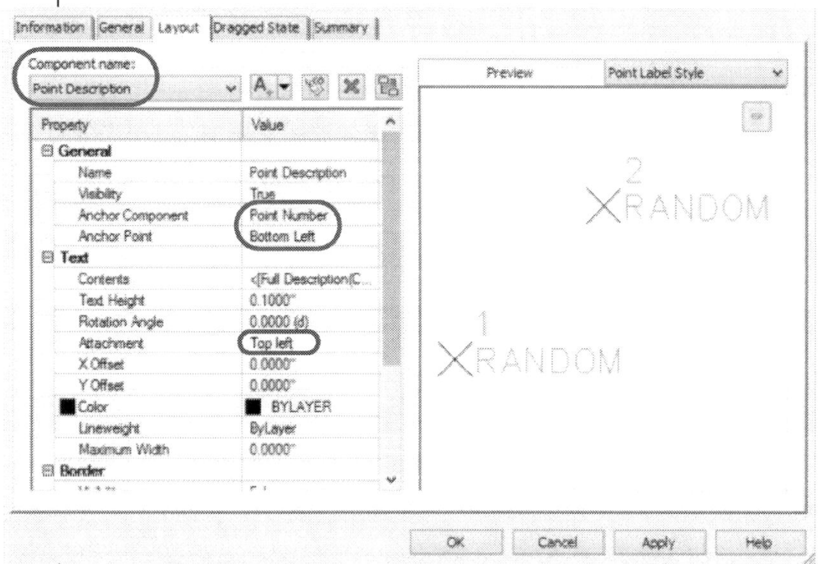

Figure 1–60

You will now add a new text component to display the Northing and Easting.

8. Expand the **Create Text Component** flyout (shown in Figure 1–61) and select **Text** to create a text component.

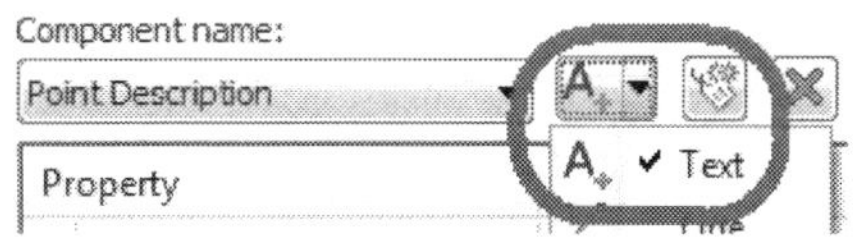

Figure 1–61

9. Change the default *Name* **text.1** to **Coordinates**, and then do the following:
   - Set the *Anchor Component* to **Point Description**.
   - Set the *Anchor Point* to **Bottom Left**.
   - Set the *Attachment* to **Top Left**.

You will now change the contents from the default label set by the AutoCAD Civil 3D software to display the coordinates.

10. Click ... in the *Contents* cell, next to *Label Text*, as shown in Figure 1–62.

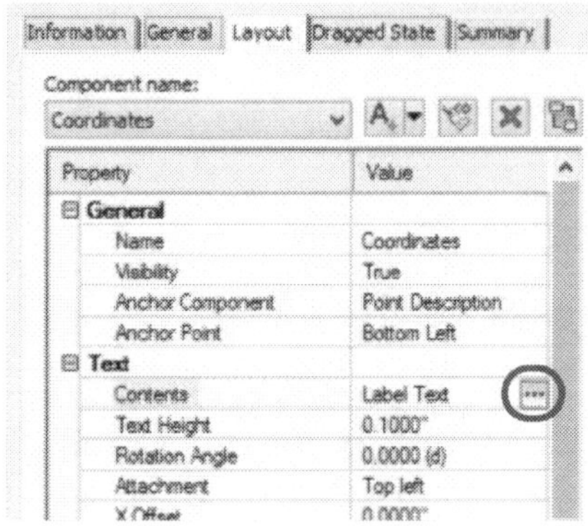

Figure 1–62

11. In the Text Component Editor dialog box, double-click on the text in the right side panel to highlight it and type **N**.

12. Select **Northing** in the Properties drop-down list. Change the *Precision* to **0.001** and click the arrow button, as shown in Figure 1–63, to add the code to display the northing.

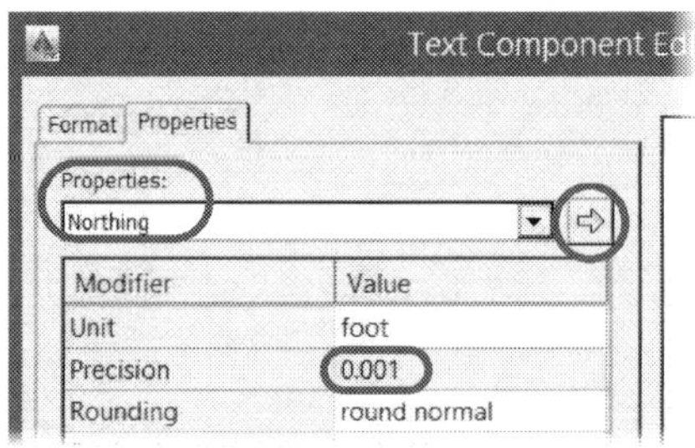

Figure 1–63

13. Click at the end of the code. Press **<Enter>** to insert a new line followed by the letter **E**. Then select **Easting** in the Properties drop-down list and add it to post the code in the right side panel. The following should be displayed:

    N<[Northing(Uft|P3|RN|AP|GC|UN|Sn|OF)]>

    E<[Easting(Uft|P4|RN|AP|GC|UN|Sn|OF)]>

In the easting, the value will be displayed to the 4th decimal, P4. Change it so that it matches the northing.

14. Select all of the code for the easting. Change the *Precision* to **0.001** and click the arrow button to revise the easting code.

15. Select the *Format* tab and verify that *Justification* is set to **Left**. Click **OK** to accept the changes in the Text Component Editor dialog box, and click **OK** again to accept the changes in the Label Style Composer.

16. Save the drawing.

Task 3 - Apply Style Components.

1. Continue working with the drawing from the previous task or open **SUV1-B3-Survey.dwg**.

2. In the Toolspace, select the *Prospector* tab and expand the *Point Groups* collection until the *Street Light* point group displays. Select the **Street Light** group, right-click, and select **Properties**.

3. In the *Information* tab, expand the Point Style drop-down list and select **Light Pole**. Then expand the Point label style drop-down list and select **Point#-Description-N-E**, as shown in Figure 1–64.

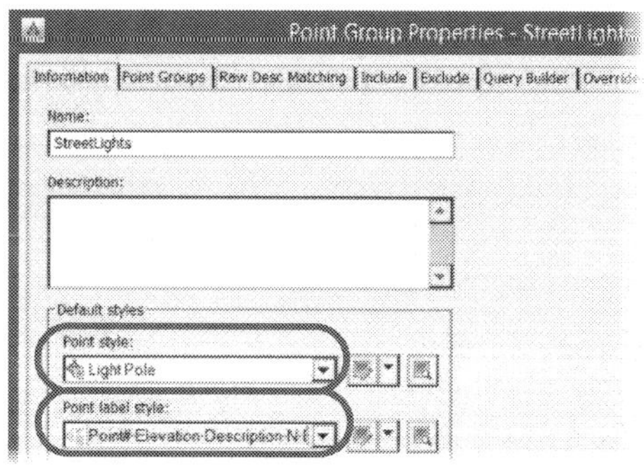

Figure 1–64

4. Click **OK** to accept the changes and close the dialog box.

5. The symbols for the Light pole points have now been changed. Additionally, both the point symbols and point labels are annotative. In the Status Bar, expand the Annotation Scale drop-down list and change the scale of the drawing from *1"=40'* to **1"=30'** as shown in Figure 1–65. The size of the labels and point symbols change.

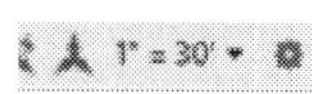

Figure 1–65

6. Save the drawing.

Chapter 2

Lines and Curves

This chapter includes instructional content to assist in your preparation for the following topic and objectives for the AutoCAD® Civil® 3D 2016 Certified Professional exam.

Autodesk Certification Exam Objectives in this Chapter

Exam Topic	Exam Objective	Section
Lines and Curves	• Use the line and curve commands	• 2.1
	• Use the Transparent commands	• 2.2

2.1 Use the Line and Curve Commands

Often, the first thing that has to be drawn up is the legal description of the property being subdivided. Designers need to enter into the computer, in the form of lines and curves, what they are given in a text description. The AutoCAD Civil 3D software makes this task easy with the many options under the **Lines** and **Curves** commands in the *Home* tab>Draw panel. Expanding the lines or curves commands displays several new options that are not found in the AutoCAD® software, as shown in Figure 2–1.

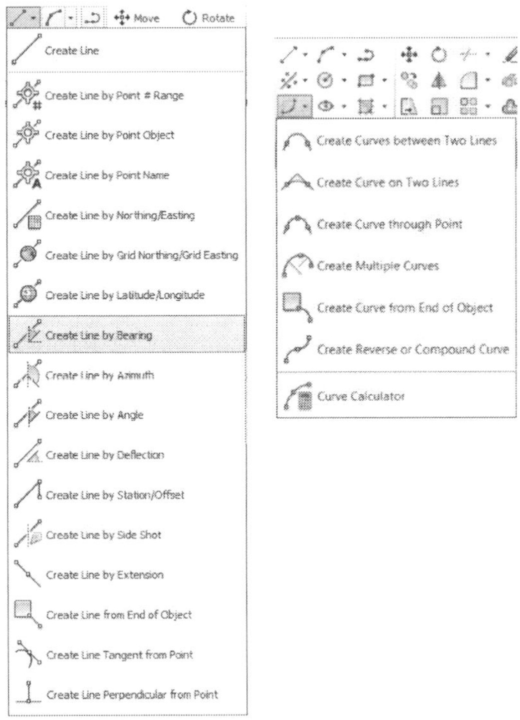

Figure 2–1

2.2 Use the Transparent Commands

A second option is to use transparent commands. These are similar to Object Snaps because they can only be accessed while in another command. Once the required command has been started, you can click the **Transparent** tool or type an apostrophe letter combination in the Command Line for the required **Transparent** command. The benefit to using these to draw parcels over the **Lines** and **Curves** options (shown in Figure 2–1) is that a **Polyline** command can be used to create one entity rather than many individual lines that would need to be joined later.

Transparent Commands

Icon	Command Line	Description
	'AD	Angle Distance: Specifies a point location at an angle and distance from a known point and direction.
	'BD	Bearing Distance: Specifies a point location at a bearing and distance from a known point (or the last point occupied).
	'ZD	Azimuth Distance: Specifies a point location at an azimuth and distance from a known point (or the last point occupied).
	'DD	Deflection Distance: Specifies a point location at an angle and distance from a known point and previous direction.
	'NE	Northing Easting: Specifies a point location using northing and easting coordinates.
	'GN	Grid Northing Grid Easting: Specifies a point location using a grid northing and grid easting. (Note: You must have the drawing zone, coordinate system, and transformations set for grids.)
	'LL	Latitude Longitude: Specifies a point location using latitude and longitude. (Note: You must have the drawing zone, coordinate system, and transformations set.)

	'PN	Point Number: Specifies a point location using a point number found in the drawing or active project.
	'PA	Point Name: Specifies a point location using a point name found in the drawing or active project.
	'PO	Point Object: Specifies a point location by picking any part of an existing COGO point in the drawing.
	'ZTP	Zoom to Point: Zooms to a point in the drawing or active project by specifying the point number or name.
	'SS	Side Shot: Specifies a point location at an angle and distance from a known point and direction (uses the last two entered points to set the reference line).
	'SO	Station Offset: Specifies a point location at a station and an offset from an alignment in the current drawing.
	.g	Point Object Filter: Specifies a point location by picking any part of an existing COGO point in the drawing.
	'STAE	Profile Station from Plan: Specifies a profile view point location by specifying an alignment station in plan and an elevation.
	'SSE	Profile Station and Elevation from Plan: Specifies a profile view point location by specifying a surface, an alignment station, and a point in plan view.
	'SPE	Profile Station and Elevation from COGO Point: Specifies a profile view point location by specifying a COGO point and an alignment station in plan view.
	'PSE	Profile Station Elevation: Specifies a profile view point location by specifying a station and an elevation.
	'PGS	Profile Grade Station: Specifies a profile view point location using grade and station values from a known point.
	'PGE	Profile Grade Elevation: Specifies a profile view point location using grade and elevation values from a known point.

	**'PGL**	Profile Grade Length: Specifies a profile view point location using grade and length values from a known point (or the last point occupied).
	**'MR**	Match Radius: Specifies a radius equal to that of an existing object.
	**'ML**	Match Length: Specifies a length equal to that of an existing object.
	**'CCALC**	Curve Calculator: Calculates curve parameters based on input.

Practice 2a Beginning a Subdivision Project

Estimated time for completion: 20 minutes

Practice Objective

- Draw a parcel from a legal description.

In this practice you will use the legal description below to draw a parcel. Later you will create a parcel from the linework.

From the **POINT OF BEGINNING**; thence, S 00° 26' 42.2" W for a distance of 922.4138 feet to a point on a line. Thence, S 00° 24' 20.8" W for a distance of 508.3493 feet to a point on a line. Thence, S 66° 03' 35.8" W for a distance of 92.1845 feet to the beginning of a curve.

Said curve turning to the right through 42° 35' 49.2", having a radius of 627.1788 feet, and whose long chord bears S 87° 21' 30.4" W for a distance of 455.6165 feet to the beginning of another curve.

Said curve turning to the left through an angle of 19° 13' 40.4", having a radius of 154.4828 feet, and whose long chord bears N 80° 57' 25.2" W for a distance of 51.6000 feet.

Thence, S 89° 25' 44.6" W for a distance of 724.9442 feet to a point on a line. Thence, N 00° 11' 09.9" E for a distance of 1904.2647 feet to a point on a line. Thence, S 61° 50' 15.3" E for a distance of 135.9034 feet to a point on a line. Thence, S 64° 05' 35.8" E for a distance of 77.8201 feet to a point on a line. Thence, S 78° 09' 29.2" E for a distance of 63.8821 feet to a point on a line. Thence, S 66° 23' 19.5" E for a distance of 379.2248 feet to a point on a line. Thence, S 66° 17' 17.4" E for a distance of 278.5122 feet to a point on a line. Thence S 84° 58' 37.7" E a distance of 466.8116 feet to the **POINT OF BEGINNING.**

Task 1 - Draw a parcel from a legal description.

1. Open **PCL1-A1-Parcels.dwg** from the *C:\Civil 3D Projects\Civil3D-Training\Parcels* folder.
2. Start the **Line** command. For the starting point, type **6257490.0191,2037127.1292**.
3. In the Transparent Command toolbar, click (Bearing Distance).

The legal description at the beginning of the practice was used to find the bearings and distances to type.

4. For the first line, type **3** for the southwest quadrant. Type **0.26422** for the bearing. Type **922.4138** for the distance. Stay in the **Line** command with the **Bearing Distance Transparent** command running for the next few lines.

5. For the next two line segments, use the following values:

Quadrant	Bearing	Distance
3	0.24208	508.3493
3	66.03358	92.1845

6. Press <Esc> twice to end the command.

7. Click (Create Curve from End of Object) in the *Home* tab>Draw panel. Select the last line that was drawn using the **Bearing Distance** command.

8. Select **Radius** from the command options, and set the *radius* to **627.1788**.

9. Select **Chord** from the command options, and set the *chord length* to **455.6165**.

10. Click (Create Reverse or Compound Curve) in the *Home* tab>Draw panel. Select the last curve drawn.

11. Select **Reverse** from the command options, and set the *radius* to **154.4828**.

12. Select **Chord** from the command options, and set the *chord length* to **51.6**.

13. Start the **Line** command. For the starting point, pick the endpoint of the last arc drawn.

14. In the Transparent Command toolbar, click (Bearing Distance).

15. For the remaining line segments:, use the following values:

Quadrant	Bearing	Distance
3	89.25446	724.9442
1	0.11099	1904.2647
2	61.50153	135.9034

2	64.05358	77.8201
2	78.09292	63.8821
2	66.23195	379.2248
2	66.17174	278.5122

16. Press <Esc> once to exit the **Bearing Distance** command. Hold <Ctrl> as you right-click and select **Endpoint**, select the starting point of the parcel to close on the point of beginning.

17. Start the **Polyline Edit** command by typing **PE**. In the model, select one of the lines or curves you just created and press <Enter> to turn it into a polyline.

This prevents closure errors from occurring later.

18. Select the **Join** option and then select all the lines and curves you just created. Press <Enter> to create one closed polyline. Press <Esc> to end the command.

19. Save the drawing.

Chapter 3

Points

This chapter includes instructional content to assist in your preparation for the following topic and objectives for the AutoCAD® Civil® 3D 2016 Certified Professional exam.

Autodesk Certification Exam Objectives in this Chapter

Exam Topic	Exam Objective	Section
Points	• Create points using the Point Creation command	• 3.1
	• Create points by importing point data	• 3.2
	• Use point groups to control the display of points	• 3.3

3.1 Create Points Using the Point Creation Command

You can create points using the commands in the Create Points toolbar. These commands include:

- **Miscellaneous - Manual:** Creates a new point at specified coordinates.
- **Alignments - Station/Offset:** Creates a point at an alignment's specific station and offset. These points and their descriptions do not update if the alignment is modified or the point is moved. If you prefer a dynamic station and offset labels, consider using an Alignment label instead.
- **Alignments - Measure Alignment:** Creates point objects at a set interval, which is useful for construction staking. Again, these points do not update if the alignment changes.
- **Surface - Random Points:** Creates points whose elevation is from a specified surface. These points do update, but you must manually force the update. If you prefer a dynamic spot label, consider a Surface label instead.

Each icon in the Create Points toolbar has a drop-down list. If you expand it, you can select a command from the list to run, as shown in Figure 3–1.

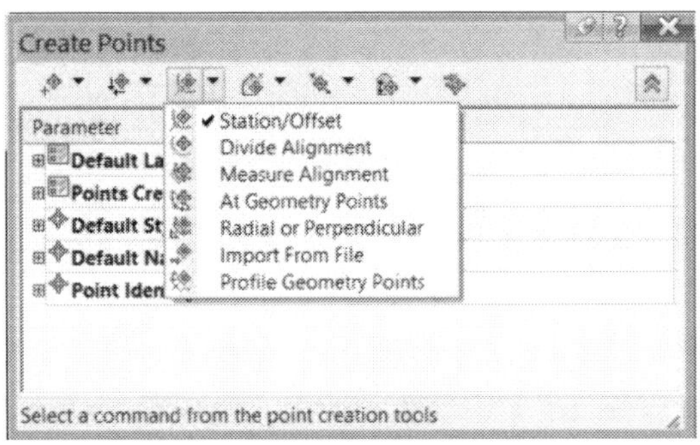

Figure 3–1

3.2 Create Points by Importing Point Data

The AutoCAD Civil 3D software has methods to import point data from ASCII text files, AutoCAD Land Desktop point databases, and Autodesk LandXML files, as well as methods to convert AutoCAD Land Desktop points to AutoCAD Civil 3D points. The *Survey* tab also inserts points from a survey to a drawing.

Import Points Only

There are two methods of launching the import point feature, one is by using the *Insert* tab and the other is using the **Points** creation tool in the *Prospector* tab.

How To: Use the *Insert* tab method

Alternatively, you can click (Import Points) in the Create Points toolbar.

1. In the *Insert* tab, click (Points from File).This opens the Import Points dialog box.
2. In the Import Points dialog box, set the file format, select the files to import, set any advanced options, and click **OK** to import the points.

How To: Use the Point Creation tools method

1. Open the Create Points dialog box by expanding Points in the *Home* tab, expanding the drop-down list and selecting a **Create Points** option, as shown on the left in Figure 3–2. Alternatively, in the *Prospector* tab, select **Points**, right-click and select **Create...**, as shown on the right.

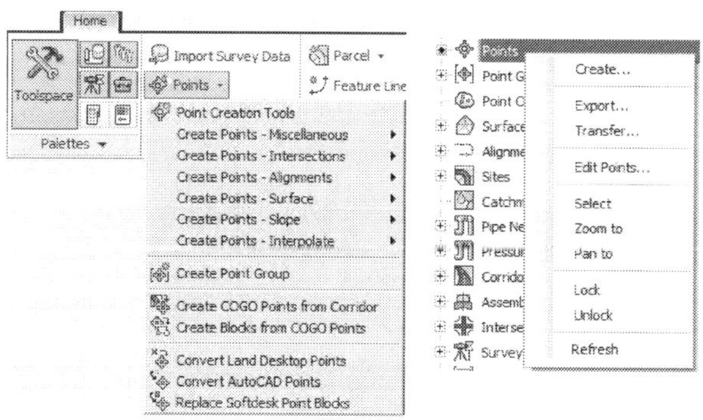

Figure 3–2

All commands in the Points drop-down list can also be accessed in the Create Points toolbar, as shown in Figure 3–3.

Figure 3–3

2. Click  (Import Points) to open the Import Points dialog box.
3. In the Import Points dialog box, expand the Format drop-down list and select a point file format.
4. After setting the format, click  on the right to open the Select Source File dialog box.
5. In the Select Source File dialog box, browse to the import point file, select it, and select **Open**. You can assign the imported points to a new or existing point group by selecting the **Add Points to Point Group** option and selecting the point group in the drop-down list. Select any **Advanced options** as required. The Import Points dialog box is shown in Figure 3–4.

You can select multiple files if they have the same file format.

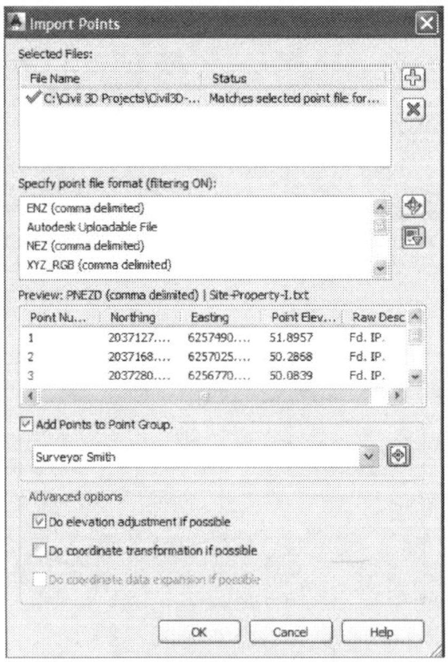

Figure 3–4

To import points directly from an AutoCAD Land Desktop point database, select the External Project Point Database format and browse for the project's COGO subfolder. Then locate and select the **Points.mdb** file.

If a drawing contains all or a subset of all points, you only need to convert the points into AutoCAD Civil 3D cogo points.

Duplicate Point Numbers

If an imported file creates duplicate point numbers, the AutoCAD Civil 3D software overwrites, merges, or reassigns them during the import process. When encountering duplicate point numbers, the AutoCAD Civil 3D software can assign the next available number, add an offset value (add 5000 to each point number that conflicts), overwrite points (replaces the current point values with the file's values), or merge points (add the file's values to an existing point's values). If using the offset method, the new point numbers are kept unique in the drawing. If using the next available number method, the new points blend into the original points and are difficult to identify.

The offset method is preferred when resolving duplicate point numbers. When importing points that will potentially duplicate point numbers, the Create Points toolbar's *Point Identity* settings, as shown in Figure 3–5, is the default when handling duplicate point numbers.

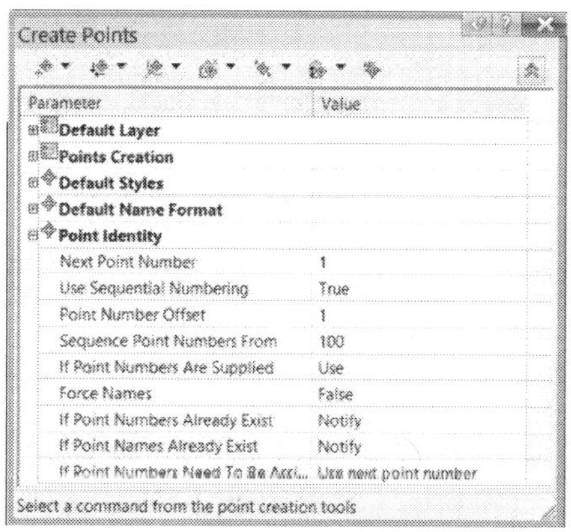

Figure 3–5

In the *Point Identity* settings, set the duplicate point resolution method for the *If Point Numbers Already Exist* variable. The four methods are **Renumber**, **Merge**, **Overwrite**, and **Notify**, as shown in Figure 3–6. The import process never overwrites point data unless you specify that it should do so.

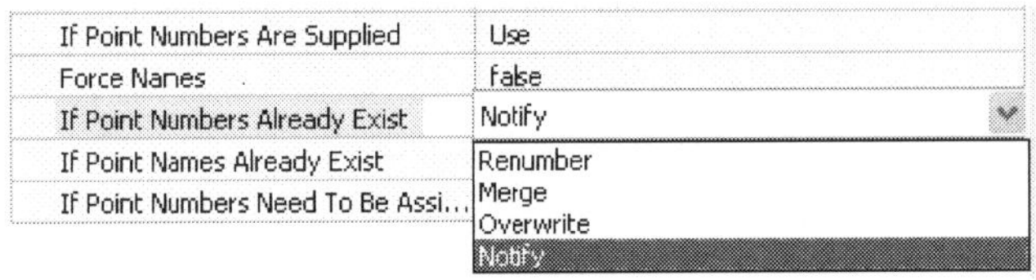

Figure 3–6

When encountering a duplicate point, the Duplicate Point Number dialog box opens. After you define a resolution, it can be assigned to the current duplicate point or to all encountered duplicate points.

Survey Toolspace

The Survey Toolspace displays a panel through which all surveys are processed. Survey uses graphics to display field book imports, figure and network previews, and points. If you toggle off these graphics, you can process a survey without a drawing being open. If you want to display these graphics, you need to have a drawing open. Survey prompts you to open a drawing if you do not have one open.

The Survey Toolspace contains Survey settings, Equipment defaults, Figure Prefixes, and Linework Code Sets. Survey's settings can be on a local or network folder. It is preferred to use a network folder in larger offices because all users can then standardize the file values.

How To: Display the Survey Toolspace

If your Toolspace does not display the *Survey* tab, click (Survey Toolspace) in the *Home* tab>Palettes panel, as shown in Figure 3–7.

Figure 3–7

Import Points and Figures Using the Survey Database

After collecting and coding the data, and then downloading and converting it, the next step in Survey is to import the survey data, review it, and place the survey points and figures into a drawing. A working folder defines where the local Survey Database is located. The preferred location is a network folder, in which you place the local Survey Databases. The Survey User Settings dialog box sets the defaults for all new Survey Databases. You should set these before starting Survey. The Survey Working Folder is the location for all of the Survey Databases and can be local or on the network. The default working folder is *C:\Civil 3D Projects*.

How To: Set the Working Folder for the Survey Database

1. In the *Survey* tab, select **Survey Databases**.
2. Right-click and select **Set working folder...** as shown in Figure 3–8.

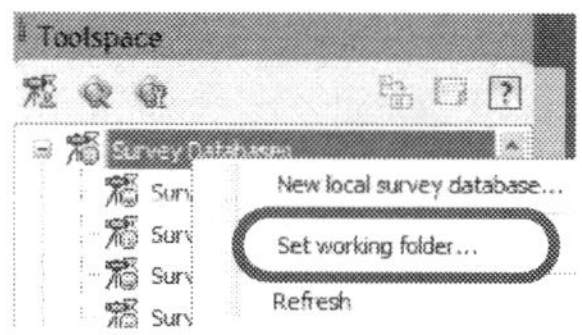

Figure 3–8

Survey Database

Survey Database Folders cannot be deleted in AutoCAD Civil 3D Survey. If you want to delete the working folder, this process must be done manually, external to the AutoCAD Civil 3D software.

A Survey Database is a subfolder in the working folder. The Survey Working Folder contains the Survey's settings and observation database. This database contains the Survey's Networks, Figures, and Survey Points.

To import a field book, you use the Survey's *Import Events* collection. *Import Events* provides access to an Import wizard, which guides you through the steps of importing a file. To open the Import wizard, select **Import Events** in the Survey, right-click, and select **Import survey data...**

The Specify Database page is shown in Figure 3–9. It sets the survey, creates a new survey, and edits the Survey's settings.

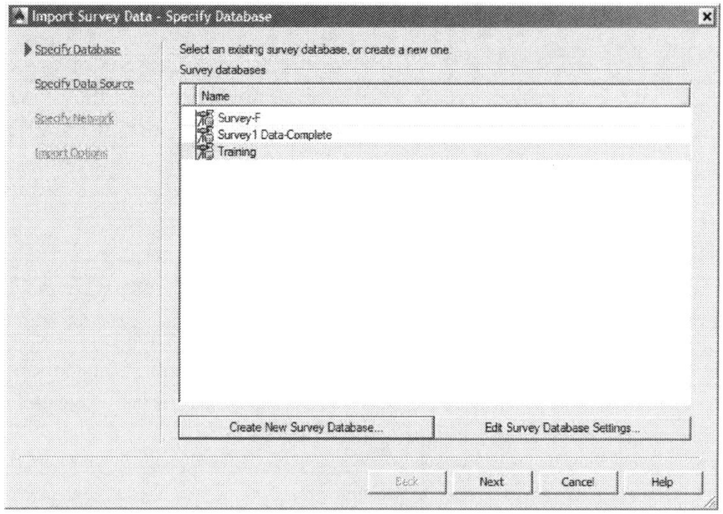

Figure 3–9

Click **Next**. The *Specify Data Source* page (shown in Figure 3–10), defines the file import type, the file's path, and its format (if it is a coordinate file).

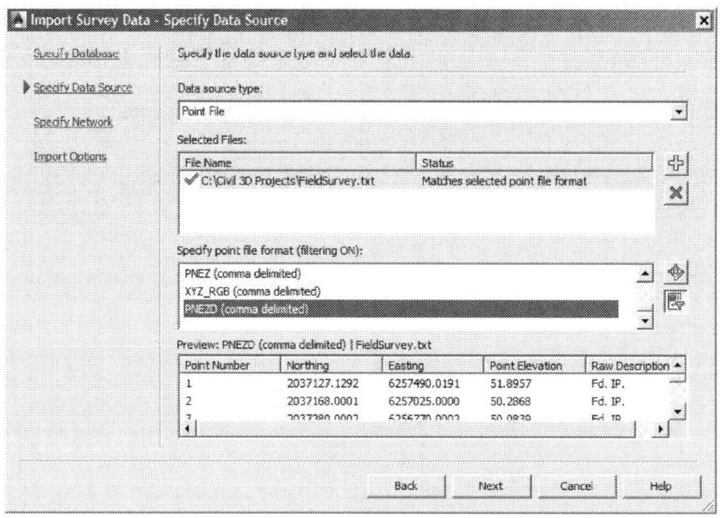

Figure 3–10

Click **Next**. The *Specify Network* page (shown in Figure 3–11), enables you to change the network or create a new survey network.

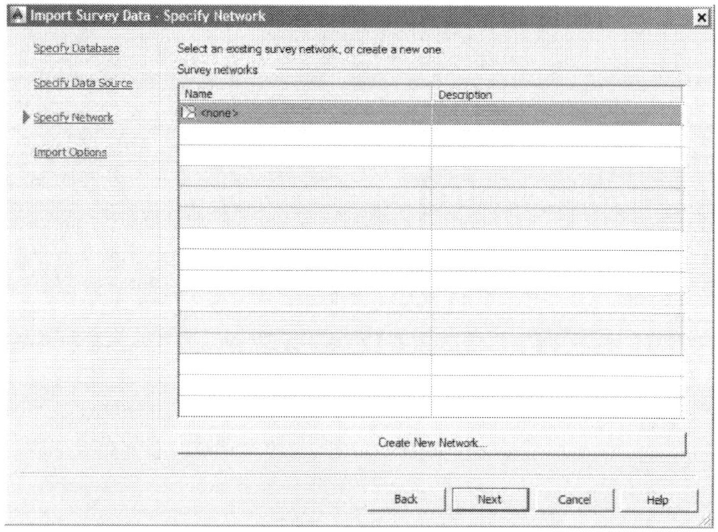

Figure 3–11

Click **Next**. The *Import Options* page (shown in Figure 3–12), sets the values for the import. These settings affect what the import does and which support files it uses.

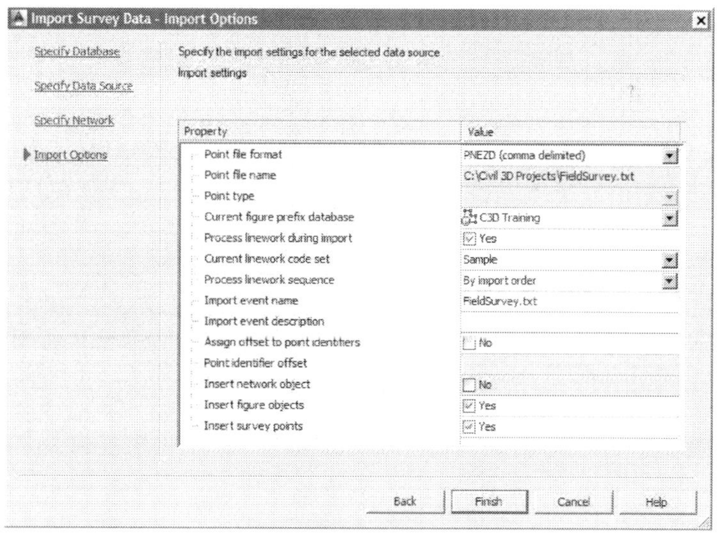

Figure 3–12

If the field book has figure coding from a conversion, you do not need to toggle on the *Process linework during import* property. This is for ASCII files other than field books that have ***Linework Code Set*** commands included in the point's description.

Inserting figures requires entries to be in the Figure Prefix database and figure styles to be in the drawing. This is required to point the figure and linework to the correct layers in the drawing and to specify whether the figure is also a breakline in a surface.

When inserting points, it is necessary to have a Description Key Set defined to assign points, point label styles, and layers, and to translate raw descriptions to full descriptions.

Open a Survey Database for Editing

Only one Survey Database can be edited at a time. When opened for editing, this prepares the survey for reading and writing.

There are options to set the path or location for the Survey Database project files, and for all of the settings. When you create a new Survey Database, a Windows folder is created with the same name. If you close a drawing with a survey open, the Survey Database closes automatically. You must start a new drawing and then open the required Survey Database. You can only have one Survey Database open at a time.

How To: Open a Survey Database

1. Expand the Survey Database branch.
2. Select the survey database that you want to open, right-click, and select **Open for edit** or **Open for read-only**, depending your requirements, as shown in Figure 3–13.

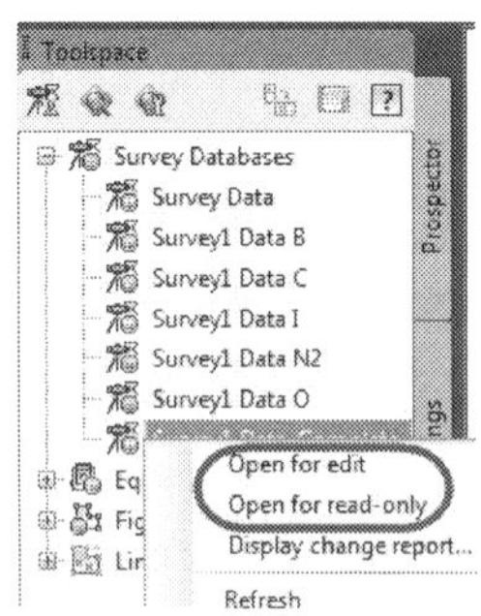

Figure 3–13

3.3 Use Point Groups to Control the Display of Points

Point groups organize points that share common descriptions and characteristics (such as existing storm, gas lines, building corners, etc.). Point groups also enable points to display different point or label styles. For example, a Landscape Architect needs to display different symbols for each tree species, while an Engineer only needs to display a generic tree symbol. The Description Key Set enables you to assign the tree species symbols for the Landscape Architect, and a point group enables generic tree symbols to override the symbols for the Engineer. Another function of a point group is to hide all of the points.

In the AutoCAD Civil 3D software, point groups can be defined in the template along with a Description Key Set. When you create a new drawing from this template and import points, they are assigned their symbols and can be sorted into point groups.

All points in a drawing belong to the **_All Points** point group. Consider this point group as the point database. It cannot be deleted and initially is not in a drawing until you add points. All new point groups include all drawing points or a subset of drawing points (referenced points from the **_All Points** point group).

Defining Point Groups

To create a new point group, select the *Prospector* tab, right-click on the *Point Groups* collection and select **New...** Alternatively, in the *Home* tab, expand Points and select **Create Point Group**.

When you select **New...** or **Create Point Group**, the Point Group Properties dialog box opens. It has nine tabs, each affecting the point group's definition.

The *Point Groups*, *Raw Desc Matching*, *Include*, and *Query Builder* tabs add points to the point group. The *Exclude* tab removes points from a point group.

The *Information* tab defines the point group's name. The *Point style* and *Point label style* should remain at their defaults, unless you want to use either style to override the assigned styles of the points in the point group. The points in the point group display their originally assigned styles until you toggle on the override. A point group can be locked by toggling on the **Object locked** option to prevent any changes to the group. The Point Group Properties dialog box is shown in Figure 3–14.

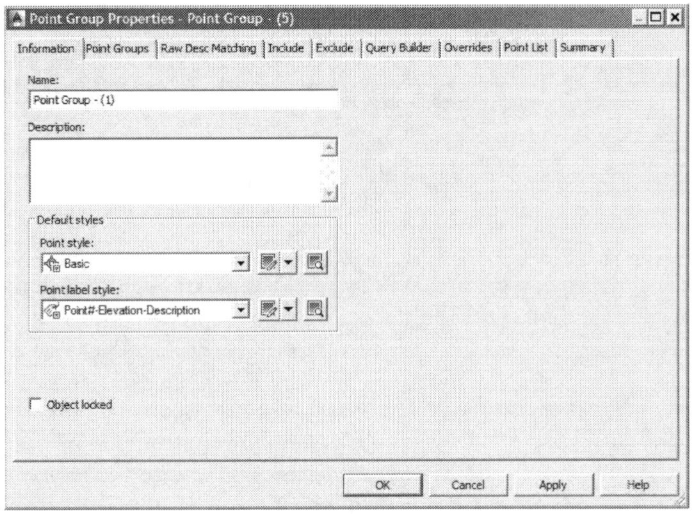

Figure 3–14

The *Point Groups* tab lists the drawing's groups. A point group can be created from other point groups. When you select a point group name, the group and its points become members of the new point group. For example, the point group **Trees** is created from the point groups *Maple*, *Walnut*, *Oak*, etc.

The *Raw Desc Matching* tab lists codes from the Description Key Code set. When you toggle on the code, any point matching the code becomes part of the point group.

If you cannot select a point with the previous two methods, the *Include* tab enables you to include points by specifically entering in the selection criteria. The criteria include the point number (point number list or by selection), elevation, name, raw description, full description, and all points.

- **With numbers matching:** Selects points by a point number range or list. When creating a list, sequential point numbers are hyphenated (1-20) and individual numbers are in a comma delimited list. A point list can include sequential and individual points (1-20, 14, 44, 50-60). Select **Selection Set in Drawing** to select the points in the drawing and list their point numbers at the top of the *Include* tab.

- **With elevations matching:** Enables you to select points by entering a specific elevation or by specifying a minimum and/or maximum elevation. For example, valid entries include >100,<400, and >100. The first entry only includes points whose elevation is above 100, but less than 400. The second entry only includes points whose elevation is greater than 100. A point without an elevation cannot be selected using this method. An elevation range, defined by separating the start and end numbers with a hyphen, includes points whose elevation falls in the range (1-100). This can be combined with greater or less than symbols.

- **With names matching:** Selects points based on matching their point names. Enter one or more point names separated by commas.

- **With raw/full descriptions matching:** Selects points based on matching an entered raw or full description. Enter one or more descriptions separated by commas. You can use the same wildcards as the Description Key Set. Generally, this method uses the asterisk (*) as the wildcard after the description (e.g., PINE*, CTV*, CL*, etc.).

- **Include all points:** Assigns all points in the drawing to the point group. When this option is toggled on, all other **Include** options are disabled.

The *Exclude* tab has the same options as the *Include* tab, except for the **Include All Points** option.

The *Query Builder* tab creates one or more expressions to select points. Each query is a row selecting points. As with all SQL queries, you combine expressions using the operators AND, OR, and NOT. You can also use parentheses to group expressions.

The *Overrides* tab overrides the points in the point group's raw description, elevation, point style, and/or point label style. For example, you can override specific tree species symbols with a generic tree symbol, override a label style when displaying this group, or override the point and label style with none (to hide all points).

The point group display order affects points and their overrides. To change how the point groups display, modify the Point Group display order.

The *Point List* tab displays the point group's points. This tab enables you to review points that are currently in the point group.

The *Summary* tab displays the point group's settings. You can print this tab as a report by cutting and pasting it into a document.

Updating Out-of-Date Point Groups

After defining point groups and adding points to a drawing, the group becomes out of date before assigning the points to the group. This enables you to verify that the point(s) should become part of the group. To review why a group is out of date, select the group, right-click, and select **Show Changes...** If the changes are correct, select **Update** to add the points to the group. If you know that all of the groups displaying as out of date should be updated, right-click on the *Point Groups* collection and select **Update**. At this level, the command updates all of the point groups.

Overriding Point Group Properties

When working with points, you might want them to display different labels, not be displayed, or display different symbols. Each required change is a function of a point group override. A point group that contains all of the points and overrides their symbols and labels with none does not display any points. This is similar to freezing all of the layers involved with points. A point group that changes the symbols that a group displays overrides the label styles assigned to the point in the point group. To display a different symbol, the point group overrides the assigned point styles. To set the style and override the assigned styles, toggle on the point group in the *Overrides* tab and set the styles in the *Override* column of the point group, as shown in Figure 3–15.

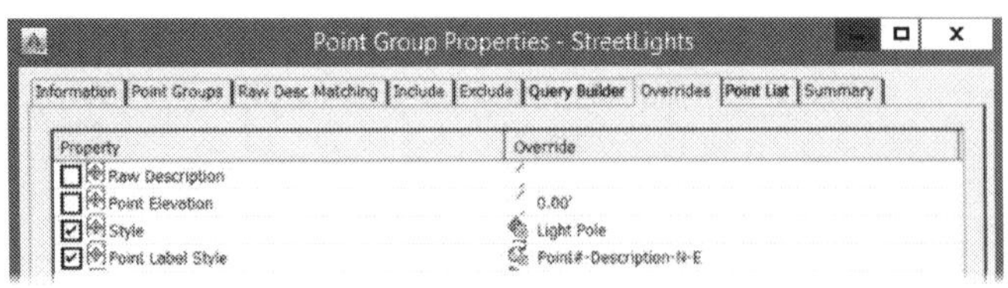

Figure 3–15

Point Groups Display Properties

When creating a point group, it is placed at the top of the point group list. The point group list is more than a list of point groups; it is also the AutoCAD Civil 3D's point draw order. The AutoCAD Civil 3D software draws the point groups starting from the bottom of the list to the top. If **_All Points** is the first drawn point group and the remaining point groups are subsets of all points, the individual point group does not display, but all of the points display.

To display point groups that are a subset of all points, you must create a point group whose purpose is to hide all points. This popular point group is commonly called *No Display*. With this group, any point group drawn after it displays its members without *seeing* the other points.

The AutoCAD Civil 3D software draws point groups from the bottom to the top of the list. To manipulate the display order, right-click on the *Point Groups* collection in the *Prospector* tab and select **Properties**. The Point Groups dialog box opens, enabling you to modify the point group display order using the arrows on the right, as shown in Figure 3–16.

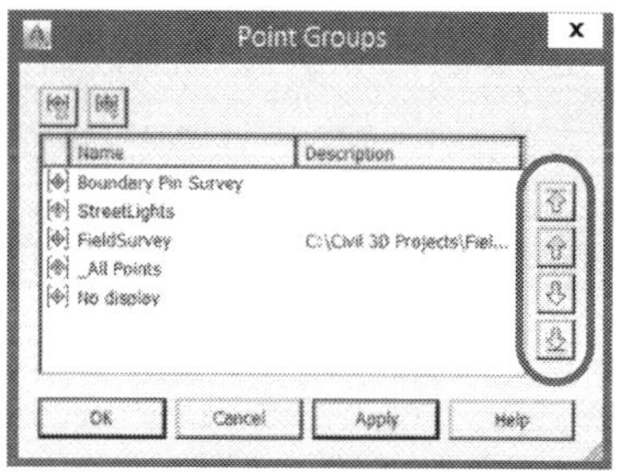

Figure 3–16

These arrows enable you to select the required point group and move it up or down in the list (or all the way to the top or bottom of the list with one click, ) in the hierarchy for display purposes. The Point Groups dialog box has two additional icons at the top. The first icon displays the difference between point groups and the second icon updates them all.

If you use Description Key Sets, a point displays the assigned point and label style when it is part of any point group. The only time the point displays another style is when you override the style (in the Point Group Properties dialog box, in the *Overrides* tab).

With the Description Key Set and display order shown in Figure 3–17, the points display their originally assigned point label styles.

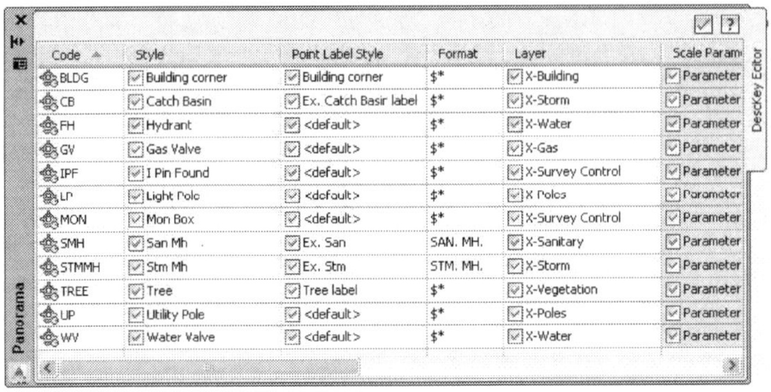

Code	Style	Point Label Style	Format	Layer	Scale Param
BLDG	Building corner	Building corner	$*	X-Building	Parameter
CB	Catch Basin	Ex. Catch Basir label	$*	X-Storm	Parameter
FH	Hydrant	<default>	$*	X-Water	Parameter
GV	Gas Valve	<default>	$*	X-Gas	Parameter
IPF	I Pin Found	<default>	$*	X-Survey Control	Parameter
LP	Light Pole	<default>	$*	X-Poles	Parameter
MON	Mon Box	<default>	$*	X-Survey Control	Parameter
SMH	San Mh	Ex. San	SAN. MH.	X-Sanitary	Parameter
STMMH	Stm Mh	Ex. Stm	STM. MH.	X-Storm	Parameter
TREE	Tree	Tree label	$*	X-Vegetation	Parameter
UP	Utility Pole	<default>	$*	X-Poles	Parameter
WV	Water Valve	<default>	$*	X-Water	Parameter

Figure 3–17

The *No Display* point group includes all of the points, but overrides the originally assigned point style and point label styles with **<none>**. When *No Display* is moved to the list's top, no points display. The Point Groups dialog box is shown in Figure 3–18.

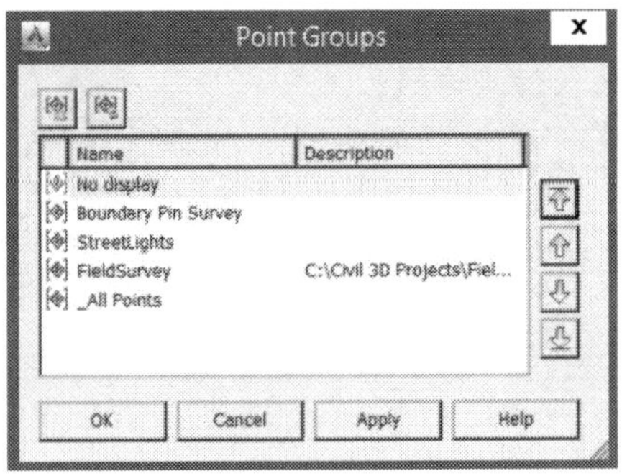

Figure 3–18

Practice 3a

Creating AutoCAD Civil 3D Points

Practice Objective

- Create a point manually then zoom to it using transparent commands.

Estimated time for completion: 10 minutes

In this practice, a fire hydrant was located by GPS. You will add a point object to locate it manually.

1. Open **SUV1-C1-Survey.dwg**.
2. In the *Home* tab>Create Ground Data panel, select **Points> Point Creation Tools** to display the Create Points toolbar.

   Expand the toolbar by clicking , as shown in Figure 3–19.

Figure 3–19

3. In the *Point Identity* area in the dialog box, set the *Next Point Number* to **260** and collapse the toolbar, by clicking .
4. Select the **Manual** option in the miscellaneous group in the toolbar as shown in Figure 3–20.

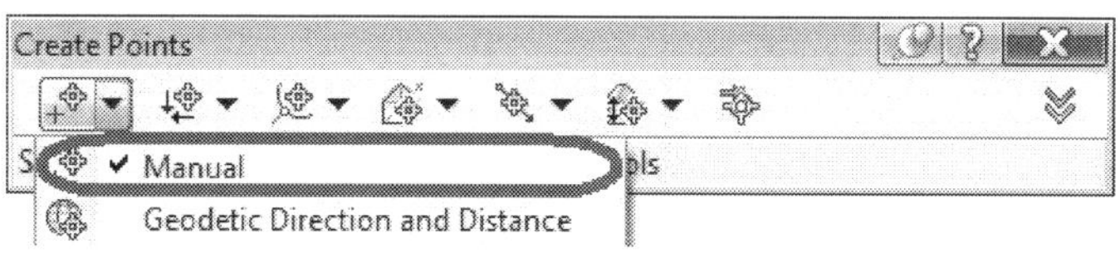

Figure 3–20

5. When prompted for a location, type **6256069.30,2036634.25** and press <Enter>.
   - When prompted for a description, type **HYD** and press <Enter>.
   - When prompted for an elevation, press <Enter> to accept the default value of **<.>** (period), because it is unknown.

The period is a placeholder for the elevation field. Typing zero is not correct because 0 is a valid elevation.

- Press <Enter> again to finish the command and select **X** in the Create Points dialog box to close it.
- In the Transparent Command toolbar, click (Zoom to Point), and type **260**.

6. Save the drawing.

Practice 3b

Importing Survey Data

Estimated time for completion: 25 minutes

Practice Objective

- Import points from and export points to ASCII files created from the field survey.

In this practice you will import an ASCII file created in the field.

Task 1 - Import an ASCII file.

1. Open **SUV1-E1-Survey.dwg** from the *C:\Civil 3D Projects\Civil3D-Training\Survey* folder.

2. In the *Home* tab>Create Ground Data panel, click (Import Survey Data).

3. On the Specify Database page, click **Create New Survey Database...**, as shown in Figure 3–21.

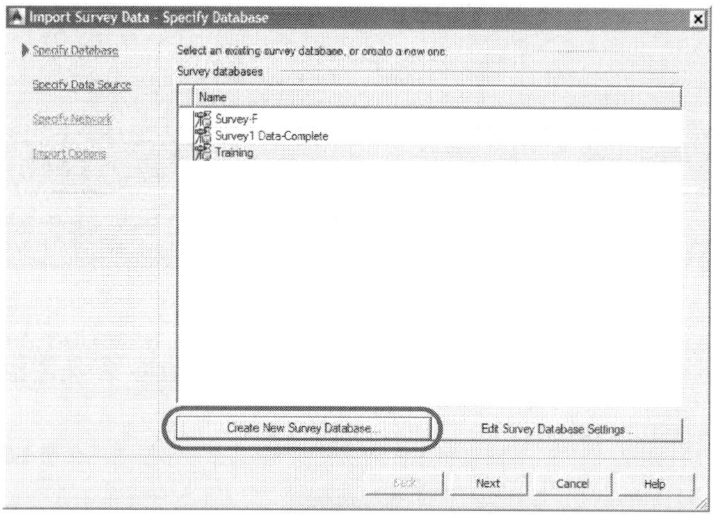

Figure 3–21

4. Type **Training** for the name and click **OK**.

5. Click **Edit Survey Database Settings...** as shown in Figure 3–22.

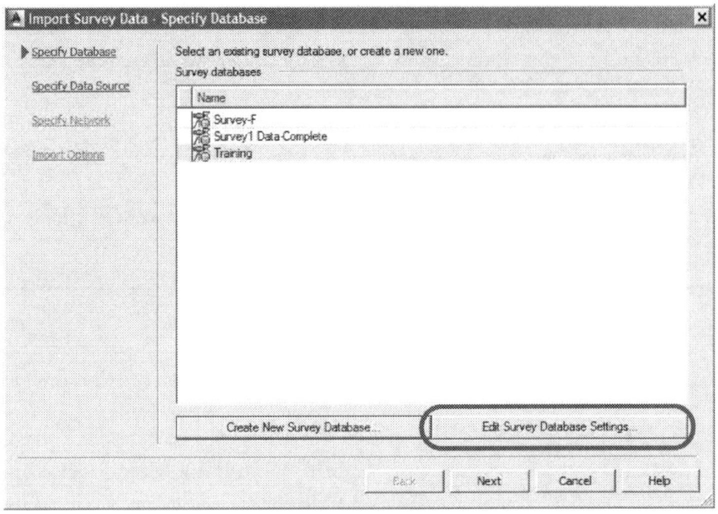

Figure 3–22

6. Under *Units* in the Survey Database Settings dialog box, for the *Coordinate Zone*, click the **Browse** icon. In the Select Coordinate Zone dialog box, select **NAD83 California State Planes, Zone VI, US Foot** (as shown in Figure 3–23). Click **OK** twice and then click **Next**.

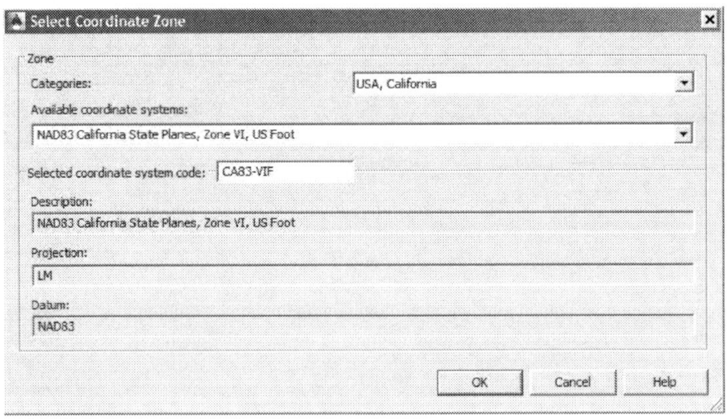

Figure 3–23

7. On the Specify Data Sources page, expand the Data source type drop-down list and select **Point File**, as shown in Figure 3–24. Click (Add file) and browse to *C:\Civil 3D Projects\Civil3D-Training\Survey*. Select **Field Survey.txt** and open it. Finally, for the file format, select **PNEZD (comma delimited)**. Click **Next**.

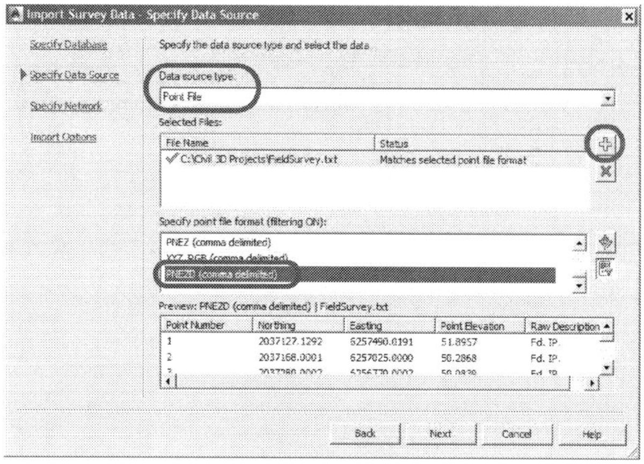

Figure 3–24

8. On the Survey Network page, click **Next**.

9. On the Import Options page, select **Process linework during import**, **Insert figure objects**, and **Insert survey points**, as shown in Figure 3–25. Click **Finish**.

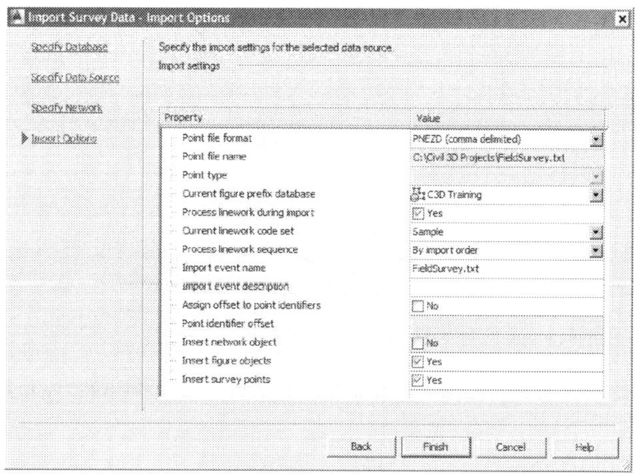

Figure 3–25

10. Save the drawing.

Practice 3c Creating Point Groups

Practice Objective

- Draw Parcels from a legal description using lines and curves or polylines and transparent commands.

Estimated time for completion: 10 minutes

In this practice you will create point groups.

Task 1 - Create Point Groups (Boundary Pin Survey).

1. Open **SUV1-F1-Survey.dwg**.
2. In the *Prospector* tab, select **Point Groups**, right-click, and select **New...**, as shown in Figure 3–26.

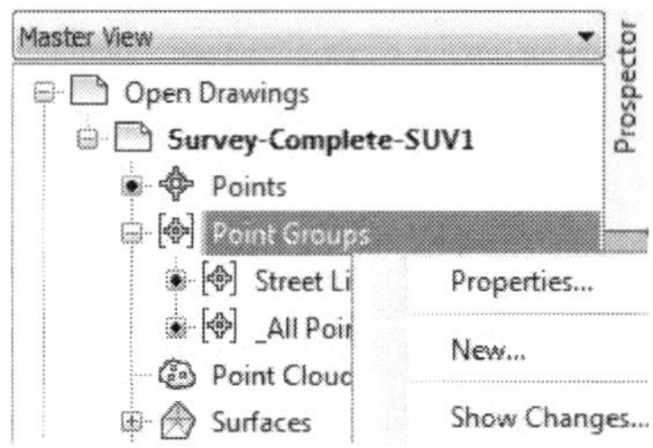

Figure 3–26

3. In the Point Group Properties dialog box, in the *Information* tab, type **Boundary Pin Survey** in the *Name* field, set the *Point style* to **Iron Pin**, and set the *Point label style* to **Elevation and Description**, as shown in Figure 3–27.

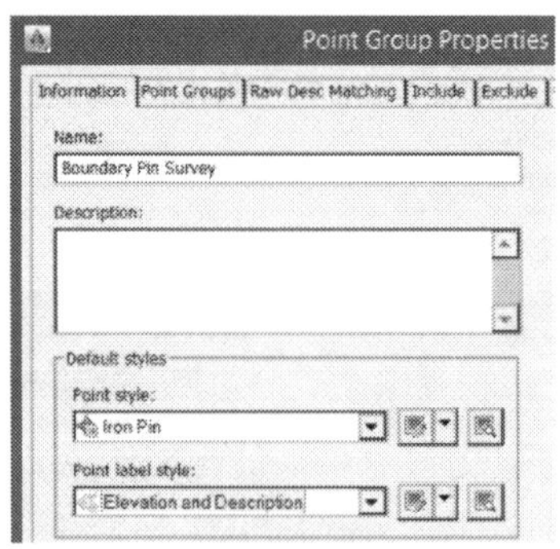

Figure 3–27

4. Select the *Include* tab. Select the **With raw description matching** option. Type ***IP.** (verify that a period follows IP) in the field to select all of the points that have the last three characters *IP.* (iron pin). You can confirm this in the *Point List* tab, as shown in Figure 3–28.

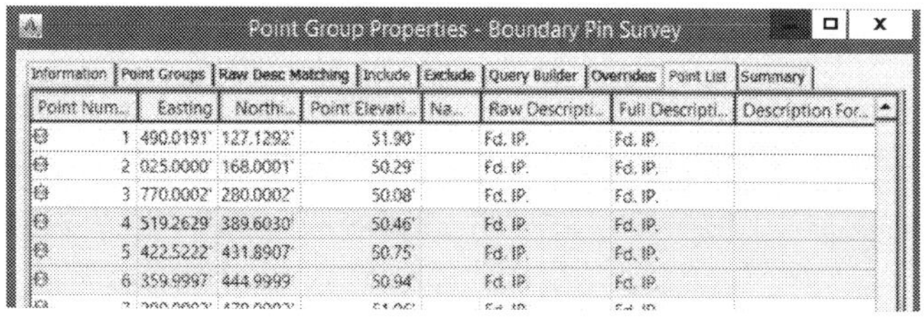

Figure 3–28

5. Click **OK** to close the dialog box and apply the changes.

Task 2 - Create point groups (No display).

Continue working with the drawing from the previous task. In this task you will use the point group to control the points display. Not only will you be able to display the same point differently, but you will also be able to control the visibility of the points. This eliminates needing to use the Layer command to thaw and freeze layers.

1. As in Task 1, select **Point Groups**, right-click, and select **New...** to create a new point group. In the *Information* tab, type **No display** for the *Name*.

2. Select **<none>** for both the *Point style* and the *Point label style*, as shown in Figure 3–29.

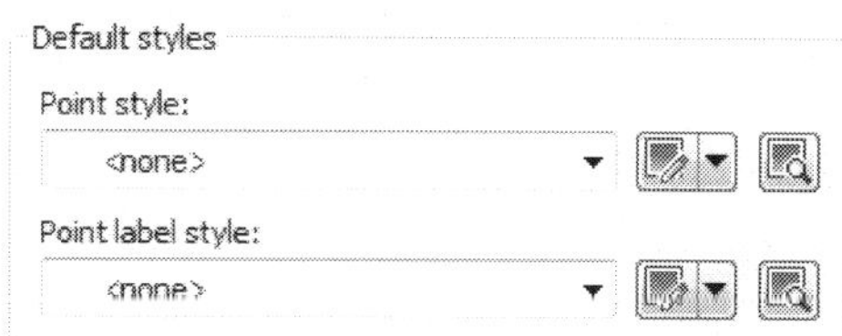

Figure 3–29

3. Select the *Overrides* tab and select **Style** and **Point Label Style**, as shown in Figure 3–30.

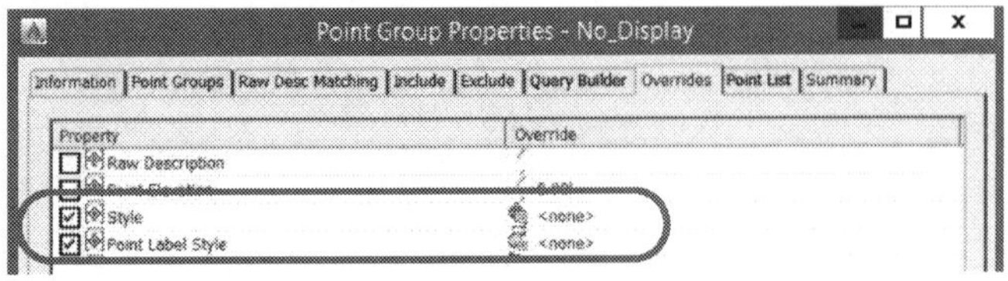

Figure 3–30

4. Select the *Include* tab, select the **Include all points** option, and set it to **True**. Select the *Point List* tab to confirm that all of the points have been included.

5. Click **OK** to create the point group. Note that the points have disappeared.

6. To control the hierarchy and the display of the point group style, select the *Prospector* tab, select **Point Groups**, right-click, and select **Properties**.

7. In the Point Groups dialog box, select the **Boundary Pin Survey** point group and move it to the top of the list by clicking . Click **OK** to apply the changes. Only the points in the Boundary Pin point group are displayed. If the property pins are not displayed you might need to **regen** the drawing (type **RE**, and press <Enter>).

8. Experiment with moving point groups up and down the list to control the display of points.

9. Save the drawing.

Chapter 4

Surfaces

This chapter includes instructional content to assist in your preparation for the following topic and objectives for the AutoCAD® Civil® 3D 2016 Certified Professional exam.

Autodesk Certification Exam Objectives in this Chapter

Exam Topic	Exam Objective	Section
Surfaces	• Identify key characteristics of surfaces	• 4.1
	• Create and edit surfaces	• 4.2
	• Use styles and settings to display surface information	• 4.3
	• Create a surface by assembling fundamental data	• 4.4
	• Use styles to analyze surface display results	• 4.5
	• Annotate surfaces	• 4.6

4.1 Identify Key Characteristics of Surfaces

The *Information* tab enables you to rename the surface, edit the description, apply a surface object style, and render material, which controls how the surface displays in a rendered view.

The *Statistics* tab displays the current surface slope, elevation, and triangulation. It contains three areas:

- **General:** Provides an overall view of the surface. The **Minimum**, **Maximum**, and **Mean** elevations are the important entries in this area and provide the first hint of bad or incorrect data.
- **Extended:** Reports the **2D** and **3D** surface areas and **Minimum**, **Maximum**, and **Mean** slope values.
- **TIN:** Reviews the number of triangles, minimum and maximum triangle areas, and leg lengths in the surface.

The areas of triangles, along with the minimum and maximum triangle side lengths are indicators of data consistency. Generally, the longest triangles form around the perimeter of the surface. Limiting the length of triangle edges removes these types of triangles from the surface. You can delete these lines rather than try to set an optimum length, or you can create a boundary to prevent these types of triangles from being created.

When surfaces are created, they are assigned properties based on the *Build Options* area in the Edit Command Settings dialog box, as shown on the right in Figure 4–1. To open this dialog box, right-click on the **Create Surface** command and select **Edit Command Settings**, as shown on the left in Figure 4–1.

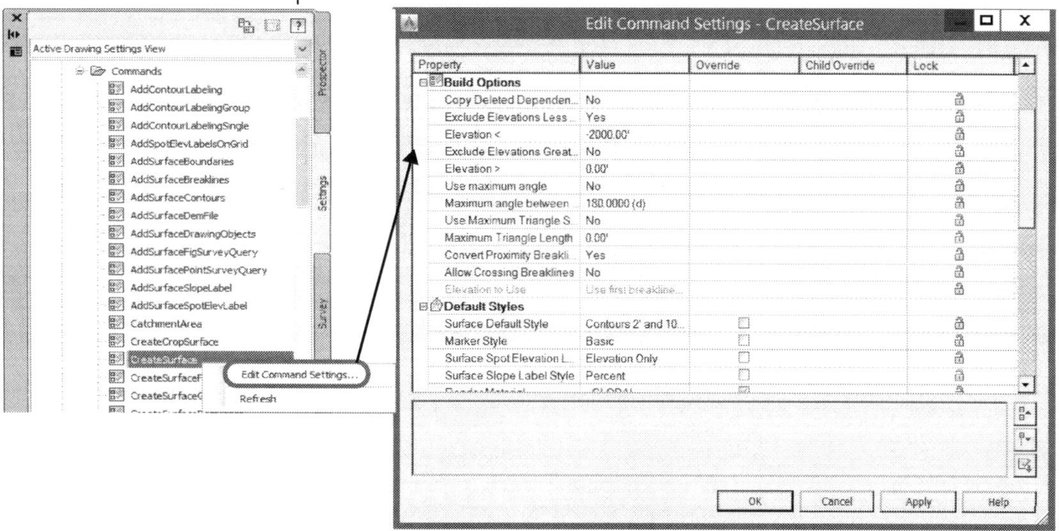

Figure 4–1

Surface Rebuilding

Some surface edits and point modifications can render a surface out of date. At that point, the surface is flagged as being out of date in the *Prospector* tab, as indicated by the **Drawing Item Modifier** icon shown in Figure 4–2.

Figure 4–2

When this occurs, you can right-click on the surface in the *Prospector* tab and select **Rebuild**. This updates the surface to reflect the recent changes. Alternatively, you can right-click on the surface in the *Prospector* and select **Rebuild-Automatic**, which updates the surface automatically without input from you. However, toggling this option on increases the strain on the computer resources and graphics capabilities so it is recommended that you leave it toggled off.

4.2 Create and Edit Surfaces

Contour data is available from many sources. Large sites are often surveyed using aerial photogrammetry, which provides contour polylines and spot elevations. Contour data can also be obtained from other AutoCAD Civil Engineering applications, such as AutoCAD Land Desktop.

In the AutoCAD Civil 3D software, polylines with elevation are useful as custom contour objects. Whether using polylines or AutoCAD Land Desktop contour objects, the AutoCAD Civil 3D software builds a surface by triangulating between contours. The end of each triangle side connects to a vertex of two different contours.

When processing contours for surface data, the AutoCAD Civil 3D software inspects the contour vertices for two conditions: too many data points representing similar data (e.g., 10 vertices on 15 units of contour length in an almost straight line), and not enough data points over the length of a contour.

You can set the values for these conditions in the Add Contour Data dialog box (as shown in Figure 4–3) when you add contour data.

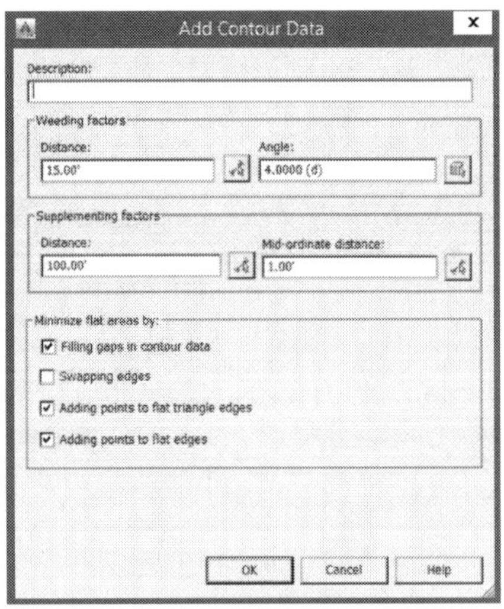

Figure 4–3

Weeding Factors

The *weeding* process removes redundant vertices from contours. The first step in the weeding process is to inspect three adjacent contour vertices, whose overall distance is shorter than a user-specified distance (e.g., three vertices in less than 15 units of contour). When encountering this situation, the weeding process prompts you about the change in direction between the three vertices. For example, does the direction from vertex 1 to vertex 2 change more than four degrees when going from vertex 2 to vertex 3? If not, the vertices are almost in a straight line and are too close. The AutoCAD Civil 3D software considers vertex 2 to be redundant and removes it from the surface data. This process repeats for the next three vertices. If the distance is under 15 units and the change of direction is less than four degrees, the next vertex 2 is removed from the data.

If a contour has three vertices in less than 15 units, and turns more than four degrees, vertex 2 is kept because the change in direction is significant. If there are more that 15 units between the three vertices, the AutoCAD Civil 3D software moves on to the next group.

An important feature of weeding is not what it removes from the data, but what is left over. If not enough data remains, the numbers for the weeding factors should be set to lower values.

Supplementing Factors

When the AutoCAD Civil 3D software inspects contour data, it uses supplementing factors to add vertices to the surface data. The first supplementing factor is the distance between contour vertices. When the distance between vertices is over 100 units, The AutoCAD Civil 3D software adds a vertex to the data along the course of the contour. The second supplementing factor is a mid-ordinate distance for the curve segments of a contour. If curves are distributed throughout the contour data, a setting of 0.1 is a good starting point.

- All weeding and supplementing factors are user-specified.
- Weeding and supplementing does not modify the contours or polylines in a drawing, only their data.
- There is no *correct* setting for weeding and supplementing. Varying the values creates more or less surface data.

Contour Issues

You should be aware of two issues when working with contour data: bays and peninsulas within the contours and the lack of high and low point elevations. These two issues affect triangulation and the quality of a surface.

Bays and peninsulas within contours represent gullies or isolated high points on a surface. As long as there is data to work with, the AutoCAD Civil 3D software builds a surface by triangulating between contours of different elevations. When the software cannot triangulate between different contours, the triangulation switches to connecting vertices on the same contour.

The **Minimize Flat Faces** command helps mitigate this situation by forcing the triangulation to target different contours, as shown in Figure 4–4. However, this method, similar to the edge swap method, does not correct every problem on a contour surface.

- To launch the **Minimize Flat Faces** command, right-click on the *Edits* heading in the *Definition* collection of a surface and select the command.

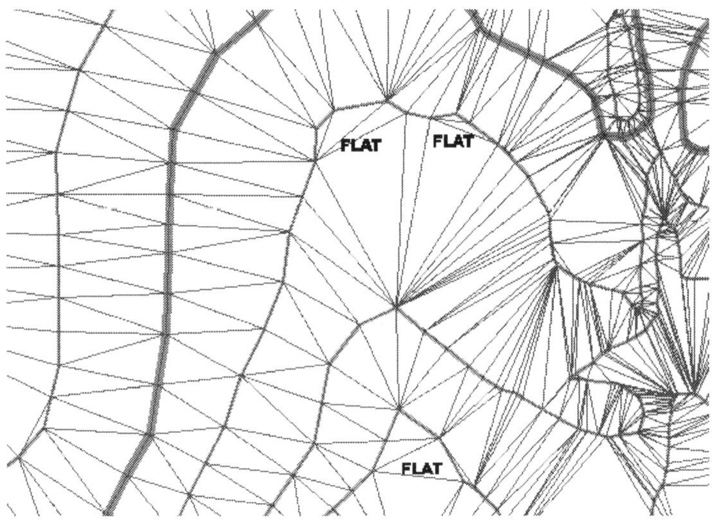

Figure 4–4

The second issue with contour data regards the loss of high and low points. Contours represent an elevation interval (120, 122, 123, etc.). However, the top of a hill could be 123.04 or 136.92 and the only contours present are for the elevations of 123 or 136. Spot elevations are needed in the surface data to help correctly resolve the high and low spots of a surface.

- Flat spots and the loss of high and low points affect the calculation of volumes for earthworks, as shown in Figure 4–5.

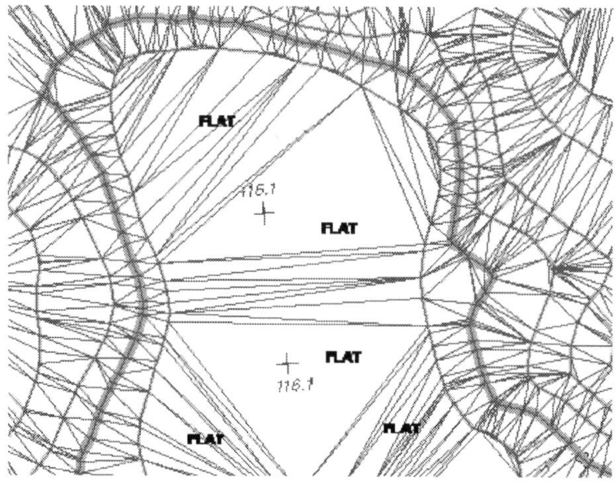

Figure 4–5

Minimizing Flat Triangle Strategies

By default, the Add Contour Data dialog box suggests using the **Minimize flat areas by:** options shown in Figure 4–6.

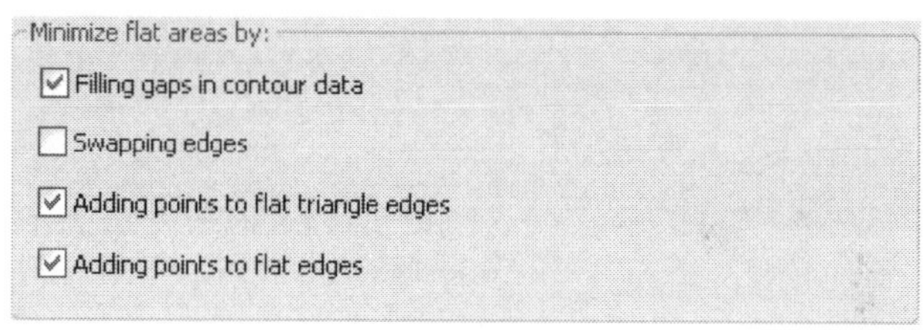

Figure 4–6

Together, these three methods attempt to detect and resolve peninsulas, bays, and other issues by adding additional points and filling in gaps based on surface trends. Generally, these provide the most expected results. The **Swapping edges** option is provided as a way of emulating how other terrain modeling software (such as AutoCAD Land Desktop) traditionally approached minimizing flat areas.

DEM Files

Digital Elevation Models (DEMs) are grid-based terrain models primarily used by GIS applications to represent large areas. Since they are large-scale and grid-based, they are generally only used in the AutoCAD Civil 3D software for preliminary design and other approximate tasks.

Drawing Objects

AutoCAD points, text, blocks, and other objects can be used as surface data. Individual AutoCAD Civil 3D point objects can also be selected using the **Drawing Objects** option. Selected objects need to have a valid elevation value.

- All data added as drawing objects is considered point data.
- You can add 3D lines and polyfaces using this method, but each end point is treated as if it were a point object. Linework is not treated as contours or breaklines. The Add Points From Drawing Objects dialog box is shown in Figure 4–7.

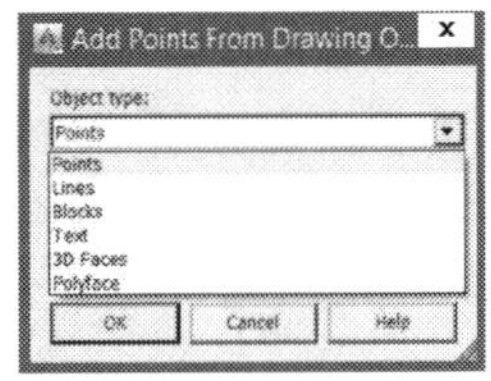

Figure 4–7

Point Files

Points in an ASCII point file can be used as surface data.

- You can use any import/export file format.
- This is an excellent way to create a large surface from a massive number of points, as it bypasses creating point objects, thereby reducing drawing overhead.

Point Groups

Using previously defined points groups in a surface definition enables you to isolate only the points on the ground to ensure that the tops of walls and invert elevations do not distort the surface.

Point Survey Queries

Select points in a survey database can be used as surface data by creating a survey query. The point data is used, but point objects are not created.

- Dynamic references to the points provide a more seamless update if changes to the database or query are made.
- This is an excellent way to create a large surface from a massive number of points, as it bypasses creating point objects, thereby reducing drawing overhead.
- Points from a survey query display under point groups in the surface definition.

Figure Survey Queries

Select figures in a survey database can be used as surface data. The figures are used as breaklines, but 3D polylines are not created in the drawing.

- Dynamic references to the figures provide a more seamless update if changes to the database or query are made.
- This is an excellent way to create a large surface from a massive number of figures, as it bypasses creating 3D polylines and turning them into breaklines, thereby reducing drawing overhead.
- Figures from a survey query display under breaklines in the surface definition.

Breaklines and Boundaries

A surface can include data from boundaries, breaklines, contours, Digital Elevation Model files (DEMs), drawing objects (AutoCAD points, individual AutoCAD Civil 3D points, lines, 3D faces, etc.), manual edits, and point files. The *Boundaries* collection displays above the *Breaklines* collection under the surface's *Definition* (in the *Prospector* tab), as shown in Figure 4–8. However, you should generally add boundaries after adding breaklines to a surface. If you use the Data Clip boundary type, any data that you add to the surface (point file, DEM file, or breakline) is only added to the area within the boundary. In that case, breaklines can be added to the surface after a Data Clip boundary type. Surface edit operations are not affected by the Data Clip boundary.

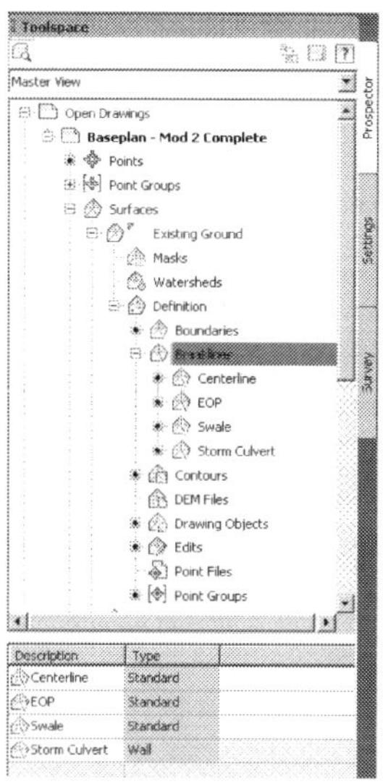

Figure 4–8

Breaklines

Breaklines affect surface triangulation and are important in point-based surfaces. They ensure that terrain models are triangulated correctly along linear features, as shown in Figure 4–9.

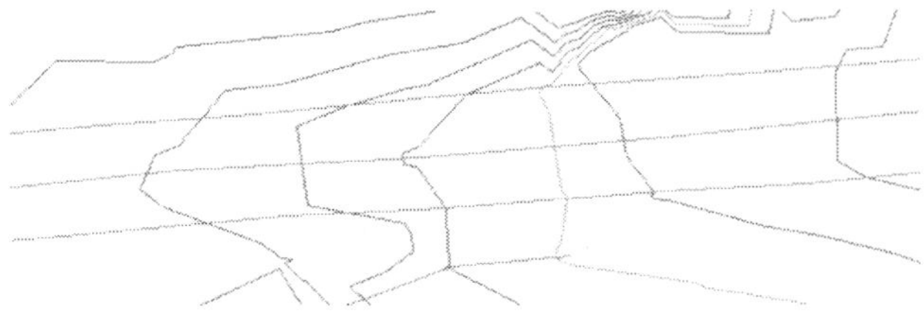

Surface before breaklines have been applied along the center line of a road.

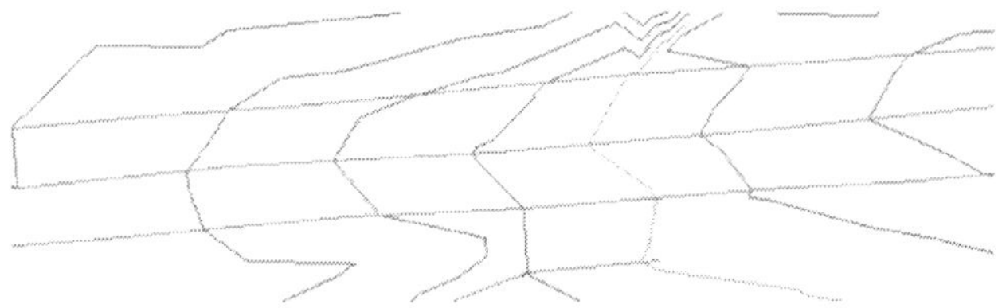

Surface after breaklines have been applied along the center line of a road.

Figure 4–9

- When adding a breakline to a surface, the AutoCAD Civil 3D software creates an entry under the *Breakline>Definition* collections, based on a description that you supply.
- When you define multiple breaklines at the same time, the AutoCAD Civil 3D software creates a single entry under the *Breaklines* collection. However, they are listed separately in the *Prospector* tab's List View.
- Breaklines can be defined as one of four types: **Standard**, **Proximity**, **Wall**, and **Non-Destructive**.

Standard Breaklines

A standard breakline is one that has valid elevations assigned at each vertex.

- Standard breaklines can be defined from 3D lines, 3D polylines, survey figures, or grading feature lines.
- The number of points generated along a breakline can be reduced by specifying a *Weeding* factor or increased by specifying a *Supplementing* factor, similar to weeding and supplementing factors for contour data.

- Curves in standard breaklines are approximated through the use of a mid-ordinate distance, similar to the way curved boundaries are resolved.
- For AutoCAD Land Desktop users, tasks that you might have applied to 3D polylines in AutoCAD Land Desktop should use grading feature lines in the AutoCAD Civil 3D software. This is because grading feature lines are more efficient in many ways, including their support of 3D curves.
- When drafting 3D lines, polylines, or feature lines, you can use AutoCAD Civil 3D's transparent commands. For example, using the **Point Object** (**'PO**) transparent command to select a point as a vertex of a 3D polyline prompts the AutoCAD Civil 3D software to assign the point's elevation to the vertex of the polyline.
- Standard breaklines can also be defined from ASCII breakline data files (.FLT file extension).

Proximity Breaklines

Proximity breaklines do not need to have elevations at their vertices. A polyline at elevation 0 could be used as a proximity breakline. When a proximity breakline is defined, the AutoCAD Civil 3D software automatically assigns vertex elevations from the nearest TIN data point, such as a nearby point object or contour line vertex.

- The AutoCAD Civil 3D software can define proximity breaklines from 2D polylines or grading feature Lines.
- The AutoCAD Civil 3D software does not support curves in proximity breaklines. Arc segments are treated as if they were straight line segments.
- One of the default options in the surface *Build* area enables the conversion of all proximity (2D) breaklines into standard (3D) breaklines. After conversion, the breakline is listed as a standard breakline and has the same elevations as the point objects that are at each vertex.

Wall Breaklines

- A wall breakline can be used to represent both the top and bottom of a wall, curb, or other sheer face.
- Wall breaklines are defined by 3D lines, 3D polylines, or feature lines. When defining them from linework, the object itself is meant to define either the top or bottom of the wall.
- The other end of the wall (top or bottom) is defined interactively by entering the absolute elevations or height differences from the defining line.
- If a Wall breakline starts as a 2D polyline or feature line, it can contain curve segments.
- The number of points generated along a breakline can be reduced by specifying a *Weeding* factor or increased by specifying a *Supplementing* factor.

Survey Figures as Breaklines

Figures created by surveyors can be used as breaklines if a connection exists between the drawing and the survey database.

How To: Add Survey Figures as Breaklines

1. Open the survey database for editing.
2. In the *Survey* tab, expand the *Survey Data* collection and select **Figures**. The list of figures in the grid view is displayed at the bottom of the Toolspace.
3. Select the figures, right-click, and select **Create breaklines...**, as shown in Figure 4–10.

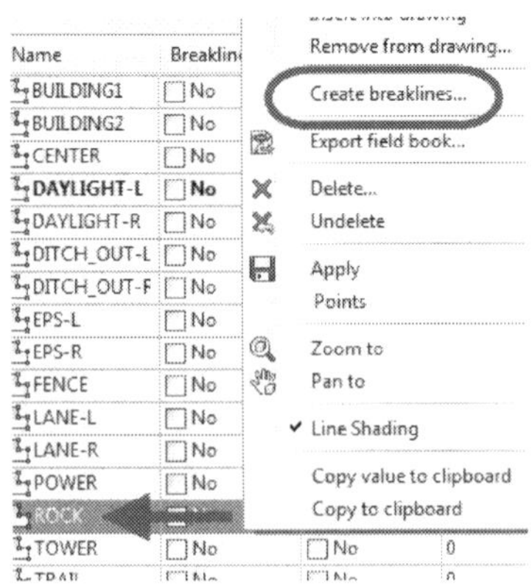

Figure 4–10

4. In the Create Breaklines dialog box, select the surface on which to place the breaklines, and then in the *Breakline* column, select the **Yes** option to create the breaklines, as shown in Figure 4–11. Click **OK** to close the dialog box.

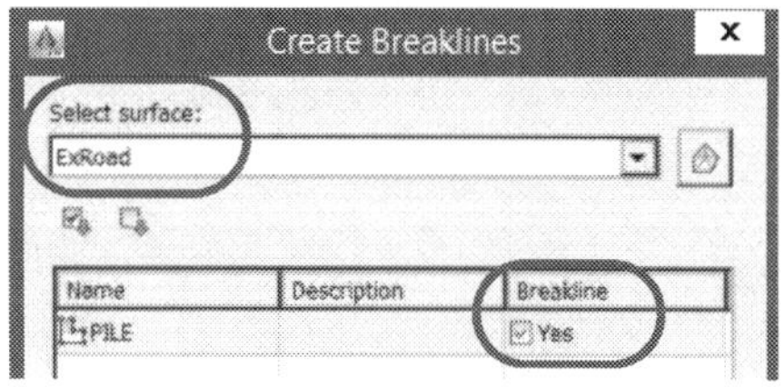

Figure 4–11

Boundaries

Boundaries provide interior or exterior limits to the surface triangulation. Boundaries are typically created from 2D closed polylines. There are four types of boundaries: **Outer**, **Hide**, **Show**, and **Data Clip**. An outer boundary should be one of the last items added to a surface, because adding data outside an existing boundary extends the surface past the boundary.

- An **Outer** boundary hides or excludes data outside its edge.
- A **Hide** boundary hides an interior portion of a surface to delineate features (such as water bodies and building footprints).
- A **Show** boundary displays a portion of a surface within a Hide boundary (e.g., to display an island in a pond).
- A **Data Clip** boundary acts as a filter on all data, including points, DEMs, and breaklines added to the surface after the creation of the Data Clip boundary. If a data clip boundary is used, any data added after it, that falls outside the data clip boundary, is ignored.

A boundary can contain arc segments. To better represent surface elevations around an arc, the AutoCAD Civil 3D software uses a mid-ordinate value to calculate where the triangles interact with the boundary. The mid-ordinate value is the distance between the midpoint of the cord and the arc. The smaller the mid-ordinate value, the closer the surface data is to the original arc. An example is shown in Figure 4–12.

Figure 4–12

A boundary can limit a surface to the data within it. When you want to extend the triangulation exactly to a boundary line, select the **Non-destructive breakline** option in the Create Boundary dialog box. A non-destructive breakline fractures triangles at their intersection with the boundary. The resulting triangles preserve the original elevations of the surface at the boundary intersection as close as possible.

The example in Figure 4–13 shows the following:

1. The surface with a polyline is used as an outer boundary.
2. The boundary is applied without the **Non-destructive breakline** option. This is typically used when the boundary polyline is approximate and not meant to represent a hard edge.
3. The boundary is applied with the **Non-destructive breakline** option. Non-destructive breaklines are often used to create a specific termination limit for the surface (such as at a parcel boundary).

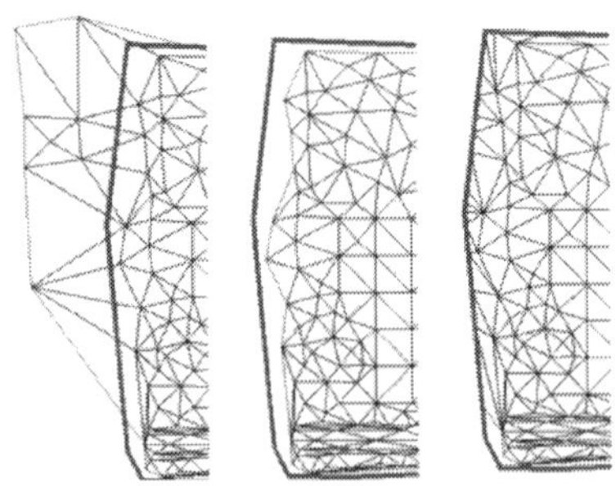

1 *2* *3*

Figure 4–13

Surface Editing

There are three ways of adjusting surfaces graphically: using lines, points, and area edit tools (such as **Minimize Flat Areas** and **Smooth Surface**). All of these tools are available by right-clicking on the *Edits* heading in a surface's *Definition* area (*Prospector*), as shown in Figure 4–14.

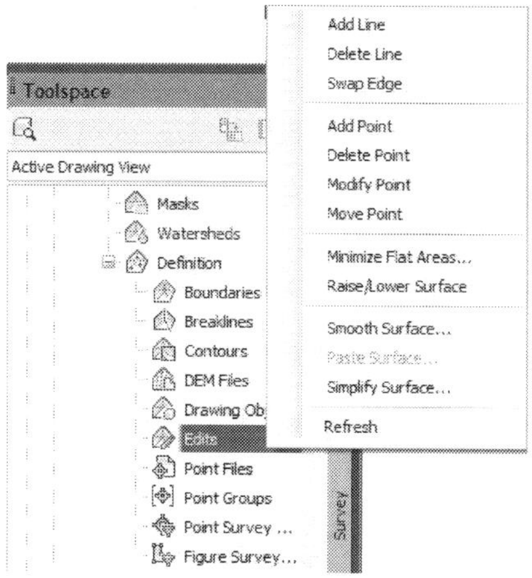

Figure 4–14

- The AutoCAD Civil 3D software considers each graphical surface edit to be additional data that can be removed later.
- Most surface edits apply immediately. If the drawing item modifier icon displays (as shown in Figure 4–15), then an edit has rendered the surface out of date. When this happens, a surface should be rebuilt by right-clicking on the surface name in the *Prospector* tab and selecting **Rebuild**.

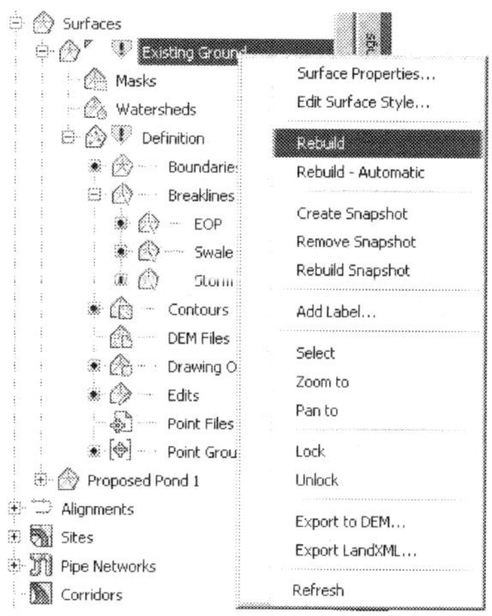

Figure 4–15

- To have a surface automatically rebuild as required, right-click on the surface name in the *Prospector* tab and select **Rebuild-Automatic**. However, toggling this option on increases the use of computer resources and graphics capabilities, so it is recommended that you leave it toggled off.
- To delete an edit from a surface permanently, remove it from the *Edits* list in *Prospector's* preview area or from the *Operations Type* list in the *Definition* tab in the Surface Properties dialog box.

Line Edits

The line editing commands include **Add Line**, **Delete Line**, and **Swap Edge**. The **Add Line** and **Delete Line** commands add or remove triangle lines. The **Delete Line** command is often only applied around the outside edge of a surface to remove unwanted edge triangulation. Deleting lines in the interior of a surface causes both of the triangles next to the removed line to be deleted, leaving a hole in the surface that needs to be repaired by adding another line.

If you are considering deleting a line only to replace it with the opposite diagonal, such as the central line shown in Figure 4–16, using the **Swap Edge** command instead might be more efficient.

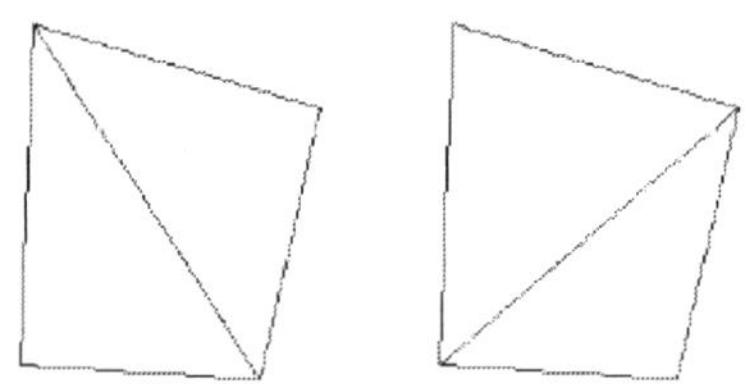

Figure 4–16

Adding an interior line that crosses many existing triangles swaps them where possible to adhere to the geometry represented by the added line. This method can be a good way of swapping multiple edges at the same time.

Point Edits

The Point editing commands can **Add**, **Delete**, **Modify**, or **Move** surface points. They do not affect point objects in the drawing, but rather the surface points created from them. Surface points can be adjusted or deleted as required.

When an AutoCAD Civil 3D point object is adjusted (e.g., moved), the surface containing that point data might not be identified as being out of date nor update automatically. In this situation, you should rebuild the surface.

Simplify Surface

As the collection methods of surface data continue to evolve, yielding significantly larger data sets, the drawing file size increases in proportion to the surface data contained in the drawing. The AutoCAD Civil 3D software has a limit of 2.5 million vertices for a surface. Once it exceeds this limit, the software prompts you to store surface data to an external file with an .mms extension. The resulting external surface files can be quite large. To avoid this, you can simplify your surface using the Simplify Surface wizard. Extra points can be removed from a surface without compromising its accuracy. Points that you might want to remove include points that are in an external point file or database, or redundant points in areas of high data concentration where the value of this extra information is minimal. There are two simplification methods available.

- **Edge Contraction:** This method simplifies the surface by using existing triangle edges. It contracts triangle edges to single points by removing one point. The location of the point to which an edge is contracted is selected so that the change to the surface is minimal.
- **Point Removal:** This method simplifies the surface by removing existing surface points. More points are removed from denser areas of the surface.

When you simplify a surface, you specify which regions of the surface the operation should address. The region options include using the existing surface border, or specifying a window or polygon. The **Pick in Drawing** icon enables you to select the region from the drawing. If a closed line exists in the drawing that you want to use as the region boundary, you can select the **Select objects** option and then use the **Pick in Drawing** icon to select the boundary. Curves in the boundary are approximated by line segments. The line segment generation is governed by a *Mid Ordinate Distance* value that you determine.

Once you have selected the region, the dialog box displays the *Total Points Selected In Region* value. You can refine the surface reduction options by setting a percentage of points to remove, the maximum change in elevation, or the maximum edge contraction error.

Smooth Contours

Although not a true surface edit, AutoCAD Civil 3D surface contours can be smoothed to reduce their jagged appearance using the Surface Object Style settings. There are two approaches to this: the *Add Vertices* method and the *Spline Curve* method. The *Add Vertices* method enables you to select a relative smoothness from the slider bar at the bottom of the Surface Style dialog box, as shown in Figure 4–17.

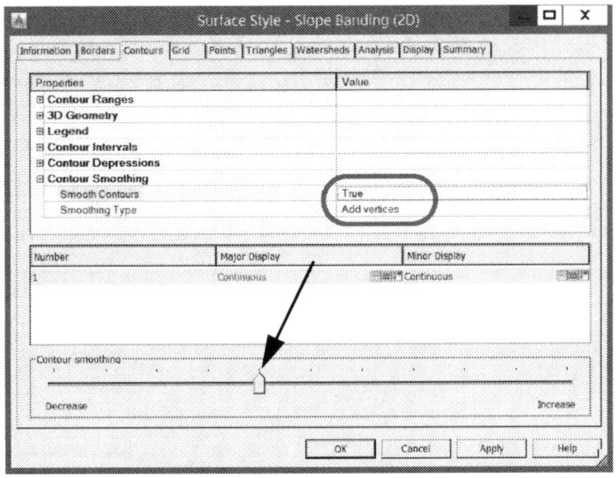

Figure 4–17

The *Spline Curve* method generates very smooth contours, but the contours are more liberally interpolated and might overlap where surface points are close together. This approach is best applied to surfaces with relatively few data points or in areas of low relief, as shown in Figure 4–18.

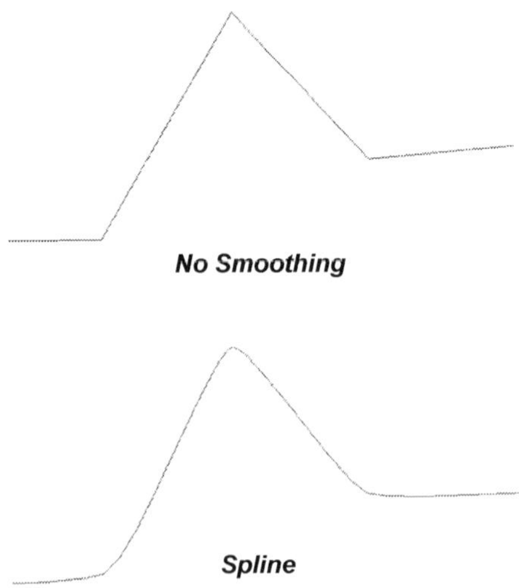

Figure 4–18

Smooth Surface

The Smooth Surface edit introduces new, interpolated elevations between surface data. It is used to create a more realistic-looking terrain model, though not necessarily a more accurate one. Generally, surface smoothing works best with point-based surface data.

The AutoCAD Civil 3D software has two smoothing methods: *Natural Neighbor* and *Kriging*.

- *Natural Neighbor* interpolates a grid of additional data points that produce a smoother overall terrain model.
- *Kriging* reads surface trends to add additional data in sparse areas.

Surface smoothing is applied by right-clicking on the *Edits* collection under a surface's *Definition* and selecting **Smooth Surface**. The Smooth Surface dialog box and example of surface smoothing are shown in Figure 4–19.

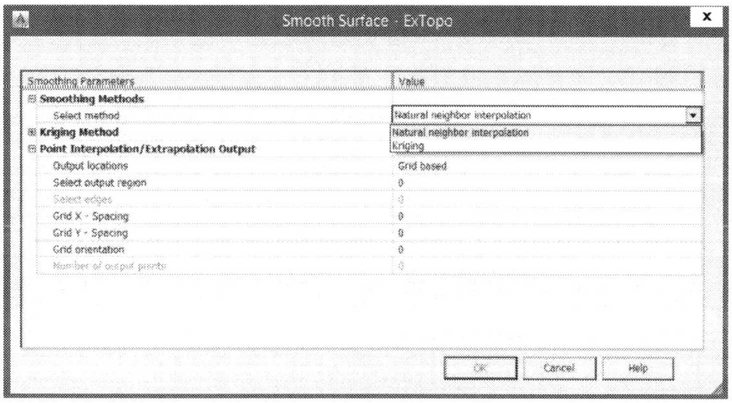

Figure 4–19

Copy Surface

The AutoCAD Civil 3D software does not have a copy surface command, but surface objects can be copied using the AutoCAD **Copy** command (**Modify>Copy**). When copying surface objects, select the same base and then a second point to ensure that the surface is not moved during the copy. After a copy, a duplicate surface is created and is displayed in the *Prospector* tab. The copy has the same name as the original followed with a number in parenthesis, such as (1). These copied surfaces can be renamed as required. Surface copies are independent of each other and can be edited.

Surface Paste

The **Surface Paste** command enables the AutoCAD Civil 3D software to combine multiple surfaces into a single surface. You might want to paste into a copy of a surface if you want to keep the original unmodified. For example, a finished condition surface is needed that includes a proposed surface (*Proposed*) along with the existing ground (EG) around its periphery. In this situation, you would first create a new surface and name it **Finished Ground**. In the *Surfaces* collection in the *Prospector* tab, right-click on the Finished Ground surface's *Edit* collection and select **Paste** to merge in the **Existing ground (EG)** and **Proposed** surfaces.

Once the command has executed, the surface's **EG** and **Proposed** surfaces are left unchanged, and the **Finished Ground** surface represents a combination of the two. If you did not create the **Finished Ground** surface, but pasted the **Proposed** surface into the **EG** surface, you would not have the original **EG** surface for reference in profiles and other places. If surfaces are pasted in the wrong order, the order can be rearranged using the *Definition* tab in the Surface Properties dialog box.

Surfaces remain dynamically linked after pasting. Therefore, if the **Proposed** surface changes, the **Finished Ground** surface updates to display the change.

Raise/Lower Surface

The **Raise/Lower Surface** command adds or subtracts a specified elevation value. This adjustment is applied to the entire surface. It is useful for modeling soil removal and changing a surface's datum elevation.

Adjusting Surfaces through Surface Properties

In addition to the graphical edit methods, you can adjust surfaces by changing their surface properties. Surface property adjustments include setting a *Maximum triangle length* or *Exclude elevations* greater or less than certain values. You can also enable or disable the effects of certain surface data (such as breaklines and boundaries) by disabling them in the dialog box.

To locate these options (as shown in Figure 4–20), right-click on a surface in the *Prospector* tab and select **Surface Properties**.

Definition Options	Value
Build	
Copy deleted dependent objects	No
Exclude elevations less than	No
Elevation <	0.000'
Exclude elevations greater than	No
Elevation >	0.000'
Use maximum triangle length	No
Maximum triangle length	0.000'
Convert proximity breaklines to standard	Yes
Allow crossing breaklines	No
Elevation to use	Use average breakline elevation at intersection
Data operations	
Edit operations	

Figure 4–20

4.3 Use Styles and Settings to Display Surface Information

The AOTG content that is recommended to review for the Identify Key Characteristics of Surfaces certification objective is covered in Section 4.1 Identify Key Characteristics of Surfaces. Refer to this section to review the content.

4.4 Create a Surface by Assembling Fundamental Data

The surface building process can be divided into the following steps:

1. Assemble the data.
2. Assign the data to a surface.
3. Evaluate the resulting surface.
4. Add breaklines, assign more data, modify the data, or edit the surface as required.

1. Assemble data.

The first step in surface building is to acquire the initial surface data. This can be points, contours, 3D polylines, feature lines, AutoCAD® objects, ASCII coordinate files, or boundaries. Each data type provides specific information about a surface.

2. Assign data to a surface.

Acquired data is assigned to a surface. Once assigned, the AutoCAD Civil 3D software immediately processes this data and a surface object is created.

Surfaces are listed individually in the *Surfaces* collection in the *Prospector* tab. Each surface contains content information, as shown in Figure 4–21. The surface content includes *Masks, Watersheds,* and *Definition* elements. The *Definition* contains a list of all of the surface data that has been applied, including boundaries, breaklines, and points. The *Prospector* tab displays data for each type of surface data in the list view when one of these types is selected.

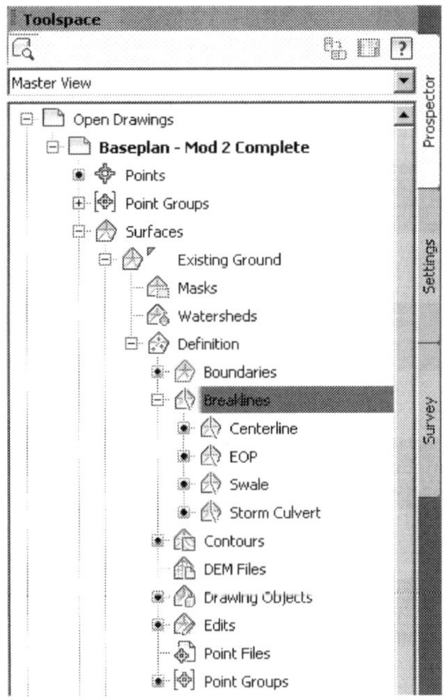

Figure 4–21

The *Definition* tab in the Surface Properties dialog box displays the permitted **Build**, **Data**, and **Edit** operations for a surface. The *Operation Type* column is a record of the surface data addition and edits. Using the checkboxes, you can toggle off individual actions in the history and display the resulting changes to the surface. The entries can be toggled on or off no matter where they display in the history. This helps to isolate possible errors or review features (such as surface slopes) that are greatly affected by the addition of a headwall or retaining wall.

You can change the order of items in the list of operations. Operations higher in the list are applied to the surface before items further down in the list. Open this dialog box by right-clicking on the surface name in the *Prospector* (or by selecting the surface in the drawing and right-clicking) and selecting **Surface Properties...**. The dialog box is shown in Figure 4–22.

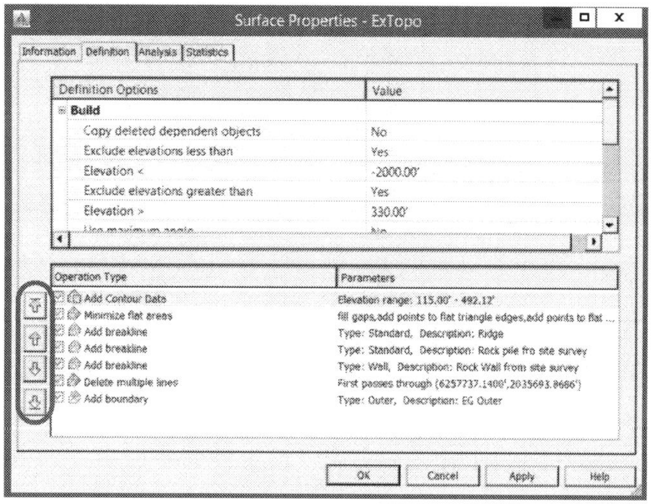

Figure 4–22

The AutoCAD Civil 3D software processes the initial data into one of two types of surfaces. The first type, the **Triangulated Irregular Network** (TIN) surface, is the most common. With triangulated surfaces, surface points are connected to adjacent points by straight lines, resulting in a triangular mesh. Surfaces generated from contour lines have surface points created at their vertices, modified by weeding and supplementing factors. An example of this type of surface is shown in Figure 4–23.

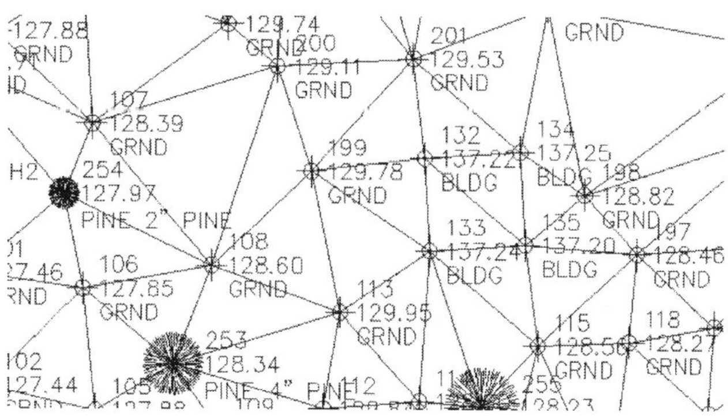

Figure 4–23

The second type of surface is a *Grid* surface. This surface interpolates and assigns an elevation from the surface data to each grid intersection. Most of the elevations at grid intersections are interpolated. **Digital Elevation Models** (DEMs) are a type of grid surface used in GIS applications. An example of this type of surface is shown in Figure 4–24.

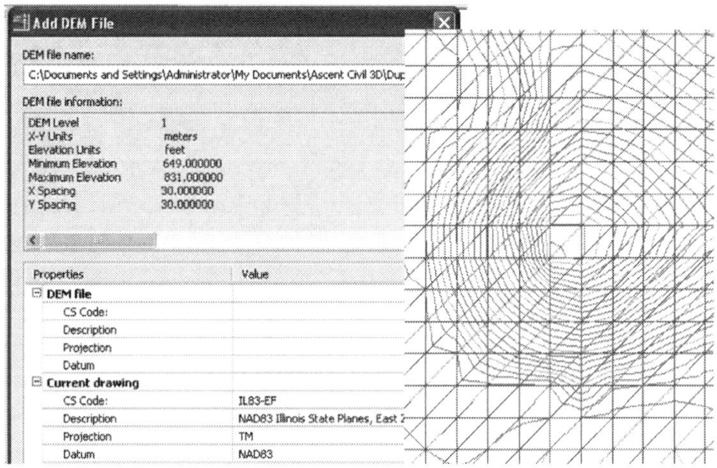

Figure 4–24

3. Evaluate the resulting surface.

Surfaces, especially ones created from points, typically need some attention to represent them as accurately as possible. For any four adjacent surface points, there are two possible triangulations, as shown in Figure 4–25.

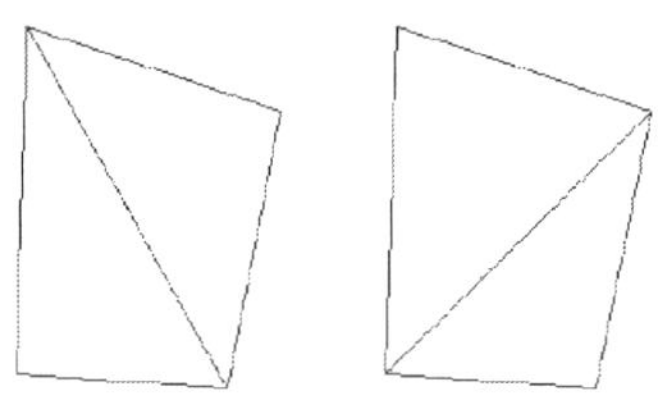

Figure 4–25

The differences can be difficult to envision when viewing the triangles from above, but these two configurations provide entirely different geometries. For example, note the surface shown in Figure 4–26.

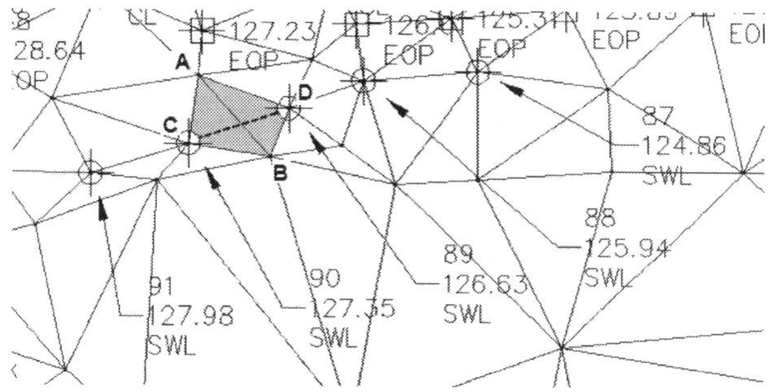

Figure 4–26

The triangulated points A, B, C, and D have a TIN line running from A to B. This configuration ignores the fact that C and D are both part of a continuous swale (SWL), indicated by the dashed line. In a 3D view, this configuration would resemble the example shown on the left in Figure 4–27. The correct triangulation has the triangle line *following* the linear feature rather than *crossing* it, as shown on the right.

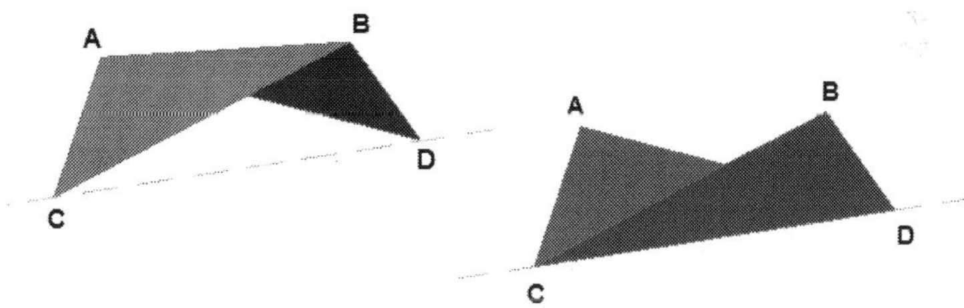

Figure 4–27

When creating surfaces, representing linear features correctly is extremely important. Examples of linear features include road center lines, edges-of-pavement, road shoulders, swales, berms, tops and bottoms of banks, and headwalls. Adding breaklines that follow linear features ensures that a terrain model is triangulated correctly along the features, rather than across them.

Other types of issues to watch out for include bad elevations (blown shots), elevations at 0 where there should be no chance of such elevation values, and points that were surveyed above or below the ground (e.g., the tops of fire hydrants). Unwanted triangles along the edges of the surface might connect points that should not be connected, which could also present problems.

In addition to the casual inspection of the triangles, surfaces can be evaluated by creating contour lines, reviewing the surface in 3D, and using the **Quick Section** command.

4. Add breaklines, assign more data, modify the data, or edit the surface as required.

After you have evaluated the surface, you can add the necessary breaklines or edit the surface directly to make adjustments. If the triangulation errors are isolated, editing the surface directly might be faster than creating and applying breaklines. For example, the triangulation issue above could be addressed by *swapping* the edge that crossed the swale center line. To do so, right-click on Edits under a Surface's definition in the *Prospector* tab and select **Swap Edge**, as shown in Figure 4–28.

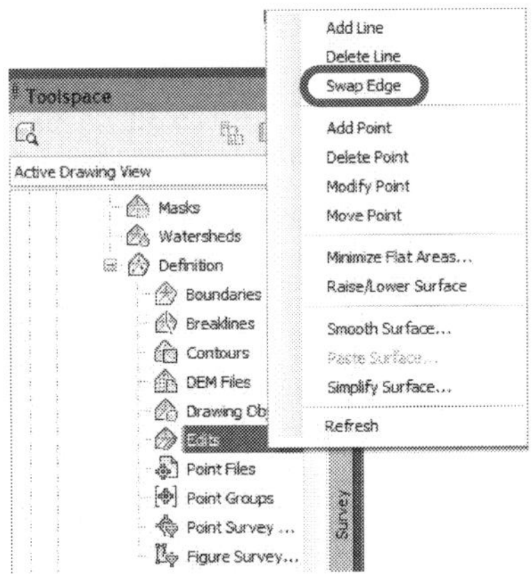

Figure 4–28

Other options enable you to add, move, modify, or remove points from the surface (but not change or erase the point object on which they were based), as well as add or remove triangle lines directly. **Minimize Flat Areas** is a group of algorithms that can be used to minimize the number of flat areas created by contour data. **Raise/Lower Surface** enables you to raise and lower the entire surface by a set amount, and a **Smooth Surface** enables you to smooth surfaces using the **Natural Neighbor** or **Kriging** method. (Contour smoothing is handled through surface styles. These techniques smooth the actual surface geometry.)

4.5 Use Styles to Analyze Surface Display Results

The AutoCAD Civil 3D software can calculate and display many different surface analyses, including:

- **Contours:** This analysis can display contours differently based on their elevation ranges.
- **Directions:** This analysis can render surface triangles differently depending on which direction they face.
- **Elevations:** This analysis can render surface triangles differently depending on their elevation ranges.
- **Slopes:** This analysis can render surface triangles differently depending on their slope ranges.
- **Slope Arrows:** This analysis creates a dynamic slope arrow that points downslope for each triangle, colorized by slope range.
- **User-Defined Contours:** This analysis can display user-defined contours differently based on their elevation ranges.
- **Watersheds:** This analysis can calculate watershed areas, and render them according to area type. The AutoCAD Civil 3D watershed analysis usually results in a very large number of individual watersheds. Although a **Catchment Areas** command is available to assist in drawing the catchment areas, it is still up to the engineers to draw their own conclusions on how these should be merged together into catchment areas.

The above analyses are calculated on demand for each surface and their results are stored under the surface's Surface Properties.

In addition, the following separate utilities might be helpful when analyzing surfaces:

- **Check for Contour Problems:** Used to locate problems with the contour data, including crossing or overlapping contours. To access this command, in the *Surface* tab>expanded Analyze panel, select **Check for Contour Problems**, as shown in Figure 4–29.

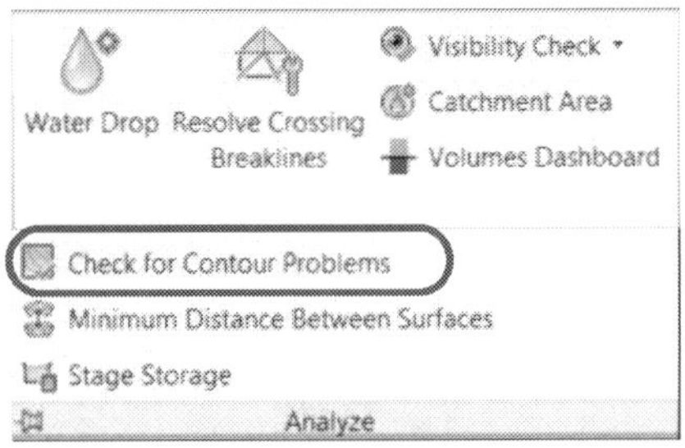

Figure 4–29

- **Resolve Crossing Breaklines:** Identifies and fixes any breaklines that create an invalid condition when two elevations exist at the intersection point of two breaklines. The breaklines can be found in the drawing, in a survey figure, or in the survey database. To access this command, in the *Surface* tab>Analyze panel, click (Resolve Crossing Breaklines).
- **Water Drop:** Draws a 2D or 3D polyline indicating the expected flow path of water across the surface from a given starting point. To access this command, in the *Surface* tab> Analyze panel, click (Water Drop).
- **Catchment Area:** Draws a 2D or 3D polyline indicating the catchment boundary and catchment point marker for a surface drainage area. To access this command, in the *Surface* tab>Analyze panel, click (Catchment Area). You should use this command in conjunction with the **Water Drop** command to determine an accurate placement of catchment regions and points.

- **Visibility Check>Zone of Visual Influence:** Analyzes the line of sight for 360 degrees around a single point. To access this command, in the *Surface* tab>Analyze panel, click (Visibility Check>Zone of Visual influence). This command is good for analyzing if towers, buildings, and other objects can be seen within a certain radius.

- **Minimum Distance Between Surfaces:** Identifies the (X,Y) location where two overlapping surfaces are the closest elevation. To access this command, in the *Surface* tab> Analyze panel, click (Minimum Distance Between Surfaces). If there is more than one location with the shortest distance between the two surfaces (because it is flat), then the location might be represented by a series of points, a line, or a closed polyline.

- **Stage Storage:** Calculates volumes of a basin from a surface, using either a surface or polylines to define the basin. To access this command, in the *Surface* tab>Analyze panel, click (Stage Storage). Either the *Average End Area* or the *Conic Approximation* method, or both are used to calculate volumes for the stage storage table.

Analysis Settings

You apply a surface analysis using the *Analysis* tab in the Surface Properties dialog box. In this tab, you can select the number of ranges and a legend table to be used. All of the remaining analysis settings are located in the *Surface Object* style, including whether to display in 2D or 3D, the color scheme, elevations, range groupings, etc. If you want to change the number of ranges or the range values, use the settings in this tab at any time.

Analysis Data Display

Overall visibility, layer, linetype, and related controls for analysis elements are managed using the *Display* tab in the Object Style dialog box, as shown in Figure 4–30. The component entries for *Slopes, Slope Arrows, Watersheds*, etc., are displayed. These can be set to display different settings and combinations of elements in 2D and 3D.

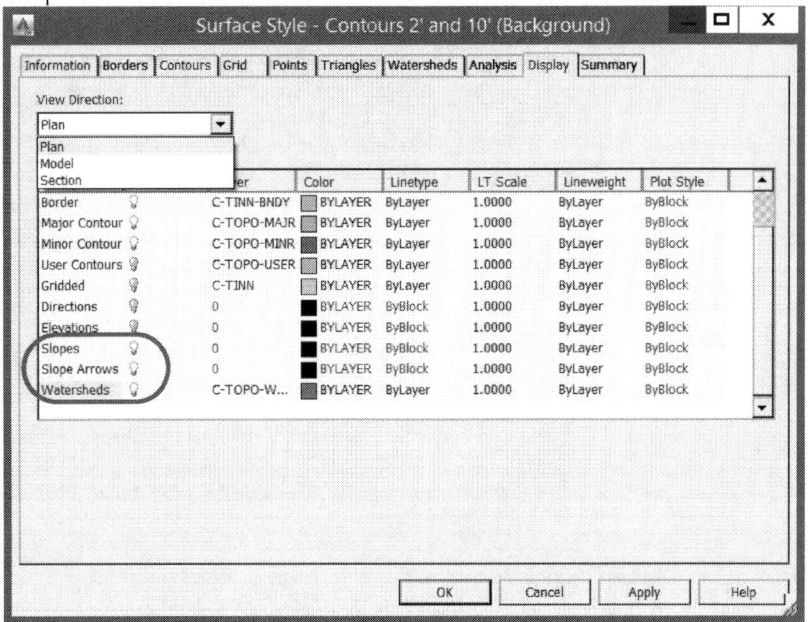

Figure 4–30

4.6 Annotate Surfaces

Surface labels can be used to label contour elevations, slope values, spot elevations, and watershed delineations. Label values update if the surface changes.

To create surface labels, in the *Annotate* tab>Labels & Tables panel, expand Add Labels and select **Surface** to access the surface label flyout menu, as shown in Figure 4–31.

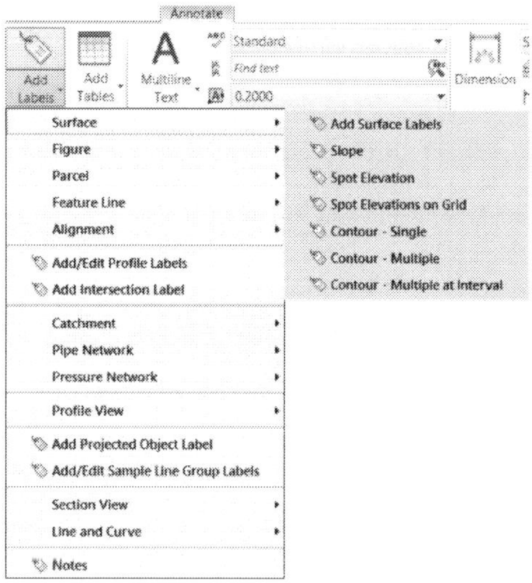

Figure 4–31

You can also click  (Add Labels) to open the Add Labels dialog box, as shown in Figure 4–32. This dialog box enables you to select the feature and label type while being able to control the label style on the fly.

Figure 4–32

Contour Labels

Contour labels can be created individually, as multiples along a linear path, or as multiples along a linear path with repeated labels at a set interval. Multiple contours are aligned along an object called a *Contour Label Line*, which can be repositioned as needed, and in turn updates the position of its labels. These label lines have a selectable property that can make them visible only when an attached label is selected. If they are left visible, they should be placed on a non-plotting layer.

Spot and Slope Labels

Spot elevation and slope labels can be created as needed to annotate a surface. These are dynamic surface labels and not point objects, although they might look similar to points. Slopes can be measured at a single point or averaged between two points.

Practice 4a

Creating an Existing Ground Surface

Estimated time for completion: 15 minutes

Practice Objective

- Add contour data and point data to a surface that already exists in the drawing.

In this practice you will define the surface with surface data. You will use this model to create existing ground contours and for reference during the design. You will begin the model with the provided contours and the previously created **Existing Ground** point group.

Task 1 - Create a surface and set properties.

1. Open **SUF1-A1-Surface.dwg**.
2. In the *Prospector* tab, select **Surfaces**, right-click, and select **Create Surface**.
3. For the *Type*, select **TIN surface**. For the *Name*, type **ExTopo** and for the *Style*, select **Contours 2' and 10' (Background)**, as shown in Figure 4–33.

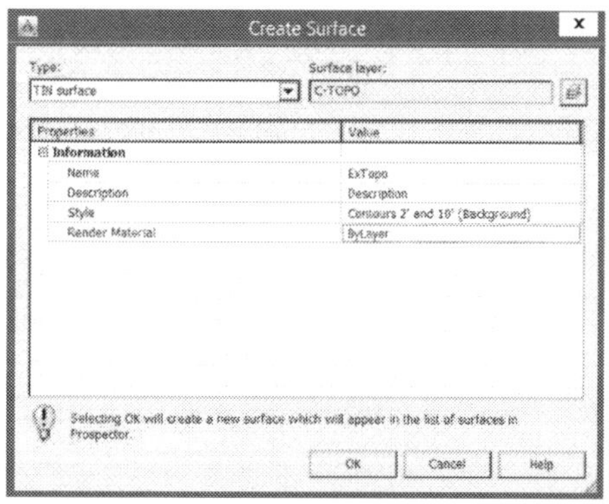

Figure 4–33

4. Click **OK** to accept the changes and close the dialog box.
5. Save the drawing.

Task 2 - Define surface with contour data.

1. Continue working with the drawing from the previous practice or open **SUF1-A2-Surface.dwg**.

2. Click  (Insert Block) in the *Insert* tab>Block panel to insert *C:\Civil 3D Projects\Civil3D-Training\Surface* **Site-Contours.dwg** into the drawing with an insertion point of **0,0,0**, uniform scale of **1**, and rotation of **0**. Ensure that you explode the file as you insert it, as shown in Figure 4–34.

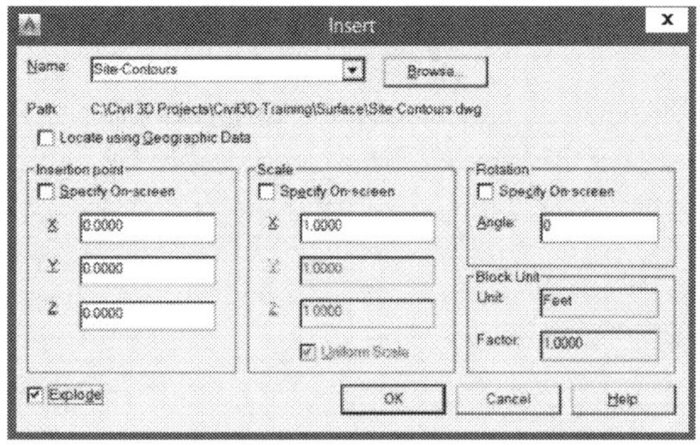

Figure 4–34

3. Isolate the layers **A-TOPO-MAJR** and **A-TOPO-MINR**. Do this by using AutoCAD's  (Isolate) or type **layiso** at the Command Line. Type **S** for **Settings**. Select **Off** and then select **Off** again to ensure that **layiso** does not lock the layer by changing the settings to toggle off isolated layers. (If this setting is not changed, the **C-TOPO** layer will lock and the AutoCAD Civil 3D software will not create the surface.) Select one major and one minor contour for the **Site-Contours.dwg**.

4. Expand the *Surfaces* collection in the *Prospector* tab.

5. Expand the *ExTopo* surfaces collection and the *Definition* collection.

6. Select the **Contours** data element, right-click, and select **Add...**, as shown in Figure 4–35.

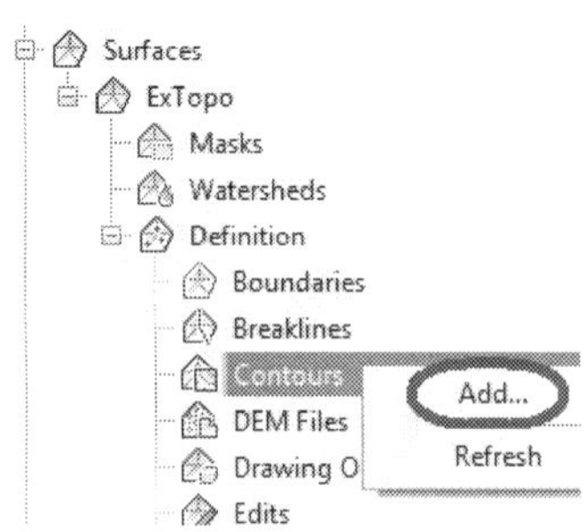

Figure 4–35

7. In the Add Contour Data dialog box, accept the defaults, as shown in Figure 4–36, and click **OK**.

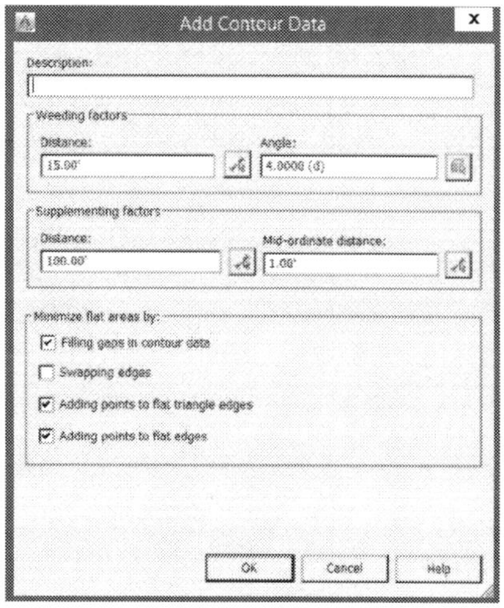

Figure 4–36

8. When prompted to select contours, use the AutoCAD window or crossing selection method to select all of the AutoCAD contour objects on the screen, as shown in Figure 4–37. Press <Enter> to end the command.

Figure 4–37

9. The AutoCAD Civil 3D software has created a surface. However, only the original two isolated contour layers are displayed, the surface is not displayed. You need to restore the previous layer state. To do so, click  (Unisolate) in the *Home* tab>Layer panel as shown in Figure 4–38.

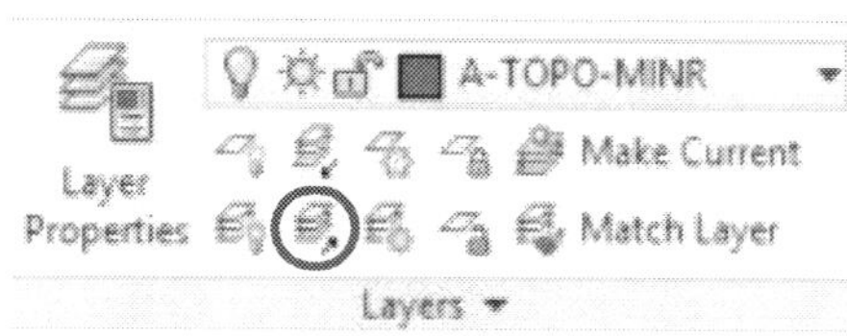

Figure 4–38

After freezing the original contours, if the contours for the new surface are not displayed, verify that the C-TOPO layer is not frozen.

10. Freeze the layers **A-TOPO-MAJR** and **A-TOPO-MINR** by clicking (Layer Freeze) and selecting the contours you selected when adding contours to the surface. This will clean up the drawing while ensuring that you do not accidentally modify the surface by changing any of the original contour polylines.

11. If you select the green surface boundary or any contour line, the *Tin Surface: ExTopo* contextual tab displays, as shown in Figure 4–39.

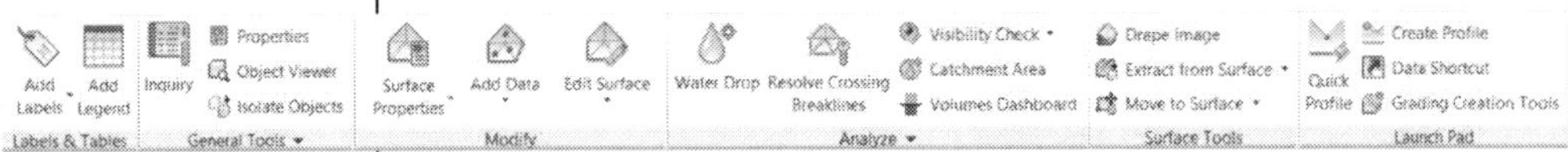

Figure 4–39

12. Save the drawing.

Task 3 - Define surface with point data.

In examining the **ExTopo** surface more closely, note that although the internal site contours correctly reflect the surveyed point elevations, the original contours are out of date or have missing information in the area of the existing road, **Mission Avenue** (the road running east to west at the top of the site). However, you have a detailed survey of the road. Using this data, you will generate a surface.

1. Continue working with the drawing from the previous task or open **SUF1-A3-Surface.dwg**.

*If the points still display in the model, you might have to right-click on Point Groups and select **Update**.*

2. Although the point group that you use in this practice has been created, you should change the display order of the point groups to display them clearly. To do so, in the *Prospector* tab, right-click on Point Groups and select **Properties**. Move the **_No Display** point group to the top and then move the **ExRoad** point group above it.

3. In the *Prospector* tab, select the **Surfaces** collection, right-click, and select **Create Surface**.

4. In the Create Surface dialog box, select **TIN surface** for the surface type, type **ExRoad** for the surface name, and type **Contours 2' and 10' Background** for the style.

5. Click **OK** to accept the changes and close the dialog box.
6. Expand the *Surfaces* collection in the *Prospector* tab and expand the *ExRoad* collection.
7. Expand the *Definition* collection, select **Point Groups**, right-click, and select **Add...**, as shown in Figure 4–40.

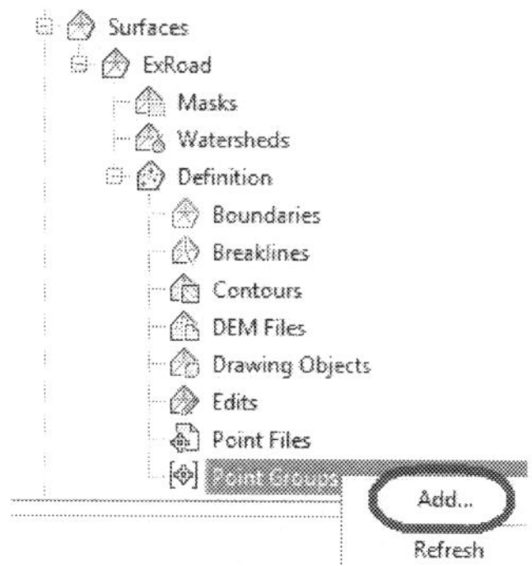

Figure 4–40

8. In the Point Groups dialog box, select the **ExRoad** points group, as shown in Figure 4–41. Click **OK** to accept the changes and close the dialog box.

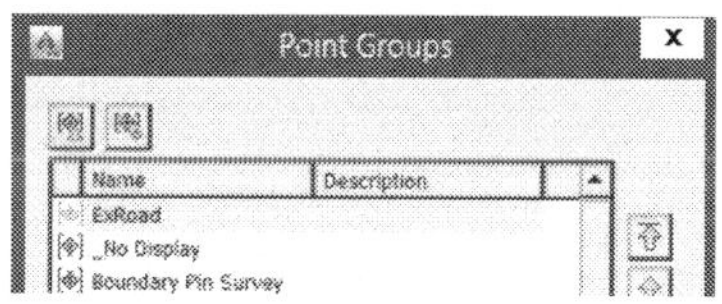

Figure 4–41

9. Save the drawing.

Task 4 - Create a surface contour style.

1. Continue working with the drawing from the previous task or open **SUF1-A4-Surface.dwg**.
2. Since there is very little grade change along the road, the frequency of the contours is small, making the surface difficult to see. Expand the *Surfaces* collection, right-click **ExRoad** and select **Surface Properties**.

3. In the Surface Properties dialog box, in the *Information* tab, expand  to the right of the *Surface style* field and select **Copy Current Selection**, as shown in Figure 4–42.

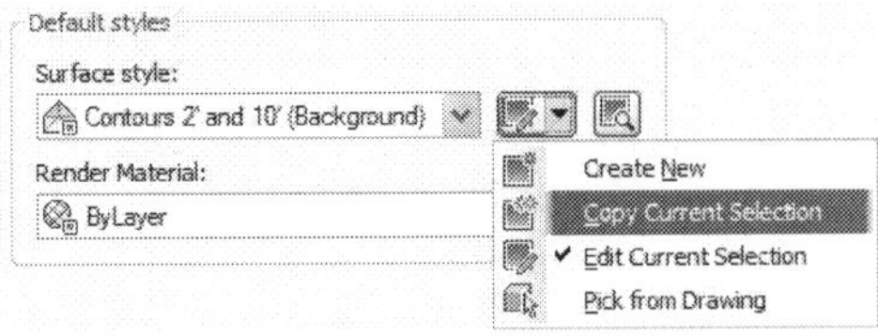

Figure 4–42

4. In the *Information* tab, type **Contours 0.5' and 2.5' (Background)** for the style name, as shown in Figure 4–43.

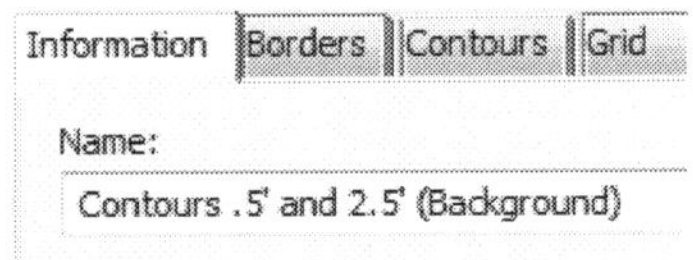

Figure 4–43

5. In the *Contours* tab, expand the *Contour Intervals* collection and type **0.5'** for the *Minor Interval* and **2.5'** for the *Major Interval*, as shown in Figure 4–44.

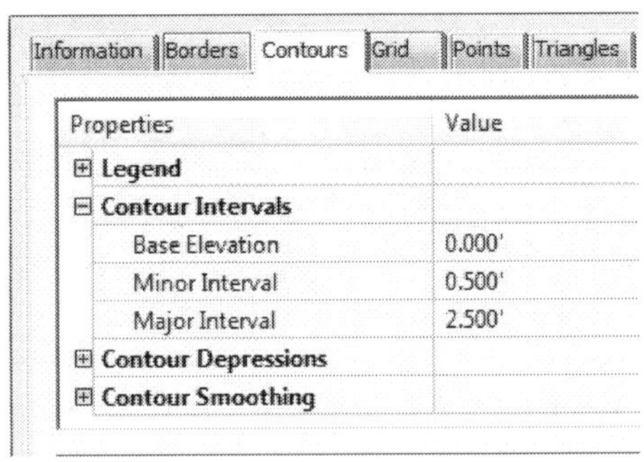

Figure 4–44

6. Click **OK** to accept and close the Edit Style dialog box, and click **OK** to close the Surface Properties dialog box.

7. Zoom into the existing road at the north end of the site and note the detail contours identifying the crown of the road.

8. Save the drawing.

Practice 4b Add Additional Data to an Existing Ground Surface

Practice Objective

- Improve the accuracy of a surface by adding various breaklines, such as standard breaklines, wall breaklines, and breaklines from survey figures.

Estimated time for completion: 20 minutes

Task 1 - Add surface breaklines.

TIN lines are generally created using the shortest distance between points. To further define a surface, you might need to supplement it with breaklines of ridges, ditches, walls, etc., that accurately define the surface. These breaklines prevent the software from triangulating directly between points that are bisected by a breakline. The breakline becomes part of the triangulation between the two adjacent points.

1. Continue working with the drawing from the previous practice or open **SUF1-B1-Surface.dwg**.

The contextual tab displays.

2. Select any part of the **ExTopo** surface in Model Space.
3. In the contextual *Surface* tab>Modify panel, select Surface Properties as shown in Figure 4–45. The Surface Properties dialog box opens.

Figure 4–45

4. In the *Information* tab, expand the Surface style drop-down list and select **Contours and Triangles**, as shown in Figure 4–46. Click **OK** to close the dialog box.

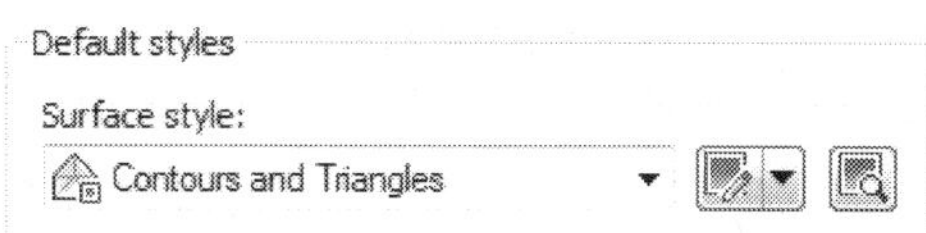

Figure 4–46

Now that the triangulations are displayed, you will examine how adding a feature line impacts the surface.

5. In the *View* tab>Views panel, expand the drop-down list and select **Surf-Breakline**. This zooms into the breakline that is located north of the existing road as shown in Figure 4–47.

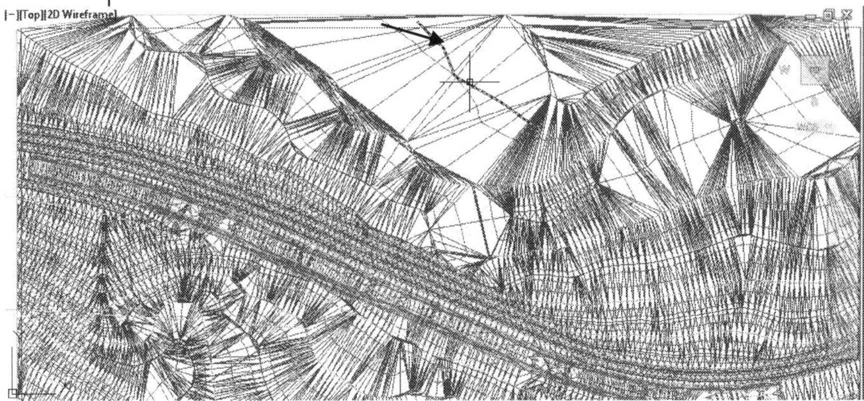

Figure 4–47

The triangulation crosses the breakline.

6. Expand the *Current Drawing* collection in the *Prospector* tab and then expand the *Surfaces>ExTopo>Definition* collections. Select **Breaklines**, right-click, and select **Add**, as shown in Figure 4–48.

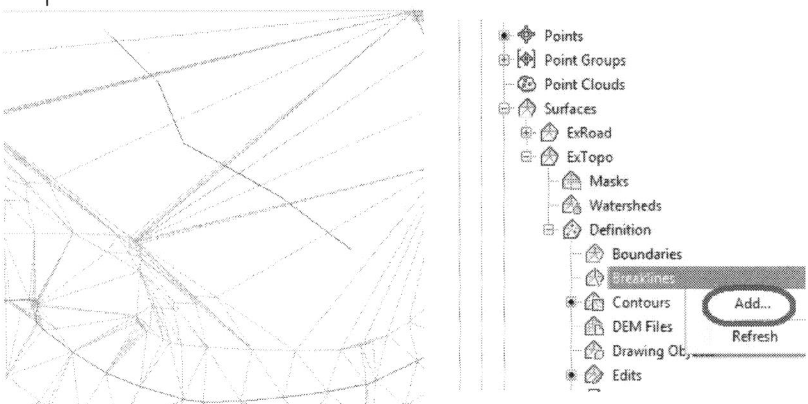

Figure 4–48

7. Type **Ridge** in the *Description* field, as shown in Figure 4–49. Accept all of the defaults and click **OK** to close the dialog box.

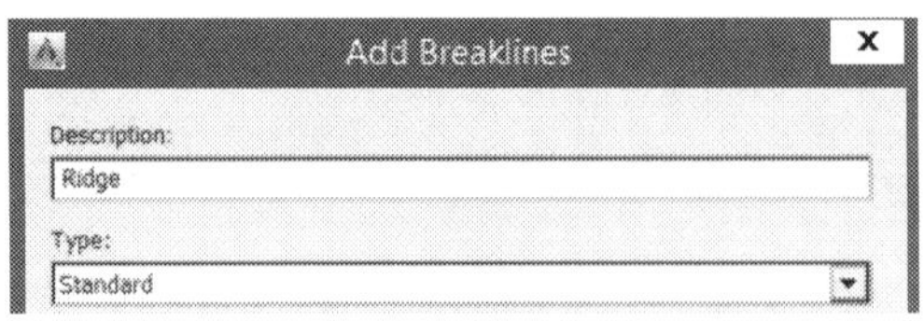

Figure 4–49

8. When prompted to select objects, select the red 3D polyline and press <Enter> to complete the command.

9. The surface should rebuild automatically. Note that the triangulation now takes the breakline into consideration, as shown in Figure 4–50.

*If the **ExTopo** surface is marked as out-of-date . Select the **ExTopo** surface, right-click, and select **Rebuild Automatic**.*

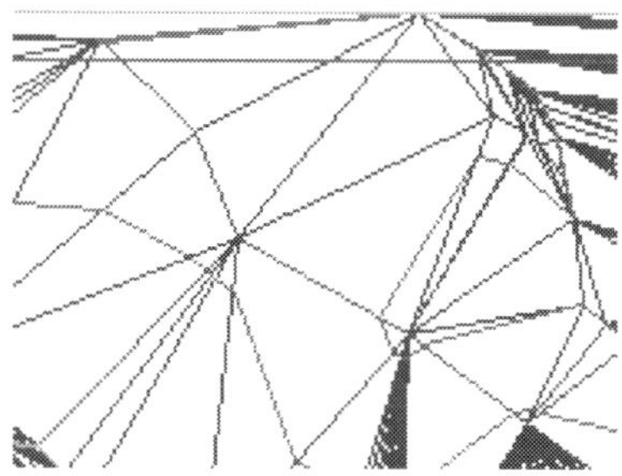

Figure 4–50

10. Save the drawing.

Task 2 - Set up the survey database.

In this practice you will need to incorporate survey data into the surface. To do so, you must first establish a connection to the survey database. If you have not completed the practices in the Survey section you will need to open the survey database **Survey1 Data_Complete** to open the connection.

1. Continue working with the drawing from the previous task or open **SUF1-B2-Surface.dwg** from the *C:\Civil 3D Projects\Civil3D-Training\Surface* folder.

2. In the *Survey* tab>Toolspace, right-click on Survey Databases and select **Set working folder**, as shown in Figure 4–51.

If the Survey tab in the Toolspace is not enabled, click in the Home tab>Palettes panel to toggle it on.

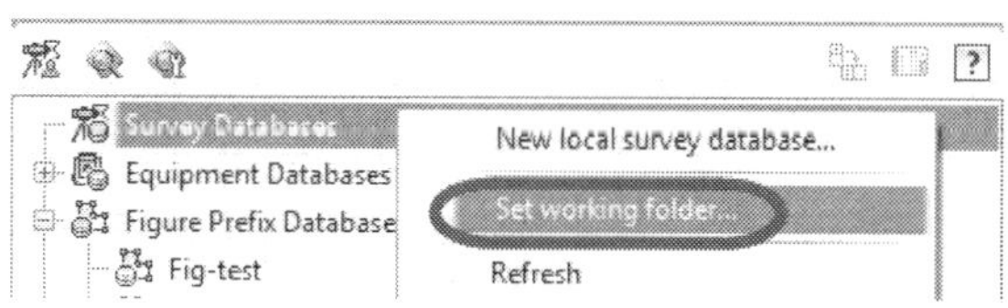

Figure 4–51

3. Select the *Survey Databases* folder in the *C:\Civil 3D Projects\Civil3D-Training\Survey* folder, as shown in Figure 4–52.

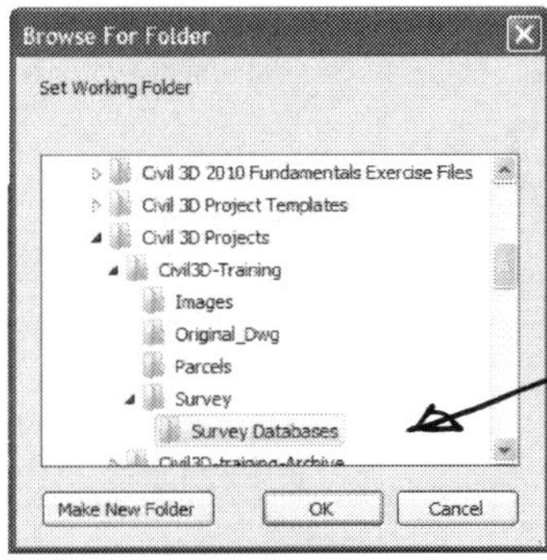

Figure 4–52

4. Select the survey database **Survey Data_Complete**, right-click, and select **Open for edit**, as shown in Figure 4–53.

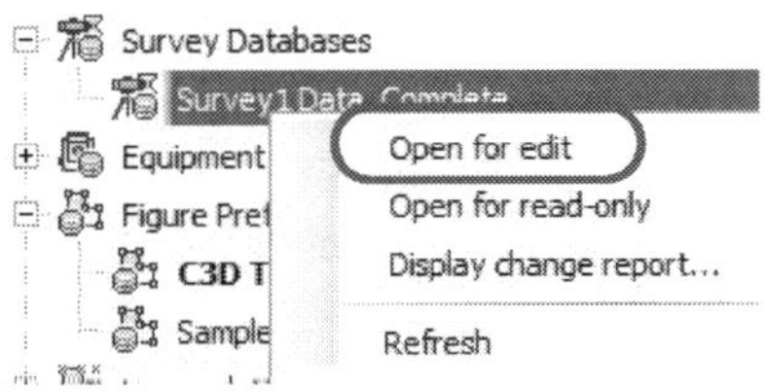

Figure 4–53

Task 3 - Add field book figures as breaklines.

In the task, you will add breaklines to the surface from figures that were created when the field books were imported.

1. Continue working with the drawing from the previous task or open **SUF1-B3-Surface.dwg**.
2. Open the survey database **Survey1 Data_Complete,** if it is not already open.
3. In the *Survey* tab, expand the *Survey Data* collection and select **Figures**. The list of figures in the grid view is displayed at the bottom of the Toolspace.

4. Select the figure **Pile**, right-click, and select **Create breaklines...**, as shown in Figure 4–54.

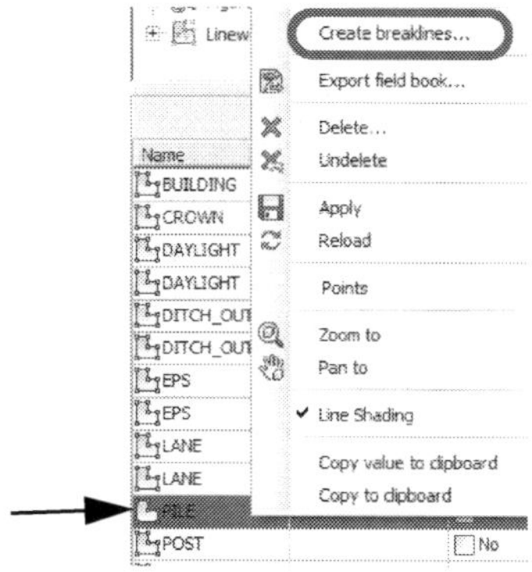

Figure 4–54

5. In the Create Breaklines dialog box, select **ExTopo** for the surface, and select the **Yes** option in the *Breakline* column to create breaklines, as shown in Figure 4–55. Click **OK** to close the dialog box.

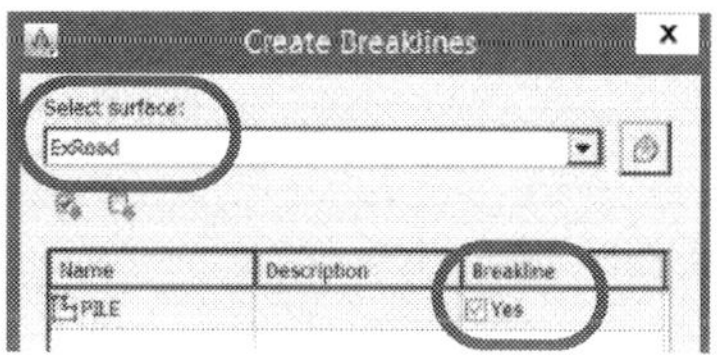

Figure 4–55

6. The AutoCAD Civil 3D software will zoom in to the location of the breakline, and open the Add Breaklines dialog box. Type **Rock pile from site survey** in the *Description* field, and ensure that **Standard** is selected in the Type drop-down list, as shown in Figure 4–56. Click **OK** to close the dialog box.

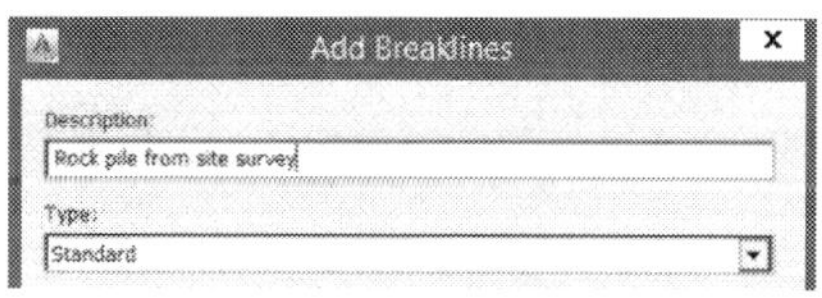

Figure 4–56

   The Event Viewer vista in the Panorama opens. You have received a number of errors with crossing breaklines. You can Zoom to the error by selecting **Zoom to** in the far right column. For now you need to clear these errors from the event log file.

7. Click **Action** in the Panorama and select **Clear All Events**, as shown in Figure 4–57.

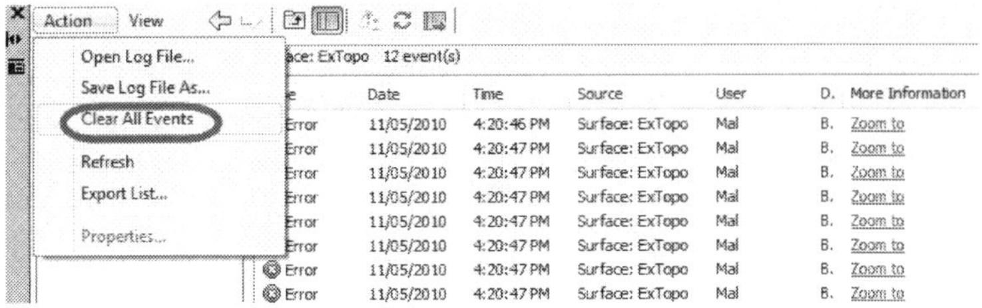

Figure 4–57

8. Close the Panorama by clicking (checkmark) in the dialog box.

9. In Model Space, select the **ExTopo** surface. The *Tin Surface: ExTopo* contextual tab displays. In the Modify panel, select **Surface Properties** as shown in Figure 4–58.

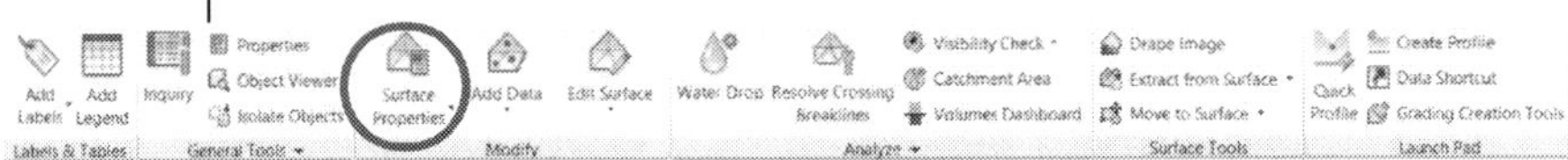

Figure 4–58

10. The Surface Properties - ExTopo dialog box opens. In the *Definition* tab, expand the *Build* collection and set the value of *Allow crossing breaklines* to **Yes**. Set the value for the *Elevation to use* field to **Use last breakline elevation at intersection**, as shown in Figure 4–59. When you have finished, click **OK**.

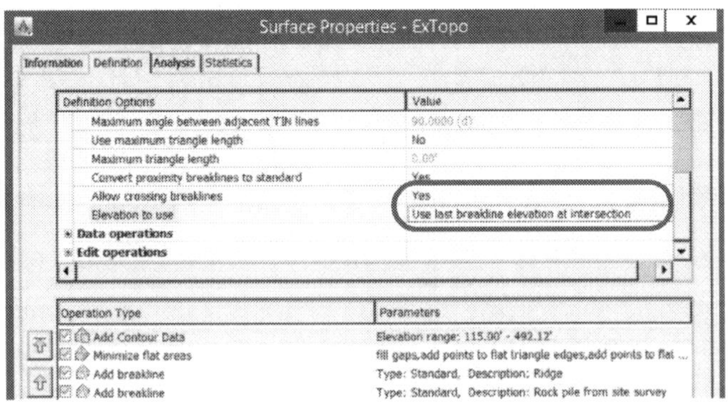

Figure 4–59

11. When prompted to *Rebuild the surface* or *Mark as out of Date*, select **Rebuild the surface**. When you review the surface contours, note that the surface has used the figure as a breakline.

12. Save the drawing.

Task 4 - Add a Wall Breakline.

In the task, you will add a wall breakline to the surface from figures that were created when the field books were imported.

1. Continue working with the drawing from the previous task or open **SUF1-B4-Surface.dwg**.
2. Open the survey database **Survey1 Data_Complete**, if it is not already open.
3. In the *Survey* tab, expand the *Survey Data* collection and select **Figures**. Note the list of figures in the grid view at the bottom of the Toolspace.
4. Select the **Wall** figure, right-click, and select **Create breaklines**.
5. In the Create Breaklines dialog box, select the **ExTopo** surface and select the **Yes** option in the *Breakline* column to create breaklines. Click **OK** to close the dialog box.
6. The AutoCAD Civil 3D software zooms in to the location of the breakline, and opens the Add Breaklines dialog box. Type **Rock wall from site survey** in the *Description* field, and ensure that **Wall** is selected in the Type drop-down list, as shown in Figure 4–60. Click **OK** to close the dialog box.

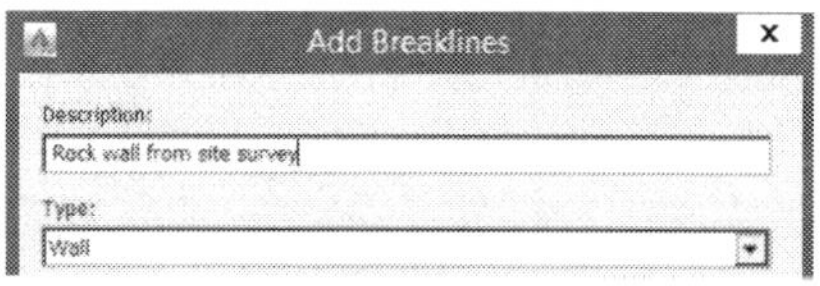

Figure 4–60

7. At the prompt to pick the offset side, select a point to the south of the wall break line, as shown in Figure 4–61.

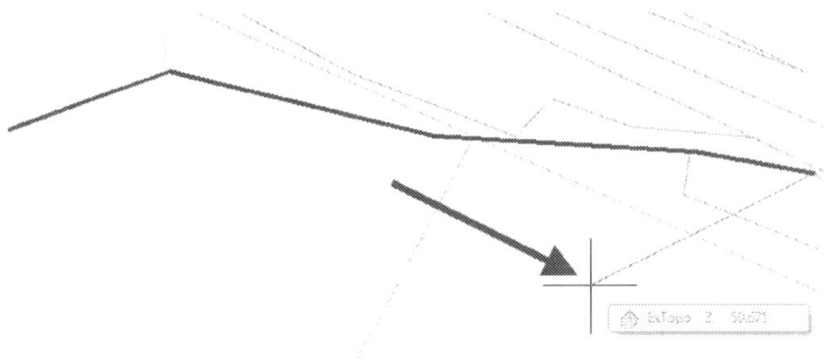

Figure 4–61

8. When prompted to select the option for the wall height, select the default **All** option because the wall has a constant height.

The wall has a constant height of 1.5' from the base.

9. When prompted for the elevation difference or elevation, type **1.5'** and press <Enter>.

10. Save the drawing.

Practice 4c

Surface Edits

Practice Objective

- Edit a surface using definition options in the surface properties and commands found in the Toolspace.

Estimated time for completion: 30 minutes

In this practice you will refine a previously created surface. The **ExTopo** surface has some triangulations that are not valid. You will eliminate these TIN lines using three methods: you will set the maximum triangle edge length, delete TIN lines (triangle edges), and add a boundary to the surface. Each of these methods has advantages and disadvantages and should be used appropriately.

Task 1 - Set the maximum triangle length.

1. Continue working with the drawing from the previous practice or open **SUF1-C1-Surface.dwg** from the *C:\Civil 3D Projects\Civil3D-Training\Surface* folder.

2. Select the preset view **Surface-Edit**, as shown in Figure 4–62.

*Ensure that the **ExTopo** surface is using the **Contours and Triangles** surface style.*

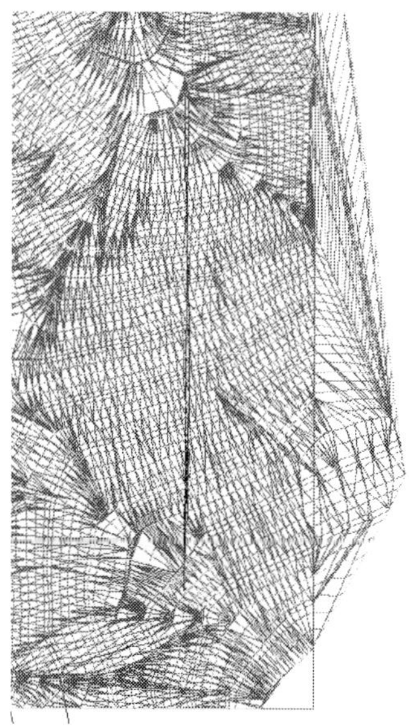

Figure 4–62

3. In Model Space, select the **ExTopo** surface. The *Tin Surface ExTopo* contextual tab will display. In the *Modify* panel, select **Surface Properties**, as shown in Figure 4–63.

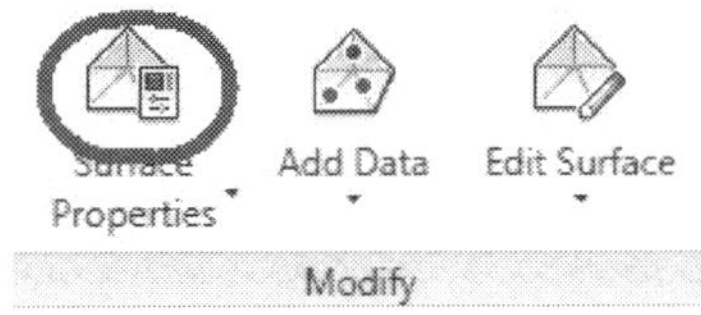

Figure 4–63

4. The Surface Properties dialog box opens. Select the *Definition* tab and expand the **Build** options in the *Definition Options* area.

Although there are invalid triangle lengths that are less than that length in this area, entering a smaller number might remove some valid triangles in the site.

5. Set the *Use maximum triangle length* value to **Yes** and the *Maximum triangle length* value to **330'**, as shown in Figure 4–64. Click **OK** to close the dialog box and accept the changes.

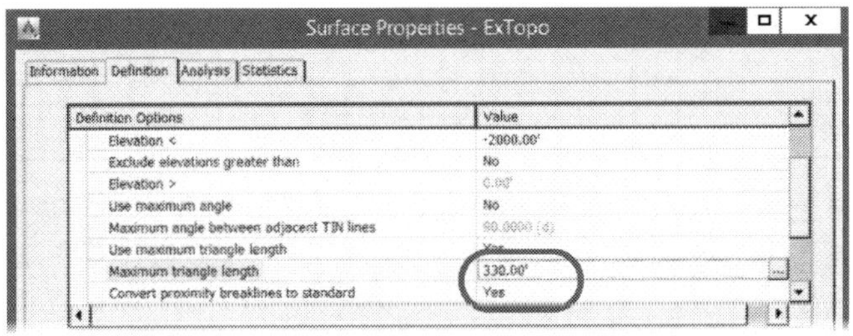

Figure 4–64

All triangles that have edge lengths greater than 330' are removed from the surface.

6. When prompted to *Rebuild the surface* or *Mark the surface as out-of-date*, select **Rebuild the surface**.

7. Save the drawing.

Task 2 - Delete lines.

Although you have eliminated triangle edge lengths greater than 330', you still have some triangles that you will remove using a scalpel (i.e., deleting selected lines).

1. Continue working with the drawing from the previous task or open **SUF1-C2-Surface.dwg**.

*If you are not still in the drawing view from the previous task, select the View tab>Views panel, and select the preset view **Surface-Edit**.*

Figure 4–65 shows the lines that you will be deleting.

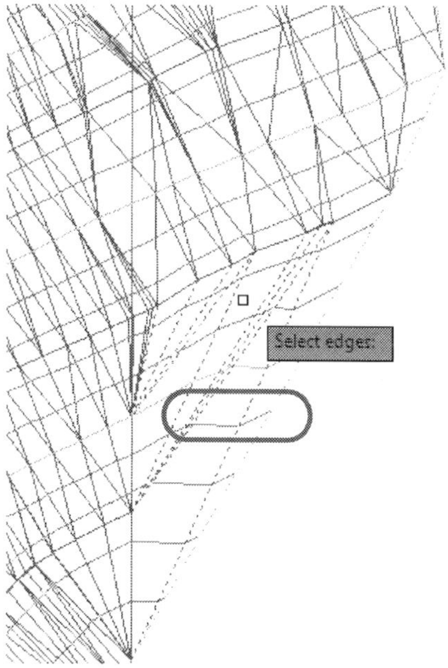

Figure 4–65

2. In Model Space, select the **ExTopo** surface. The *Tin Surface ExTopo* contextual tab will display. In the *Modify* panel, expand the (Edit Surface) drop-down list, and select **Delete Line**, as shown in Figure 4–66.

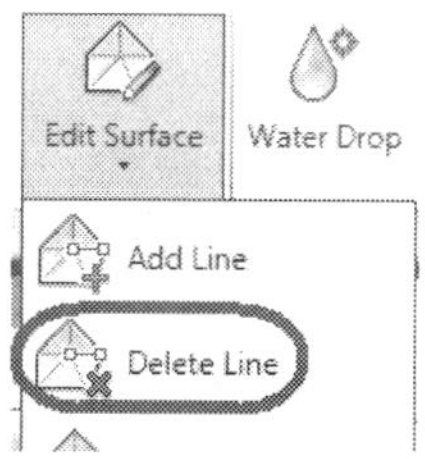

Figure 4–66

3. Select each of the required TIN lines in Model Space, as shown in Figure 4–67. When you have finished, press <Enter> to end the selection and press <Enter> to end the command.

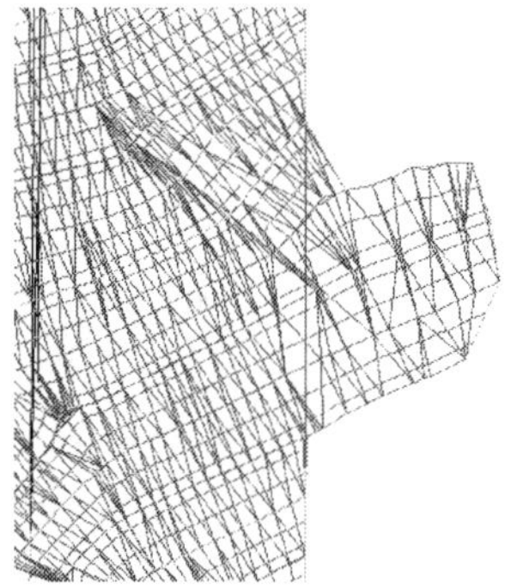

Figure 4–67

4. Save the drawing.

Task 3 - Add a boundary.

The **Delete Line** command can be effective, but might not efficiently clean up the edges of large surfaces. A surface boundary might be useful if you have a well-defined boundary.

1. Continue working with the drawing from the previous task or open **SUF1-C3-Surface.dwg**.
2. If you are not still in the drawing view from the previous task, select the *View* tab>Views panel and select the preset view **Surface-Edit**.
3. In Model Space, select the **ExTopo** surface. The *Tin Surface ExTopo* contextual tab will display. In the *Modify* panel, click (Add Data), expand the drop-down list and select **Boundaries**, as shown in Figure 4–68.

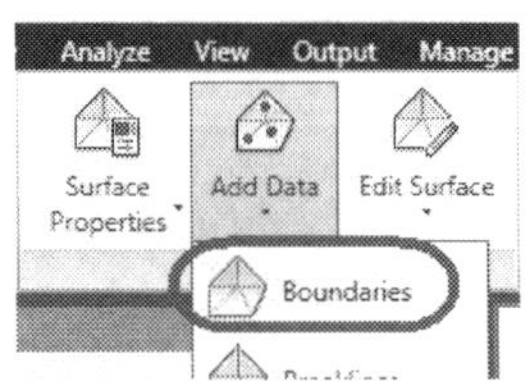

Figure 4–68

4. The Add Boundaries dialog box opens, as shown in Figure 4–69. Type **EG Outside** in the *Name* field, and select **Outer** in the Type drop-down list. Do not select the **Non-destructive breakline** option, because you do not want to trim to this polyline shape. Instead, the dialog box options selected will erase all of the triangle lines that cross or are beyond the boundary. Click **OK** to accept the changes and close the dialog box.

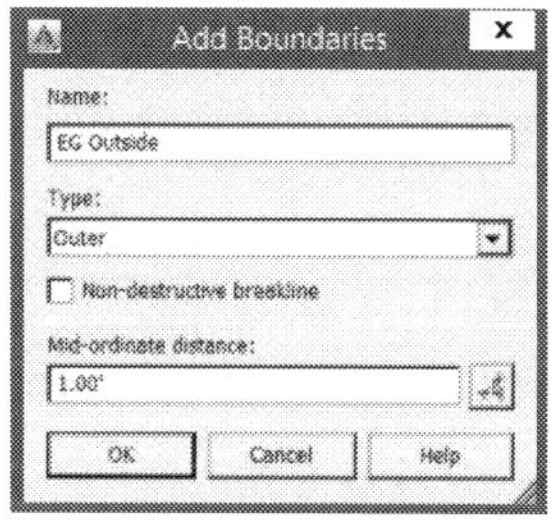

Figure 4–69

You might have to regen the screen to display the boundary.

5. When prompted to select an object, select the red polyline that represents the boundary, as shown in Figure 4–70.

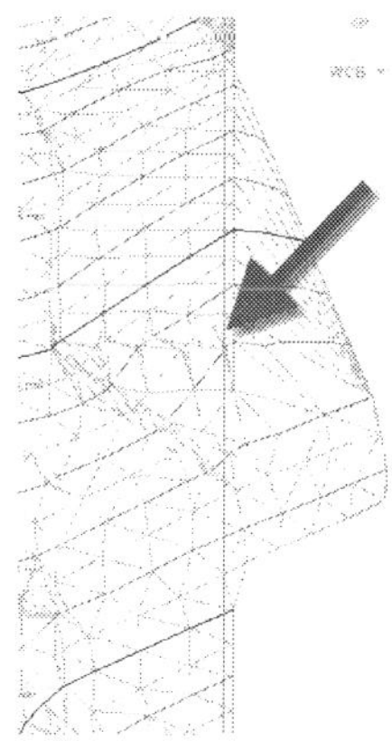

Figure 4–70

6. Examine how this boundary affected the surface. The boundary excluded all data that crossed or fell beyond it. This boundary is a dynamic part of the **ExTopo** surface.

7. (Optional) Select the boundary line and move the grips. Note how the surface expands or contracts to match the change in the boundary. Undo the changes.

8. Save the drawing.

Task 4 - Set the elevation range.

In reviewing the drawing, you need to address an error in the site. The original topographical contour file contains an invalid piece of data that has transferred to the surface.

1. Continue working with the drawing from the previous task or open **SUF1-C4-Surface.dwg**.
2. Select the preset view **Surf Elev Edit**.
3. In Model Space, as shown on the left in Figure 4–71, select the **ExTopo** surface, right-click, and select **Object Viewer**.
4. In the Object Viewer, click and drag the view, as shown on the right in Figure 4–71, to rotate the 3D view to identify the issue.

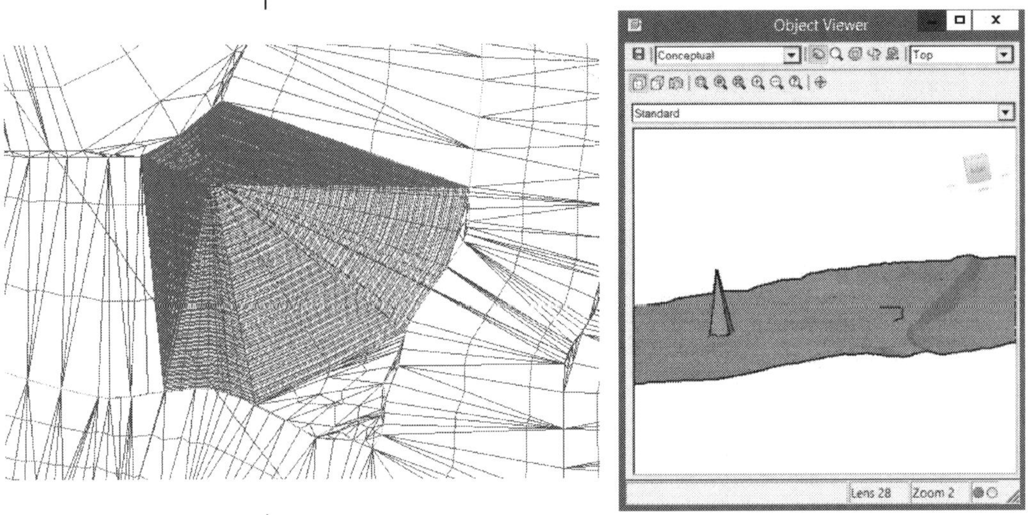

Figure 4–71

5. Close the Object Viewer by selecting **X** in the top right corner of the dialog box.
6. In Model Space, select the **ExTopo** surface. The *Tin Surface ExTopo* contextual tab will display. In the Modify panel, select **Surface Properties**, as shown in Figure 4–72. The Surface Properties dialog box opens.

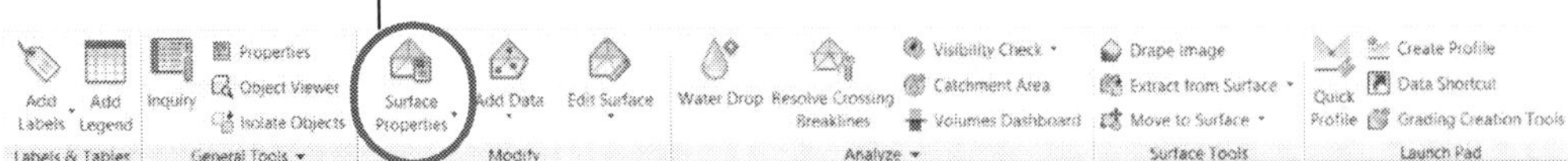

Figure 4–72

7. Select the *Statistics* tab and expand the value list in the *General* area.

8. When you review the site conditions, note that the site ranges from an elevation of roughly 100' to 330'. However, the statistics indicate that the surface ranges from an elevation of 110' to 500', as shown in Figure 4–73.

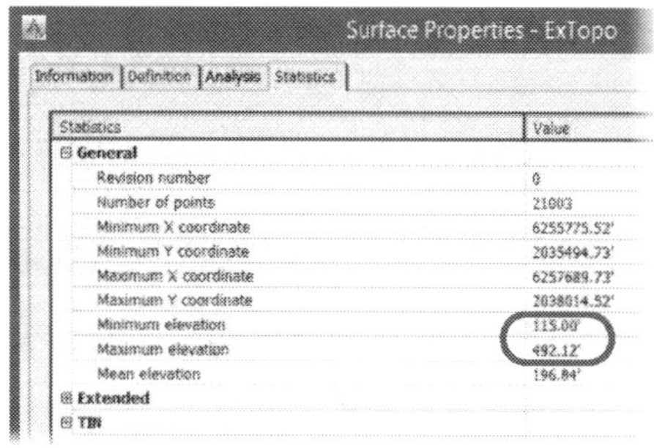

Figure 4–73

9. To correct the surface, select the *Definition* tab. Expand *Build* properties and set the *Exclude elevation less than* value to **Yes**. Set the *Elevation* < value to **100'**, the *Exclude elevation greater than* value to **Yes**, and the *Elevation* > value to **330'**, as shown in Figure 4–74.

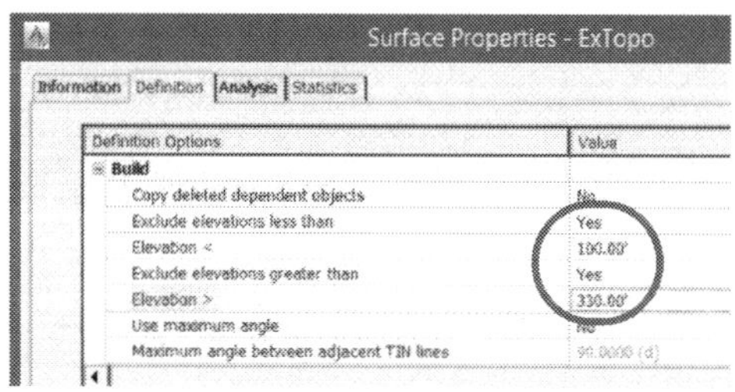

Figure 4–74

10. Click **OK** to accept the changes and close the dialog box.

All points that are above an elevation of 330' are removed and the error is fixed.

11. When prompted to *Rebuild the surface* or *Mark the surface as out-of-date*, select **Rebuild the Surface**.

12. Save the drawing.

Task 5 - Review edits in the *Prospector* tab and the Surface Properties dialog box.

The history of all of the changes made to a surface is saved in the drawing. You can apply and remove these changes selectively to the surface.

1. Continue working with the drawing from the previous task or open **SUF1-C5-Surface.dwg**.
2. Select the preset view **Surface-Edit**.
3. In the *Prospector* tab, expand the *Surfaces* collection and select the **ExTopo** surface. Right-click and select **Surface Properties**. In the Surface Properties dialog box, clear the **Add boundary** *Operation Type* (as shown in Figure 4–75), and click **Apply**.

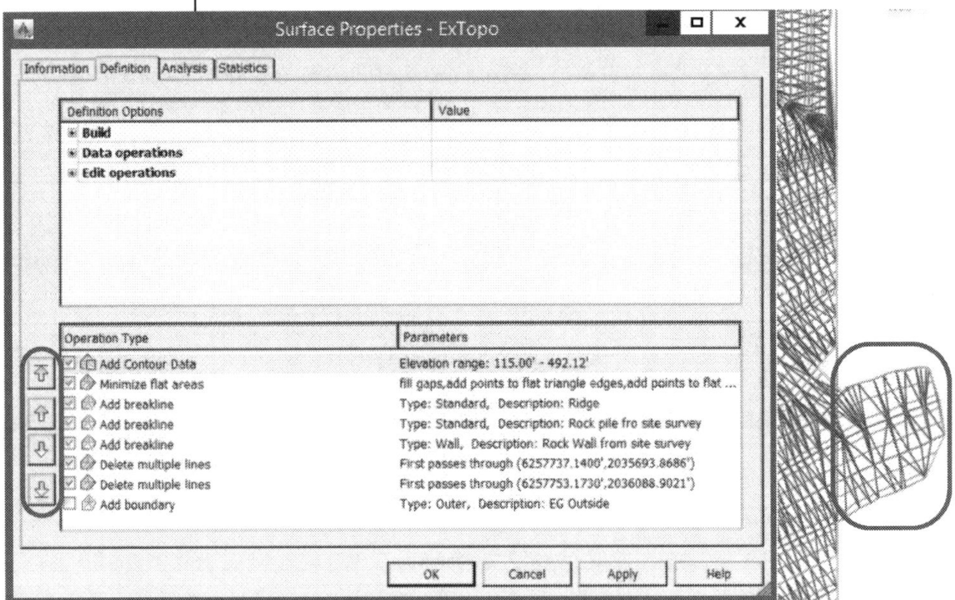

Figure 4–75

4. When prompted, select **Rebuild the Surface** in the Warning dialog box that opens. The boundary is ignored.

The boundary is once again used in the surface definition.

5. Re-select the **Add boundary** *Operation Type* and click **Apply**. When prompted, select **Rebuild the Surface** in the Warning dialog box that opens.
6. Save the drawing.

Task 6 - Create a composite surface.

In the preceding tasks, you created a surface from available contour data. However, the data around the existing road, **Mission Avenue** (the road running east to west at the top of the site), was inaccurate, so you surveyed the road and created a surface. You need to create a composite surface that represents the site condition combined with the road.

1. Continue working with the drawing from the previous task or open **SUF1-C6-Surface.dwg**.

2. Select the preset view **Survey Main**.

3. In the *Prospector* tab, right-click on the *Surfaces* collection and select **Create Surface**.

4. Select **TIN surface** for the surface *Type*. Type **Existing-Site** for the surface name and **Composite surface of ExTopo and ExRoad** for the *Description*. Select **Contours 2' and 10' (Background)** for the surface *Style*. Click **OK** to close the dialog box and create a surface.

5. In the *Prospector* tab of the Toolspace, select the Surfaces category. In the preview list area, select the **ExRoad** and **ExTopo** surfaces. Right-click on the *Style* column heading and select **Edit**, as shown in Figure 4–76.

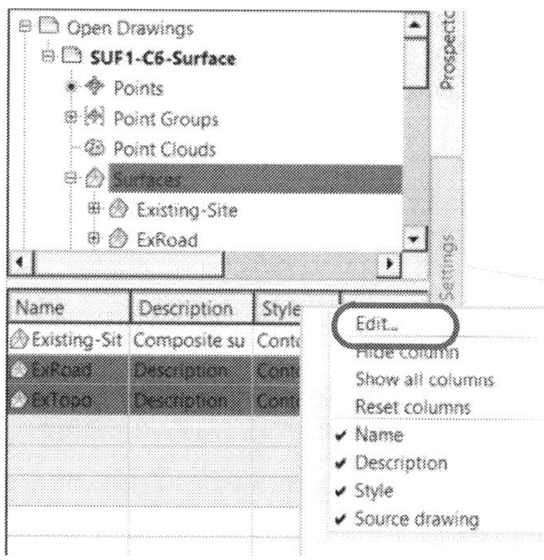

Figure 4–76

6. Set the surface style to **_No Display** and click **OK** to accept the changes and close the dialog box.

7. In the *Prospector* tab, expand the *Surfaces>Existing-Site>Definition* collections for that surface and select **Edits**. Right-click and select **Paste Surface...**, as shown in Figure 4–77.

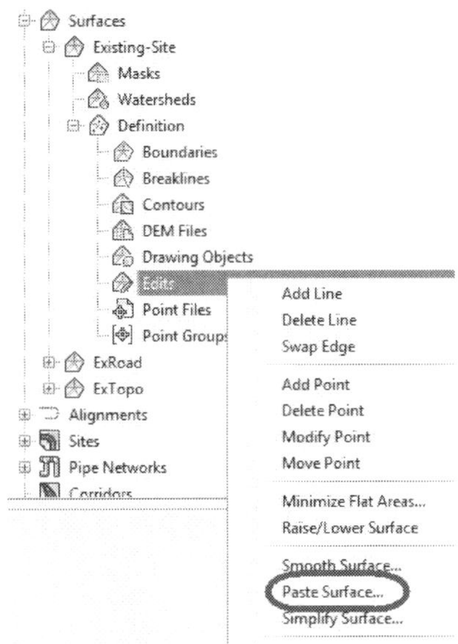

Figure 4–77

To select both surfaces, hold <Ctrl> when selecting the second surface.

8. In the Select Surface to Paste dialog box, select the **Ex Topo** and **Ex Road** surfaces, as shown in Figure 4–78. Once selected, click **OK** to close the dialog box.

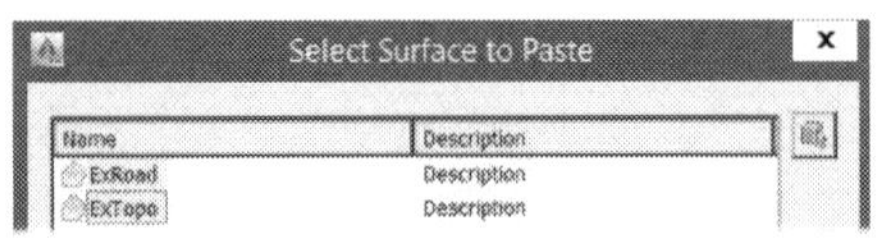

Figure 4–78

Note that the **ExRoad** surface was pasted first, followed by the **ExTopo** surface. In the area of overlap along the road, the **ExTopo** surface data will take precedence. This is not the required result.

9. In Model Space, select the **Existing-Site** surface from the surfaces listed in the *Surfaces* collection in the *Prospector* tab. The contextual tab for the surface object will display. Select **Surface Properties** in the Ribbon panel. The Surface Properties - Existing Site dialog box opens. In the *Definition* tab, note the order of the paste operations, as shown in Figure 4–79.

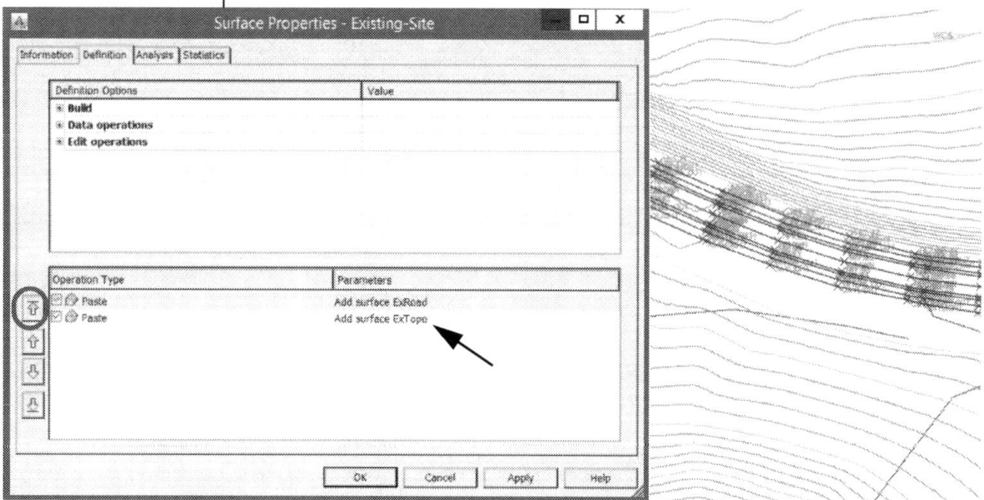

Figure 4–79

10. Select the **Paste** operation with the value **Add surface ExTopo** and move it to the top of the list by clicking .

11. Click **Apply**. When prompted to *Rebuild the surface* or *Mark the surface as out-of-date*, select **Rebuild the Surface**.

12. Click **OK** to exit the dialog box.

    As a consequence of the AutoCAD Civil 3D software's dynamic abilities, any changes to either the **ExTopo** or **ExRoad** surface will be reflected in the **Existing-Site** surface.

13. Save the drawing.

Practice 4d Surface Labeling and Analysis

Estimated time for completion: 20 minutes

Practice Objective

- Communicate information about the surface by labeling and analyzing it.

Task 1 - Add surface labels.

1. Continue working with the drawing from the previous practice or open **SUF1-D1-Surface.dwg** from the *C:\Civil 3D Projects\Civil3D-Training\Surface* folder.
2. Select the preset view **Surface Label**.
3. Select the **Existing-Site** surface in Model Space. In the contextual *Surface* tab>Labels & Tables panel, expand Add Labels and select the **Contour - Multiple**, as shown in Figure 4–80.

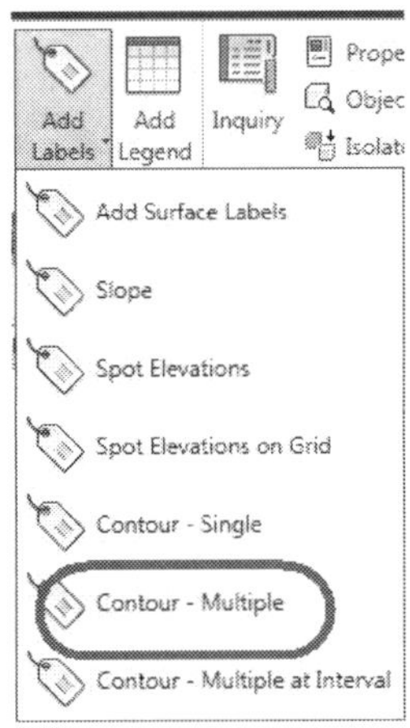

Figure 4–80

4. When prompted to select the first point, specify any point. When prompted for the next point, select a second and third point that creates a line intersecting all of the contours that you want to label, as shown in Figure 4–81. Press <Enter> when done.

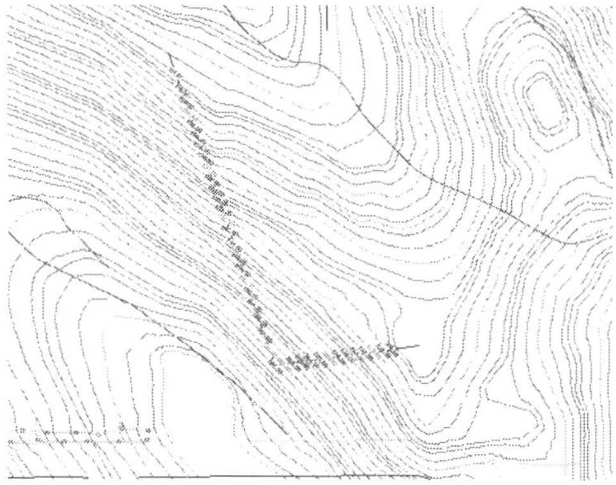

Figure 4–81

5. Move and reorient the contour label line. The labels update.

6. The *Display Contour Label Line* property can be set to only be visible when contour labels are selected. To change the visibility property, select the line in Model Space and select **Properties** in the contextual *Label* tab>General Tools panel. In the Properties dialog box, set the *Display Contour Label Line* property and the *Display Minor Contour Labels* property to **False,** as shown in Figure 4–82.

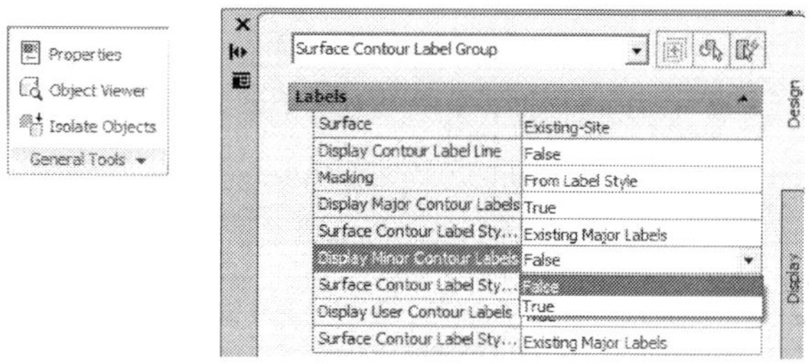

Figure 4–82

Once the grips disappear, the line is no longer dispalyed. Select a contour label to have the contour label line temporarily display for editing.

7. Close the Properties dialog box and press <Esc> to cancel your selection.

8. To have all of the future contour label lines behave this way in this drawing, select the *Settings* tab in the Toolspace. Select **Surface**, right-click, and select **Edit Feature Settings...**,as shown in Figure 4–83.

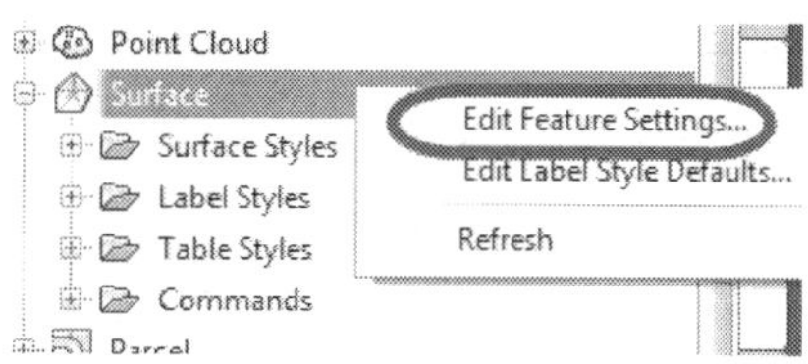

Figure 4–83

9. In the Edit Feature Settings dialog box, expand *Contour Labeling Defaults* and set the *Display Contour Label Line* property to **False** and change *Surface Contour Label Style Minor* to **<none>**, as shown in Figure 4–84. Click **OK** to accept the changes and close the dialog box.

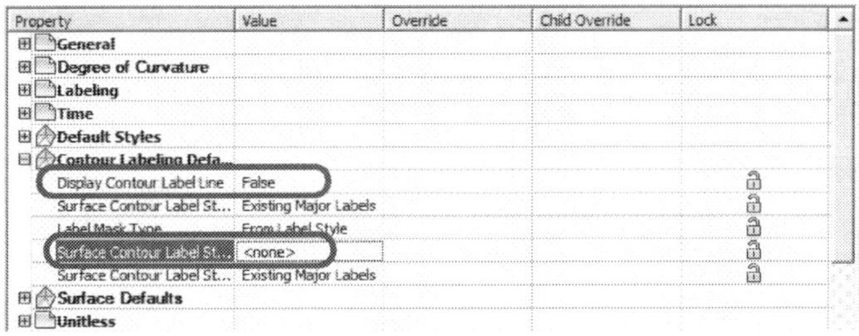

Figure 4–84

10. Select the **Existing-Site** surface again in Model Space. In the contextual *Surface* tab>Labels & Tables panel, expand Add Labels and select **Contour - Multiple**.

11. Select two points that will draw a line across some contours and press <Enter> when done. The contour label line and minor contour labels do not display.

12. Select the **Existing-Site** surface in Model Space. In the contextual *Surface* tab>Labels & Tables panel, expand Add Labels and select **Slope**.

13. To accept the prompt for the default One-point label, press <Enter>, and select a point in Model Space within the surface boundary. The AutoCAD Civil 3D software will place the slope value at that point. When you finish placing the labels, press <Enter> to exit the command.

14. (Optional) Using the process from Steps 10 and 11, experiment with labeling the surface with spot elevations and two point slopes. Note that you will be able to copy a label and place it at a different location. As the labels are dynamic, the values will change to reflect the surface information at the location of the label.

Task 2 - Perform a slope analysis.

The AutoCAD Civil 3D software calculates a range of values to fit within the specified number of ranges.

1. Continue working with the drawing from the previous task or open **SUF1-D2-Surface.dwg**.
2. Select the preset view **Surface**.
3. Select the **Existing-Site** surface in Model Space. In the contextual *Surface* tab>Modify panel, select **Surface Properties**.
4. In the *Information* tab in the Surface Properties dialog box, select **Slope Banding (2D)** as the surface style.
5. In the *Analysis* tab, select **Slopes** for the *Analysis type* and select **5** for the number of ranges to use. Click (Run Analysis).
6. Change the range values for Range1 to 0-2%, Range2 to 2-5%, Range3 to 5-10% Range4 to 10-20%, and Range5 to 20-70000%, as shown in Figure 4–85.

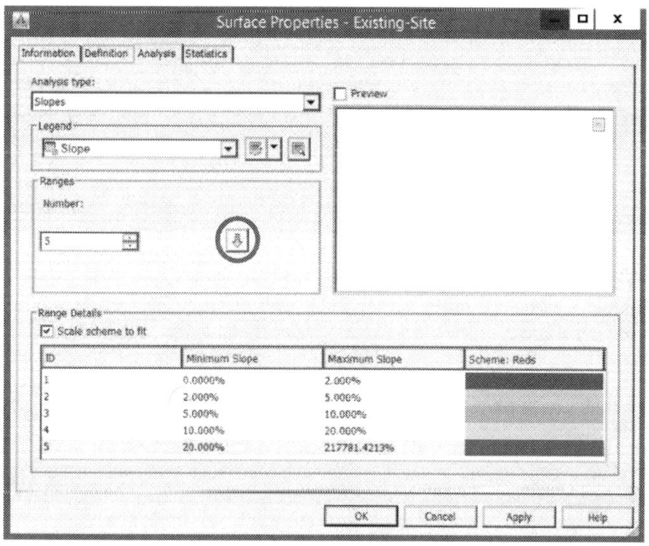

Figure 4–85

7. Change the range of colors for the slope range to match those shown in Figure 4–85. To change the color, click on it to open the Select Color dialog box, as shown in Figure 4–86, and select the required color. Click **OK** to close the dialog box.

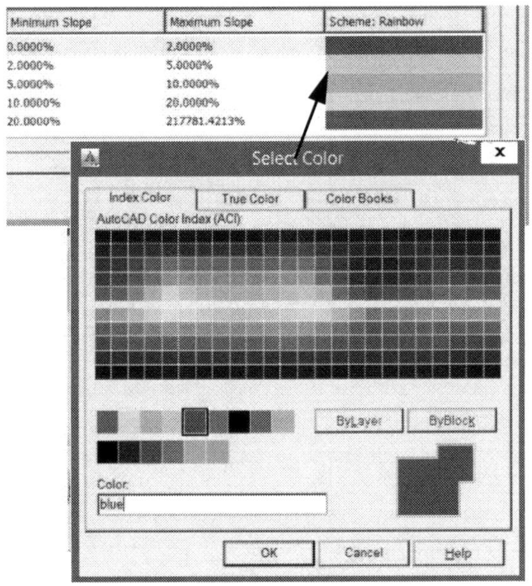

Figure 4–86

8. Click **OK** to close the dialog box and apply the changes. Press <Esc> to exit the surface selection.

9. Review the area that you want to develop. The slope ranges will be an issue.

10. You need to create a slope values table. Select the **Existing-Site** surface in Model Space. In the contextual *Surface* tab>Labels & Tables panel, select **Add Legend**.

11. Select **Slopes** from the command options, and then select **Dynamic** for a dynamic table.

12. When prompted for the top corner of the table (top left), select a location in an open area to the right of the surface, as shown in Figure 4–87. Press <Esc> to exit the selection.

Because this table is dynamic, any changes made to the surface or to the ranges in the analysis will update the table automatically.

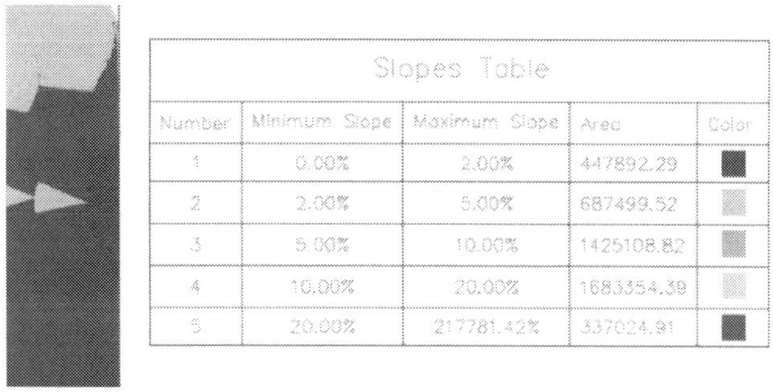

Slopes Table

Number	Minimum Slope	Maximum Slope	Area	Color
1	0.00%	2.00%	447892.29	
2	2.00%	5.00%	687499.52	
3	5.00%	10.00%	1425108.82	
4	10.00%	20.00%	1683354.39	
5	20.00%	217781.42%	337024.91	

Figure 4–87

13. (Optional) Open the Surface Properties dialog box (Steps 3 to 7) and change the number of slope ranges or the values. The Model Space Legend table will be updated.

14. Save the drawing.

Parcels

This chapter includes instructional content to assist in your preparation for the following topic and objectives for the AutoCAD® Civil® 3D 2016 Certified Professional exam.

Autodesk Certification Exam Objectives in this Chapter

Exam Topic	Exam Objective	Section
Parcels	• Design a parcel layout	• 5.1
	• Select parcel styles to change the display of parcels	• 5.2
	• Select styles to annotate parcels	• 5.3

5.1 Design a Parcel Layout

A Site under development (as shown in Figure 5–1), is the starting point for defining smaller parcels. The development's zoning agreement or covenants determine the size, setback, and other criteria for the new parcels. If a parcel is residential, there might be restrictions affecting minimum parcel areas, setbacks, and where to locate a house. If it is a commercial property, there might be restrictions or specific mandates for access, traffic control, parking spaces, etc. The **Parcel Layout** commands are used for subdividing larger parcels.

Figure 5–1

Sites, parcels, and alignments are closely related. Each can exist by itself and you do not need to have any alignments associated with the parcels. However, you often start with a site boundary and then divide the site into smaller parcels by placing alignments within its boundary.

- Parcels are listed in the *Prospector* tab in the Sites branch, as shown in Figure 5–2.

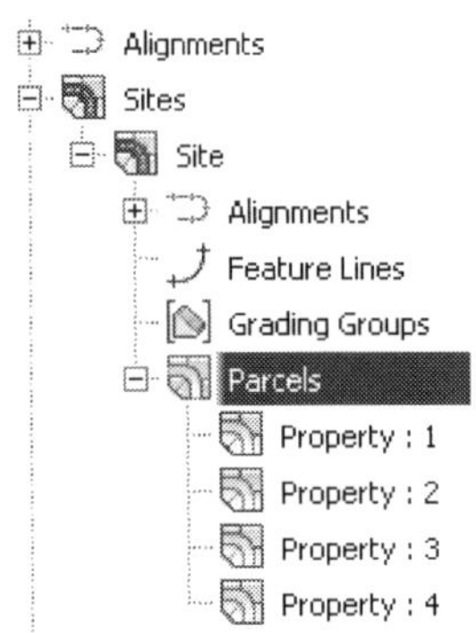

Figure 5–2

- When adding alignments to a site, the Parcels list is updated in the *Prospector* tab.

- As in all other AutoCAD Civil 3D objects, Parcel object layers are controlled in the *Object Layers* tab of the Drawing Settings dialog box, as shown in Figure 5–3.

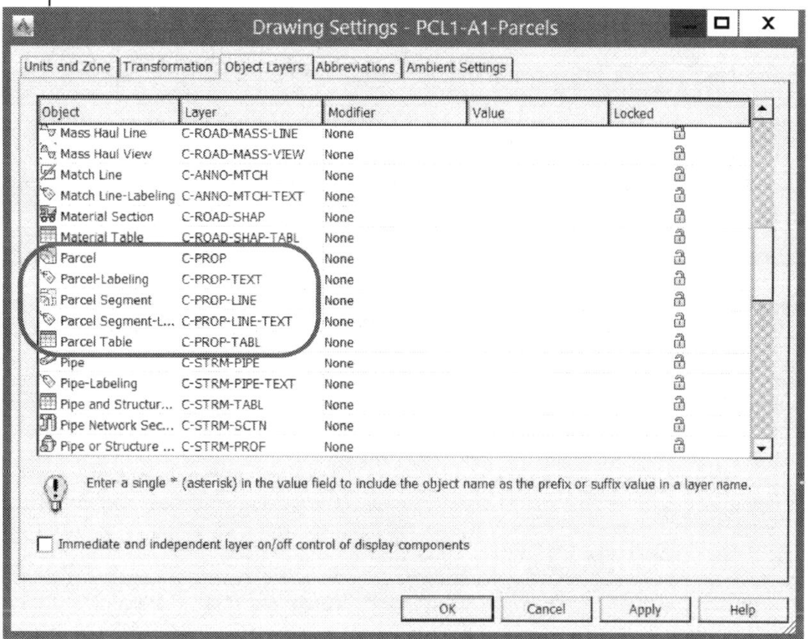

Figure 5–3

ROW Parcel

The right-of-way (ROW) parcel is related to the alignment and parcels. This special parcel represents land that is owned, maintained, and used for the community by a regulatory body (usually the local municipality or Department of Transportation). Typically, the ROW contains road, sidewalks, and utilities. The contents of the ROW depend on the covenants or agreements made before the site is developed. For example, in some cases the sidewalks and utilities might be located in an easement outside the road ROW.

- The AutoCAD Civil 3D software contains a **ROW** command, which creates a parcel using offsets from an alignment.

- A ROW parcel can represent the front yard definition of several potential parcels.

- While normal parcels automatically adjust to changes to an alignment, ROW parcels are static as shown in Figure 5–4. Therefore, you should only create ROW parcels after determining a final location for an alignment.

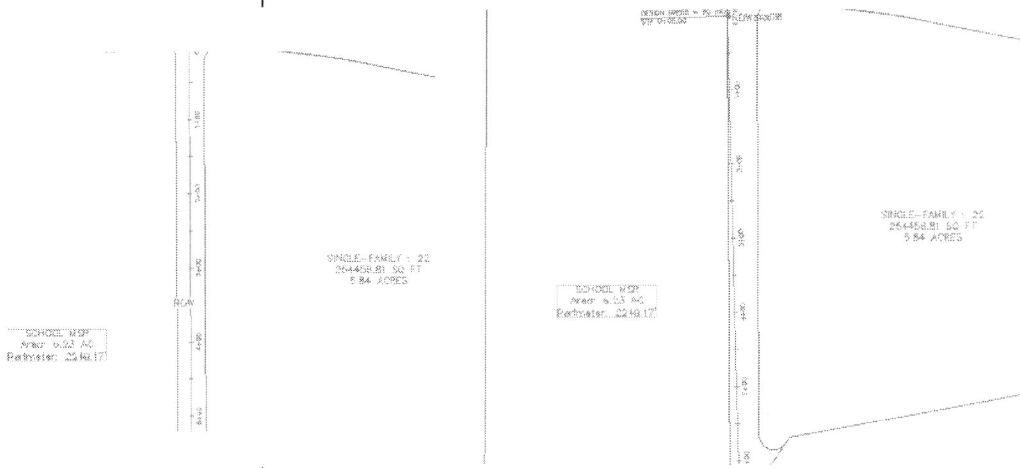

Figure 5–4

Parcel Layout Tools

In addition to creating parcels from polylines, arcs, and lines, the AutoCAD Civil 3D software can also intelligently create (and adjust) parcels using commands in the Parcel Layout Tools toolbar. To open the Parcel Layout Tools toolbar, expand Parcel in the Create Design panel, and select **Parcel Creation Tools**, as shown in Figure 5–5.

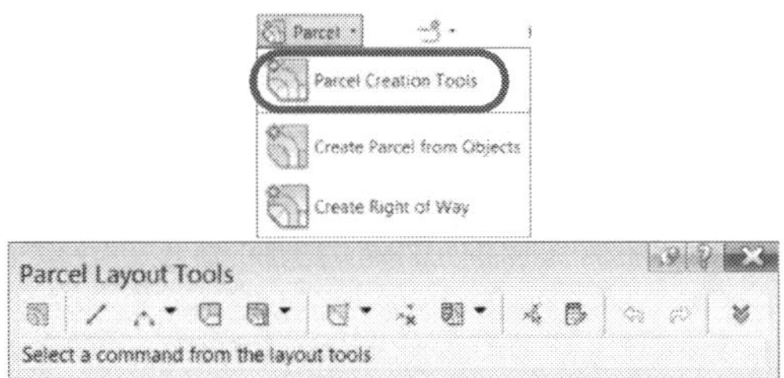

Figure 5–5

-  (Create Parcel) assigns parcel creation settings, such as parcel type, labeling styles, and other parameters.

- The Line and Curve commands can be used to create individual line and curve parcel segments. Segments created with these tools are considered *fixed*.

- (Draw Tangent - Tangent with No Curves) enables you to create a series of connected parcel line segments.

- The Parcel Sizing flyout (shown in Figure 5–6), contains a list of commands for creating and editing parcels. The methods used to create parcels include defining the last parcel segment by slide direction, slide angle, swing line, or freehand drawing of a parcel boundary. The most frequently used method is **Slide Line**.

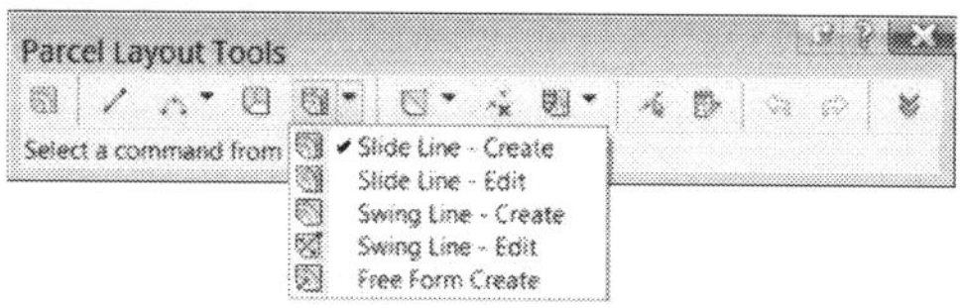

Figure 5–6

- The commands at the center of the toolbar (shown in Figure 5–7), enable you to further edit parcel segments. These commands include inserting or deleting PIs (points of intersection), deleting parcel segments, or creating or dissolving parcel unions.

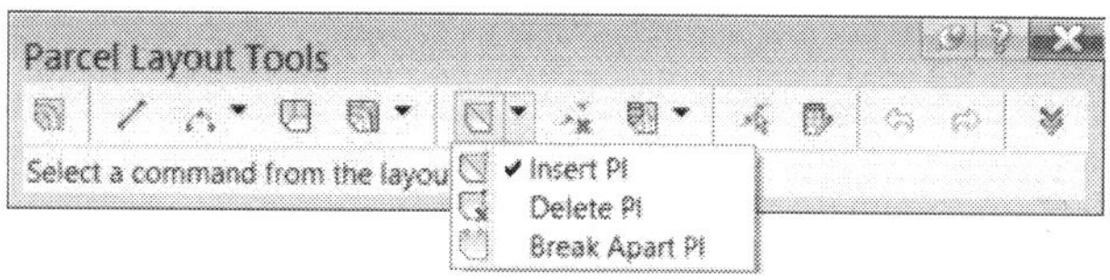

Figure 5–7

- (Pick Sub-Entity) enables you to select a parcel line and display its details in the Parcel Layout Parameters dialog box.

- (Sub-entity Editor) opens and closes the Parcel Layout Parameters dialog box.

- The next two commands enable you to **Undo** and **Redo** parcel edits. These can be used while the Parcel Layout Tools have been opened.

- The drop-down arrow ( ) expands the toolbar to display the Parcel Creation parameters, as shown in Figure 5–8 (also accessible through the Command Settings of *CreateParcelByLayout* in the *Settings* tab).

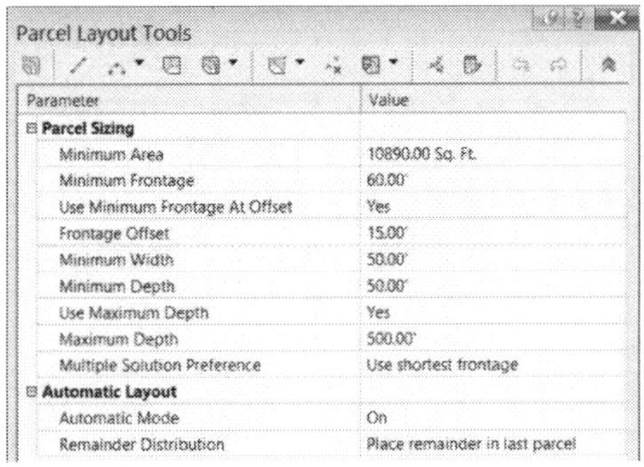

Figure 5–8

- The *Parcel Sizing* area sets the minimum area for parcels to be laid out. *Minimum Frontage* sets the minimum width of a parcel at the ROW or at a setback from the ROW.

- *Use Minimum Frontage At Offset* specifies whether or not to use frontage offset criteria.

- *Frontage Offset* sets the default value for the frontage offset from the ROW.

- *Minimum Width* sets the default minimum width at the frontage offset.

- *Minimum Depth* sets the minimum depth of new or existing parcels at the mid-point and is perpendicular to the frontage of the parcel.

- *Use Maximum Depth* specifies whether or not to use maximum depth criteria.

- *Maximum Depth* sets the maximum depth for new parcels or when editing parcels.

- *Multiple Solution Preference* specifies whether or not to use the shortest frontage or the smallest area when multiple solutions are encountered.

- *Automatic Layout* affects how parcel auto-sizing subdivides a parcel block.

Create Parcels

The **Create Parcel by Layout** tools can help you to quickly create a subdivision plan. Although these tools can make your job easier and are faster than manual drafting, they are only effective in creating the last side of new parcels. Therefore, you might need to create additional (or adjust) parcel lines manually to guide the AutoCAD Civil 3D software to the best solution. For example, the area shown in Figure 5–9, requires you to create minimum 10,225 sq ft (0.23 acres) parcels.

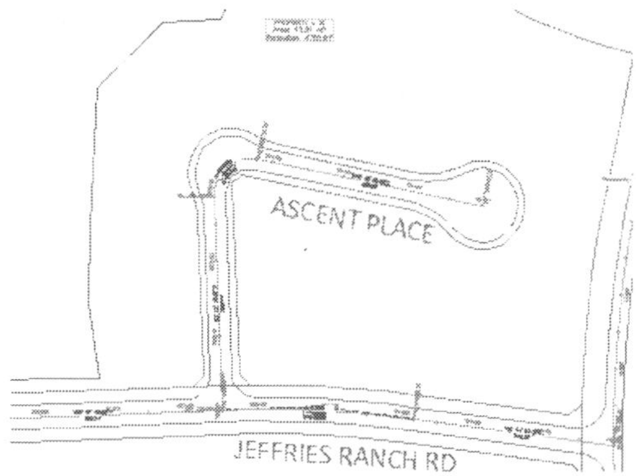

Figure 5–9

The back parcel lines (those along the west and south of the Cul-De-Sac area, and between Jeffries Ranch Rd and Ascent Place) were drawn manually and saved in a separate drawing file. Once inserted, they are used to guide the creation of the parcels next to Ascent Place. If you ask the AutoCAD Civil 3D software to automatically subdivide this area, the result is a total of 15 residential lot parcels, as shown in Figure 5–10.

Figure 5–10

The various creation and editing techniques available in the Create Parcel by Layout toolbar are as follows:

Freehand

The **Line** and **Curve** commands and  (Draw Tangent - Tangent with No Curves) enable you to create lot lines without having to specify an area. In contrast, the following commands all create parcels based on a specified area.

Slide Line

The **Slide Line - Create** command enables you to subdivide a larger parcel by creating new parcel lines that hold a specific angle relative to the Right-of-Way, such as 90º or a specific bearing or azimuth. The **Slide Line - Edit** command enables you to modify a parcel to a specified area while holding the same angle from the ROW or a specific bearing or azimuth. The commands are shown in Figure 5–11.

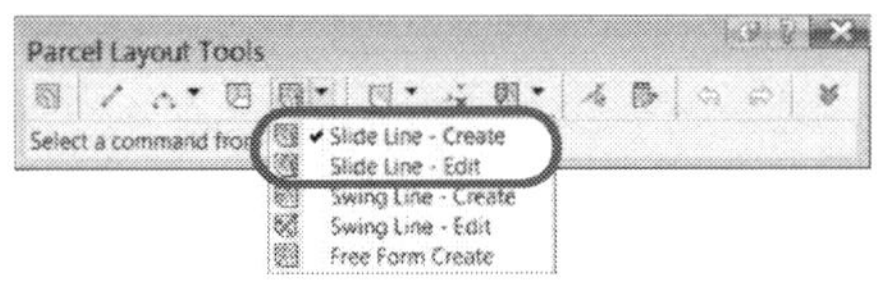

Figure 5–11

Swing Line

The **Swing Line - Create** command enables you to create a new parcel by creating a parcel segment that connects to a specified point, such as a property corner. The **Swing Line - Edit** command enables you to resize a parcel while specifying a lot corner. These commands are shown in Figure 5–12.

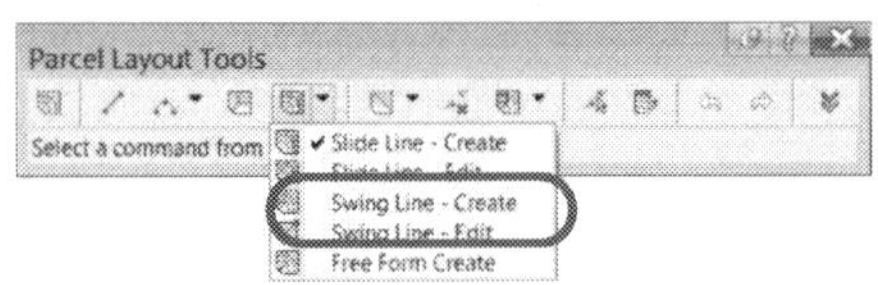

Figure 5–12

Free Form Create

The **Free Form Create** command enables you to create a new lot by specifying an area, attachment point and angle, or two attachment points.

Frontage

When using these routines, you are prompted to select a parcel interior point and trace its frontage geometry. This is a critical step. As you trace the frontage, the command creates a jig (heavy highlight) that recognizes the changing geometry of the frontage line work.

5.2 Select Parcel Styles to Change the Display of Parcels

Parcel Style Display Order

Parcel segment display is controlled by parcel styles, and parcel lines can abut parcels with different styles. Select the **Parcels** collection (under *Sites*), right-click, and select **Properties**, as shown in Figure 5–13, to open the Site Parcel Properties dialog box. You can select which parcel style should take precedence in the *Parcel style display order* area in the Site Parcel Properties dialog box, as shown in Figure 5–13. Placing the style for the overall parent tract (the Site Parcel Style) at the top of the list causes the outside parcel lines to display differently than those inside.

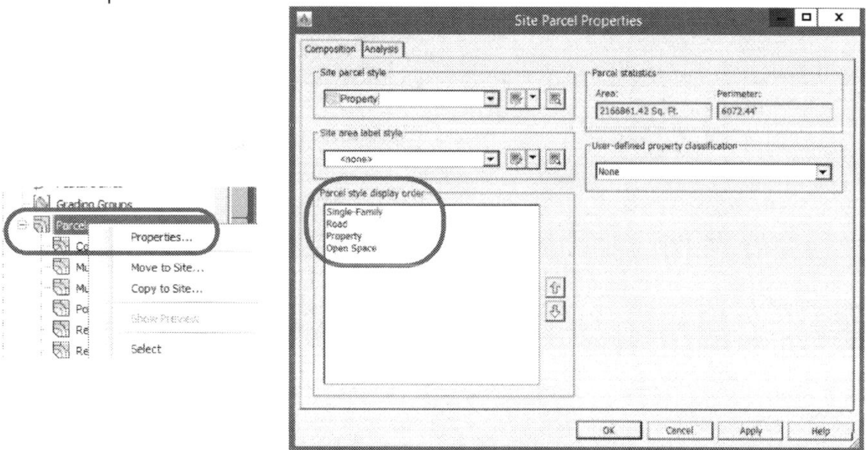

Figure 5–13

Parcel Properties

The properties of a parcel include its name, style, and an *Analysis* tab containing the parcel's area, perimeter, and point-of-beginning (POB). The Parcel Property's *Composition* tab displays the label style, area, and perimeter, as shown in Figure 5–14.

Figure 5–14

The *Analysis* tab contains a parcel boundary Inverse or Mapcheck analysis. In the upper right area of the tab, you can change the POB location and the analysis direction, as shown in Figure 5–15.

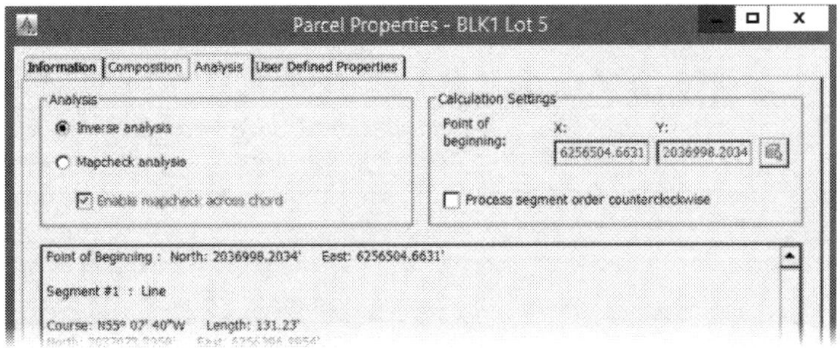

Figure 5–15

- The Mapcheck analysis precision is the same as the drawing distance precision.
- The Inverse report precision is set to the precision of the AutoCAD Civil 3D software (10 to 12 decimal places).
- The default direction of a Mapcheck or Inverse analysis is clockwise. You can change the direction to counter-clockwise if needed.
- A POB can be any vertex on the parcel's perimeter.

The *User Defined Properties* tab contains site-specific details, such as the *Parcel Number, Parcel Address, Parcel Tax ID*, and other properties you might want to define, as shown in Figure 5–16. Custom properties can be assigned to a drawing by using the *User Defined Property Classifications* area in the *Settings* tab, under the *Parcels* collection.

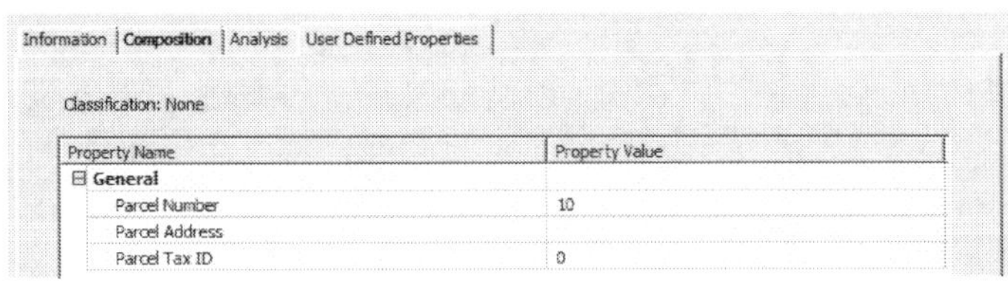

Figure 5–16

5.3 Select Styles to Annotate Parcels

Parcel Labels and Styles

There are two types of parcel annotation: an area label for the parcel itself and the segments defining the parcel.

A parcel area label usually consists of a parcel's number or name, area, and perimeter, as shown in Figure 5–17. Most offices define their own parcel label styles. A parcel label style can include several additional parcel properties, address, PIN, Site name, etc. In the AutoCAD Civil 3D software, you select a parcel by selecting a parcel area label, not the parcel segments.

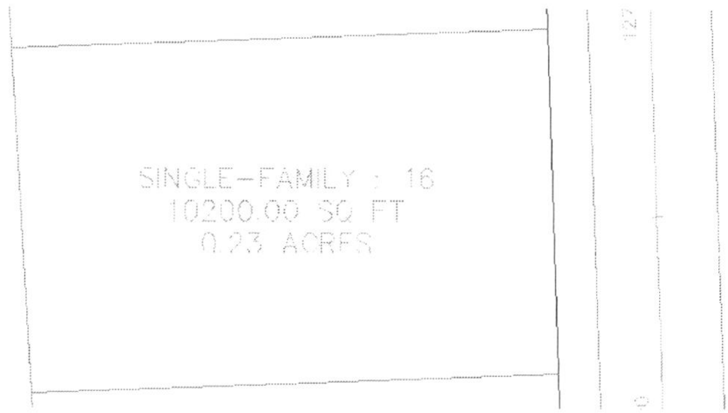

Figure 5–17

Parcel Labels

Parcel area labels are a means of graphically selecting a parcel, such as when creating Right-of-Ways. In the Parcel creation and editing examples, the parcel segment labels were created for you automatically. This section explores the functionality of these labels in more depth.

The Add Labels dialog box (**Annotate>Add Labels>Parcel> Add Parcel Labels...**) can be used to assign the required label styles and place labels in the drawing. It can set the line, curve, and spiral styles and toggle between single and multiple segment labeling, and to access the Tag Numbering Table. The dialog box is shown in Figure 5–18.

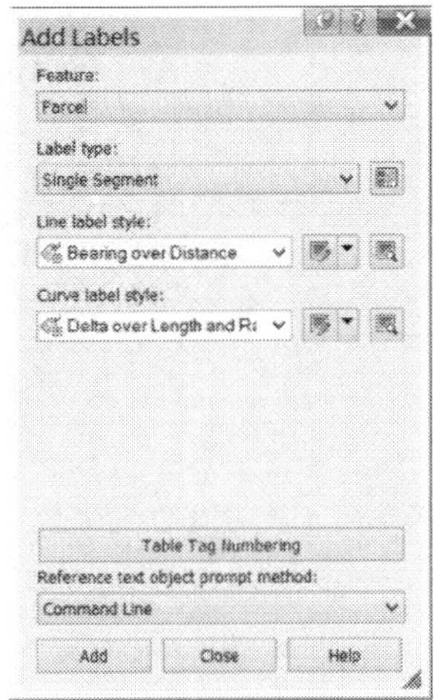

Figure 5–18

- Parcel labels, as with all AutoCAD Civil 3D labels, are capable of rotating and resizing to match changes in the viewport scale and rotation.
- A segment label has two definitions: composed and dragged state. A dragged state can be quite different from the original label definition.
- The AutoCAD Civil 3D software can label segments while sizing parcels.
- Labeling can be read clockwise or counter-clockwise around the parcel.
- Labels can be added through an external reference file using the same commands that label objects in their source drawing. This makes it easier to have multiple plans that need different label styles.
- The **Replace Multiple Labels** option is useful when you want to replace a number of parcel segment labels with another style. However, if you are labeling through an external reference file, labels created in the source drawing cannot be modified.

Parcel Area labels are controlled using Parcel Area Label Styles, which control the display of custom information (such as the parcel number, area, perimeter, address, etc.). For example, you can create more than one parcel area label if you need to show different parcel information on different sheets, as shown in Figure 5–19.

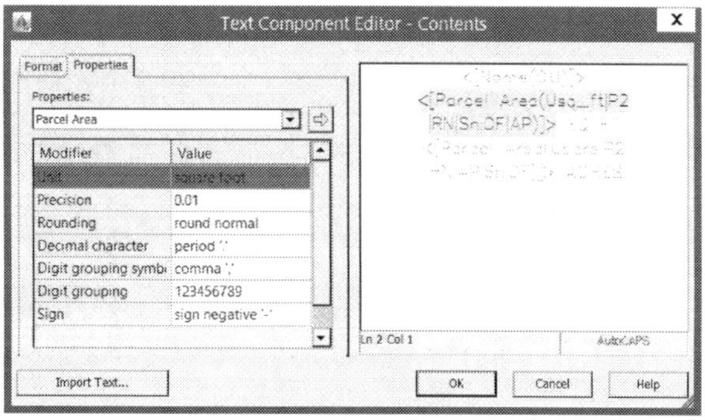

Figure 5–19

Parcel Segment labels annotate the line and curve segments of a parcel, as shown in Figure 5–20. You can label all of the segments of a parcel with one click or only label selected parcel segments.

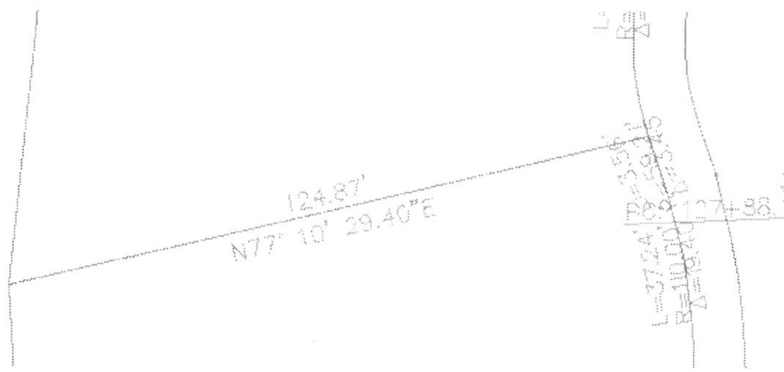

Figure 5–20

All labels have two definitions: one for the original location, and another when it is moved from its original location. A dragged label can remain as originally defined or can be changed to stacked text.

Renumbering Parcels

Creating parcels using the methods that have already been taught results in inconsistent parcel numbering. AutoCAD Civil 3D parcels can be renumbered individually using Parcel Properties, or in groups using **Modify>Parcel>Renumber/ Rename**.

This command enables you to specify a starting parcel number and the increment you want to have between parcels. (It also enables you to rename your parcels based on a different name template.) When renumbering, the command prompts you to identify parcels in the order in which you want to have them numbered. The Renumber/Rename Parcels dialog box is shown in Figure 5–21.

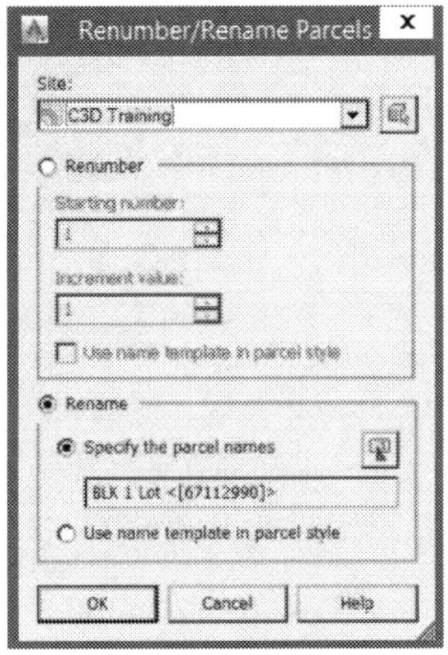

Figure 5–21

Parcel Tables

Parcel tables are an alternative to labeling individual parcel areas and segments. An example is shown in Figure 5–22.

Parcel Line and Curve Table			
Line #/Curve #	Length	Bearing/Delta	Radius
L76	112.01	N4° 08' 12.22"W	
L77	395.08	N85° 33' 05.19"E	
L78	471.49	N85° 33' 05.19"E	
L79	210.99	N4° 17' 33.13"W	
L80	211.55	N4° 17' 33.13"W	
L81	115.43	S25° 31' 05.98"W	

Figure 5–22

When creating a table, the AutoCAD Civil 3D software changes the parcel segment labels to an alpha-numeric combination, called a *tag*. A tag with an **L** stands for line and a **C** stands for curve. A segment's tag has a corresponding entry in the table.

- A table can only represent a selected set of label styles.
- The **Add Existing** option (shown in Figure 5–23) creates a table from existing objects. New objects are not added to the table. The **Add Existing and New** option creates a table with existing and new objects.

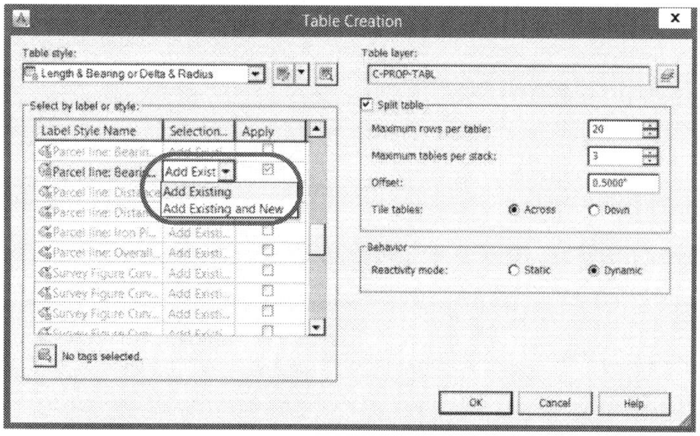

Figure 5–23

- A table can have a dynamic link between a segment's tag and table entry. If the segment changes, the table entry updates.
- The AutoCAD Civil 3D software switches a label to a tag by changing the *Display* mode from **Label** to **Tag**, as shown in Figure 5–24.

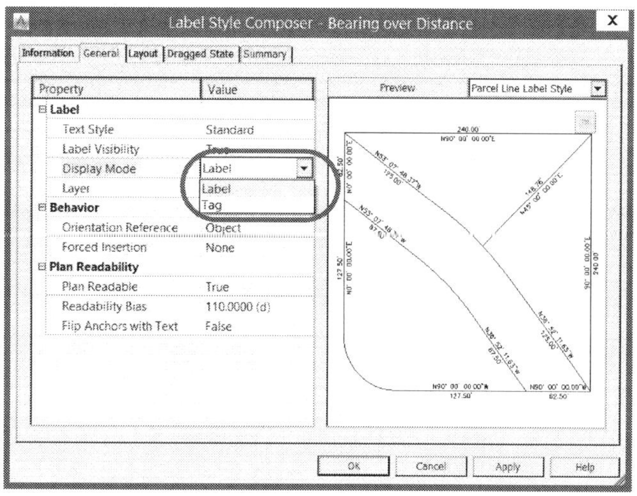

Figure 5–24

Parcel Reports

The AutoCAD Civil 3D software contains several types of parcel reports. Parcel Inverse and Mapcheck data is available in the *Analysis* tab in the Parcel Properties dialog box, as shown in Figure 5–25. The report can be generated clockwise or counter-clockwise, and the point of beginning can be specified.

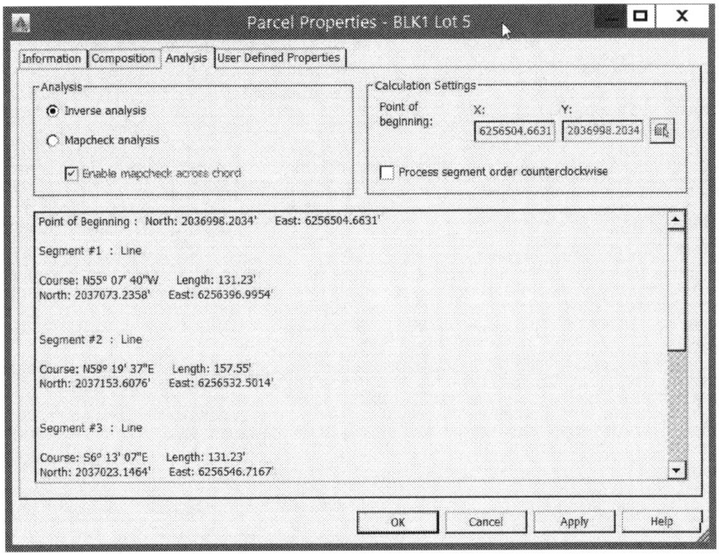

Figure 5–25

This dialog box does not enable output. If you want to generate a printable report, use the AutoCAD Civil 3D Toolbox. It includes several stock Parcel-related reports (such as Surveyor Certificates, Inverse and Mapcheck reports, Metes and Bounds), as shown in Figure 5–26.

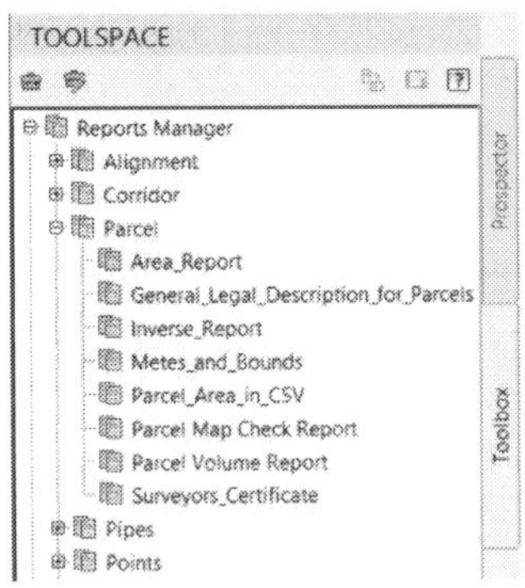

Figure 5–26

Practice 5a

Create Parcels From Objects

Practice Objective

- Create parcels from objects in the drawing or external reference file.

Estimated time for completion: 15 minutes

Task 1 - Create a Site parcel from objects.

1. Open **PCL1-B1-Parcels.dwg**.
2. In the *Home* tab>Create Design panel, expand Parcel and select **Create Parcels from Objects**, as shown in Figure 5–27.
3. In the model, select the polyline that represent the property boundary and press <Enter>.
4. In the Create Parcels dialog box, set the following parameters, as shown in Figure 5–28, and then click **OK**.
   - Site: **Site 1**
   - Parcel style: **Property**
   - Area Label style: **Name Area & Perimeter**
   - Automatically add segment labels: **Select this option.**
   - Parcel line segment label style: **(Span) Bearing and Distance with Crows Feet**.
   - Erase existing entities: **Select this option**.

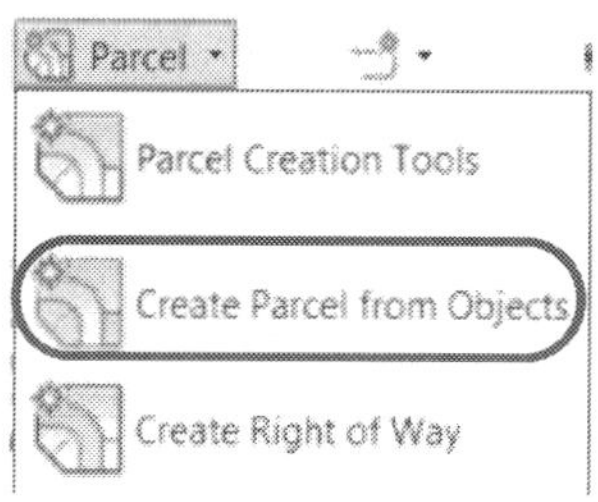

Figure 5–27

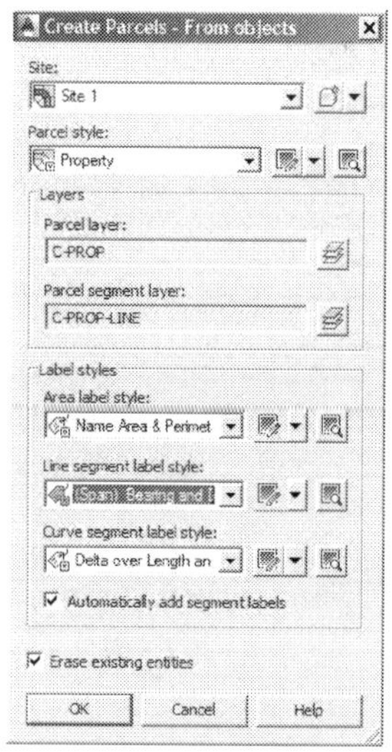

Figure 5–28

One parcel will be created with the parameters entered.

*Note: If the **+** is not displayed next to Parcels, press <F5> to refresh the Prospector tab view.*

5. In the *Prospector* tab, expand the current drawing**>Sites>** *Parcels*, as shown in Figure 5–29.

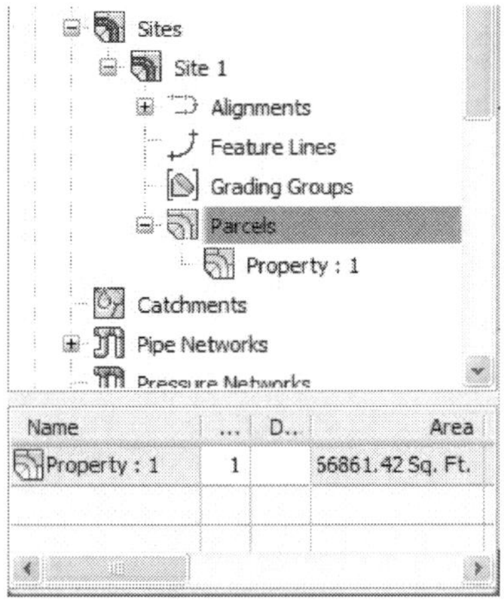

Figure 5–29

Task 2 - Create a new site and parcel from referenced objects.

You have received a drawing from the Land planning department that displays the street layout and different parcels. Using this plan, you will create parcels from XREF objects.

1. Continue working with the drawing from the previous task or open the file **PCL1-B2-Parcels.dwg**.
2. In the *Prospector* tab, right-click on the Sites branch and select **New**. Type **C3D Training** as the name and click **OK** to close the dialog box.
3. You now need to move the Property:1 Parcel from Site 1 to the C3D Training site. Expand the *Site1* collection, expand the *Parcels* collection, right-click on Property:1 parcel and select **Move to Site**, as shown on the left in Figure 5–30.
4. In the Move to Site dialog box, select **C3D Training**, as shown on the right in Figure 5–30. Click **OK** to close the dialog box.

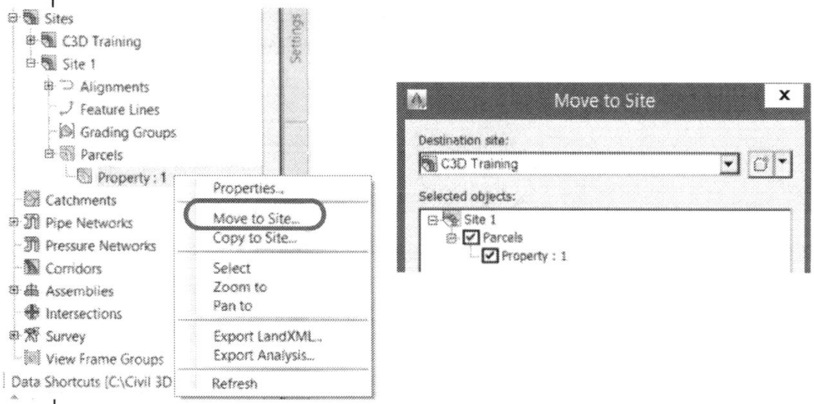

Figure 5–30

Note: To save time, the x-referenced drawing **Base-original Property**, has already been referenced. The zone and units for the project drawings were set. This enables you to geo reference the drawings using **Locate using Geographic data**, as shown in Figure 5–31.

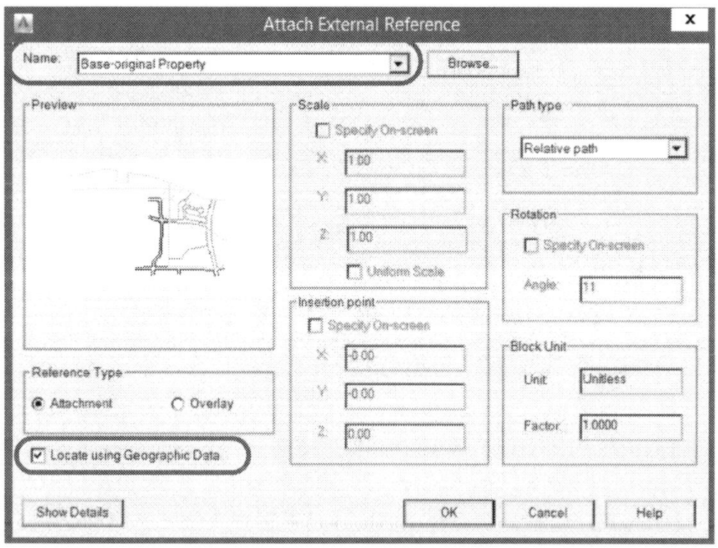

Figure 5–31

5. Thaw the layer **Base-originalProperty|A-Property-Future**.

6. In the *Home* tab>Create Design panel, expand Parcel and select **Create Parcels from Objects**. Select XREF from the command options.

7. Draw a rectangle around the linework to select it. Press <Enter> to end the **XREF selection** command.

8. In the Create Parcels - From Objects dialog box, verify that the Site name is **C3D Training** and accept the remaining defaults, as shown on the right in Figure 5–32. Click **OK** to close the dialog box.

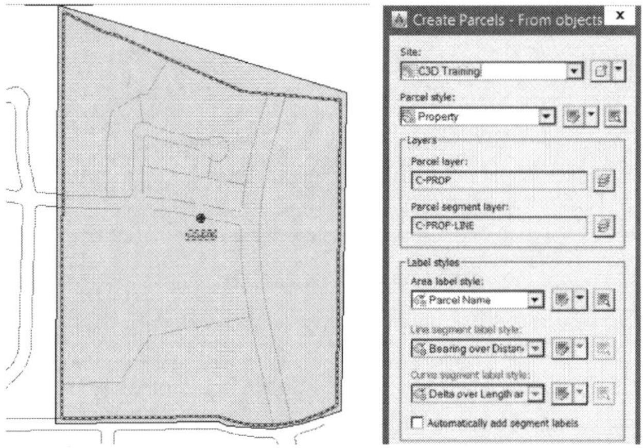

Figure 5–32

9. The project site has nine parcels. Select each parcel label and click  (Parcel Properties) on the contextual *Parcels* tab > Modify panel.

It may be necessary to clear the ***Use name template in parcel style*** *option.*

10. In the Parcel Properties dialog box, on the *Information* tab, rename the parcels according to Figure 5–33 and the table in Step 11. Note that your default parcel numbers might be different because the parcels are randomly numbered.

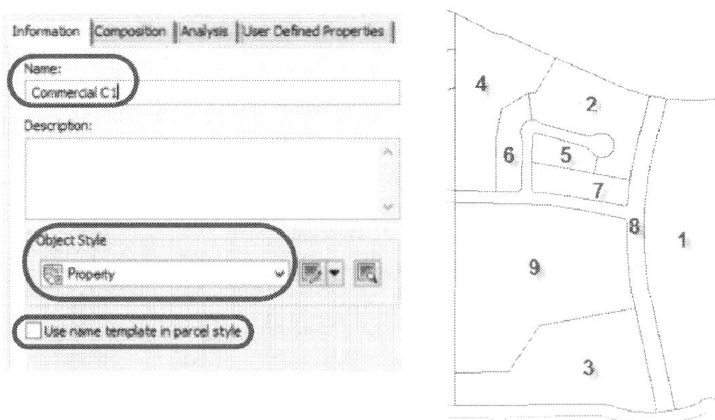

Figure 5–33

11. Using Figure 5–33 as a reference, set the parcel styles as follows:

Property Name	Style
1. Commercial C1	Property
2. Multi Family MF	Property
3. Municipal Reserve MR	Property
4. Pond PUL	Open Space
5. Residential BLK2 R1	Property
6. Residential BLK1 R1	Property
7. Residential BLK3 R1	Property
8. Right Of Way	Road
9. School MSR	Property

12. In the *Prospector* tab, expand Sites, expand the C3D Training site, right-click on Parcels, and select **Properties**, as shown in Figure 5–34.

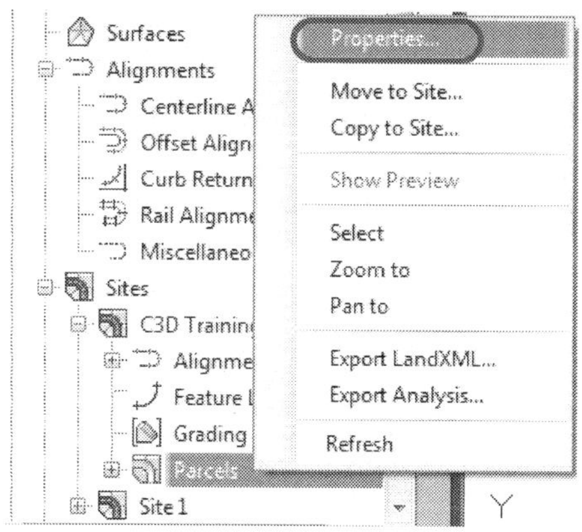

Figure 5–34

If the drawing does not look different after completing Step 13, you might need to adjust the draw order so that the XREF drawing is behind the existing drawing linework.

13. In the Site Parcel Properties dialog box, select **Property** in the *Parcel style display order* area, as shown in Figure 5–35.

    Click to move it up in the list.

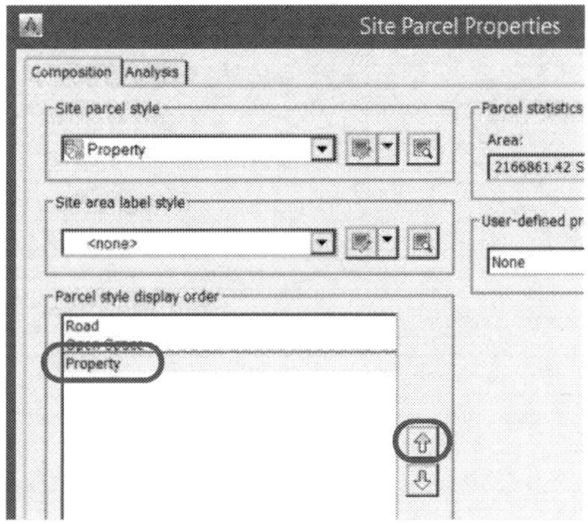

Figure 5–35

14. Click **OK**.

15. Save the drawing.

Practice 5b Creating and Editing Parcels

Estimated time for completion: 15 minutes

Practice Objective

- Create and edit parcels to maximize the number of lots you can create with the required area and frontage.

You have three parcels zoned as single-family residential: Block 1 (1.31ac), Block2 (0.94ac), and Block3 (1.47ac). Your client, the land developer, requires you to maximize the number of lots in these three parcels, while noting the minimum area and frontages as required by the Land Use bylaws.

Task 1 - Create parcels by slide angle.

1. Open **PCL1-C1-Parcels.dwg** from the *C:\Civil 3D Projects\Civil3D-Training\Parcels* folder.
2. Select the preset view **Parcel-Create**.
3. In the *Home* tab>Create Design panel, expand Parcel and select **Parcel Creation Tools**. The Parcel Layout Tools toolbar displays as shown in Figure 5–36.

Figure 5–36

4. Click to expand the *Parcel Creation Tools* and enter the values shown in Figure 5–37. When finished, click to collapse the expanded toolbar.

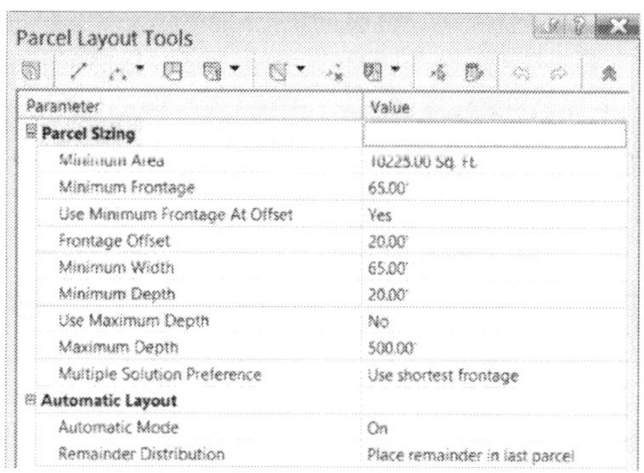

Figure 5–37

5. In the Parcel Layout Tools toolbar, expand  and select **Slide Line - Create**, as shown in Figure 5–38.

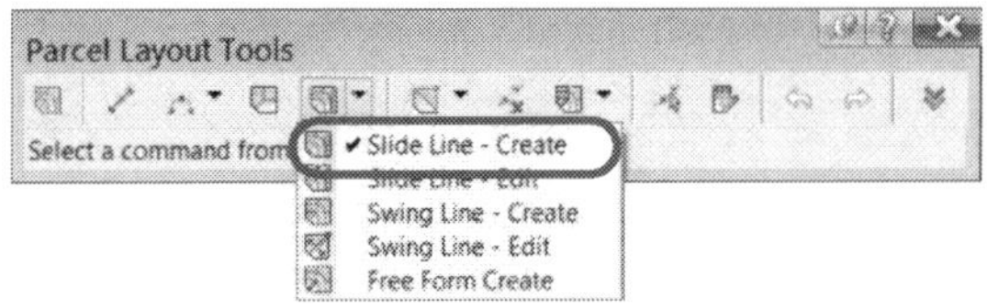

Figure 5–38

6. In the Create Parcels - Layout dialog box, set the following parameters, as shown in Figure 5–39:

   - Site: **C3D Training**
   - Parcel style: **Single-Family**
   - Area label style: **Name Square Foot & Acres**

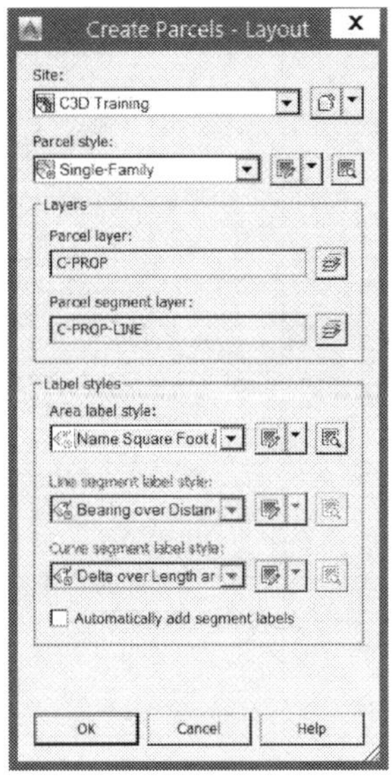

Figure 5–39

7. Click **OK** to accept the changes and close the dialog box.

8. When prompted to select the parcel to be subdivided, select the area label for parcel **RESIDENTIAL BLK1 R1**, as shown in Figure 5–40.

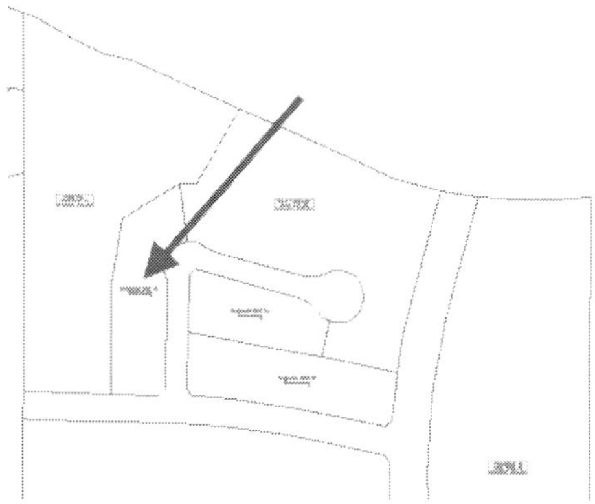

Figure 5–40

9. When you are prompted for the *starting point on frontage*, select the south end of the corner cut. Press <Ctrl>, right-click, and select **endpoint**. Then select the corner cut, **Pt 1**, shown in Figure 5–41.

10. When prompted for the *end point of the frontage*, set the end point of the property line to the north, **Pt 2**, as shown in Figure 5–41. Use the same process as the previous step to set the end point.

11. When prompted for the *angle of the property line* that will be used to define each lot, select a point east of the parcel near **Pt 3**, as shown in Figure 5–41. For the second point, press <Ctrl>, right-click, and select **Perpendicular**. Then select the line at Pt 4.

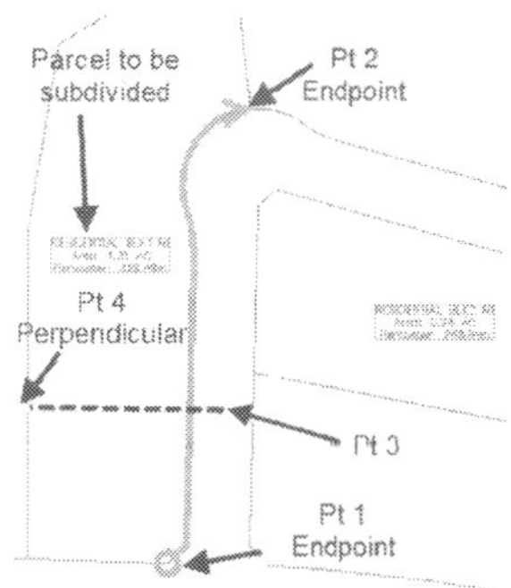

Figure 5–41

12. When prompted to *Accept results*, press <Enter>.

13. When prompted to select another parcel to subdivide, press <Esc> to end the command.

14. Save the drawing.

Practice 5c Rename/Renumber Parcels

Estimated time for completion: 15 minutes

Practice Objective

- Renumber the lots created so that they are in sequential order.

Task 1 - Rename and renumber parcels.

1. Open **PCL1-D1-Parcels.dwg**.
2. Select the preset view **Parcel-Create**.
3. Before renaming the newly created parcels, you need to change the label style of the original parcel. Select the parcel label **RESIDENTIAL BLK1 R1**, right-click, and select **Edit Area Selection Label Style**. Select **Name Square Foot & Acres** as the style and click **OK** to apply the changes and close the dialog box, as shown in Figure 5–42.

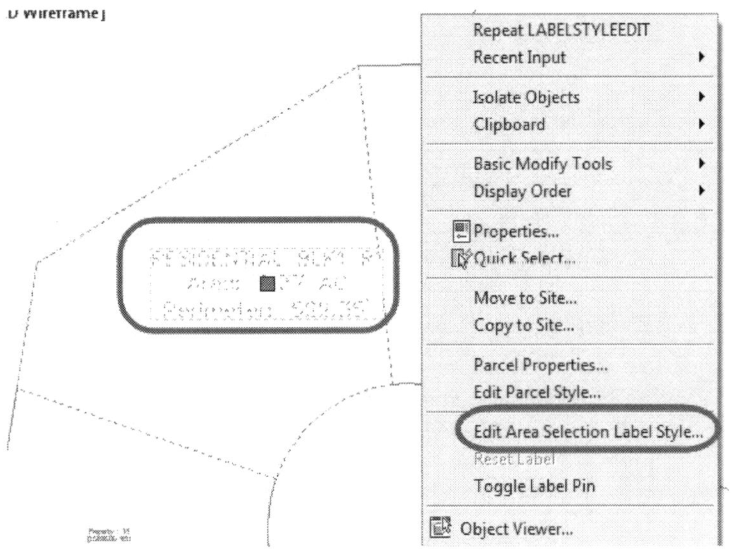

Figure 5–42

4. Rename and renumber the lots so that you have the same numbering system. In the *Modify* tab>Design panel, select **Parcel**. The *Parcel* contextual tab displays.

5. In the *Parcel* tab>Modify panel, select **Renumber/Rename**, as shown in Figure 5–43.

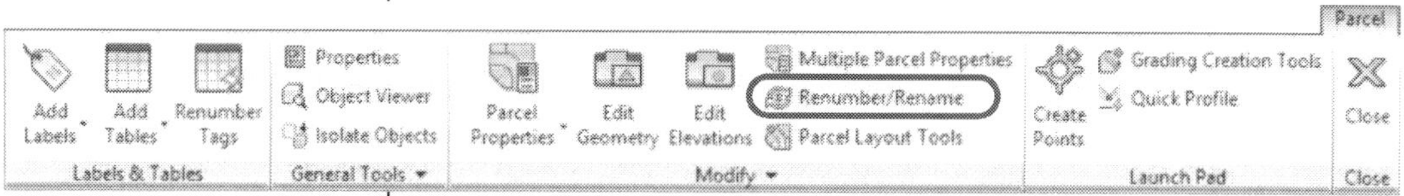

Figure 5–43

6. In the Renumber/Rename Parcel dialog box, select the **Rename** option. Select the **Specify the parcel names** option and click , as shown in Figure 5–44.

Figure 5–44

7. In the Name Template dialog box, type **BLK1 Lot** followed by a space in the *Name* field, as shown in Figure 5–45. Expand the Property Fields drop-down list, select **Next Counter**, and click **Insert**. Click **OK** to apply the changes and close the dialog box.

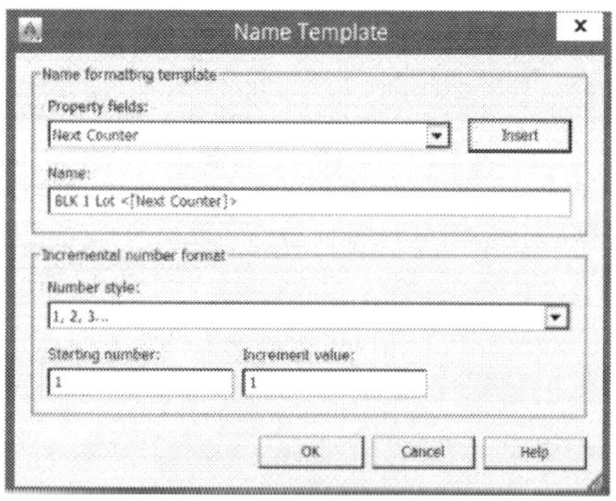

Figure 5–45

8. In the Renumber/Rename Parcel dialog box, click **OK** to accept the changes and close the dialog box.

9. When prompted for the points, select all of the parcels to be renumbered. Select the two points shown in Figure 5–46 and press <Enter> to complete the selection. Press <Enter> again to exit the command.

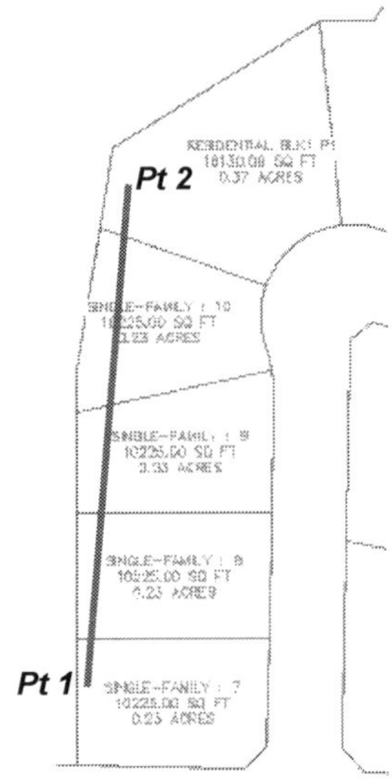

Figure 5–46

10. Save the drawing.

Task 2 - Edit parcels using Swing Line - Edit.

In this task, you adjust the last three lots of the parcel suddivision so that they are more marketable.

1. Continue working with the drawing from the previous task or open the file **PCL1-D2-Parcels.dwg**.

2. You first need to adjust the Lot line between Parcel 3 and Parcel 4. In the *Home* tab>Create Design panel, select **Parcel**. In the expanded list, select **Parcel Creation Tools**.

3. In the Parcel Layout Tools toolbar, select **Swing Line - Edit**, as shown in Figure 5–47.

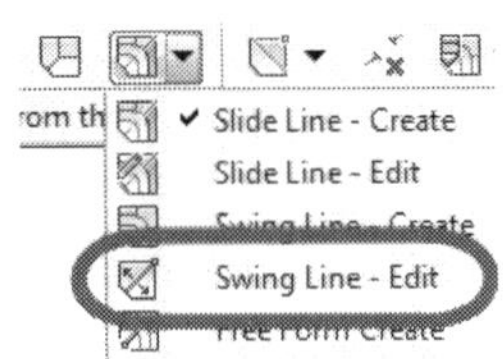

Figure 5–47

4. In the Create Parcel - Layout dialog box, set the following parameters:
    - Site: **C3D Training**
    - Parcel Style: **Single-Family**
    - Area Label style: **Name Square Foot & Acres**
5. You do not want to label segments, so do not enable this option. Click **OK** when done.
6. When prompted, complete the following, as shown in Figure 5–48:
    - To select the parcel line to adjust, select the parcel line between Lot 3 and Lot 4.
    - For the parcel to adjust, select **Lot 3**.
    - For the *start frontage*, select the bottom right corner of **Lot 3, pt1**.
    - For the *end of the frontage*, select the top right corner of **Lot 4, pt2**.
    - For the *swing point*, select the end point of **pt3**.
    - To accept the results, select **Yes**.

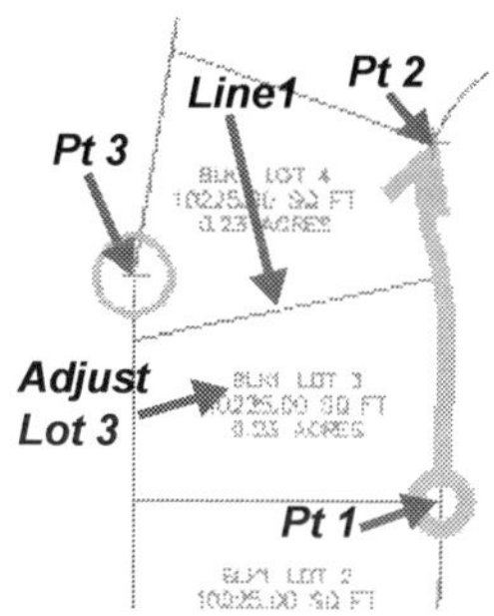

Figure 5–48

7. You have the required results for Lot 3. However, Lot 4 is 10225.00 sq ft and Lot 5 is 16130.09 sq ft. You want to create even-sized lots, each being approximately 13,177.5 sq ft. Display the Parcel Layout Tools toolbar if it is not open.
8. You should still be in the **Swing Line - Edit** command. (If not, repeat Steps 2 to 3 of this task.)

9. In the Parcel Layout Tools toolbar, click to expand it. Change the minimum area to **13,177.5 sq ft**. Collapse the toolbar if needed by clicking .

10. When prompted, complete the following, as shown in Figure 5–49:

    - To select the parcel line to adjust, select the parcel line between Lot 4 and Lot 5 (Line 1).
    - For the parcel to adjust, select **Lot 4**.
    - For the *start frontage*, select the bottom right corner of **Lot 4, pt1**.
    - For the *end of the frontage*, select the top right corner of **Lot 5, pt2**.
    - For the *swing point*, select the end point of **pt3**.

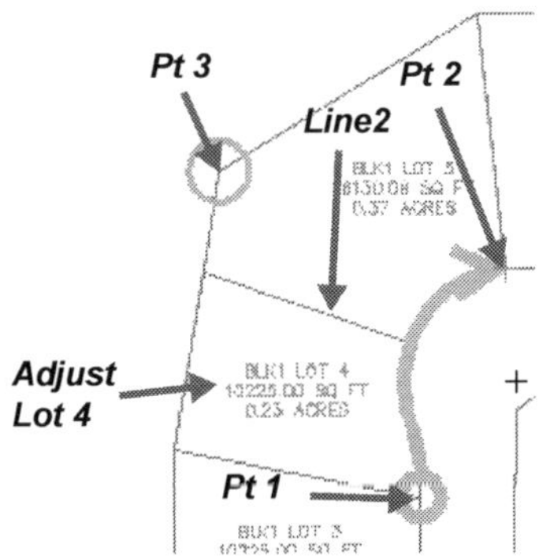

Figure 5–49

11. To accept the results, select **Yes**.

12. Press <Esc> or click **X** in the Parcel Layout Tools dialog box to close it.

13. If time permits, repeat the steps above to subdivide the Parcels Block 2 and Block 3. If you do not complete the subdivisions for Parcels Block 2 and Block 3, you will need to open **PCL-C1-Parcels** in the next practice.

14. Save the drawing.

Practice 5d Reporting On and Annotating the Parcel Layout

Practice Objectives

- Add labels, tags, and tables to the drawing to display useful parcel information.
- Create predefined reports to share useful parcel information in a textual format.

Estimated time for completion: 20 minutes

Task 1 - Add Parcel labels.

1. Open **PCL1-E1-Parcels.dwg** from the *C:\Civil 3D Projects\Civil3D-Training-I\Parcels* folder.

2. In the *Annotate* tab>Labels & Tables panel, click (Add Labels), as shown in Figure 5–50.

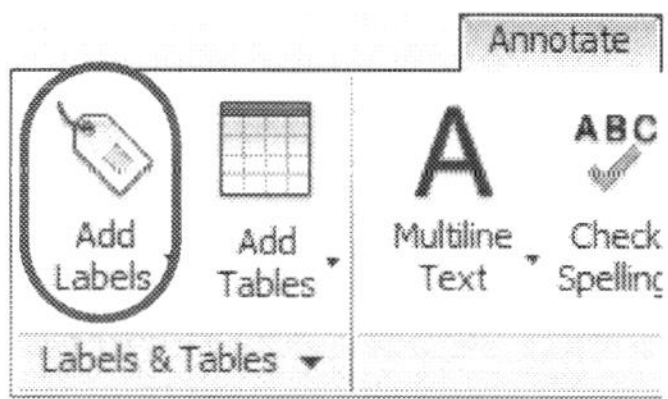

Figure 5–50

3. In the Add Labels dialog box, set the following parameters, as shown in Figure 5–51:

   - Feature: **Parcel**
   - Label type: **Multiple Segment**
   - Line label style: **Bearing over Distance**
   - Curve label style: **Delta over Length and Radius**

Figure 5–51

4. Click **Add**.
5. When prompted to select the Parcels that you want to annotate, select the single-family parcel labels in Model Space.
6. When prompted for the label direction, type **CL** for clockwise and press <Enter>.
7. Repeat the previous three steps for all remaining single-family parcels.
8. Press <Enter> when finished labeling the parcels.
9. Select **X** in the Add Labels dialog box or click **Close** to close the dialog box.

Parcels can also be labeled in an XREF file.

10. Save the drawing.

Task 2 - Create Line and Curve Segment Tables.

The labels are overlapping in a number of locations, making the drawing difficult to read. In this task, you try two methods to fix this. In the first method, you drag the label to a location in which there is no conflict. In the second method, you add a label tag and an associated table.

1. Continue working with the drawing from the previous task or open **PCL1-E2-Parcels.dwg**.
2. Select the preset view **Parcel-Tag1**.
3. Select the label **11.70'**, select the square grip, and drag to place the label in a location in which there is no conflict. Do the same for the label **21.48'**, as shown in Figure 5–52.

Figure 5–52

4. You will now add tags and a table. In the *Annotate* tab> Label & Tables panel, expand Add Tables, expand Parcel, and select **Add segment**, as shown in Figure 5–53.

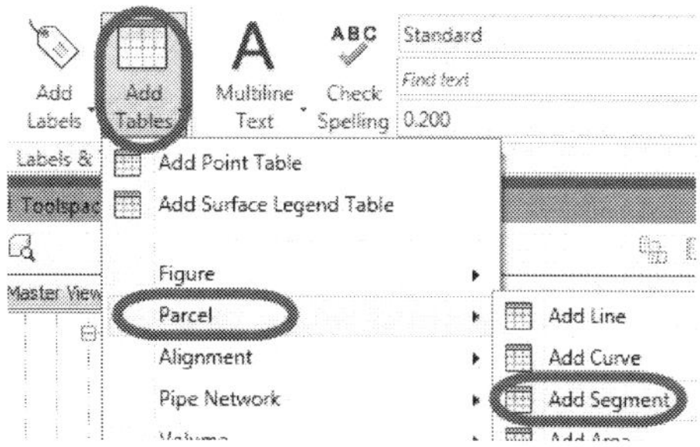

Figure 5–53

5. In the Table Creation dialog box, click (Pick on screen) and select the labels shown in Figure 5–54. Press <Enter> when done.

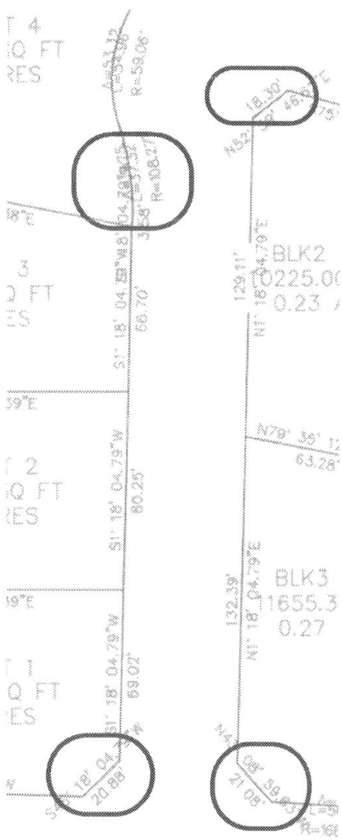

Figure 5–54

6. When prompted to convert labels to tags or to not add labels, select **Convert all selected label styles to tag mode**.

7. Click **OK** to close the Table Creation dialog box.

8. When prompted for a location for the table, select a location in an open space, as shown in Figure 5–55.

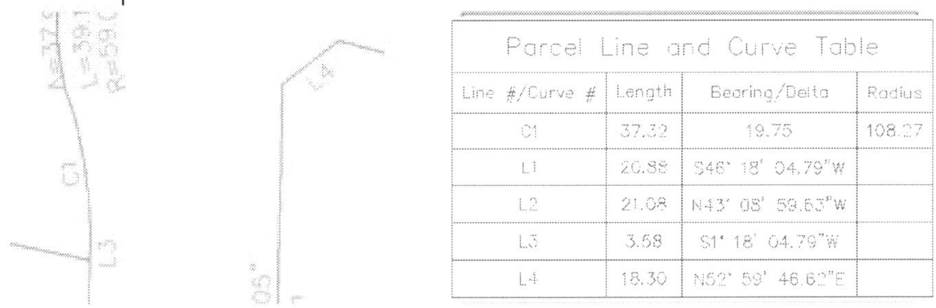

Parcel Line and Curve Table			
Line #/Curve #	Length	Bearing/Delta	Radius
C1	37.32	19.75	108.27
L1	20.88	S46° 18' 04.79"W	
L2	21.08	N43° 08' 59.63"W	
L3	3.58	S1° 18' 04.79"W	
L4	18.30	N52° 59' 46.62"E	

Figure 5–55

9. Save the drawing.

Task 3 - Create a Parcel Area Table.

---

1. Continue working with the drawing from the previous task or open **PCL1-E3-Parcels.dwg**.

2. In the *Annotate* tab>Label & Tables panel, expand Add Tables, expand Parcel, and select **Add Area**.

3. In the Table Creation dialog box, in the *Select by label* or *style* area, select the style name **Name Square Foot & Acres** as shown in Figure 5–56. All parcels with this style will be selected. Click **OK** to close the dialog box.

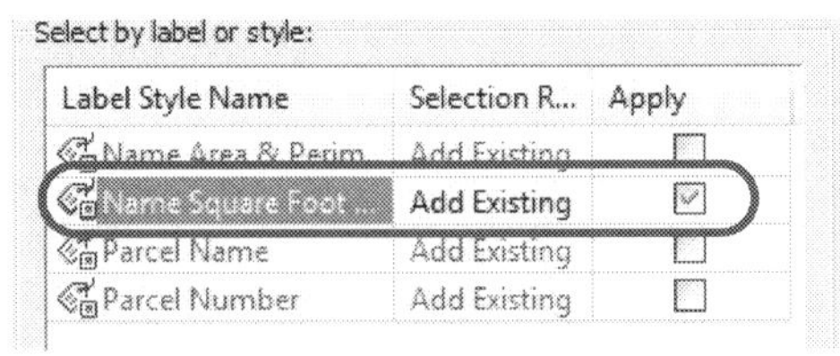

Figure 5–56

4. Select a location to insert the table into the drawing, as shown in Figure 5–57.

Parcel Area Table				
Parcel #	Area	Perimeter	Segment Lengths	Segment Bearings
3	10156.55	476.43	131.23 87.55 131.23 56.41	N55° 07' 40.10"W N39° 1[illegible]' 26.[illegible]"E S6° 13' [illegible].61"E S59° 19' 36.55"W
5	11298.21	427.15	26.72 78.21 113.57 19.73 86.[illegible]	N16° 50' 42.05"E S79° 24' 32.62"E S9° 37' 08.61"W S52° 30' 45.[illegible]"W N79° 24' 32.62"W
2	[illegible]	[illegible]	123.83 4.20 70.72 29.8[illegible] 52.59 47.65 11.70 36.39	N10° 34' 47.46"E S76° 16' 31.56"E S86° 35' 41.15"E S62° 20' 32.14"E S3° 48' 22.81"W N79° 24' 32.52"W N79° 35' 12.54"W N73° 35' 12.54"W

Figure 5–57

5. Save the drawing.

Task 4 - Create a Parcel Report.

1. Continue working with the drawing from the previous task or open **PCL1-E4-Parcels.dwg**.
2. If the *Toolbox* tab is not displayed, go to the *Home* tab> Palettes panel, and click (Toolbox), as shown in Figure 5–58.

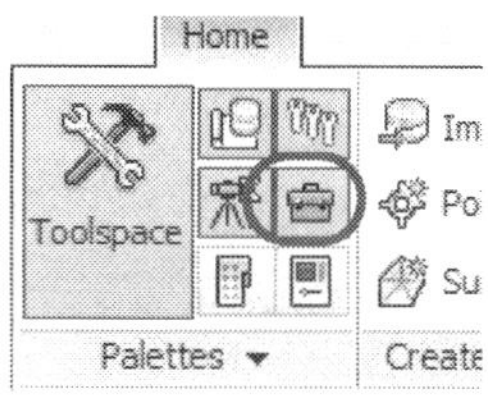

Figure 5–58

3. In the *Toolbox* tab, expand the *Reports Manager* and *Parcel* collections. Right-click on Surveyor's Certificate and select **Execute**.
4. In the Export to LandXML dialog box, click (Pick from drawing), located at the bottom left of the dialog box.
5. When prompted to select a parcel, select one of the single-family lots that you created earlier and press <Enter>.

6. In the Export to XML Report dialog box, note that only the Lots you selected now display a checkmark. Click **OK** to close the dialog box.

7. In the Save As dialog box, type the required filename for the report and click **Save** to close the dialog box.

8. Review the report (as shown in Figure 5–59), and close the web browser.

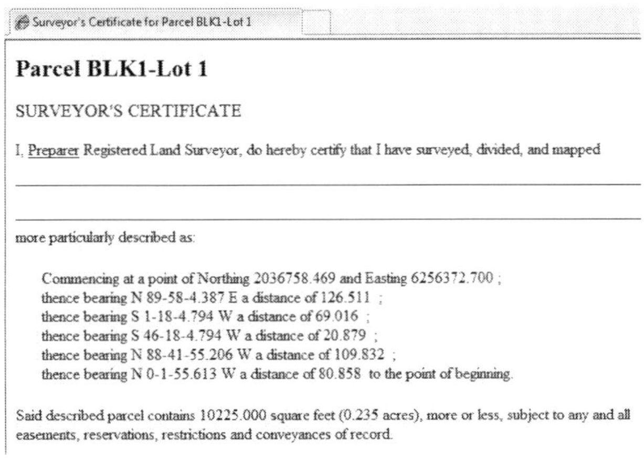
Surveyor's Certificate for Parcel BLK1-Lot 1

Parcel BLK1-Lot 1

SURVEYOR'S CERTIFICATE

I, Preparer Registered Land Surveyor, do hereby certify that I have surveyed, divided, and mapped

more particularly described as:

Commencing at a point of Northing 2036758.469 and Easting 6256372.700 ;
thence bearing N 89-58-4.387 E a distance of 126.511 ;
thence bearing S 1-18-4.794 W a distance of 69.016 ;
thence bearing S 46-18-4.794 W a distance of 20.879 ;
thence bearing N 88-41-55.206 W a distance of 109.832 ;
thence bearing N 0-1-55.613 W a distance of 80.858 to the point of beginning.

Said described parcel contains 10225.000 square feet (0.235 acres), more or less, subject to any and all easements, reservations, restrictions and conveyances of record.

Figure 5–59

9. Save the drawing.

Either of these formats can be opened in word processors, such as Microsoft Word, which can read all of the formatting displayed in the web browser. Report settings, such as the Preparer's name, can be assigned by selecting **Report Settings** in the Toolspace.

Alignments

This chapter includes instructional content to assist in your preparation for the following topic and objectives for the AutoCAD® Civil® 3D 2016 Certified Professional exam.

Autodesk Certification Exam Objectives in this Chapter

Exam Topic	Exam Objective	Section
Alignments	• Design a geometric layout	• 6.1
	• Create alignments	• 6.2

6.1 Design a Geometric Layout

An AutoCAD Civil 3D alignment is an AEC object that resembles an AutoCAD® polyline. Alignments have rule-based constraints that make them very powerful design tools. Alignments can contain tangents (line segments), circular curves, and spirals.

The appearance and annotation of alignments are controlled by object and label styles. These styles are flexible, have an extensive list of label properties, and control layer assignments for objects and their labels.

AutoCAD Civil 3D alignments can be created in the following ways:

- If previously defined, alignments can be imported from Autodesk LandXML®, directly from an AutoCAD® Land Desktop project, or from an InfraWorks model.
- A polyline can be converted directly to an alignment. Converted polylines follow the direction of the original polyline object.
- An alignment can be created interactively using the Alignment Layout toolbar.
- Individual AutoCAD lines and arcs can be converted to alignments using the Layout toolbar as well.

When creating new alignments, remember that you can use transparent commands to draw line segments by **Angle and Distance**, **Bearing and Distance**, **Azimuth and Distance**, and **Deflection Distance**. These commands are available in the Transparent Commands toolbar, as shown in Figure 6–1. They are extremely helpful when you need to stay within a specific right-of-way and you have the legal description of that right-of-way.

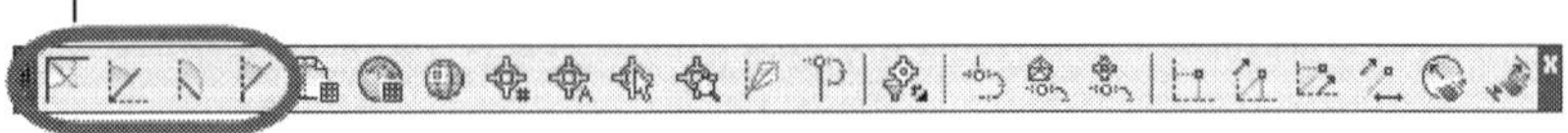

Figure 6–1

Criteria-Based Design

Default or custom standards can be used in the AutoCAD Civil 3D software to evaluate alignment and profile designs. The Design Criteria Editor enables you to view, edit, or create criteria files (such as AASHTO tables). When you create a new alignment, the Create Alignment dialog box opens, as shown in Figure 6–2. You can tell the software what type of alignment you are creating to make intersection design easier later. The dialog box includes a *Design Criteria* tab that enables you to type the starting design speed, use criteria-based design, use a design criteria file, or use a design check set.

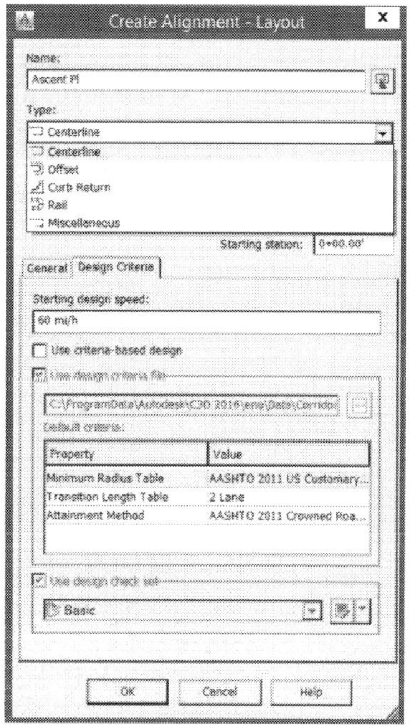

Figure 6–2

When an entity does not meet the criteria in the file it is displayed with a warning marker. Hover over the marker and note which criteria the entity violates, as shown in Figure 6–3.

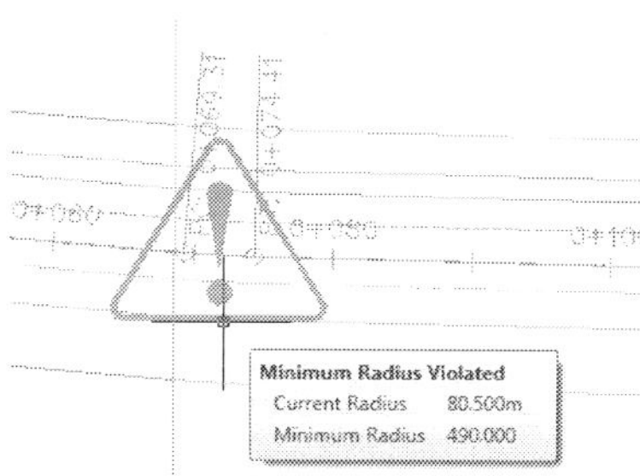

Figure 6–3

A warning marker also displays in the sub-entity and grid view editors when a violation occurs. This marker disappears when the value meets the required criteria.

Alignment Types

There are 5 different types of alignments that can be used in a design.

1. A **Centerline alignment** is the most commonly used type of alignment. You can use it when you know the location and design parameters of the centerline of the road, trail, or other linear feature being designed.
2. An **Offset alignment** is used to create transitions in a corridor design. You can use it when you want to target a transition line, such as a curb return, bus turnout lane, or other deviation from the original widths.
3. A **Curb Return alignment** is used when you want to base the design of the road from the curb location or when you need to connect the edges of two intersecting roadways.
4. A **Rail alignment** is the newest type of alignment. You can use it when you need to calculate curves along chords rather than arcs. It also enables you to set the track width and calculate cants.
5. A **Miscellaneous alignment** is available when the type of alignment you are creating does not fall into any of the other categories.

Alignment Segment Types

Each alignment tangent, circular curve, and spiral falls into one of three categories.

1. A **fixed segment** is one that is defined by specific criteria that only have a limited ability to be dynamically updated. Fixed curves hold their initial constraints (such as length and radius) and do not remain tangent at either end if a neighboring line segment is adjusted. You should avoid fixed curves in alignments that you might want to dynamically update (such as proposed alignments).

Alignments imported from the Autodesk LandXML software (and directly from the AutoCAD Land Desktop software) contain all fixed segments. Alignment segments created from individual lines and arcs are also created as fixed segments. These fixed curves can be deleted and replaced with other types as required.

2. A **floating element** is one that depends entirely on the object before it in the alignment. If a preceding object is moved, stretched, or otherwise adjusted, a floating element (and everything following it) translates accordingly while holding all of the initial constraints (length, radius, pass-through-points, etc.).

   For example, the alignment shown in Figure 6–4 begins with a fixed line followed by a series of floating curves and a floating line that together define a cul-de-sac. Changing the end point of the fixed line causes all of the floating elements to translate while maintaining the original length of the floating line, and the original length, radius, and direction of the following curves. Floating elements only stay tangent at one end to neighboring segments if they are adjusted.

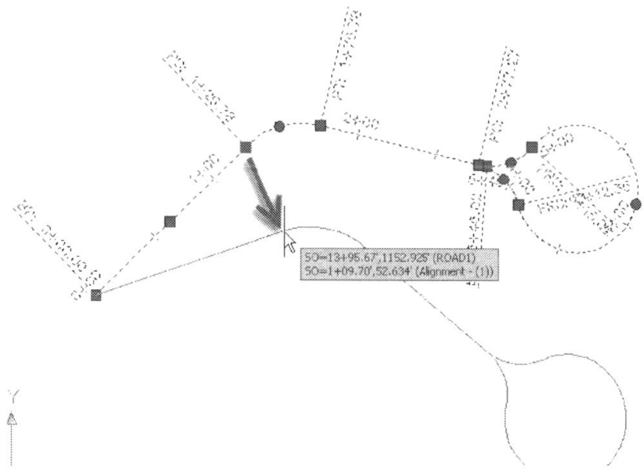

Figure 6–4

3. A **free segment** is one that is adjusted if the geometry of either neighboring segment is changed. Free segments always adjust to remain tangent to adjacent segments at both ends. For example, the free line shown in Figure 6–5 was drawn connected to two fixed arcs. If either of the arcs were assigned a different property (such as a new radius), the line would be completely redrawn to remain tangent to both.

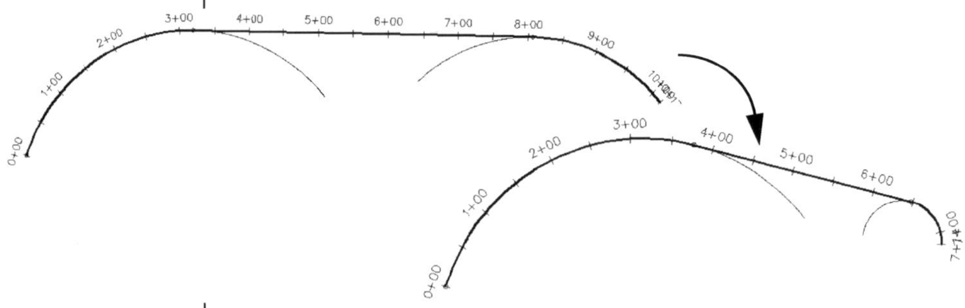

Figure 6–5

- Alignments created by layout and polyline are made of fixed lines and free curves and spirals. These tend to be the most flexible types of alignments.

- Because of their flexibility and ability to remain tangent through changes, free and floating elements are more useful in alignments that are subject to change, such as those for proposed roadway center lines.

6.2 Create Alignments

Alignments are created and edited using the Alignment Layout toolbar, which can be opened from the *Home* tab>Create Design panel. Expand Alignment and select (Alignment Creation Tools), as shown at the top of Figure 6–6. The Alignment Layout Tools toolbar displays, as shown at the bottom of Figure 6–6.

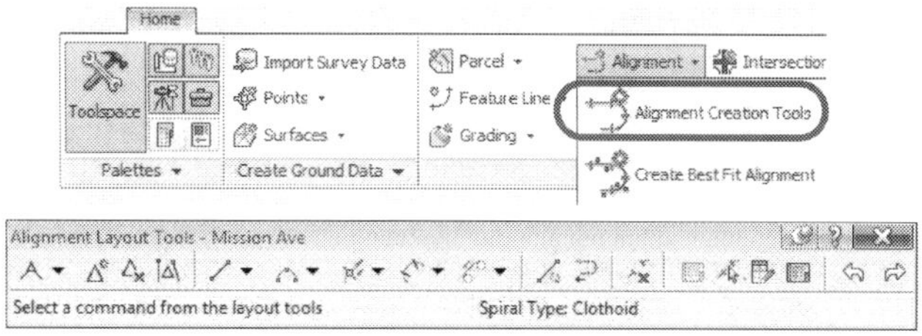

Figure 6–6

To create or add to an alignment interactively by locating new Points of Intersection (PIs), select one of the first two options in the Draw Tangents drop-down list, as shown in Figure 6–7.

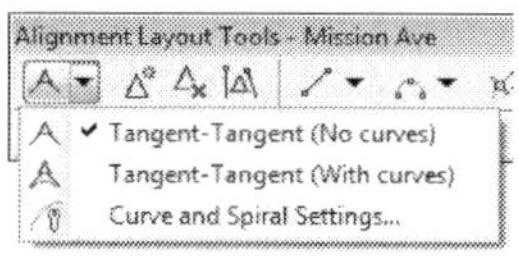

Figure 6–7

These two methods (with or without curves) are similar to drawing an AutoCAD polyline. If the **With Curves** option is selected, default curve information can be assigned in the Curve and Spiral Settings dialog box, as shown in Figure 6–8.

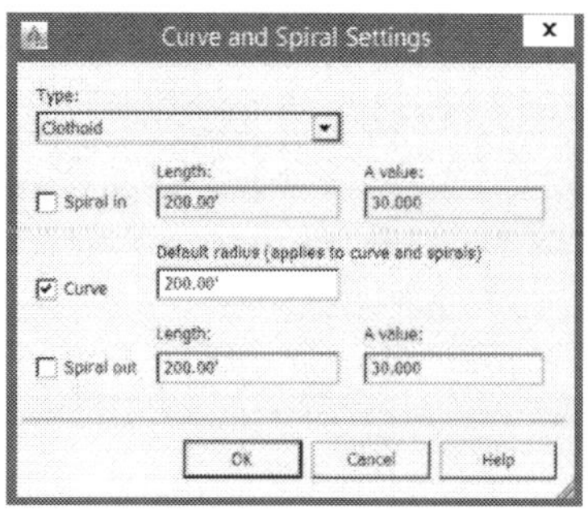

Figure 6–8

The Layout toolbar also includes tools that enable you to:

	Create new Points of Intersection (PIs).
	Delete PIs (and associated curves).
	Break apart PIs.
	Convert AutoCAD lines and arcs to alignment segments.
	Delete a line, circular curve, or spiral segment.
	Edit best-fit data for all entities.
	Select an individual segment for editing in the Sub-Entity Editor.
	Review and adjust alignment properties (length, radius, etc.) in the Alignment Entities Vista.
	Undo a recent alignment edit.
	Redo a recent alignment edit.

Most of the other tools in the Layout toolbar are intended for creating segments with various constraints.

Alignment Editing

In addition to the Edit tools available in the Alignment Layout toolbar, alignments can be edited using the AutoCAD **Modify** commands, such as **Move** and **Stretch**. Alignment entities can also be grip-edited into new positions. You can delete an alignment using the AutoCAD **Erase** command, or by right-clicking on the name of the alignment in the *Prospector* tab and selecting **Delete**. To open the Alignment Layout toolbar, expand Alignments and select **Edit Alignment Geometry**.

Practice 6a Creating Alignments from Objects

Estimated time for completion: 15 minutes

Practice Objective

- Create alignments from objects in the drawing or in an external reference file attached to the drawing.

In this practice you will create horizontal alignments using two methods. First, you will create an alignment from an existing polyline that defines a road center line alignment. Second, you will create an alignment from a XREF file that defines a proposed center line alignment.

Task 1 - Create Alignment from a Polyline.

1. Open **ALN1-A1-Alignment.dwg** from the *C:\Civil 3D Projects\Civil3D-Training\Alignments* folder.

   In the drawing, the red polyline running east-west represents the existing center line alignment of Mission Avenue, as shown in Figure 6–9.

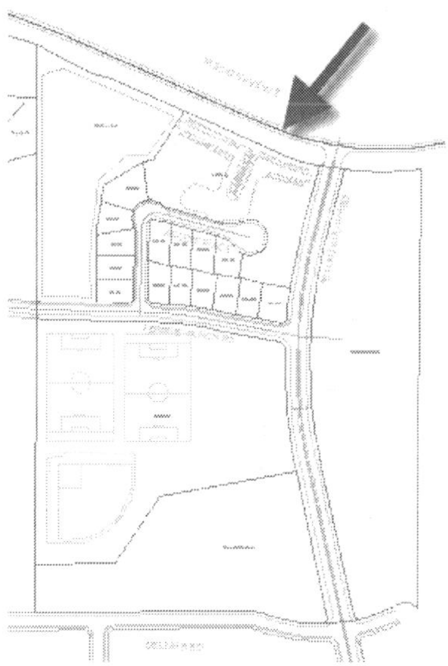

Figure 6–9

2. In the *Home* tab>Create Design panel, expand Alignment, and select (Create Alignment from Objects), as shown in Figure 6–10. Select the west end of the polyline representing **Mission Ave polyline** (as shown in Figure 6–9) and press <Enter>.

Selecting the west end of the polyline identifies the start direction of the alignment.

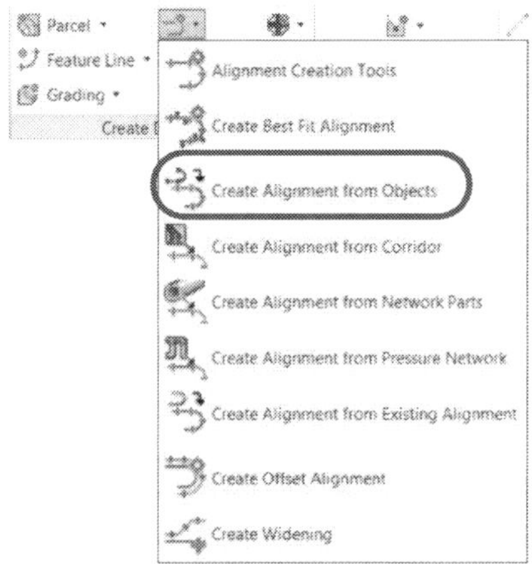

Figure 6–10

*If you want to reverse the direction of the alignment, you need to select **Reverse**.*

3. Verify that the alignment direction arrow is pointing East and press <Enter> to accept the alignment direction.
4. In the Create Alignment from Objects dialog box, assign the values shown in Figure 6–11 to define the properties of this alignment:
    - Alignment name: **Mission Ave**
    - Type: Leave as **Centerline**
    - Description: Type a description if needed
    - Starting station: **0**
    - Site (*General* tab): **None**
    - Alignment Label Set: **All Labels**
    - Clear the **Add curves between tangents** option
    - Accept the remaining default values.

Note: The difference between having an alignment in a site or not, is that if an alignment is in a site, any parcels in that same site will be divided by the alignment that bisects the parcel.

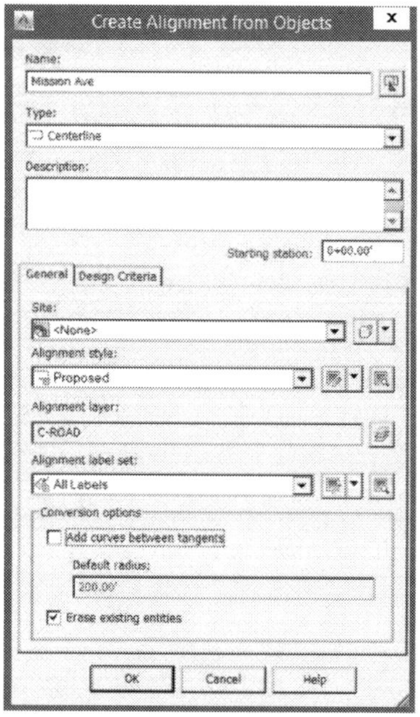

Figure 6–11

*This means that the AutoCAD Civil 3D software will reference the design criteria file **Autodesk Civil 3D Imperial (2011) Roadway Design Standards.xml**.*

An AutoCAD Civil 3D alignment is automatically created complete with labeling.

5. Select the *Design Criteria* tab shown in Figure 6–12. Ensure that the following are set then click **OK**;
   - Design speed is set to **60mi/h**.
   - Both the **Use criteria-based design** and **Use design criteria file** options should be selected.

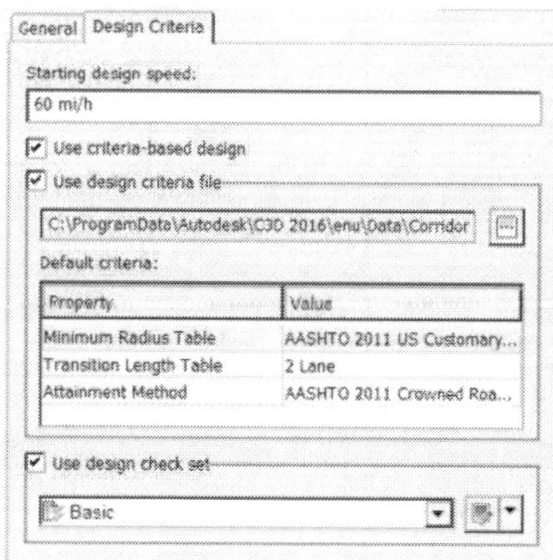

Figure 6–12

6. Select the preset view **Aln-Warning**. Hover the cursor over the exclamation mark at approximately the station 19+26 on the alignment and note which design check was violated, as shown in Figure 6–13. In this case, the radius is 1033.46, but the minimum radius for a 60mi/hr road based on the AASHTO table must be greater than 1505.

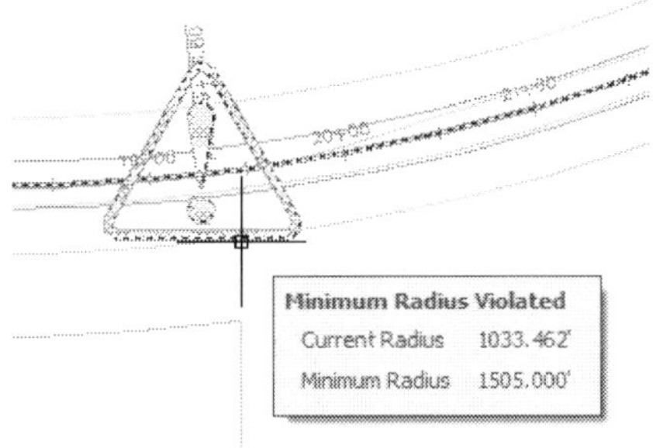

Figure 6–13

7. Save the drawing.

Task 2 - Create an Alignment by Object (XREF).

1. Continue working with the drawing from the previous task or open **ALN1-A2-Alignment.dwg**.
2. Select the preset view **Aln-xref**.
3. In the *Home* tab>Create Design panel, expand Alignment, and select (Create Alignment from Objects). When prompted to select an object, type **Xref** or **X** and press <Enter>. You will then be prompted to select a XREF object.
4. Select the west end of the polyline representing **Jeffries Ranch Rd** center line (the black line), as shown in Figure 6–14 and press <Enter>.

Selecting the west end of the XREF line identifies the start direction of the alignment.

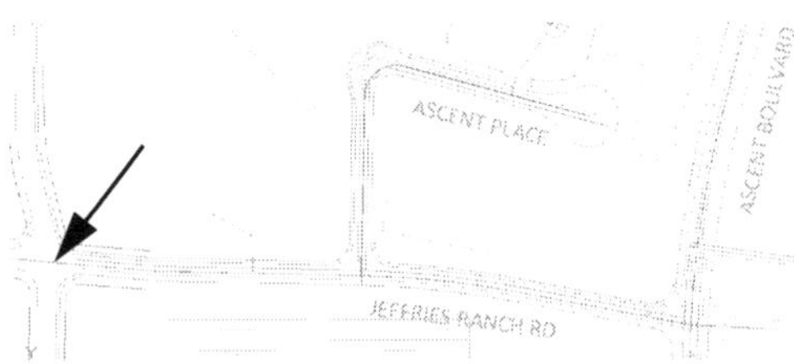

Figure 6–14

5. Verify that the alignment direction arrow is pointing East and press <Enter> to accept the alignment direction.

6. In the Create Alignment from Objects dialog box, type **Jeffries Ranch Rd** for the alignment name and accept all of the default values.

For this alignment, you will not be using design criteria.

7. In the *Design Criteria* tab, ensure that the **Use criteria-based design** option is cleared, as shown in Figure 6–15.

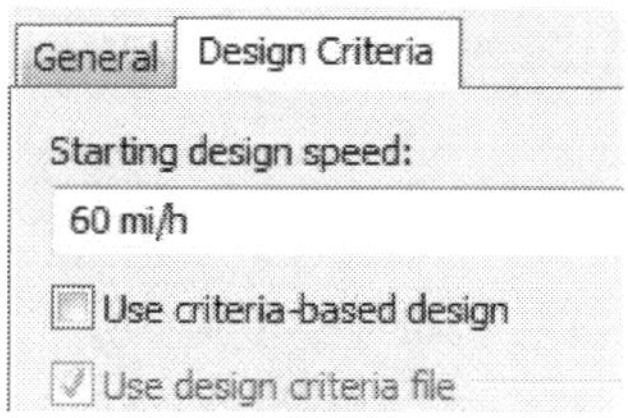

Figure 6–15

8. Click **OK** to close the dialog box and create the alignment.

9. Save the drawing.

Practice 6b Creating and Modifying Alignments

Practice Objective

- Create an alignment from scratch using the Alignment Layout tools.

Estimated time for completion: 15 minutes

In this practice you will create a free form alignment, based on some design parameters. You will create an alignment for Ascent Place based on existing design data, as shown in Figure 6–16. According to this data, the street right-of-way extends north at a bearing of N1d18'04.79"E and then east at a bearing of S75d18'31.56"E. The north center line leg is 353.17' to the point of intersection and the east leg is 381.93' from the point of intersection. In addition, the center line of Ascent Place intersects Jeffries Ranch road at sta 5+79.13'.

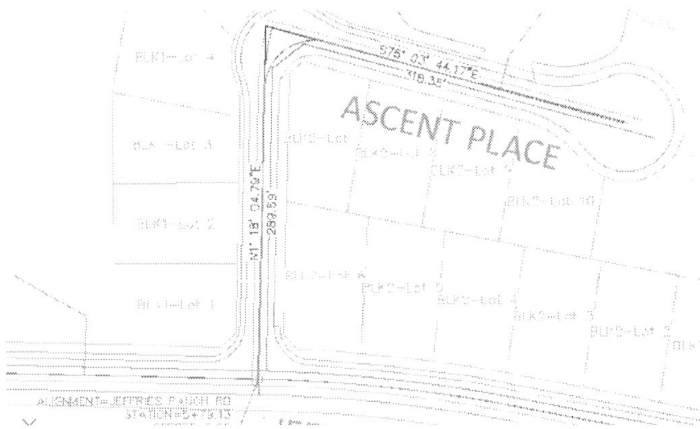

Figure 6–16

Task 1 - Create an Alignment by Layout.

1. Continue working with the drawing from the previous practice or open **ALN1-B1-Alignment.dwg**.
2. Select the preset view **Aln-Create**.
3. Toggle on *Selection* cycling by pressing <Ctrl>+<W>. The alignment object and XREF center line occupy the same location in space (as shown in Figure 6–17), and the selection cycling enables you to select the alignment.

Pressing <Shift>+<Space> to cycle through objects does not work in a transparent command.

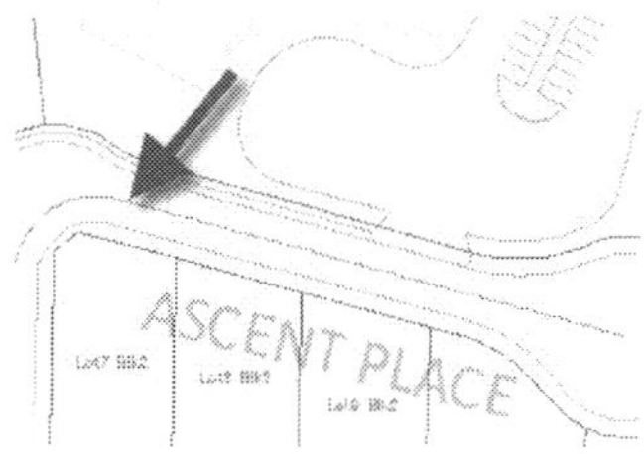

Figure 6–17

4. In the *Home* tab>Create Design panel, expand Alignment, and select (Alignment Creation Tools).
5. In the Create Alignment Layout dialog box, type **Ascent Pl** for the alignment name and accept all of the default values.

For this alignment, you will not be using design criteria.

6. In the *Design Criteria* tab, ensure that the **Use criteria-based design** option is not selected. Click **OK** to close the dialog box and create the alignment.
7. Expand the Tangent tool icon and select (Curve and Spiral Settings), as shown in Figure 6–18.

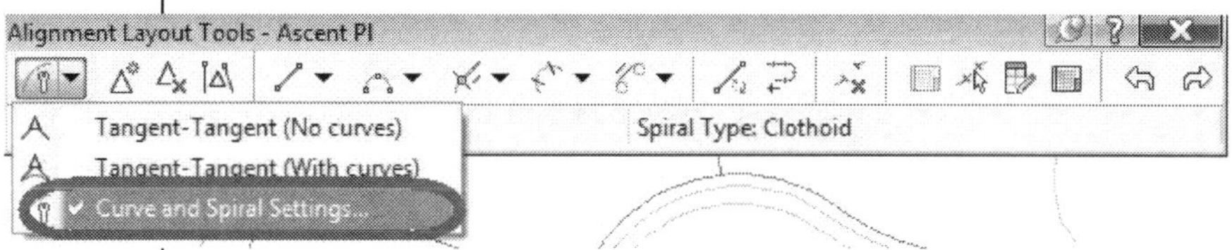

Figure 6–18

8. For the curve settings, ensure that the **curve** option is selected. Set the curve radius to **30.00'**, and click **OK** to close the Curve and Spiral Settings dialog box.
9. Expand the Tangent tool icon and select the (Tangent-Tangent (With curves)) to start creating the horizontal alignment.

You want to start the alignment at a reference station to Jeffries Ranch Rd.

10. When prompted for the start of the alignment, click (Station Offset) on the Transparent Tools toolbar.
11. When prompted for an alignment, select **Jeffries Ranch Rd**. In the Selection Cycling dialog box, click **Alignment**.
12. When prompted for a station, type **579.13'** and press <Enter>.

13. When prompted for the offset, type **0** and press <Enter>. Press <Esc> to exit the transparent command. The AutoCAD Civil 3D software has now established the starting location of the alignment by converting the station/offset to a X,Y value.

14. You will specify the next point using the transparent command to enter a bearing and a distance. Click (Bearing Distance) on the Transparent Tools toolbar and enter the following:

    - Type **1** and press <Enter> for the NE quadrant.
    - Type **1.180479** and then press <Enter> for the bearing.
    - Type a distance of **353.17'** and press <Enter>.
    - Press <Esc> to exit the transparent command.

15. You will specify the next point using the transparent command to enter a turned angle and a distance. Click (Angle Distance) on the Transparent Tools toolbar and do the following:

    - Type **C** and press <Enter>, since you will be entering a counter-clockwise include angle.
    - Type the include angle of **76.3636** and press <Enter>.
    - Type **381.93** and press <Enter> for the distance.

16. Press <Esc> to exit the transparent command and press <Enter> to complete the horizontal alignment.

17. Close the **Alignment** layout tool by clicking **X** in the top right of the dialog box.

18. Save the drawing.

Task 2 - Edit Alignments.

1. Continue working with the drawing from the previous task or open **ALN1-B2-Alignment.dwg**.

2. Set **Aln-Curv Radius** as the active view.

3. Select the alignment **Ascent PI**. In the contextual Alignment tab>Modify panel, click (Geometry Editor).

Note that the radius dynamically changes in the graphics view.

4. In the alignment Tool Layout toolbar, click (Pick Sub-entity), as shown in Figure 6–19.

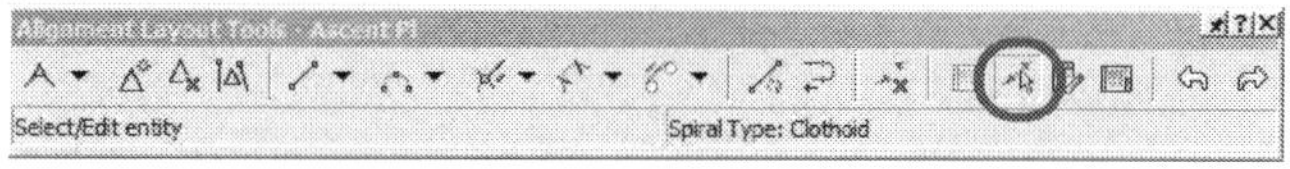

Figure 6–19

5. When prompted to select the sub-entity, select the curve. Change the radius to **50'** and press <Enter>, as shown in Figure 6–20.

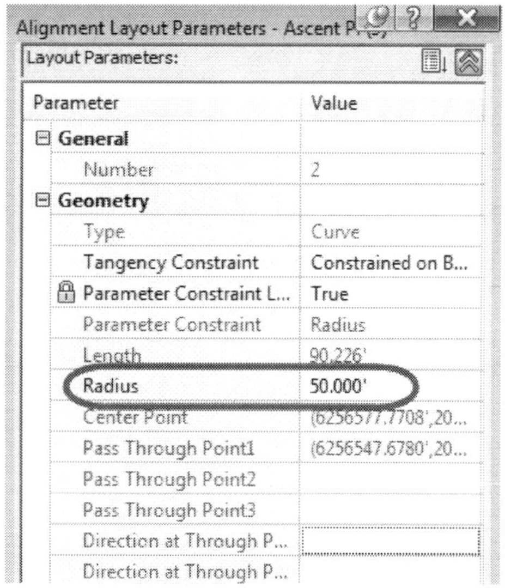

Figure 6–20

6. Select (Delete Sub-entity) in the Alignment Layout toolbar, as shown in Figure 6–21. Select the curve and press <Enter> to exit the command.

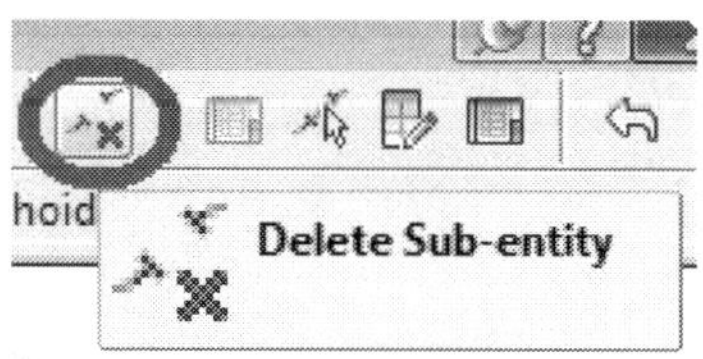

Figure 6–21

7. In the Alignment Layout toolbar, expand the curve drop-down list and select (Free Curve Fillet (between two entities, radius)) as shown in Figure 6–22.

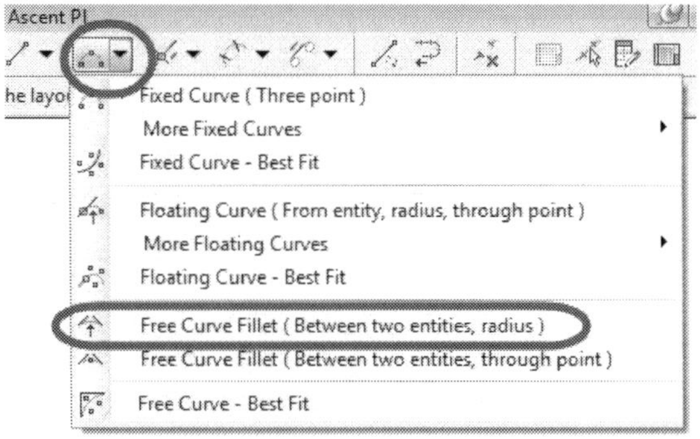

Figure 6–22

8. Select the two tangents and press <Enter> to accept that the angle is **less than 180 deg**. For the radius, type **50'**, press <Enter>, and press <Enter> again to complete the command. The results are shown in Figure 6–23.

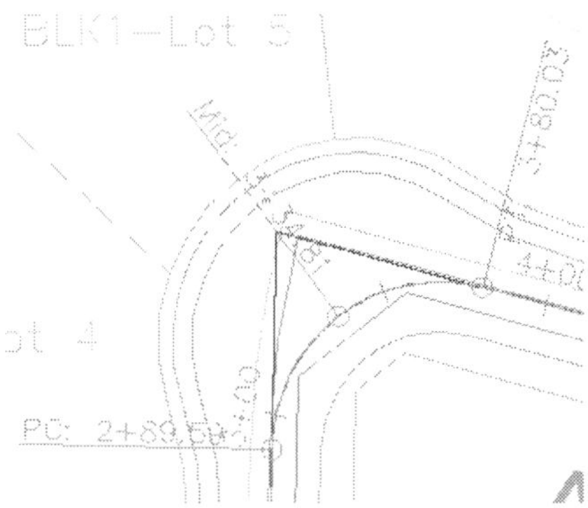

Figure 6–23

9. Close the Alignment Layout toolbar and save the drawing.

10. Save the drawing.

Chapter 7

Profiles & Profile Views

This chapter includes instructional content to assist in your preparation for the following topic and objectives for the AutoCAD® Civil® 3D 2016 Certified Professional exam.

Autodesk Certification Exam Objectives in this Chapter

Exam Topic	Exam Objective	Section
Profiles & Profile Views	• Create a surface profile	• 7.1
	• Design a profile	• 7.2
	• Create a profile view style	• 7.3
	• Create a profile view	• 7.4

7.1 Create a Surface Profile

Most profile views display at least one profile based on a surface, such as from an existing ground terrain model. To create a profile from a surface, use the following steps:

1. In the *Home* tab>Create Design panel, click  (Profile> Create Surface Profile).
2. In the Create Profile from Surface dialog box (shown in Figure 7–1), select the required alignment and surface(s).
3. Enter the required station range.
4. Click **Add>>** to sample each surface based on these settings.

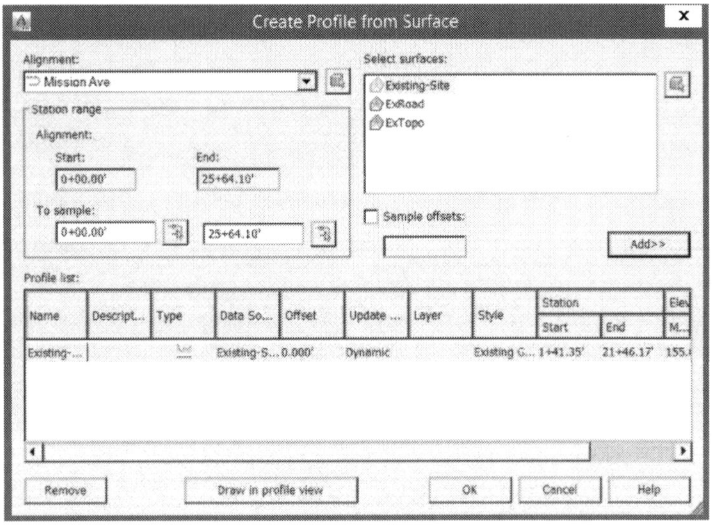

Figure 7–1

This creates a profile along the alignment itself. If you want to sample at an offset from the alignment, select the **Sample Offsets** option. Enter a positive (+) value to sample the right side and a negative (-) value to sample the left side of the alignment, and then click **Add>>**. You can sample multiple offsets by entering values one at a time and clicking **Add>>** after each or putting a comma between offset values to add them all at the same time.

There are two ways to exit this dialog box (other than clicking **Cancel**):

- If you do not have a profile view of this alignment in the drawing, click **Draw in profile view**. This opens the Create Profile View dialog box.
- If you already have a profile view of this alignment, click **OK** and any new profiles are added to the existing view. If you clicked **OK** accidentally without having a view in which to display the profile, go to the *Home* tab> Profile and Section Views panel, and click (Profile View> Create Profile View).

7.2 Design a Profile

Finished ground profiles (also referred to as proposed profiles or proposed vertical alignments) are often created interactively using the Profile Layout Tools toolbar, as shown in Figure 7–2. This is similar to how alignments are created by layout. The toolbar can be opened by going to the *Home* tab>Create Design panel and expanding Profile and selecting **Profile Creation Tools**.

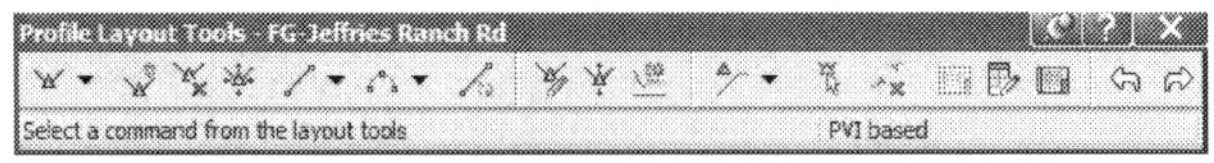

Figure 7–2

- Using these tools, you can add tangents and vertical curves.
- Vertical curves transition a vehicle from one tangent grade to another and occur in two situations: Crest (top of a hill) and Sag (valley).
- There are multiple types of vertical curves to transition between changing the tangent grades of a crest or sag: **Circular**, **Parabolic**, **Asymmetric Parabolic**, and **Best Fit**. Roadways almost always use parabolic (equal length) curves. Asymmetric parabolic curves are usually only used if layout constraints do not permit an equal-length curve. True circular curves are used in some parts of the world for low-speed rail design. Generally, they should *never* be used for roadways (which could lead to vehicle vaulting or bottoming out). Best fit curves follow the most likely path through a series of points.
- In the *Settings* tab, in the Profile heading, the Edit Features Settings set the default curve type, styles, and command settings.

Most vertical designs have regulations affecting the minimum and maximum values for tangent slopes, distances along tangents between vertical curves, and safety design parameters for passing sight and stopping sight distances. Refer to local design manuals for more information on these design constraints.

The points connecting tangents in a finished ground profile are referred to as a *Point of Vertical Intersection* (PVI).

Profile Layout Tools

Similar to the Alignments Layout toolbar, the Profile Layout Tools toolbar contains an overall vista (Profile Grid View) and Profile Layout Parameters (segment data viewer). These vistas enable you to review and edit the vertical design. The settings used when creating a finished ground profile can be selected in the Draw Tangents flyout in the toolbar, as shown in Figure 7–3. This toolbar is used to edit any kind of profile, including profiles created from surfaces.

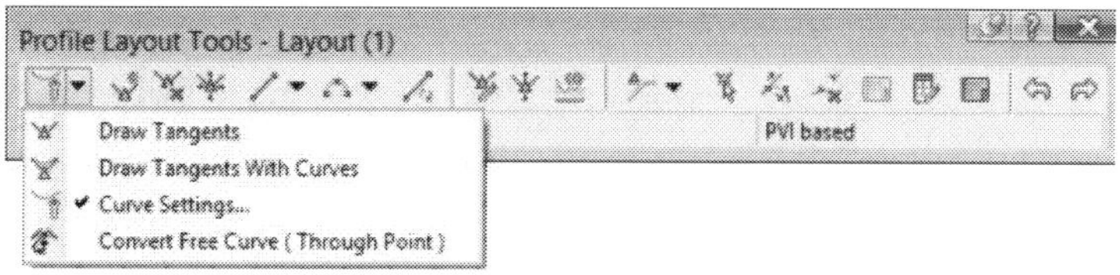

Figure 7–3

Other toolbar commands (shown in Figure 7–4), enable you to **Add**, **Delete**, or **Move** individual tangents, PVIs, or vertical curve segments.

- When editing a profile in the layout parameters or grid view, editable parameters display in black.
- You can graphically edit a design profile using grips. As soon as you select the profile, a contextual tab displays in the Ribbon that is specific to that profile.

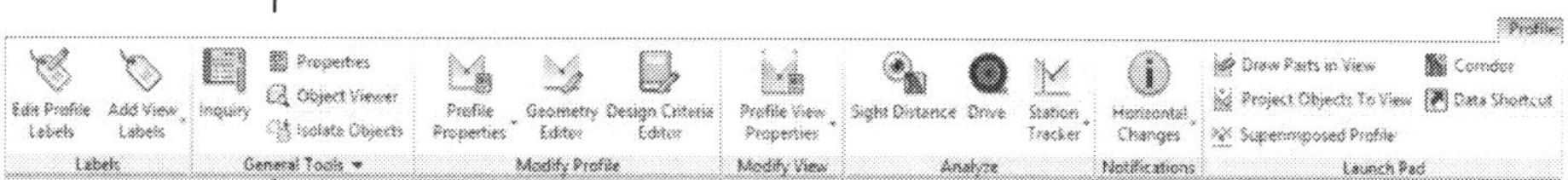

Figure 7–4

- When graphically editing a vertical alignment, the tangents, PVIs, and vertical curves display grips that represent specific editing functions, as shown in Figure 7–5.

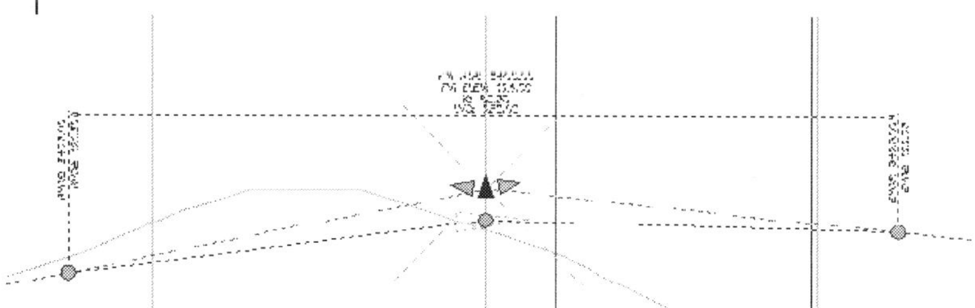

Figure 7–5

- The center triangular grip moves the PVI to a new station and/or elevation.
- The triangles left and right of the center extend the selected tangent, hold its grade, and modify the grade of the opposite tangent to relocate the PVI.
- The middle or end circular grips lengthen or shorten the vertical curve without affecting the location of the PVI.
- When you move the cursor to the original location of the grip, the cursor snaps to that location.

7.3 Create a Profile View Style

Profile view styles control the format of the grid, titles, axis annotations, and other elements used for displaying profiles. To set up a new profile view style, select the *Settings* tab in the Toolspace. Expand the Profile View tree, right-click on Profile View Styles, and select **New**. Typically, this is already set up for you in the drawing template, but you might sometimes need to change some of the settings.

Information Tab

The *Information* tab enables you to enter basic information about the style, such as the name, a description, who it was created by and when, and who it was last modified by and when, as shown in Figure 7–6.

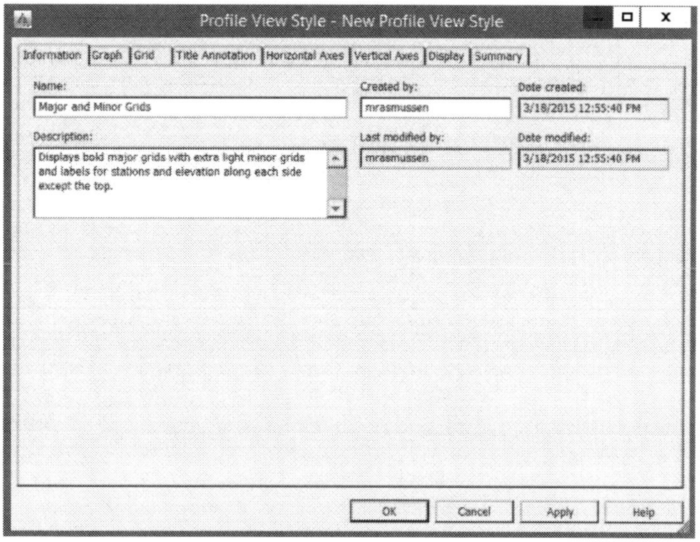

Figure 7–6

Graph Tab

The *Graph* tab enables you to set the vertical exaggeration for greater visibility in the profile view and the profile direction. The vertical scale can be set in two ways:

1. By dividing the current horizontal scale of the drawing by the vertical scale value, which gives you the vertical exaggeration value. This is usually set at a one to ten ratio. Therefore, if the horizontal scale is 1"=50', the *Vertical exaggeration* is set to **5**.
2. You can select the vertical scale from a list, as shown in Figure 7–7.

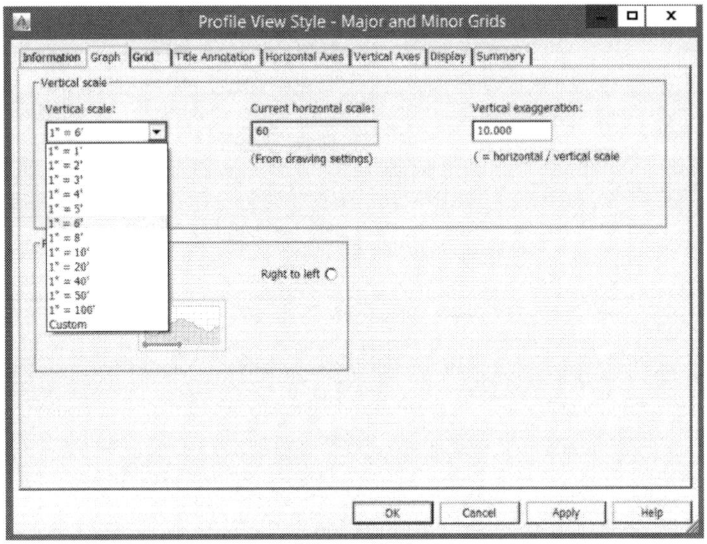

Figure 7–7

Grid Tab

The *Grid* tab is used to specify the clipping, padding, and axes offset in the profile view grid.

- The **Clip vertical grid** option enables you to trim the vertical grid lines at either the existing ground or finished ground profiles or the highest profile.
- The **Clip horizontal grid** option does the same for the horizontal grid lines, as shown in Figure 7–8.
- The **Grid padding** enables you to add extra grid boxes at the beginning and end of the profile, and to the top and bottom.
- The **Axis offset** specifies the distance to offset the axis beyond the profile extents.

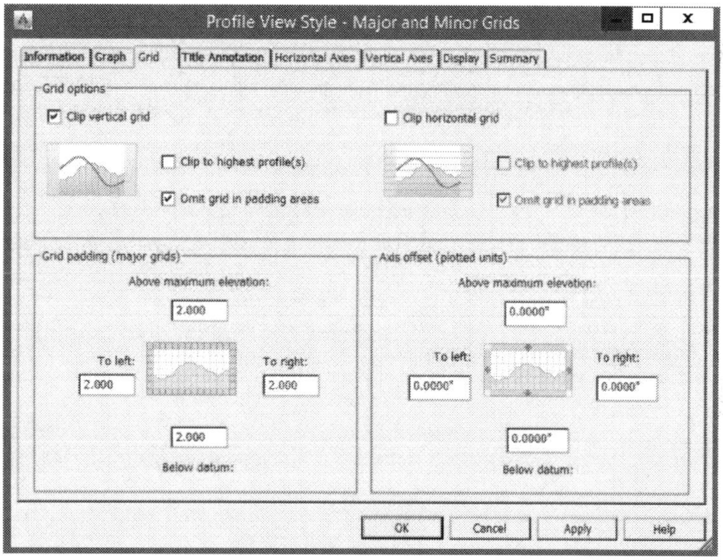

Figure 7–8

Title Annotation Tab

The *Title Annotation* tab enables you to specify the text style, contents, justification, and location of the profile view and axis titles, as shown in Figure 7–9.

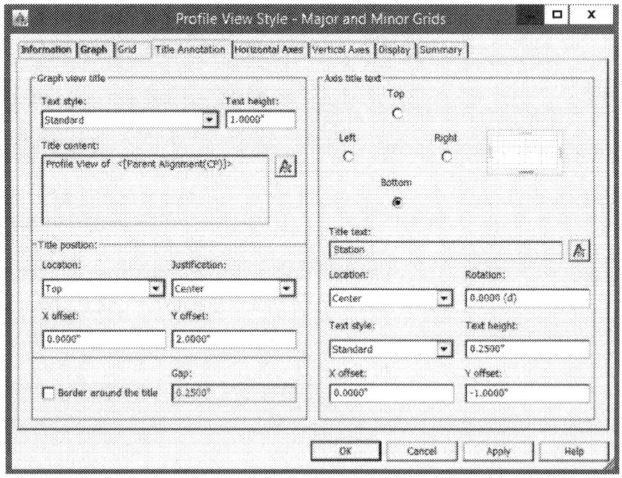

Figure 7–9

Horizontal Axes Tab

The *Horizontal Axes* tab enables you to specify the annotation for the top and bottom axes of the profile view. From here you can set the major and minor intervals for station labels and/or ticks, and the horizontal geometry tick details, as shown in Figure 7–10.

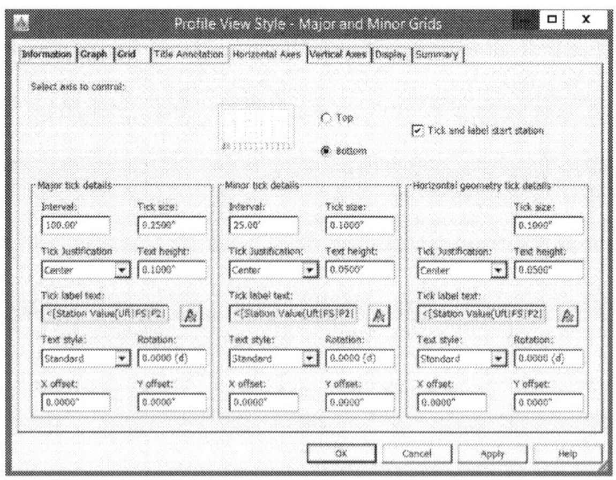

Figure 7–10

Vertical Axes Tab

The *Vertical Axes* tab enables you to specify the elevation label details, such as vertical interval, justification, content, text styles, and tick sizes, as shown in Figure 7–11.

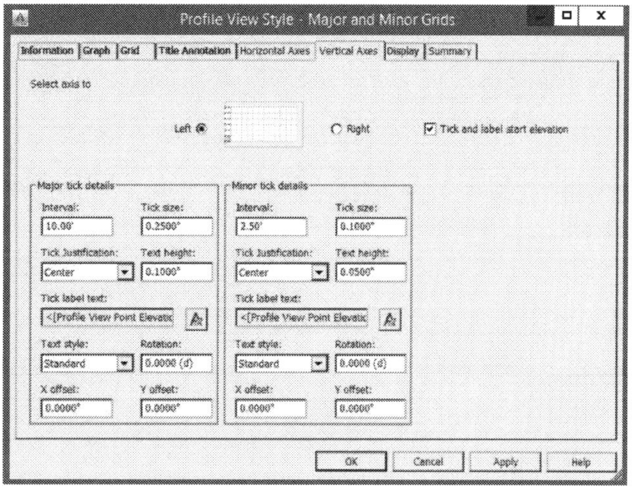

Figure 7–11

Display Tab

The *Display* tab enables you to set which components are displayed and which layer, color, linetype, and other properties they use, as shown in Figure 7–12.

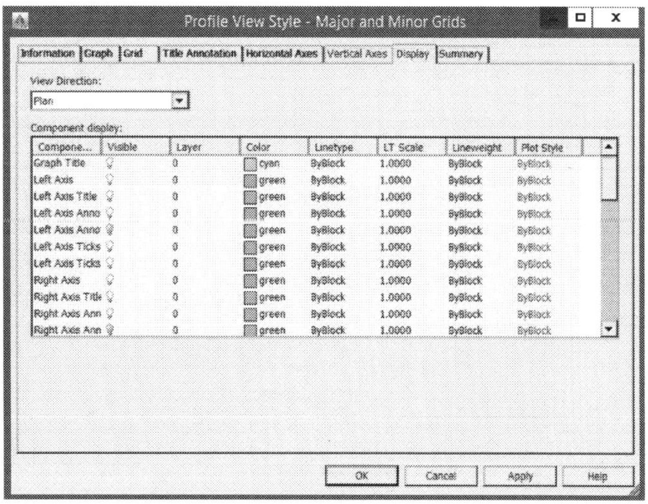

Figure 7–12

Summary Tab

The *Summary* tab enables you to review all of the settings that were selected on the other tabs for a quick reference, as shown in Figure 7–13.

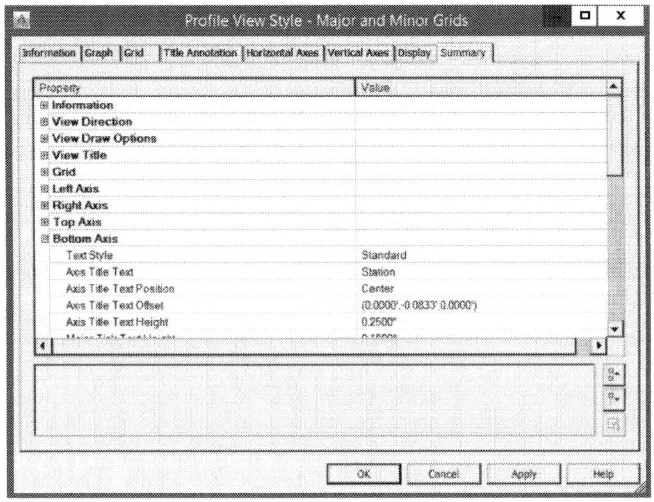

Figure 7–13

7.4 Create a Profile View

You can create a profile view at any time using (Profile View>Create Profile View). All of the settings selected in the wizard can be reassigned later using Profile View Properties (except for the alignment on which they are based).

Clicking ***Draw in profile view*** *in the Create Profile from Surface dialog box opens the same wizard.*

The *General* page in the Create Profile View wizard enables you to select the alignment that you want to work with and to assign the profile view a name, description, view style, and layer. The **Show offset profiles by vertically stacking profile views** option (shown in Figure 7–14), enables you to display offset profiles in a different view from the center line profile without overlapping.

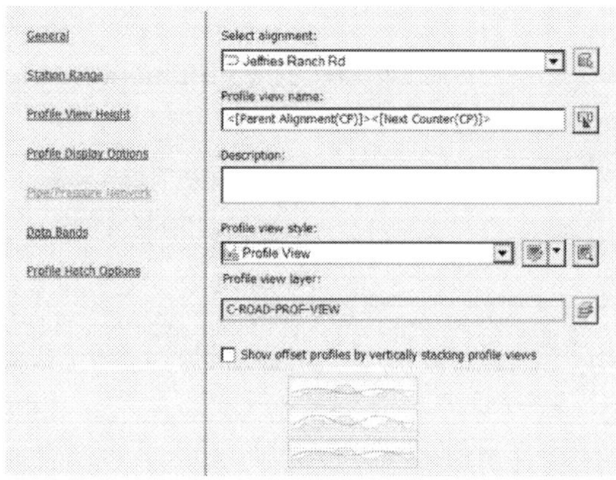

Figure 7–14

The *Station Range* page (shown in Figure 7–15), enables you to select the station range with which you want to work. The **Automatic** option includes the entire alignment's length.

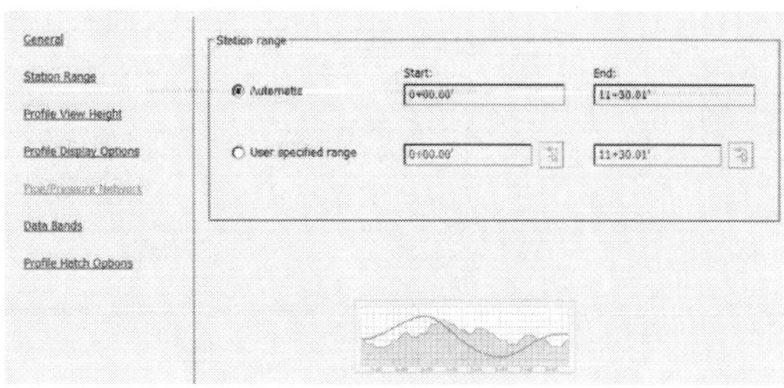

Figure 7–15

The *Profile View Height* page (shown in Figure 7–16), enables you to select the required height of the profile grid.

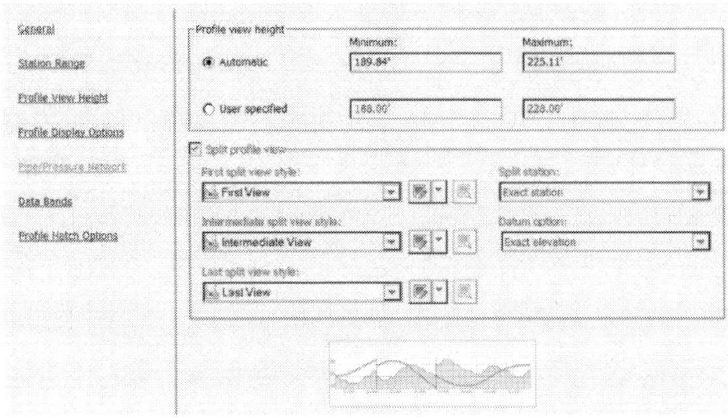

Figure 7–16

- The **Automatic** option creates a profile view that is sized to avoid having to be split.
- The **User Specified** option enables you to assign specific minimum and maximum heights to the profile view. If a profile in one of these views has an elevation below or above the specified values, the profile view is split to accommodate it. If a profile needs to be split you can assign different styles to control the different portions of the split profile.

Figure 7–17 shows a profile view that has been split.

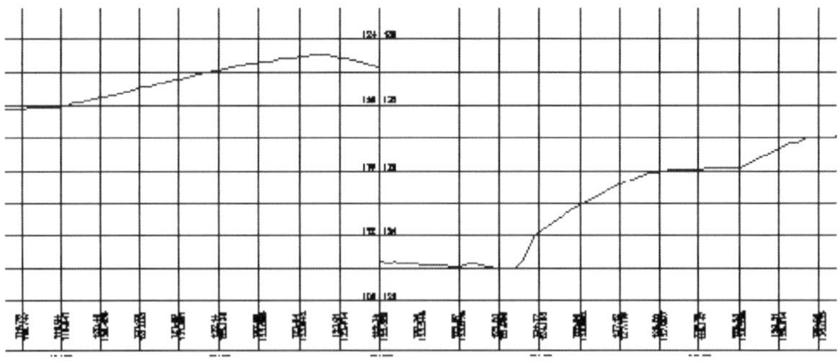

Figure 7–17

The *Stacked Profile* page (shown in Figure 7–18), enables you to set the number of stacked views, the gap between those views, and the styles for each one.

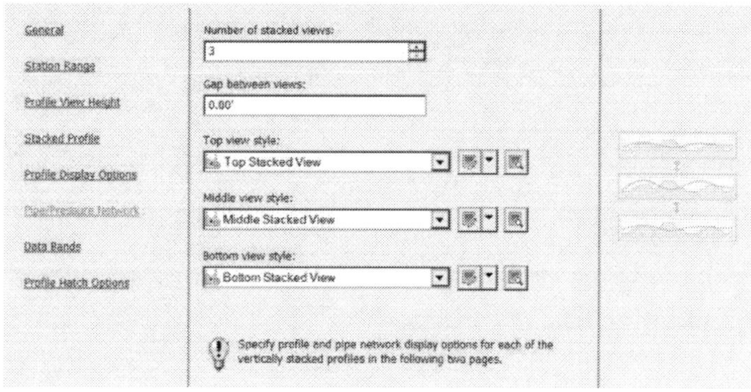

Figure 7–18

The *Profile Display Options* page (shown in Figure 7–19), enables you to apply specific controls to profiles that are displayed in the views.

Some of the most important options include:

- **Draw:** Disabling this option prevents the profile from being displayed in the view.
- **Style:** Sets the profile style to display in the profile.
- **Labels:** Sets the profile label set to display in the profile.

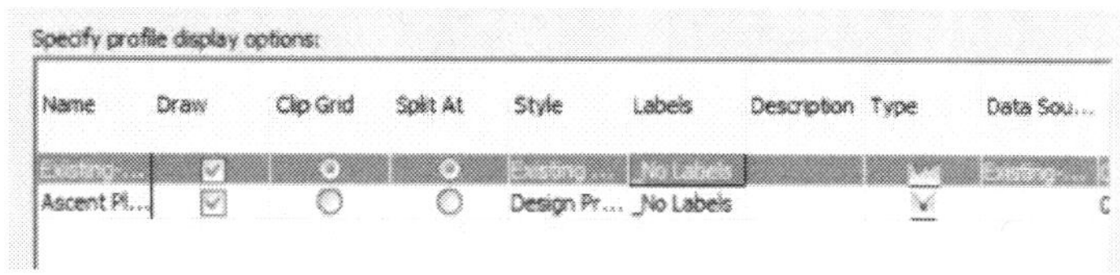

Figure 7–19

The *Data Bands* page (shown in Figure 7–20), enables you to select the bands that you want to include. Bands are additional profile information that can be included along the top or bottom of a profile. Bands are applied in this dialog box by selecting a Band Set.

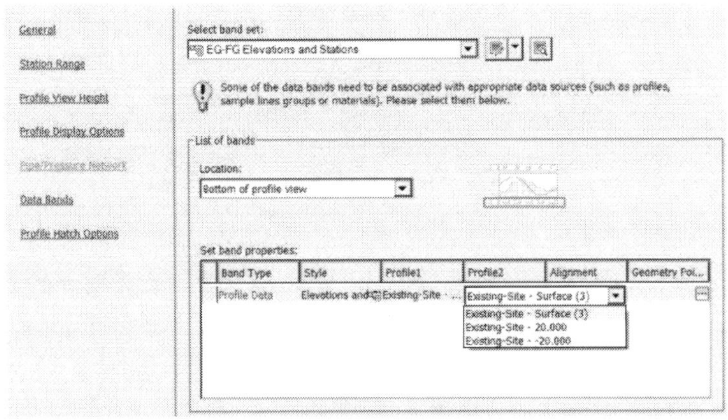

Figure 7–20

The **Profile Hatch** option is shown in Figure 7–21. You can hatch the profile according to the *Cut Area*, *Fill Area*, *Multiple boundaries*, or *From criteria* that you import. If you select one of these options, the software enables you to specify the upper and lower boundaries for the hatch area.

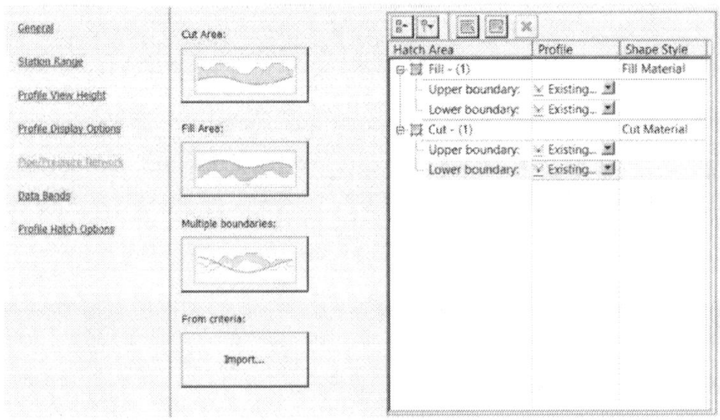

Figure 7–21

When satisfied, click **CreateProfile View** to create the profile view. After the profile view is created these settings can be reviewed and adjusted using **Profile View Properties**. To open this dialog box, select the profile view, right-click and select **Profile View Properties**.

Assigning Profile Band Elevations

Profile band elevations are assigned using Profile View Properties, in the *Bands* tab. When you create a profile view, you should review the band settings and verify that each profile band is assigned the correct profile in the *Profile1* and *Profile2* fields, as shown in Figure 7–22. The AutoCAD Civil 3D software does not make any assumptions about which profile to use in either field.

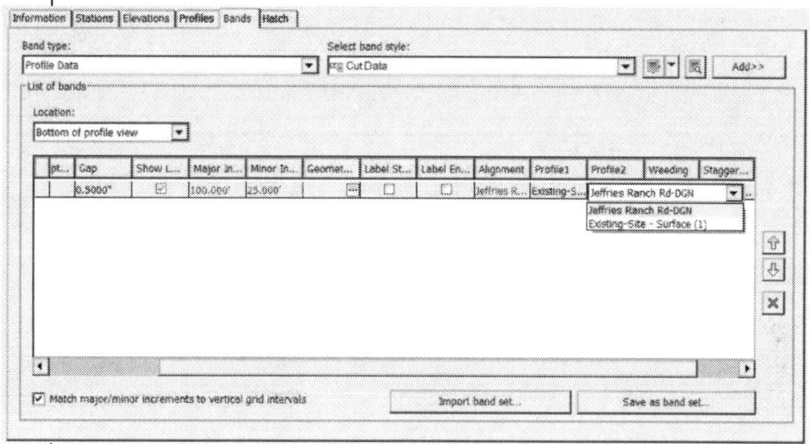

Figure 7–22

Using the styles supplied with the AutoCAD Civil 3D templates, the existing ground surface would be assigned the *Profile1* field, and the finished ground profile would be assigned the *Profile2* field.

Practice 7a Working with Profiles Part I

Estimated time for completion: 15 minutes

Practice Objective

- List the various types of projects that use alignments and profiles in their designs.

In the following practices you will create profile views and a profile vertical design. In a production collaboration environment, you will use data references to share data between team members, i.e., surfaces and horizontal alignments.

Based on specific design workflow, the horizontal alignment and design profiles might sometimes reside in the same drawing. This is the workflow that you will use. However, you can assume that the horizontal alignments are fixed and that you only need to reference them into the profile drawing. In that case, you can practice using data shortcuts or Vault shortcuts.

Task 1 - Create surface profiles.

1. Open **PRF1-A1-Profile.dwg** from the *C:\Civil 3D Projects\Civil3D-Training\Profiles* folder.

2. In the *Home* tab>Create Design panel, click (Profile>Create Surface Profile), as shown in Figure 7–23.

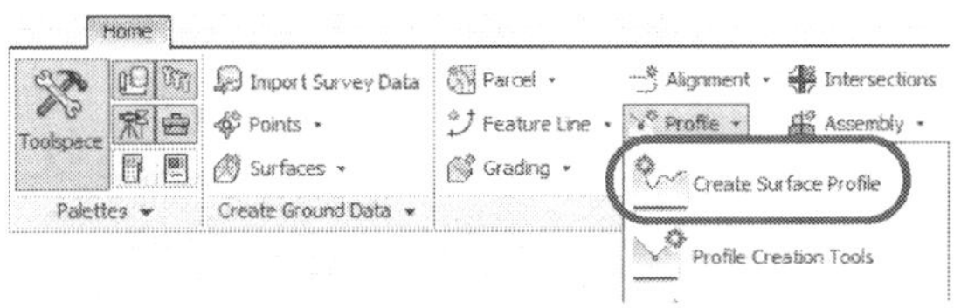

Figure 7–23

3. In the dialog box, select the **Jeffries Ranch Rd** alignment, highlight the **Existing-Site** surface and click **Add>>**, as shown in Figure 7–24.

This samples an existing ground profile along the center line, the entire length of Jeffries Ranch Rd.

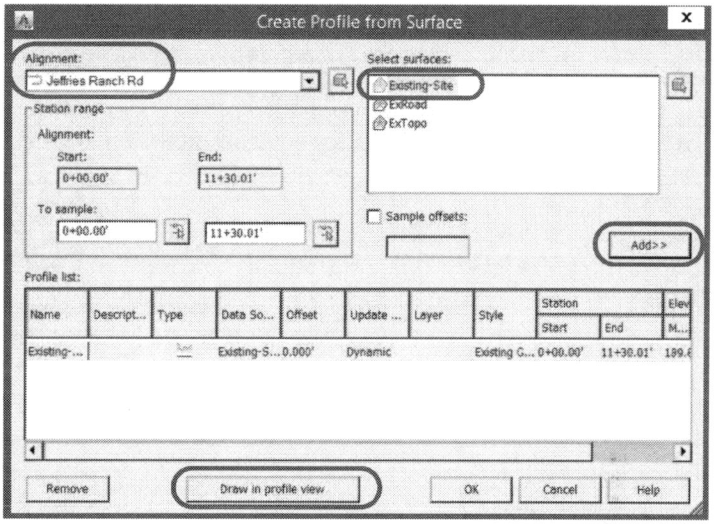

Figure 7–24

*If you clicked **OK** instead, expand Profile View and select **Create Profile View** in the Home tab>Profile & Section Views panel.*

4. Click **Draw in profile view**.
5. In the Create Profile View wizard, in the *General* page, confirm **Jeffries Ranch Rd** as the alignment and set the *Profile view style* to **Profile View**, as shown in Figure 7–25. Click **Next>**.

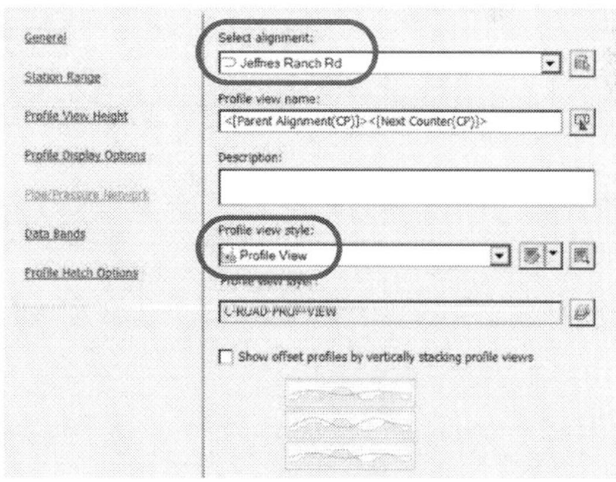

Figure 7–25

6. Accept the defaults in the *Station Range* page and click **Next>**.

7. Accept the defaults in the *Profile View Height* page and click **Next>**.

8. Accept the defaults in the *Profile Display Options* page and click **Next>**.

Note: You will set which profiles to use for profiles 1 and 2 in the data bands after a finish ground profile has been created.

9. In the *Data Bands* page, accept **EG-FG Elevations and Stations** for the band set, and click **Next>**.

10. In the *Profile Hatch Options* page, accept the default of no hatching and click **Create Profile View**

11. If the event viewer is displayed, close it by clicking the checkmark in the top right corner. When prompted for a location for the profile, click a point to the right of the plan view to define the lower left corner of the Profile View, as shown in Figure 7–26.

Note: The surface profile displays although the surface contours are not displayed in the plan view. This is because the surface exists in the drawing but is set to a ***No Display*** *style.*

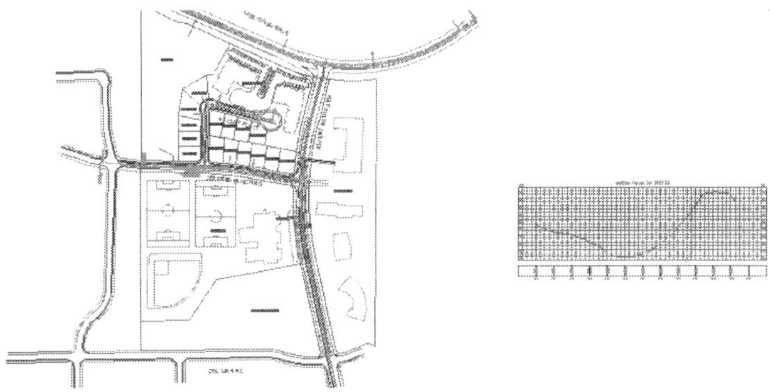

Figure 7–26

12. Repeat Step 3 to Step 12 for the alignment **Ascent Pl**.

13. Save the drawing.

Task 2 - Adjust the Profile View.

You might sometimes be required to modify some of the selections that you made in the Create Profile View Wizard, specifically, the datum elevation or grid height. In this task, you will adjust the profile view.

1. Continue working with the drawing from the previous task or open **PRF1-A2-Profile.dwg**.

2. Select the **Ascent PI** profile view, right-click, and select **Profile View Properties**, as shown on the left in Figure 7–27.

You can also select the Prospector tab and expand Alignments>Centerline Alignments>Ascent PI>Profile Views. Right-click on Ascent PI2 and select ***Properties****.*

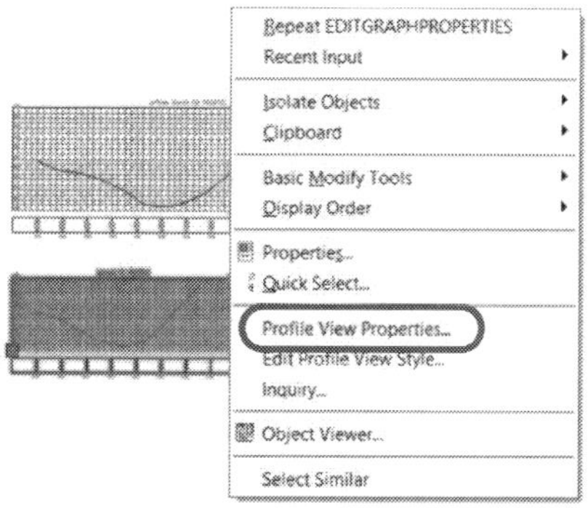

Figure 7–27

3. In the *Elevations* tab, select the **User specified height** option. Type a *Minimum* of **165** and a *Maximum* of **210**, as shown in Figure 7–28. Click **OK**.

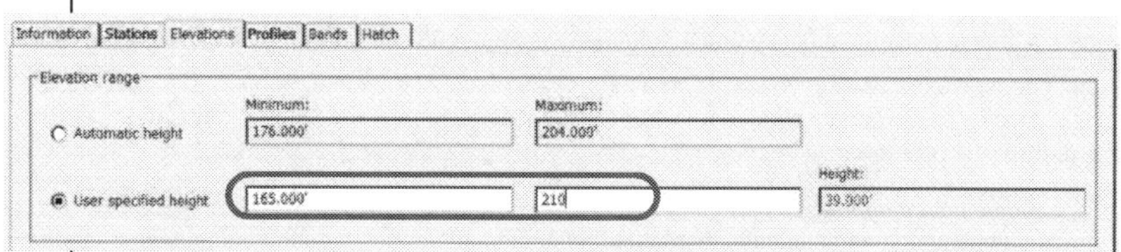

Figure 7–28

4. Save the drawing.

Practice 7b Working with Profiles Part II

Practice Objective

- Create finished ground profiles using specific design parameters.

Estimated time for completion: 20 minutes

Before starting any type of design, you need to obtain all of the constraints. The tie in elevation for Jeffries Ranch Rd at the east end is 200.02'. You also know that based on survey data that the tie in elevations at the west end at station 0+06.17' is 207.78', with an existing grade of approximately 3.79%. The cul-de-sac will be based on the grade of Jeffries Ranch Rd and an adjacent grade at Ascent Blvd. The low point overflow drainage in the Knuckle will be addressed by an overland gutter to the pond. Figure 7–29 roughly shows the type of street drainage that you want to establish.

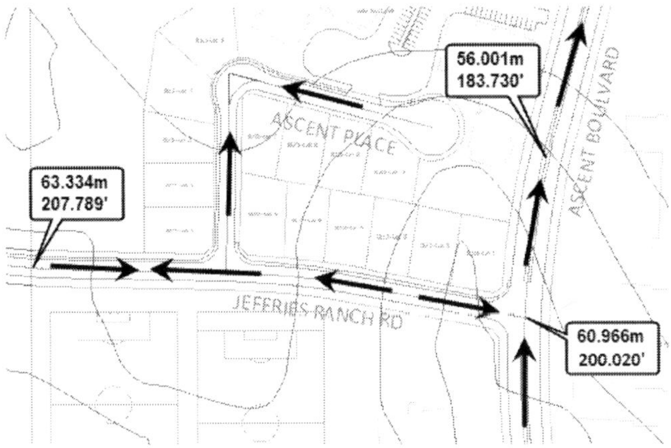

Figure 7–29

Task 1 - Create the Finished Ground Profile.

1. Open **PRF1-B1-Profile.dwg**.

Alternatively, select the ***Jeffries Ranch Rd*** *profile view, and in the contextual tab>Launch Pad panel, select* ***Profile Creation Tools***

2. Zoom to the Jeffries Ranch Rd profile view. In the *Home* tab> Create Design panel, expand Profile and select **Profile Creation Tools**. When prompted to select a profile view, select the **Jeffries Ranch Rd** profile view.
3. In the Create Profile dialog box that opens, for the *Name,* click **Edit name template** to the right. In the Name Template dialog box, select **Alignment Name** in the *Property* fields and click **Insert**. Type -**DGN** in the name and click **OK** to close the dialog box, as shown in Figure 7–30.

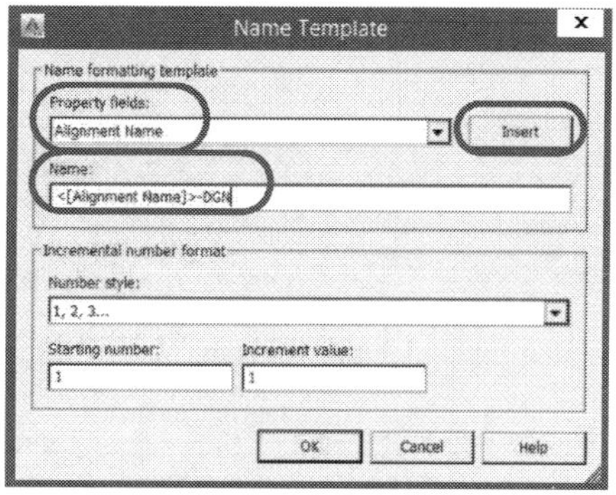

Figure 7–30

4. Set the *Profile style* to **Design Profile** and the *Profile label set* to **Complete Label Set** as shown in Figure 7–31. Click **OK**.

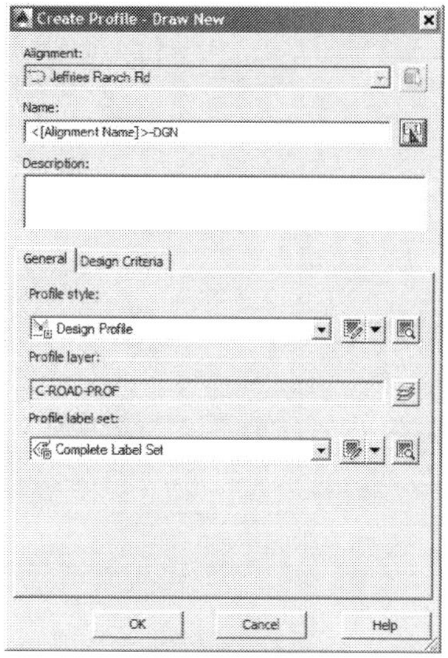

Figure 7–31

5. Expand the drop-down menu in the Profile Layout Tools toolbar and select **Draw Tangents**, as shown in Figure 7–32. The AutoCAD Civil 3D software prompts you for a start point, which indicates the location of the road's first PVI.

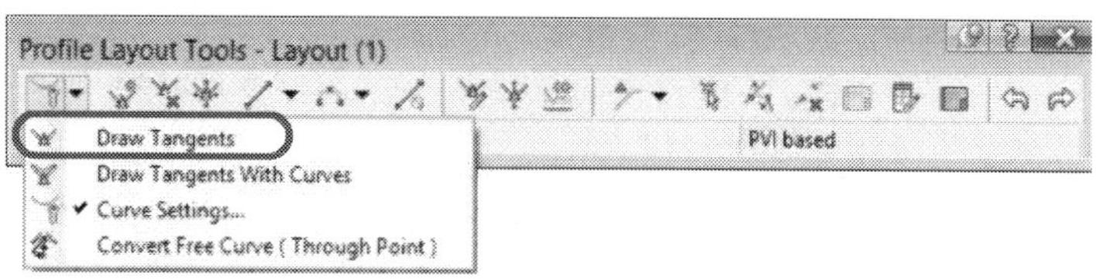

Figure 7–32

6. In the Transparent Commands toolbar, click (Profile Station Elevation).

7. When prompted, select any part of the Jeffries Ranch Rd profile view, type a starting station of **6.17'** and press <Enter>, type **207.78'**, and press <Enter> for the starting elevation. The routine prompts you for another station and elevation value. As you want to enter another method of setting the next point, press <Esc> to exit this transparent command.

*You want to set the next point based on a grade to a given station, so you will use the **Profile Grade Station** transparent command.*

8. Click (Profile Grade Station) in the Transparent Commands toolbar to enter a grade followed by a station. When prompted, type **-3.79** and press <Enter> for the slope (to indicate -3.79%) and type **328.08'** and press <Enter> for the station. Press <Esc> to end the transparent command and press <Esc> again to end the layout command.

   The profile is shown in Figure 7–33. Close the Profile Layout Tools, as shown on the top right of Figure 7–33.

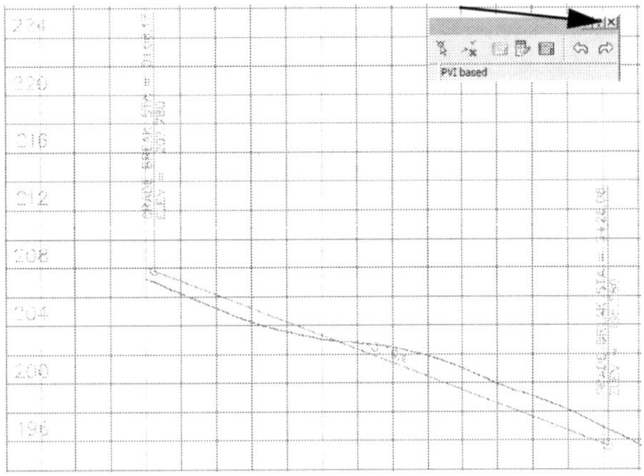

Figure 7–33

9. At any time, you can continue to edit a profile by selecting it, right-clicking, and selecting **Edit Profile Geometry**. In the Jeffries Ranch Rd profile view, select the **DGN** grade line drawn in Step 9, In the contextual tab>Modify Profile panel, click (Geometry Editor) to edit it.

10. To continue adding PVIs, return to the Profile Layout Tools toolbar and expand and select **Draw Tangents**. When prompted for the start point, snap to the end point of the last segment that you drew (i.e., sta=328.08' elev=195.58').

11. In the Transparent Commands toolbar, click (Profile Grade Length) and select the **Jeffries Ranch Rd** profile view. Type **0.8** and press <Enter> for the slope and type **482.283'** and press <Enter> for the length. Press <Esc> to exit the transparent command.

12. To tie back to the final design point, click (Profile Station Elevation) in the Transparent Commands toolbar. Type an end alignment station of **1130.01'** and press <Enter> and a tie in elevation of **200.02'** and press <Enter>.

13. Press <Esc> to exit the transparent command and press <Enter> to exit the **Draw Tangent** command.

14. In the Profile Layout Tools toolbar, click **X** to close it.

Task 2 - Adjust the FG Profile.

1. Continue with the previous drawing or open **PRF1-B2-Profile.dwg**.

2. Select the **Jefferies Ranch Rd-DGN1** profile that you drew in the previous task and note the grips that display.

3. In the contextual tab>Modify Profile panel, click (Geometry Editor).

   The PVIs do not have any vertical curves. You will add them to the design using the **Free Vertical Curve (Parameter)** option, as shown in Figure 7–34. You could have also done this at the initial stage of the design using the **Draw Tangent with Curves** tool rather than the **Draw Tangent** tool.

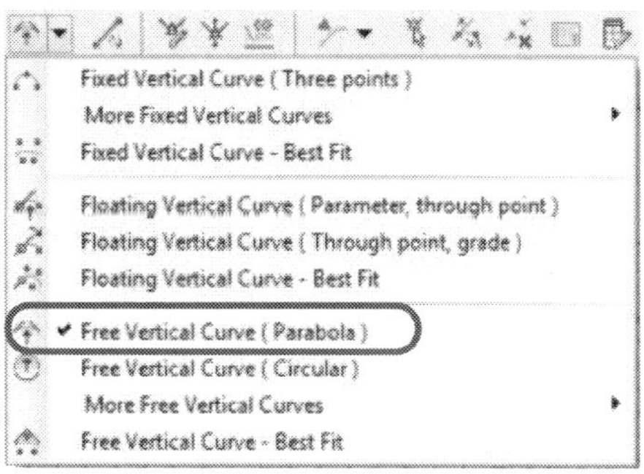

Figure 7–34

4. Click (Free Vertical Curve (Parabola)), and when prompted to select the first entity, select the incoming grade (1) and then select the outgoing grade (2), as shown in Figure 7–35. Type **100'** for the length of vertical curve.

5. Do the same for the second vertical curve. Select entities (3) and (4) (as shown in Figure 7–35) and type **100'** for the length of the vertical curve. Press <Enter> to exit the command.

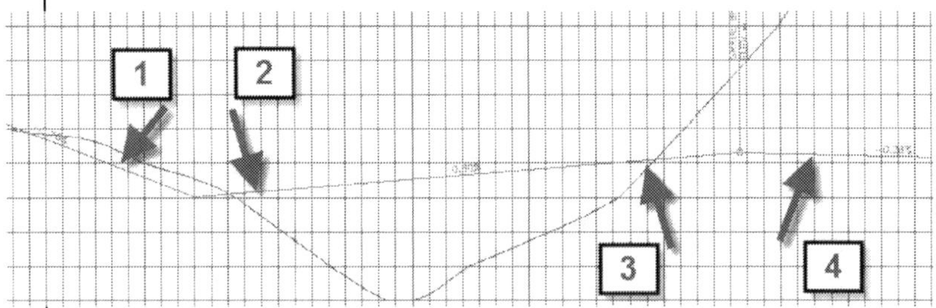

Figure 7–35

6. In the Profile Layout Tools toolbar, click (Profile Grid View).

The Profile Entities vista should display in the Panorama.

7. The *Grade In* elevation at the station 11+30.01' is 0.18%. This is less than minimum, so you need to change it to **-0.8%** while maintaining both PVI stations. However, the elevation at station 8+10.37' will be revised. Select the *Grade In* elevation and change *0.18* to **-0.8**, as shown in Figure 7–36.

No.	PVI Station	PVI Elevation	Grade In	Grade Out
1	0+06.17'	207.780'		-3.79%
2	3+28.08'	195.579'	-3.79%	0.80%
3	8+10.37'	199.438'	0.80%	0.18%
4	11+30.01'	200.020'	0.18%	

Figure 7–36

8. You will change the *Grade In* elevation at station 8+10.37' to also be **0.80%**. Select the *Grade In* elevation and change *1.45* to **0.8**, as shown in Figure 7–37. This affects the elevation at station 3+28.08.

No.	PVI Station	PVI Elevation	Grade In	Grade Out
1	0+06.17'	207.780'		-3.79%
2	3+28.08'	195.579'	-3.79%	1.45%
3	8+10.37'	202.577'	1.45%	-0.80%
4	11+30.01'	200.020'	-0.80%	

Figure 7–37

At this point, the as built grade from station 0+06.17' is no longer 3.79%. However, from a simple calculation you know that if you move the PVI from station 3+28.08', elevation 198.72' to station **2+60.04'**, elevation **198.16**', you will be able to preserve the 3.79% grade and the 0.8% minimum grade. There are two methods to accomplish this:

- Edit the station and elevation in the grid view, as shown in Figure 7–38.

No.	PVI Station	PVI Elevation	Grade In	Grade Out
1	0+06.17'	207.780'		-2.81%
2	3+28.08'	198.719'	-2.81%	0.80%
3	8+10.37'	202.577'	0.80%	-0.80%
4	11+30.01'	200.020'	-0.80%	

Figure 7–38

- Alternatively, in Model Space, move the PVI to a station and elevation. For training proposes, perform the more complex process of the two.

Use the following steps to correct the grade.

9. In Model Space, select the **DGN** grade line to display its grips.
10. At the 3+28.08' PVI station, select the center PVI grip. For the new location, click (Profile Station and Elevation).
11. When prompted for the profile view, select one of the grid lines of the Jeffries Ranch Rd profile view.
12. Type a sta value of **260.04'** and press <Enter> and an elevation value of **198.16'** and press <Enter>.
13. The grid view should have the values shown in Figure 7–39. Click the **X** in the Profile Layout Tools toolbar to close both the grid view and toolbar.

No.	PVI Station	PVI Elevation	Grade In	Grade Out
1	0+06.17'	207.780'		-3.79%
2	2+60.04'	198.160'	-3.79%	0.80%
3	8+10.37'	202.577'	0.80%	-0.80%
4	11+30.01'	200.020'	-0.80%	

Figure 7–39

Task 3 - Update profile bands.

The profile views display existing ground elevations in both the existing and proposed slots of the profile bands, as shown in Figure 7–40. In this task, you will change the right label to a finished ground profile label.

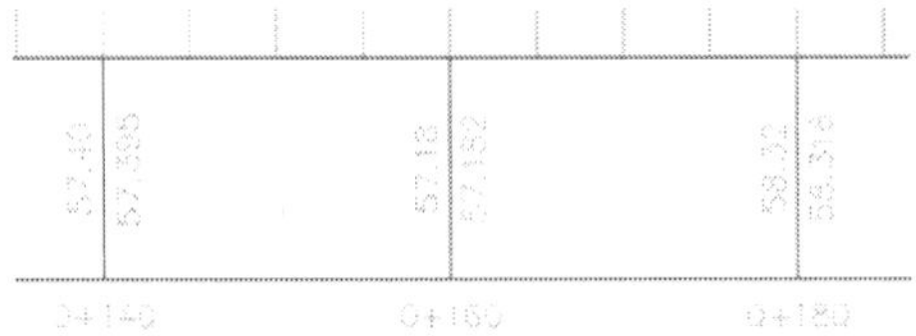

Figure 7–40

1. Continue with the drawing from the previous task or open **PRF1-B3-Profile.dwg**.

2. To update, select the Jeffries Ranch Rd profile view, right-click, and select **Profile View Properties**. In the *Bands* tab, assign Profile2 to reference Jeffries Ranch Rd-DGN, as shown in Figure 7–41. Click **OK**.

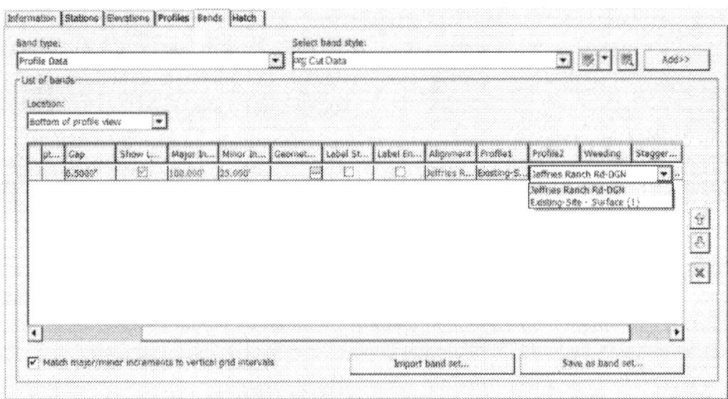

Figure 7–41

The profile band displays existing ground elevations on the left and design elevations on the right, as shown in Figure 7–42.

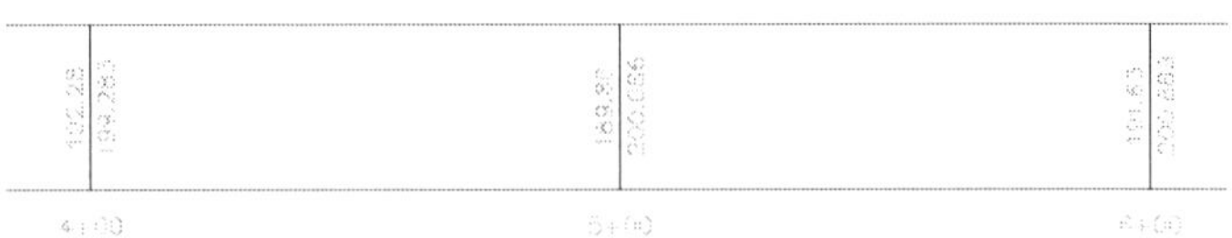

Figure 7–42

3. Save the drawing.

Practice 7c

Working with Profiles Additional Practice

Practice Objective

- Create finished ground profiles using specific design parameters.

Estimated time for completion: 15 minutes

Task 1 - (Optional) Create a second FG Profile.

In this task, you will create a design grade for Ascent Place. To do this, you will use the tie in elevation at Jeffries Ranch Rd of 200.72'. Design requirements include PVI at station 3+77.461' elev 187.237' and a slope of 0.8% to the end station of 6+98.72'.

If you are not able to complete this task on your own, use the following steps.

1. Open **PRF1-C1-Profile.dwg**.
2. Zoom into the Ascent Pl profile view. In the *Home* tab>

   Create Design panel, expand Profile, and click (Profile Creation Tools). When prompted to select a profile view, select the **Ascent Pl** profile view.
3. The Create Profile dialog box opens. Set the following, as shown in Figure 7–43:
   - Set the name as you did in the previous practice, in Steps 2 and 3, or type **Ascent Pl-DGN** for the *Name*.
   - Set the *Profile style* to **Design Profile**.
   - Set the *Profile label set* to **Complete Label Set**.
   - Click **OK**.

Figure 7–43

4. Expand the drop-down list in the Profile Layout Tools toolbar and select (Curve Settings), as shown in Figure 7–44.

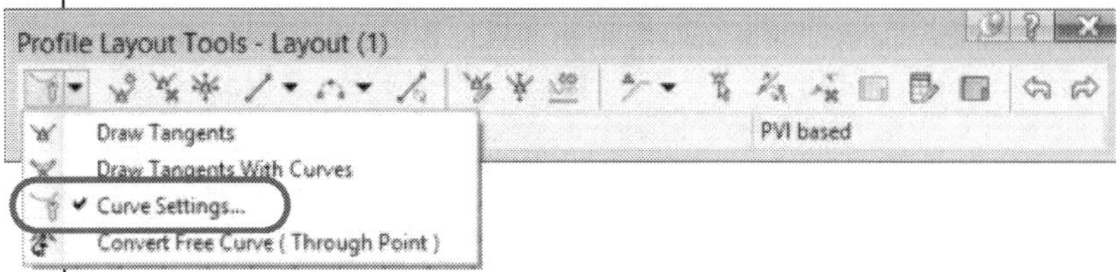

Figure 7–44

5. In the Vertical Curve Settings dialog box, set the curve type to **Parabolic** for both the Crest and Sag curves. Select the **Length** option and type **100'** as the length for both curves. Click **OK** to close dialog box.

6. Click (Draw Tangent with Curves).

7. The AutoCAD Civil 3D software prompts you for a start point, which indicates the location of the road's first PVI. In the Transparent Commands toolbar, click (Profile Station Elevation). When prompted for a profile view, select the **Ascent PI** profile view.

8. The AutoCAD Civil 3D software will prompt you for the station and elevation. Type a starting station of **0** and press <Enter>, and then type **200.72'** and press <Enter> for the starting elevation. For the next station, type **377.46'** and press <Enter> and type **187.24'** and press <Enter> for the elevation. The routine prompts you for another station and elevation value. As you want to enter another method of setting the next point, press <Esc> to exit this transparent command.

9. In the Transparent Commands toolbar, click (Profile Grade Station). Type **0.80** and press <Enter> for the grade and type **698.72'** and press <Enter> for the station.

10. Press <Esc> to exit the transparent command and press <Enter> to exit the **Profile Draw** command. Click the **X** to close the Profile Layout Tools toolbar.

11. Save the drawing.

Corridors

This chapter includes instructional content to assist in your preparation for the following topic and objectives for the AutoCAD® Civil® 3D 2016 Certified Professional exam.

Autodesk Certification Exam Objectives in this Chapter

Exam Topic	Exam Objective	Section
Corridors	• Design and create a corridor	• 8.1
	• Derive information and data from a corridor	• 8.2
	• Design and create an intersection	• 8.3

8.1 Design and Create a Corridor

Assemblies

An *assembly* defines the attachment point of a roadway cross-section to the horizontal and vertical alignments. This attachment point occurs at the midpoint of the assembly marker (or assembly baseline), as shown in Figure 8–1. The 3D progression of the attachment point along the corridor is also sometimes referred to as the *profile grade line*.

Figure 8–1

Assemblies can be placed anywhere in a drawing (centerline of roads, curb returns, sidewalks, off ramps, railways, etc). Assembly styles only affect the display of the marker itself (i.e., color, layer, etc.).

Assembly Types

The type of road or railway that an assembly represents can be very important, especially if it is used in a corridor that requires superelevation axis of rotation or cant. When a superelevation or cant is calculated for an alignment, it is important to also select an assembly type that matches these design needs. There are six types of assemblies:

- **Undivided Crowned Road:** Enables you to specify the axis about which the corridor is superelevated.
- **Undivided Planar Road:** Enables you to specify the axis about which the corridor is superelevated and the default highside location for planar roads.
- **Divided Crowned Road:** Enables you to specify the axis about which the corridor is superelevated and whether the median maintains its shape or becomes distorted as the corridor superelevates.
- **Divided Planar Road:** Enables you to specify the axis about which the corridor is superelevated and whether the median maintains its shape or becomes distorted as the corridor superelevates.

- **Railway:** Enables you to specify the cant about which the corridor is going to bank.
- **Other:** Used for all other types of corridors that are not listed above.

Subassemblies

Assemblies are assigned *subassemblies*, which represent individual components of the proposed cross-section (such as lane or curb subassemblies). Subassemblies attach to the left or right side of an assembly's attachment point. When building an assembly, you build from the middle out to the left or right edges.

- The library of stock subassemblies supplied with the AutoCAD® Civil 3D® software uses of a wide array of dynamic parameters (e.g., dimensions such as lane width and slope). If these values change, the road model can automatically update. Custom dynamic subassemblies can also be created using the .net programming language.
- You can create static subassemblies (without dynamic parameters) from polylines.
- Each point (vertex) of a subassembly can be assigned a name or *point code* for reference later. A point is a potential location for offset and elevation annotation. It is also a connection point for an adjacent subassembly. For example, points are commonly assigned at edge-of-travelways, back-of-curbs, gutters, etc. Marker styles define the properties for points and their labels.
- Corridors can generate *feature lines* at every location that is assigned a point code. These linear 3D objects can be used as input for surfaces and grading solutions.
- Lines in subassemblies are referred to as *links*. A link can be automatically given a slope or grade label in the cross-sections as required. Links can also be used as surface data. Link styles define the properties of a link and its labels.
- A subassembly *shape* is an area enclosed by links. Shapes are typically assigned material types and can be used to calculate quantities. Shape styles define the display properties of a shape.

- Marker styles, feature line styles, and link and shape styles are all assigned based on a Code Set Style. The Code Set Style assigns the styles to be applied based on the codes assigned to these objects. Code Sets and each of these styles are all configured under the *Multipurpose Styles* collection in the *Settings* tab.

The example in Figure 8–2 shows an assembly containing lane, curb, and daylight subassemblies. This assembly has been assigned to display an offset and elevation marker (point) label at the edge of the lane, a pavement slope (link) label, and shape labels displaying the area of the sub-base.

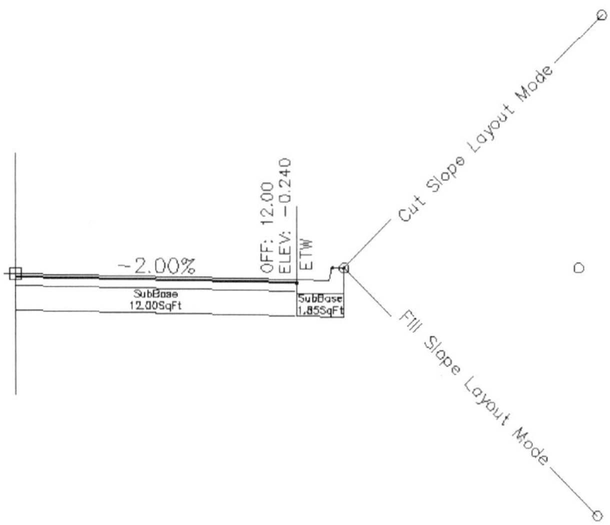

Figure 8–2

- Each subassembly attaches to the assembly connection point or to a point on an adjacent subassembly. OSNAPs are not necessary.
- You should assign each assembly and its subassemblies, a logical, unique name during creation. This is helpful later in the corridor creation process when you are working with very complex corridors that include intersections, transitions, and other components.
- AutoCAD Civil 3D Help contains extensive documentation for each subassembly.

The *Prospector* tab lists each assembly with a further breakdown of each subassembly associated with it, in a tree structure, as shown in Figure 8–3.

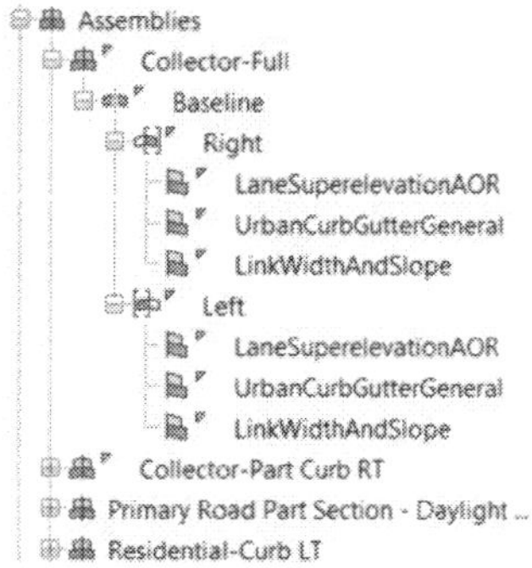

Figure 8–3

To review their interconnections and parameters, select the assembly, right-click, and select **Assembly Properties**. The Assembly Properties dialog box opens as shown in Figure 8–4.

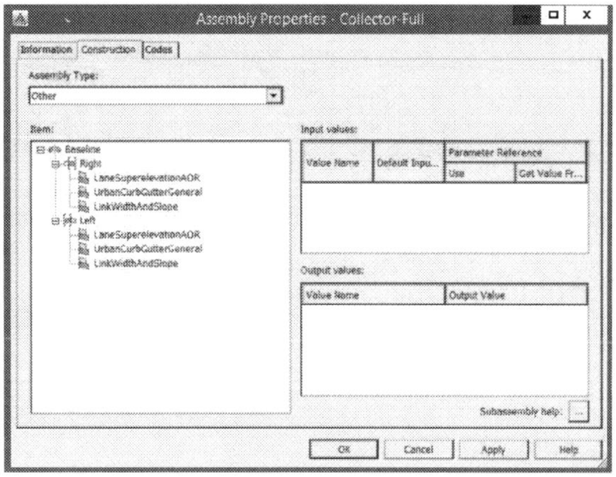

Figure 8–4

Attaching Subassemblies

The easiest way to add an AutoCAD Civil 3D subassembly to an assembly is using the Tool Palettes. You can open the Tool Palettes by clicking  in the *Home* tab>Palettes panel, as shown in Figure 8–5, or in the *View* tab>Palettes panel. You can also use <Ctrl>+<3>.

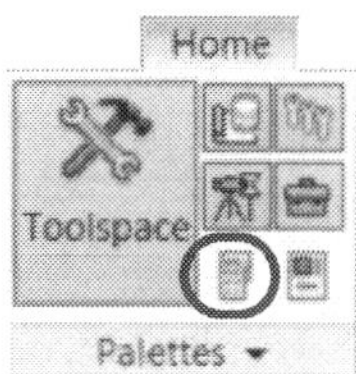

Figure 8–5

The AutoCAD Civil 3D software provides a number of stock subassembly tool palettes, as shown in Figure 8–6. In addition, it is continually updating and adding new subassemblies with every release.

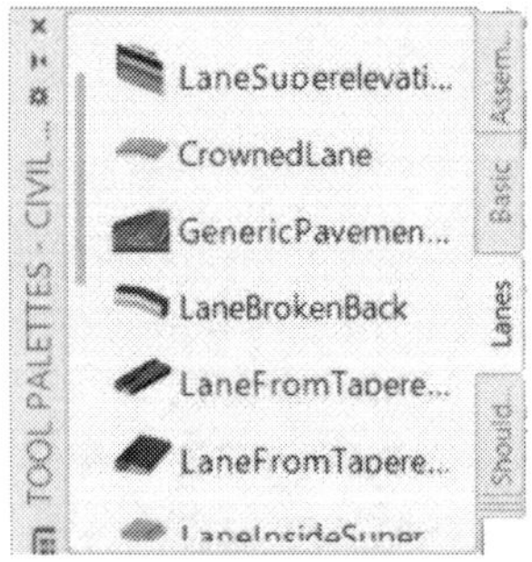

Figure 8–6

The Help file is an invaluable resource for an updated list, and information about the specific attributes and properties of each subassembly, as shown in Figure 8–7.

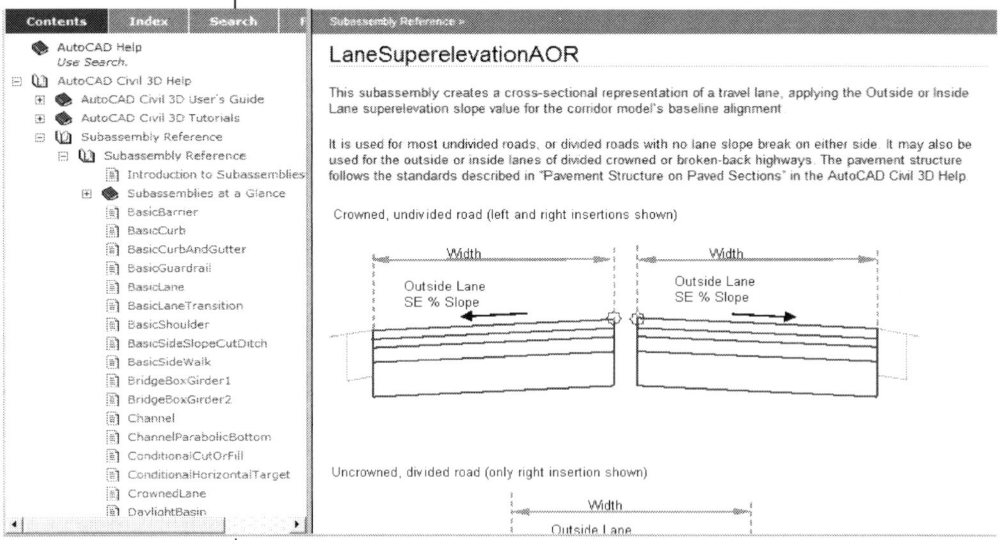

Figure 8–7

Additional subassemblies can be accessed using the Corridor Modeling catalogs. Open the catalog by selecting an assembly or subassembly from the drawing. In the *Assembly/Subassembly* tab>Launch Pad panel, click **Catalog**, as shown in Figure 8–8.

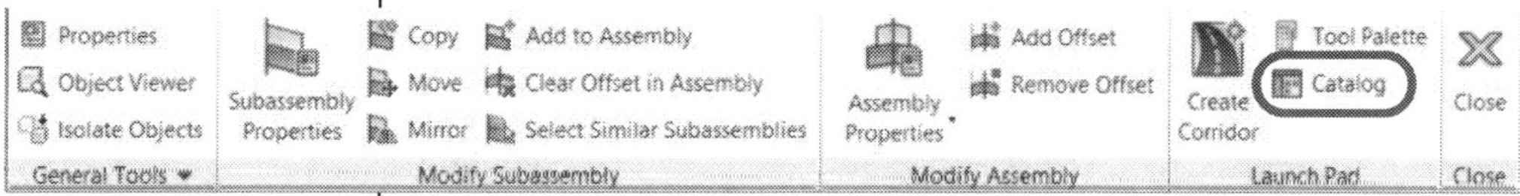

Figure 8–8

You can drag and drop the catalog onto a Tool Palette, if needed. When working with the Tool Palettes and Properties palette, you might find it helpful to toggle off the **Allow Docking** option to prevent them from docking on the sides of the screen. Right-click on the palette's title bar to set the option, as shown in Figure 8–9.

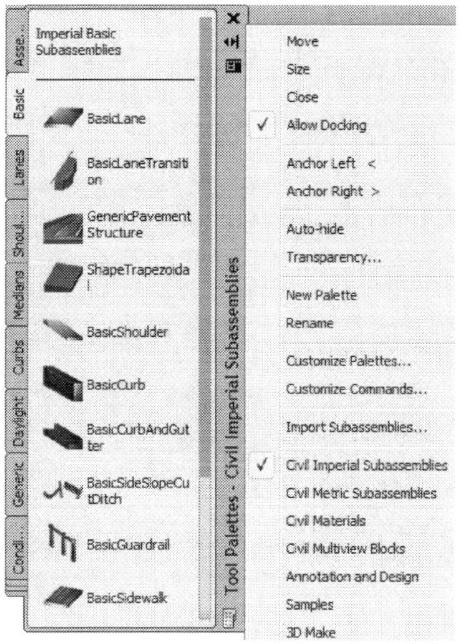

Figure 8–9

Detaching Subassemblies

Individual subassemblies can be deleted directly from an assembly with the AutoCAD® **Erase** command or using Assembly Properties. Assemblies can also be deleted with the **Erase** command.

Copying Assemblies

Assemblies can be copied with the AutoCAD **Copy** command or by clicking (Copy) in the *Assembly* tab>Modify Subassembly panel. Copying an assembly creates an independent assembly without a relationship to the original. Select the assembly by selecting the **Assembly Baseline**.

Mirroring Subassemblies

In the AutoCAD Civil 3D software, subassemblies can be mirrored across the assembly to which it is attached by selecting the subassemblies, right-clicking, and selecting **Mirror** or clicking (Mirror) in the *Assembly* tab>Modify Subassembly panel. This enables you to create one side of the roadway and to create a mirrored image for the other side in one step.

> **Hint: AutoCAD Mirror**
>
> The basic AutoCAD Mirror command does not work for this. You need to use the Mirror option from the shortcut menu or in the Modify Subassembly panel.

Select Similar Subassemblies

It is often necessary to create multiple assemblies with the same subassemblies for various purposes. For example, a corridor that includes an intersection might need a full assembly that includes both sides of the road, an assembly that includes just the right side of the road, and another that includes just the left side of the road. It might also include two other assemblies that require the assembly marker to be placed at the edge of pavement rather than the crown, as shown in Figure 8–10.

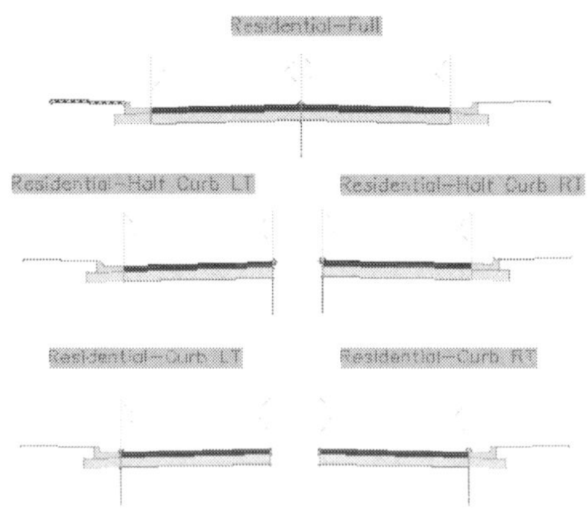

Figure 8–10

However, making changes to all of the assemblies when a design parameter changes can be time consuming. To ensure that all similar subassemblies are modified at the same time when a design change occurs you can select one subassembly, click (Select Similar Subassemblies) in the *Assembly* tab> Modify Subassembly panel, and change the parameter in the AutoCAD properties palette.

Sharing Assemblies

Assemblies can be shared with the AutoCAD Civil 3D software in three ways:

- Assemblies can be dragged from the drawing area to a Tool Palette. The Tool Palette can then be shared.
- The Content Browser can be used to add assemblies to a catalog.
- Assemblies can be placed in their own drawing files and shared by dragging the assembly drawing into the destination drawing file. If this method is used, the assembly drawing must only contain the assemblies that you want to share.

Getting More Information on Subassemblies

Many subassemblies have a large number of parameters. If you want to read the documentation on a subassembly, right-click on its tool icon in a Tool Palette and select **Help**. You can also find out more from Subassembly Properties and Assembly Properties using the **Subassembly help** icon, as shown in Figure 8–11.

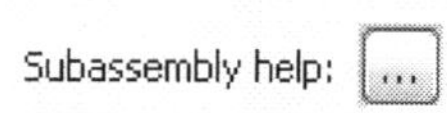

Figure 8–11

Creating a Corridor

A corridor is a 3D model of a proposed design based on alignments, profiles, and assemblies. Corridors can be used to create terrain models (such as a finished ground terrain model) and generate section data. Corridors display as complex drawing objects consisting of individual cross-sections, feature lines that connect marker points (locations where point codes are assigned), and other related data, as shown in Figure 8–12.

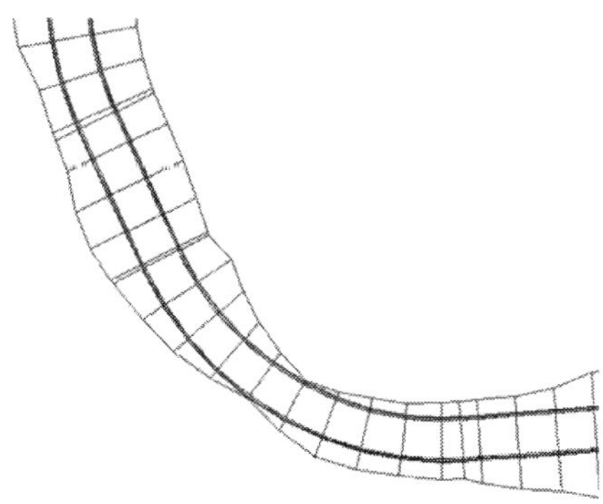

Figure 8–12

Corridors can be used to represent an individual alignment, profile, and assembly (such as for a single road) or can contain multiples of each. When modeling intersections, it is often easiest to have all intersecting roads as part of the same corridor object. However, it might not be practical to include all of the proposed roads in a single corridor on large projects. You can have any number of corridors present in the same drawing file.

To create a corridor, click (Corridor) in the *Home* tab>Create Design panel. A dialog box opens in which you can enter a description, corridor style, layer, alignment, profile, assembly, and target surface, as shown on the left in Figure 8–13. It also has an option that enables you to set the baseline and region parameters. By selecting this, when you click **OK** a second dialog box opens as shown on the right of Figure 8–13.

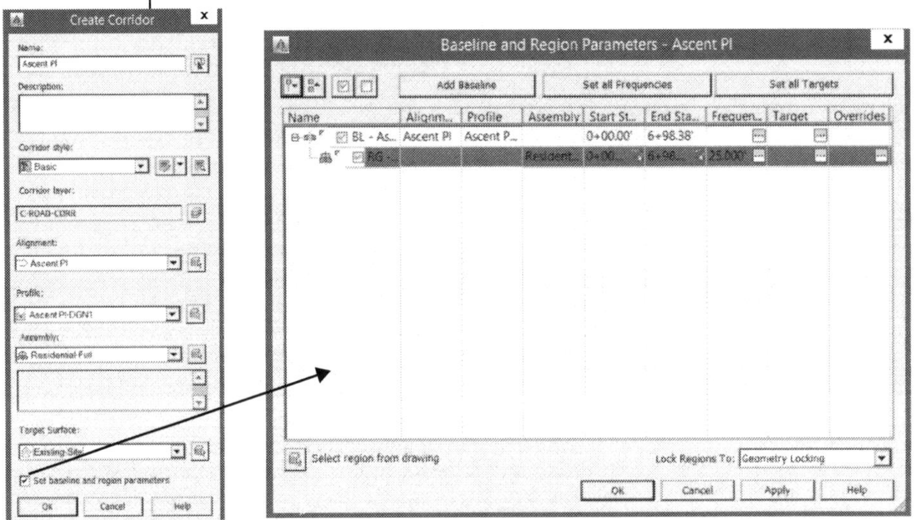

Figure 8–13

Target Mapping

Target Mapping is where you assign a surface to which daylight subassemblies are graded or alignments, feature lines, and polylines that cause lanes and other subassemblies to stretch.

Many stock subassemblies include transitional components, such as the lanes you added to the 2 Lane Road assembly. These lanes can have their outside edge-of-travelway (ETW) controlled by other alignments, feature lines, survey figures, and 3D polylines as required, which can be used to specify widening and contraction of the lanes. These lanes also include profile controls at the ETW points. These types of controls are all assigned using Target Mapping.

In the Target Mapping dialog box (shown in Figure 8–14), the subassembly name and assembly groups are listed. Giving these items logical names is important. Otherwise, it would be difficult to tell them apart in this dialog box.

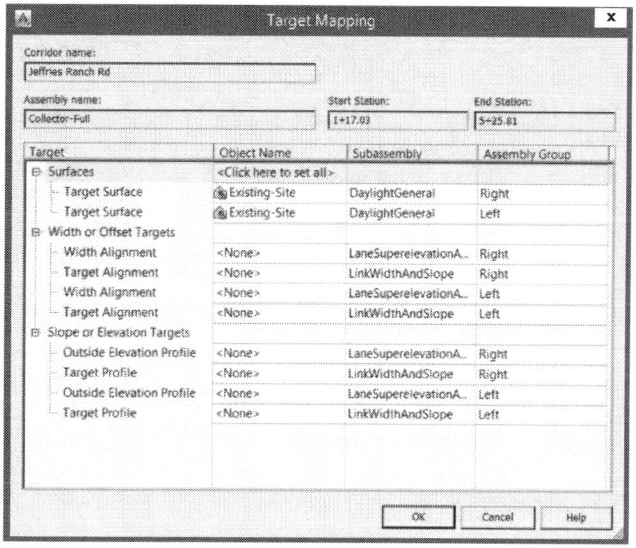

Figure 8–14

Corridor Frequency

The corridor frequency determines how often assemblies are applied to the corridor model, as shown in Figure 8–15. The frequency can be set for tangents separate from curves to provide more control over the model's size and accuracy. The more frequently the assembly is applied to the corridor model, the more accurate the model. A higher frequency also causes the model to require more computer resources, as it increases the size of the model. It is important to set the frequency at a level that balances the level of required accuracy with a reasonably sized corridor model.

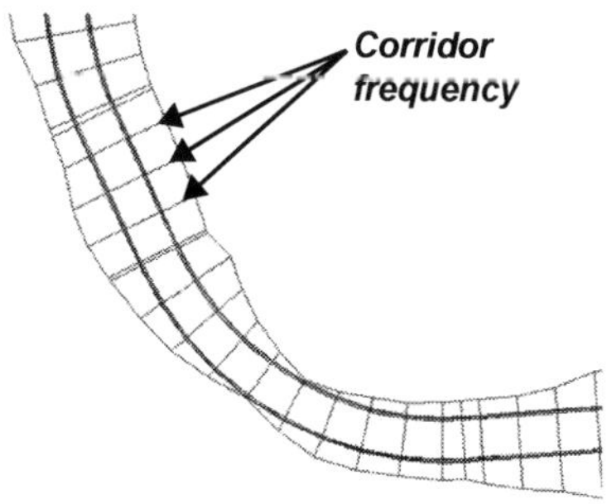

Figure 8–15

Frequency locations for curved baselines can be set **By curvature**, or **At an increment**, as shown in Figure 8–16. If the **At an increment** option is selected, assemblies are applied at a specified number of units along the curve. If the **By curvature** option is selected, the radius of the curve determines how frequently the assemblies are applied to the corridor model.

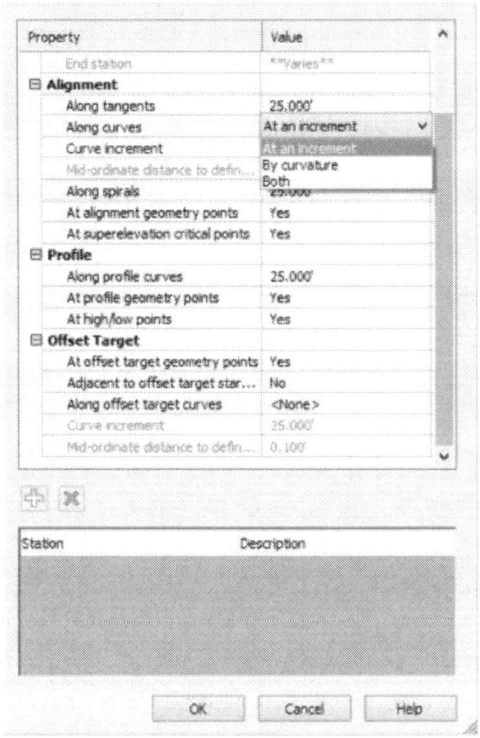

Figure 8–16

8.2 Derive Information and Data from a Corridor

The *Surfaces* tab in the Corridor Properties dialog box enables you to build the proposed surfaces based on corridor geometry. You can create these surfaces from corridor links, and/or from feature lines based on marker points (point codes). As the corridor changes, its surfaces automatically update.

The two most common types of corridor surfaces are Top and Datum surfaces.

- **Top surfaces:** Follow the uppermost geometry of the corridor. These are useful for many purposes, such as in the display of finished ground contours and as a way of determining rim elevations of proposed utility structures.
- **Datum surfaces:** Generally follow the bottommost corridor geometry. These can be used in both Surface-to-Surface volume calculations and Section-based Earthworks calculations to determine site cut and fill totals (when compared to existing ground).
- **Corridor surfaces:** As with all AutoCAD Civil 3D surfaces, these cannot contain vertical elements. Include slight offsets so that vertical curbing and similar geometry are not absolutely vertical.

Overhang Correction

In some configurations, AutoCAD Civil 3D assemblies might have top or datum points, or links in locations that might lead to incorrect surfaces, such as the datum surface represented by the heavy line in Figure 8–17.

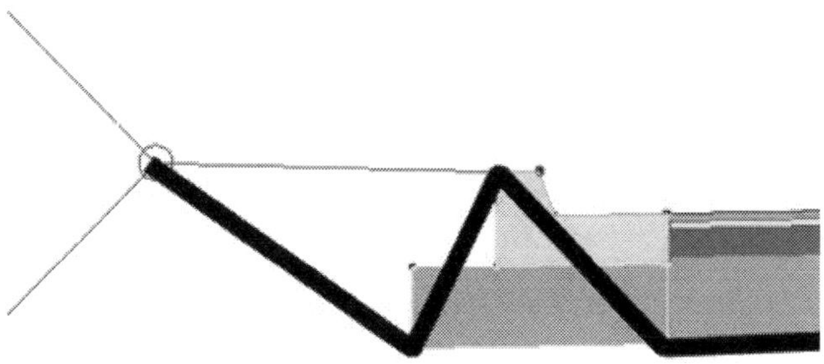

Figure 8–17

In these cases, the **Overhang Correction** option forces these surfaces to follow either the top or bottom of the corridor geometry, as shown in Figure 8–18. This setting is typically only needed for datum surfaces.

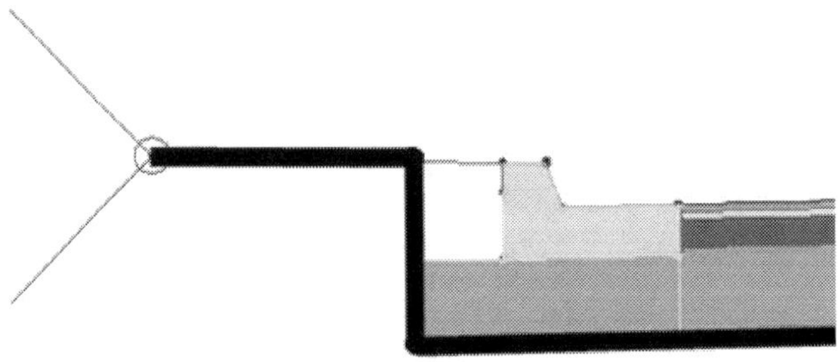

Figure 8–18

Surface Boundaries

Corridor surfaces, as with all AutoCAD Civil 3D surfaces, often benefit from a boundary to remove unwanted interpolation between points. The *Boundaries* tab in the Corridor Surfaces dialog box enables you to add these boundaries in a number of ways: by selecting a closed polyline or by interactively tracing the boundary using a jig.

The best option is often to *automatically* add a boundary that follows the daylight feature lines on both sides. This can be done using the new **Create Boundary from Corridor Extents** command.

8.3 Design and Create an Intersection

Intersection objects are complex corridor models that automatically create offset and curb return geometry where two intersecting alignments meet. As changes are made to the underlying information (alignments, profiles, assemblies, and surfaces) the intersection geometry is automatically updated. There are four types of Intersection objects, as shown in Figure 8–19. This review guide only covers the standard intersection.

Figure 8–19

To create an intersection, select the *Home* tab>Create Design panel and click (Create Intersection). You are prompted to pick the intersection of two roads. The Create Intersection Wizard then opens.

General Tab

The *General* tab enables you to name the intersection (recommended), add a description, and select intersection marker and label styles. An important element on this tab is the intersection corridor type. You can keep the primary road crown maintained or have all road crowns maintained, as shown in Figure 8–20. If you only maintain the crown of the primary road, the secondary road's profile is adjusted automatically.

Note: The intersection corridor type cannot be changed once you click ***Create Intersection*** *and exit the Create Intersection Wizard.*

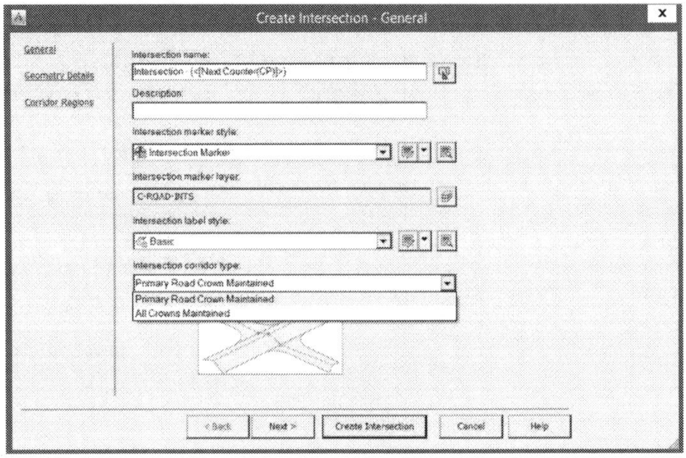

Figure 8–20

Geometry Details Tab

The *Geometry Details* tab enables you to set the road that is going to be the primary road, as shown in Figure 8–21. It is also where you set the **Offset** and **Curb Return** parameters, which include parameters for both alignments and profiles.

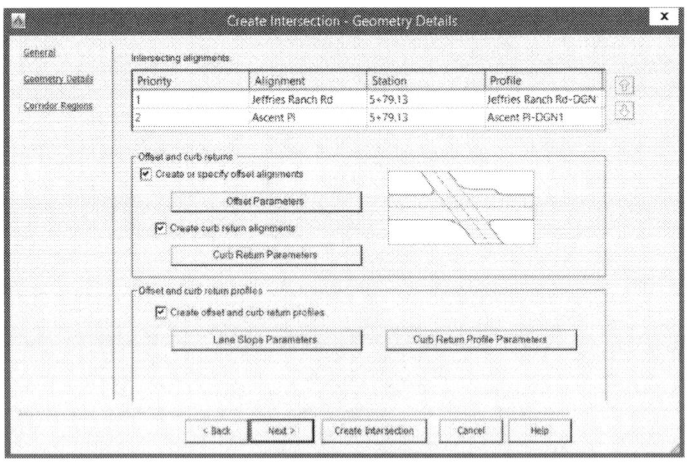

Figure 8–21

Corridor Regions Tab

The *Corridor Regions* tab enables you to create a new corridor or add the intersection corridor to an existing corridor, as shown in Figure 8–22. This is also where you select the assemblies to use in each of the corridor regions. Some assembly sets ship with the AutoCAD Civil 3D software and can be located by clicking **Browse**. By default, a Metric or Imperial assembly set displays various assemblies that are set in the window. You will click for each Corridor Region Section Type and select the appropriate assembly as required. As you select a region, the wizard highlights that region in the preview at the bottom of the window. If you select any assemblies that use daylight subassemblies, do not forget to set the target surface at the top right.

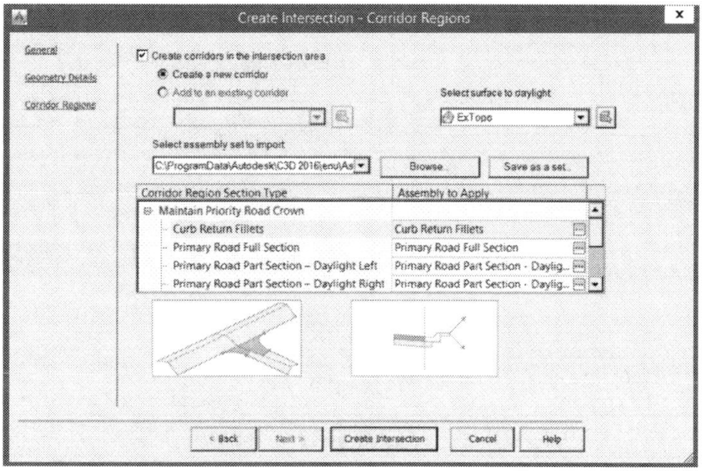

Figure 8–22

Once all of the parameters have been set, click **Create Intersection** to create the intersection object.

Practice 8a Creating Assemblies

Practice Objective

- Create and modify assemblies for use in a corridor model.

Estimated time for completion: 15 minutes

In this practice you will create two assemblies: one for Jeffries Ranch Rd and the second for the existing Ascent Pl that contains daylighting.

Task 1 - Create the Collector Road assembly.

A typical cross-section of Jeffries Ranch Rd is shown in Figure 8–23. (See Appendix A for the design criteria.)

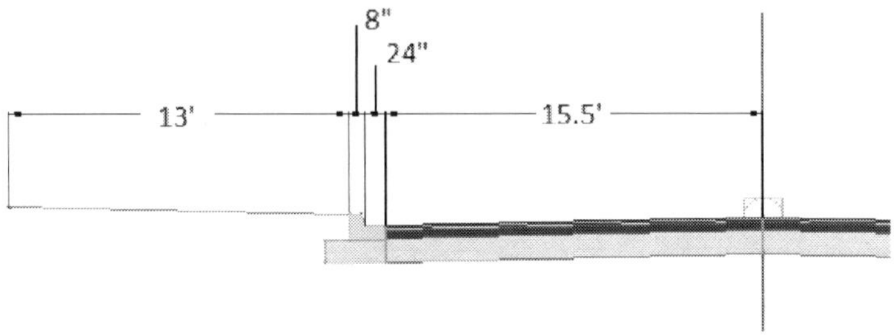

Figure 8–23

1. Continue working with the drawing from the previous task or open **COR1-A1-Corridor.dwg** from the *C:\Civil 3D Projects\Civil3D-Training\Corridors* folder.

2. In the *Home* tab>Create Design panel, click  (Create Assembly).

3. In the Create Assembly dialog box, name the new assembly **Collector-Full**. Leave the other settings at their defaults, as shown in Figure 8–24. Click **OK** to close the dialog box.

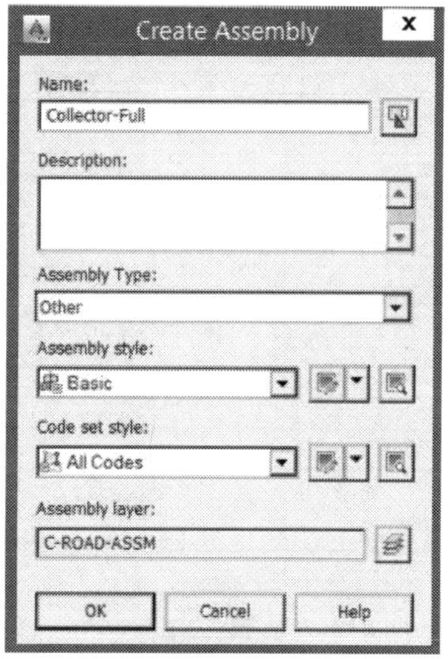

Figure 8–24

4. When prompted, locate the assembly baseline to the left of the profile view Jeffries Ranch Rd in the current drawing, as shown in Figure 8–25. Once selected, the AutoCAD Civil 3D software will change the view to zoom into the assembly baseline location.

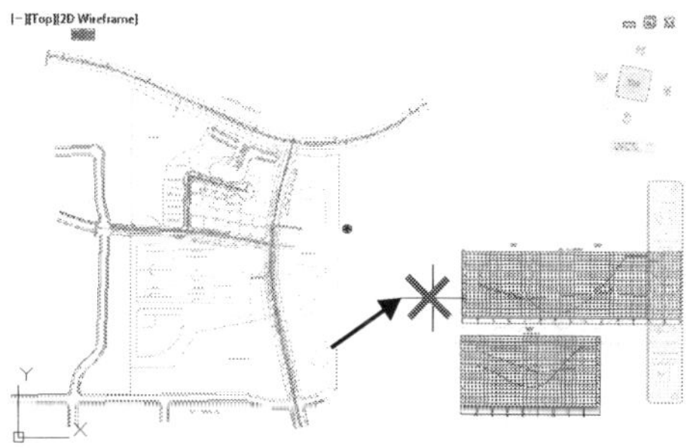

Figure 8–25

5. Open the Tool Palettes by clicking (Tool Palettes) in the *Home* tab> Palettes panel.

6. In the Lanes Tool Palette, select the **LaneSuperelevationAOR** subassembly to add it to your assembly. In the Properties palette, set the following, as shown in Figure 8–26:
    - *Side* is set to **Right**
    - *Width* is set to **15.5'**
    - *Slope* is set to **-2%**
    - Select the assembly baseline to attach the subassembly to the assembly.

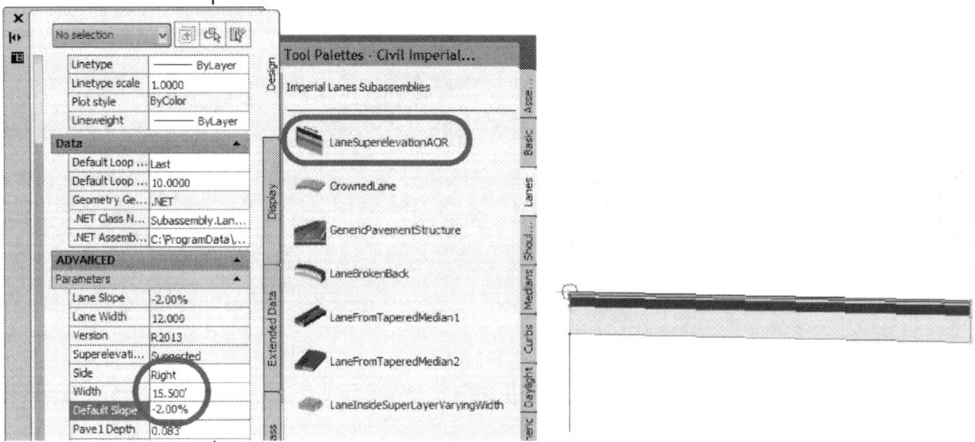

Figure 8–26

7. In the Subassemblies Tool Palette, select the *Curbs* tab and select the **UrbanCurbGutterGeneral** subassembly. In the Advanced Properties, set the following:
    - *Side* is set to **Right**
    - *Dimension B* is set to **24"**
    - Insert the subassembly by selecting the circle at the end of the **LaneInsideSuper** subassembly, as shown in Figure 8–27. Press <Esc> to exit the subassembly command.

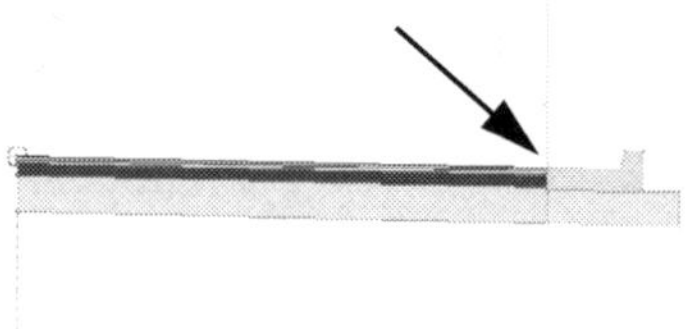

Figure 8–27

8. You will now create a subassembly that links the back of curb to property line. In the Subassemblies Tool Palette, select the *Generic* tab, and select the **LinkWidthAndSlope** subassembly. In the Advanced Properties, set the following:
    - *Side parameter* is set to **Right**
    - *Width* is set to **13'**
    - Insert the subassembly by selecting the circle at the end of the **UrbanCurbGutterGeneral** subassembly, as shown in Figure 8–28.
    - Press <Esc> to exit the subassembly command.

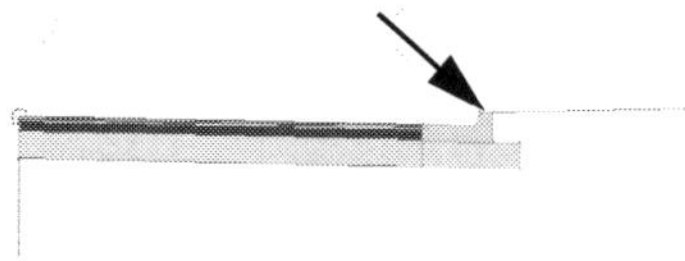

Figure 8–28

Do not select the assembly baseline, and do not use window crossing.

9. Select the three sub-assemblies that you just created on the right side, right-click, and select **Mirror**. At the *select marker point within assembly:* prompt, select the assembly baseline (the red vertical line), as shown in Figure 8–29, which represents the road center line.

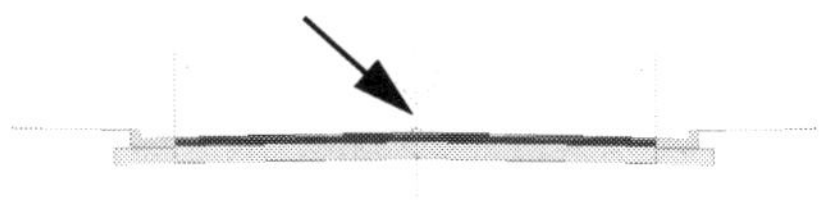

Figure 8–29

10. Save the drawing

Task 2 - Create the Residential Road assembly.

A typical cross-section of Ascent Pl is shown in Figure 8–30. (See Appendix A for design criteria.)

Note that this task is similar to Task 1. You can use this Task as a test of your knowledge in creating a residential road assembly or you can skip this task and open the backup drawing in Task 3.

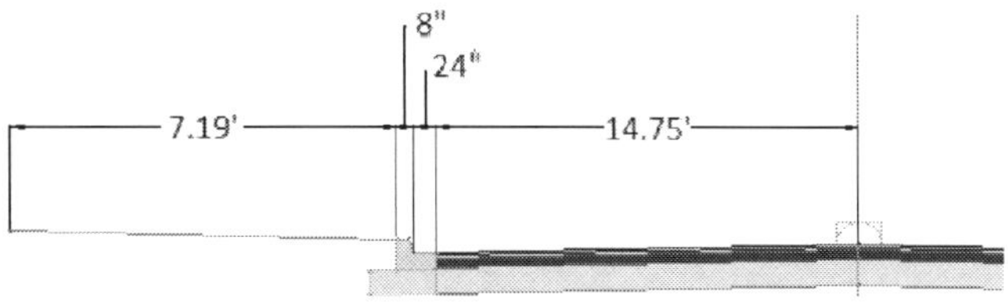

Figure 8–30

1. Continue working with the drawing from the previous task or open **COR1-A2-Corridor.dwg**.

2. In the *Home* tab>Create Design panel, click (Create Assembly).

3. In the Create Assembly dialog box, name the new assembly **Residential-Full**. Leave the other settings at their defaults and click **OK**. Click in the drawing to place the new assembly.

4. Follow the same steps in Task 1 to create the residential assembly. For this assembly:

    - Set the pavement LaneSuperelevationAOR *width* to **14.75'**
    - **UrbanCurbGutterGeneral** subassembly *Dimension B* is set to **24"**
    - LinkWidthAndSlope *width* to **7.193'**.

Task 3 - Copy and modify an assembly.

Copying an assembly can be helpful if you need another, similar assembly for other design purposes. In the following task, you will create assemblies that are required by the Intersection wizard for the intersection area of Jeffries Ranch Rd and Ascent Place. It would be helpful to understand the names and the configuration of the different assemblies.

1. Continue working with the drawing from the previous task if you completed creating all of the assemblies or open **COR1-A3-Corridor.dwg** from the *C:\Civil 3D Projects\Civil3D-Training\Corridors* folder.

2. Start the AutoCAD **Copy** command. Copy the **Collector-Full** assembly to a location just below the original, as shown in Figure 8–31.

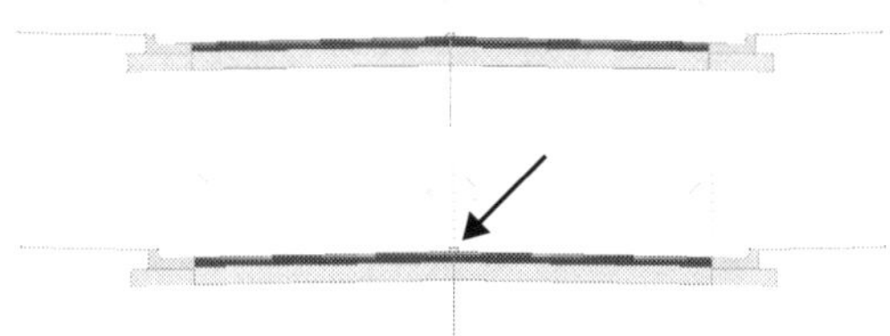

Figure 8–31

3. Select the bottom assembly baseline, right-click, and select **Assembly Properties**.

4. In the *Information* tab, change the *Name* to **Collector - Part Curb RT,** and click **OK**.

5. Start the AutoCAD **Erase** command and erase the left **UrbanCurbGutterGeneral** and the left **LinkWidthAndSlope**, as shown in Figure 8–32.

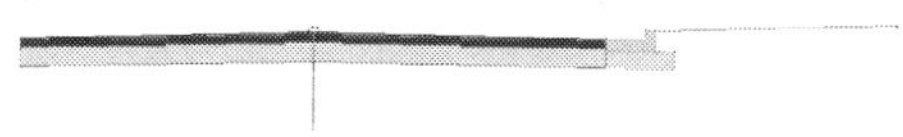

Figure 8–32

6. Save the drawing.

Practice 8b

Creating Assemblies Additional Practice

Estimated time for completion: 15 minutes

Practice Objective

- Create and modify assemblies for use in an intersection model.

In the previous practice, you created all of the Jeffries Ranch Rd assemblies that were required for the intersection. In this practice, you will create all of the required Ascent Place assemblies.

Task 1 - Create the assemblies required for the intersection.

1. Continue working with the drawing from the previous practice if you completed creating all of the subassemblies or open **COR1-B1-Corridor.dwg** from the *C:\Civil 3D Projects\Civil3D-Training\Corridors* folder.

2. Start the AutoCAD **Copy** command. Copy the **Residential -Full** assembly to two locations below the original, as shown in Figure 8–33.

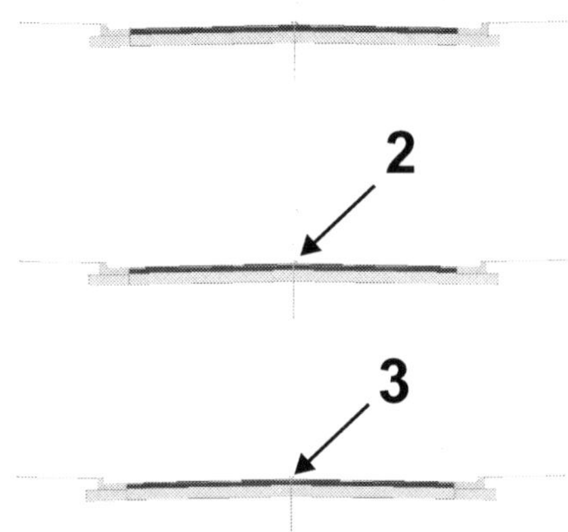

Figure 8–33

3. Select the second assembly baseline, right-click, and select **Assembly Properties**. In the *Information* tab, change the *Name* to **Residential - Half Curb LT,** and click **OK**.

4. Start the AutoCAD **Erase** command and erase the right **LaneSuperelevationAOR**, the right **UrbanCurbGutterGeneral**, and the right **LinkWidthAndSlope**.

5. Select the third assembly baseline, right-click, and select **Assembly Properties**. In the *Information* tab, change the *Name* to **Residential - Half Curb RT**, and click **OK**.

6. Start the AutoCAD **Erase** command and erase the left **LaneSuperelevationAOR**, the left **UrbanCurbGutterGeneral**, and the left **LinkWidthAndSlope**, as shown in Figure 8–34.

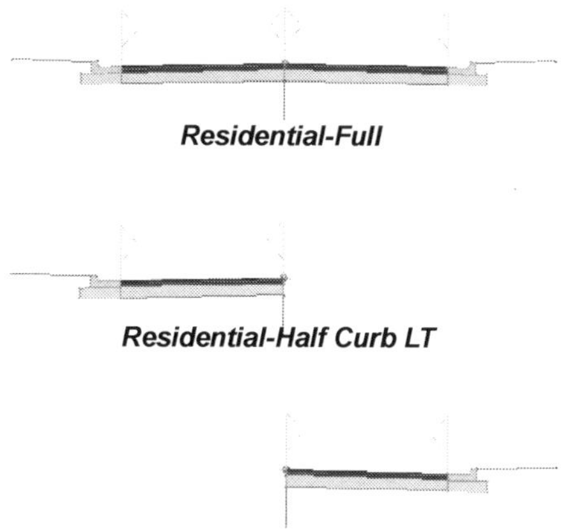

Residential-Full

Residential-Half Curb LT

Residential-Half Curb RT

Figure 8–34

Task 2 - Create a Curb Return assembly.

To include the intersection in the corridor model, you need another assembly to go around the curb returns. This assembly will have the assembly baseline at the edge of pavement or flange of the curb and gutter. It is important to create the assembly with the lane inserted first for the **Intersection** tool to be able to set the correct transitions at the centerline.

1. Continue working with the drawing from the previous task if you completed creating all of the subassemblies or open **COR1-B2-Corridor.dwg**.

Open the Tool Palettes by clicking in the View tab> Palettes panel, if it is not already open.

2. In the *Home* tab>Create Design panel, expand Assembly and select **Create Assembly**.

3. In the Create Assembly dialog box, name the new assembly **Residential-Curb Return**. Leave the other settings at their defaults, and click **OK**. Click in the drawing to place the new assembly.

4. In the Lanes Tool Palette, select the **LaneSuperelevationAOR** subassembly to add it to your assembly. Confirm the following:
    - *Side* is set to **Left**
    - *Width* is set to **14.75'**
    - *Slope* is set to **+2%**.
    - To add the Left lane subassembly, select the assembly baseline object.
5. In the Curbs tool palette, select the **UrbanCurbGutterGeneral** subassembly to add it to your assembly.
6. Confirm the following:
    - *Side* is set to **Right**
    - *Dimensions B* is set to **24"**.
    - Select the assembly baseline to add the curb and gutter, as shown in Figure 8–35.

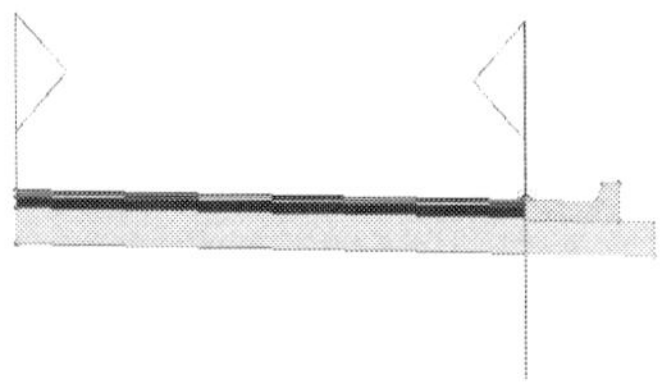

Figure 8–35

You will now create a subassembly that links the back of curb to the property line.

7. In the Subassemblies Tool Palette, select the *Generic* tab, and select the **LinkWidthAndSlope** subassembly. In the Advanced Properties, set the following:
    - *Side* is set to **Right**
    - *Width* is set to **7'**
    - Insert the subassembly at the end of the **UrbanCurbGutterGeneral** subassembly, as shown in Figure 8–36.

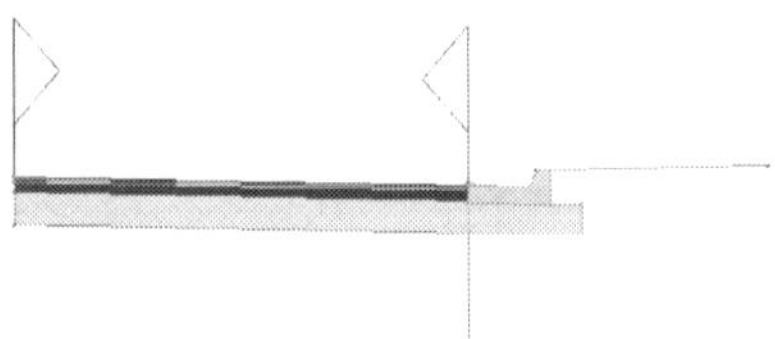

Figure 8–36

8. Press <Esc> to exit the subassembly command and save the drawing.

Practice 8c

Working with Corridors Part I

Practice Objective

- Create a corridor model using previously created alignments, profiles, and assemblies.

Estimated time for completion: 15 minutes

Task 1 - Create a corridor with regions.

In this practice, you will use the assemblies to create a corridor for both Jeffries Ranch Rd and Ascent Pl. You will also learn how to split a region.

1. Continue working with the drawing from the previous practice or open **COR1-C1-Corridor.dwg** from the *C:\Civil 3D Projects\Civil3D-Training\Corridors* folder.

2. In the *Home* tab>Create Design panel, click (Corridor). Enter the following:

    - Name it **Jeffries Ranch Rd**
    - For the alignment, select **Jeffries Ranch Rd**
    - For the profile, select **Jeffries Ranch Rd-DGN1**
    - For the subassembly, select **Collector-Full**
    - Verify that the **Set baseline and region parameters** option is selected, as shown in Figure 8–37.

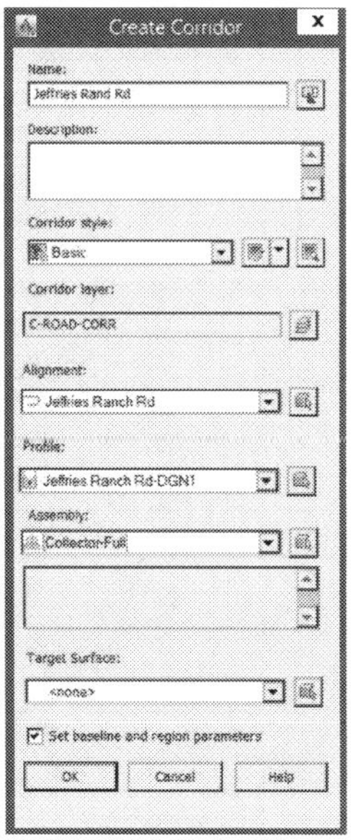

Figure 8–37

3. Click **OK**. The baseline and region parameters dialog box should open.

In this practice, you will create Jeffries Ranch Road and Ascent Pl as two independent corridors. Note that this will also create two separate surfaces. As you will be creating an intersection in the Jeffries Ranch Rd, you need to create two regions: one before the intersection and one after the intersection.

4. The dialog box identifies the Baseline (BL) as *BL-Jeffries Ranch Rd - (1)*. This baseline currently has one Region (RG). Change the region name to **RG-Before Intersection** and adjust the start station to **117.03'**, as shown in Figure 8–38. Right-click on RG-Before Intersection and select **Split Region**.

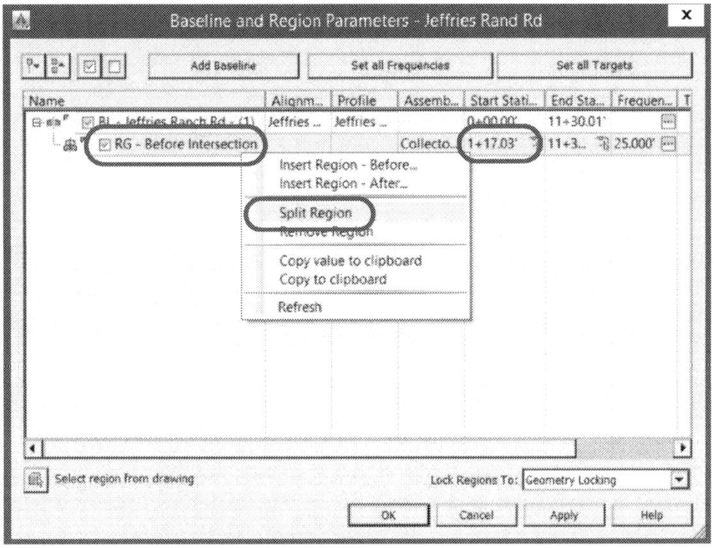

Figure 8–38

5. You now need to enter the start and end stations for the regions. You have already typed **117.03'** for the start station for the **RG-Before Intersection**. Enter the following values, as shown in Figure 8–39.
   - RG-Before Intersection End station: **525.81'**
   - RG-After Intersection Start station: **630.74'**
   - RG-After Intersection End station: **1035.92'**
   - Press <Enter> to return to the Baseline and Region dialog box.

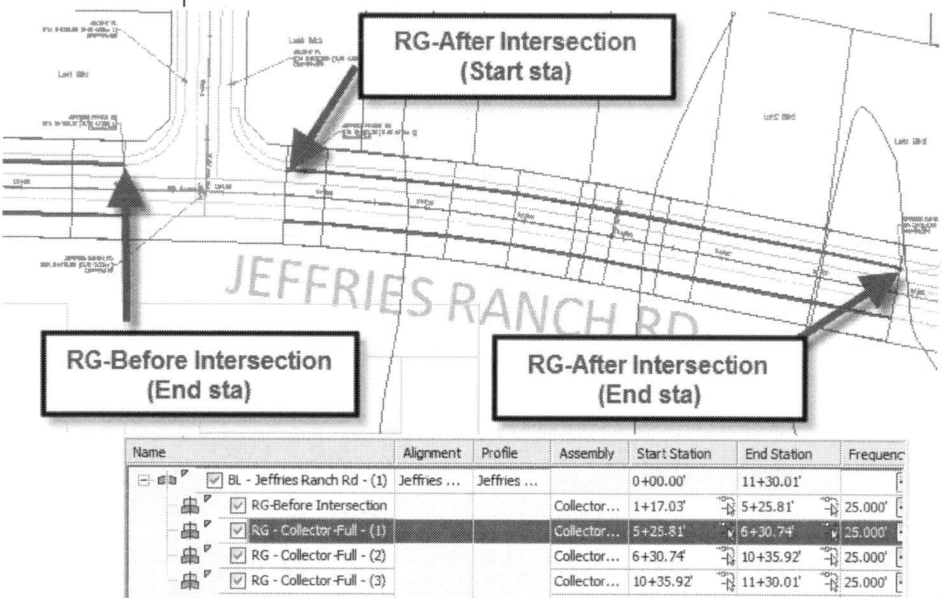

Figure 8–39

6. In the Baseline and Region Parameters dialog box, right-click on RG - Collector-Full - (1) and select **Remove Region**. Do the same for RG - Collector-Full - (3).
7. Click **OK** to apply the changes and close the dialog box. If prompted, rebuild the corridor.
8. Save the drawing.

Task 2 - Create a corridor.

In this task, you will use the assemblies to create a corridor, applying the **Residential-Full** subassembly from station to station.The steps to accomplish this are similar to those in Task 1. If you have time, you can complete this task, otherwise skip this task and open the backup drawing when instructed to do so in the next practice.

1. Continue working with the drawing from the previous task or open **COR1-C2-Corridor.dwg**.
2. In the *Home* tab>Create Design panel, click (Corridor).
3. Name it **Ascent PI**, then enter the following, as shown in Figure 8–40:
   - For the alignment, select **Ascent PI** from the list
   - For the profile, select **Ascent PI-DGN1** from the list
   - For the subassembly, select **Residential-Full**
   - Verify that the **Set baseline and region parameters** option is selected.

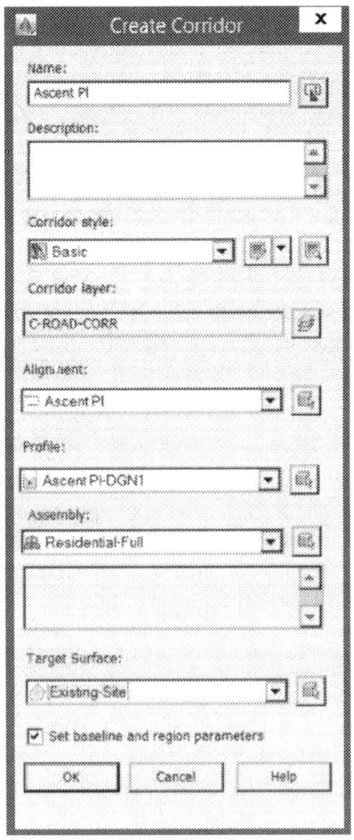

Figure 8–40

4. Click **OK**. The baseline and region parameters dialog box should open.

   The dialog box identifies the Baseline (BL) as *BL-Ascent Pl*. This baseline currently has one Region, which is assigned the **Residential - Full Assembly**. Rename the region as **RG – Start**. Adjust the *Start Station* for **RG-Start** to **54.13'** and the *End Station* to **265.48'**, as shown in Figure 8–41.

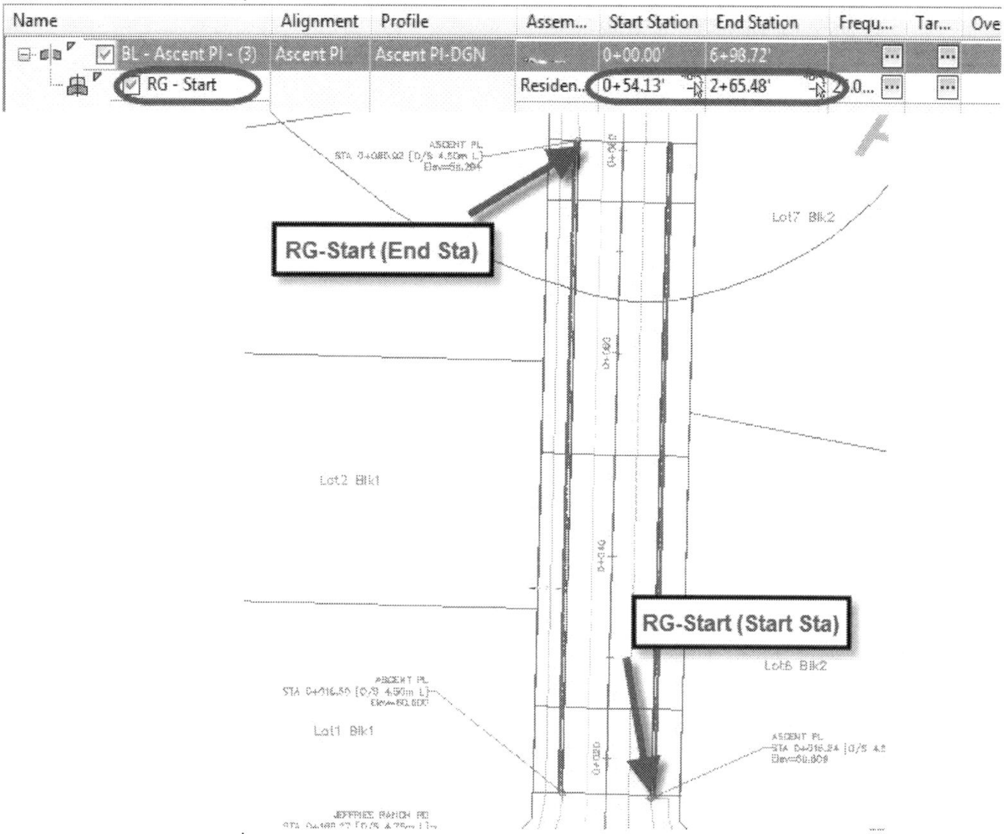

Figure 8–41

5. Click **OK** to create the corridor. If prompted, rebuild the corridor.

6. Save the drawing.

Practice 8d Working with Corridors Part II

Estimated time for completion: 25 minutes

Practice Objective

- Create an intersection object to represent how two roads should meet.

Task 1 - Create an intersection.

In this task, you will create an intersection at Jeffries Ranch Rd and Ascent Pl. This intersection will fill in the gap you left in the Jeffries Ranch Rd corridor by setting regions.

1. Open **COR1-D1-Corridor.dwg** from the *C:\Civil 3D Projects\Civil3D-Training\Corridors* folder.
2. In the *View* tab>Views panel, select the preset view **Corr-Inter**.
3. In the *Home* tab>Create Design panel, click  (Create Intersection).
4. The AutoCAD Civil 3D software sets an **Intersection** object snap and prompts you to *Select Intersection Point*.
5. Select the intersection of the Jeffries Ranch Rd and Ascent Pl alignments, as shown in Figure 8–42.

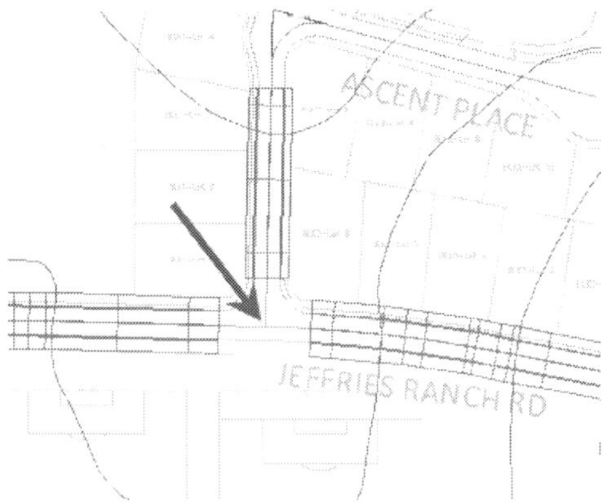

Figure 8–42

Note: If you are having problems selecting the intersection point, press <Esc> to exit the **Intersection** command. In Model Space, select the two alignments **Jeffries Ranch Rd** and **Ascent Pl**, right-click, expand Display order and select **Bring to front**. Then create the intersection.

If this were a four-way intersection, you would be prompted to select the Primary road. In this case, the AutoCAD Civil 3D software assumes that Jeffries Ranch Rd is the primary road.

6. Position the Create Intersection wizard so that the intersection is also displayed in the drawing. In the *General* page, type **Intersection–(Jeffries Ranch & Ascent Pl)** as the *Intersection Name*, and accept the *Intersection Marker Style* and *Intersection Label Style* defaults. Verify that the *Intersection Corridor Type* is **Primary Road Crown Maintained**, as shown in Figure 8–43. Click **Next>**.

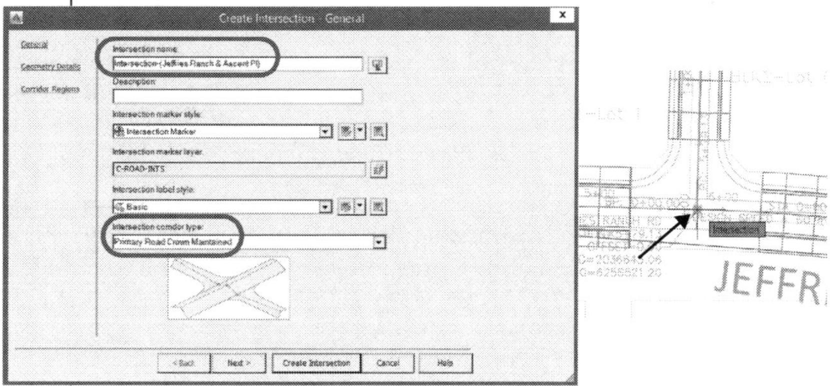

Figure 8–43

7. In the *Geometry Details* page, the alignments, intersection stations, and profiles to be used are listed. The profile can be changed here if required. In the *Offset and curb returns* area, select the **Create or specify offset alignments** option and click **Offset Parameters**, as shown in Figure 8–44.

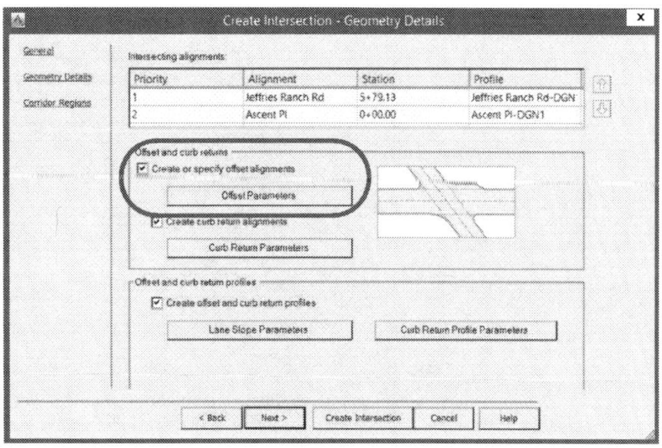

Figure 8–44

In the Intersection Offset Parameters dialog box, note that selecting the **Primary Road** or **Secondary Road** highlights the respective alignment in the drawing.

8. For this project, set the offset parameters for the Primary Road, Jeffries Ranch Rd to **15.5'** for the right and left sides, if not already set. For the Secondary Road, Ascent Pl, set the offset parameters to **14.75'** for the right and left sides. Because this is a simple intersection, you do not need to add additional offsets. Review and click **OK**.

9. In the *Geometry Details* page, select the **Create curb return alignments** option and click **Curb Return Parameters**.

10. In the Intersection Curb Return Parameters dialog box, note the preview for the **NE-Quadrant** in the drawing. Set the *Curb Return Radius* to **38.55'**, as shown in Figure 8–45, and accept the remaining default values. Note the preview as you make the edits.

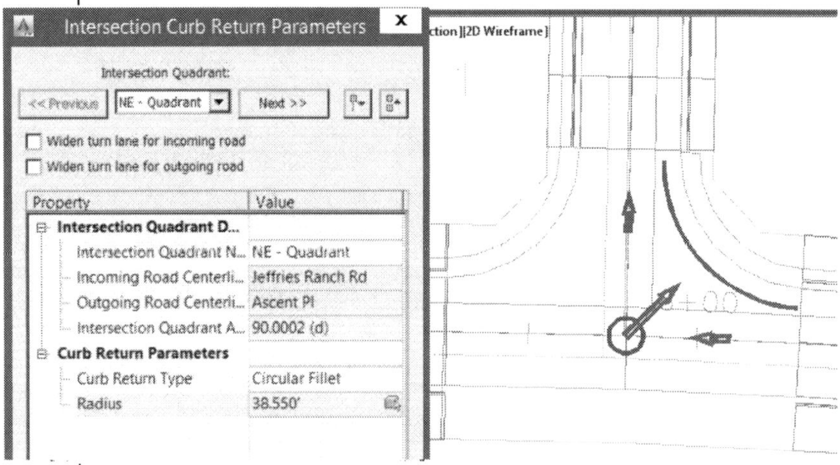

Figure 8–45

11. Click **Next>>** at the top of the dialog box to switch to the **NW-Quadrant**. Note the change in the drawing. Set the *Curb Return Radius* to **38.55'**, as shown in Figure 8–46,and accept the remaining default values. Click **OK** to return to the *Geometry Details* page.

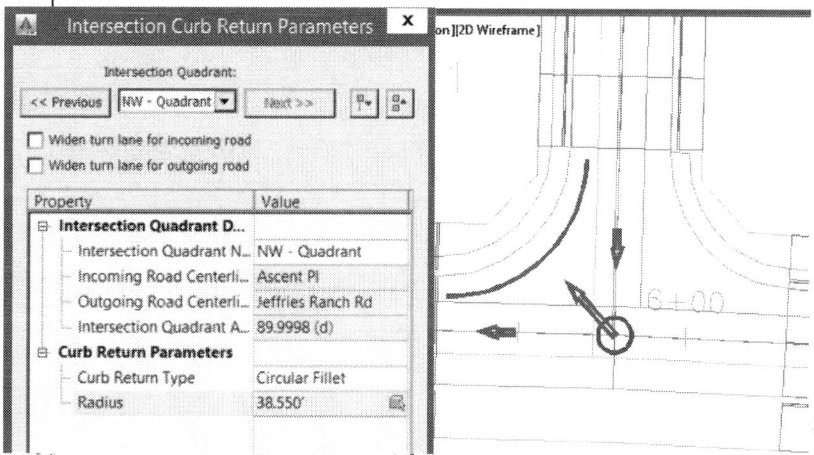

Figure 8–46

12. To automatically create curb return profiles, in the *Offset and curb return profiles* area, select the **Create offset and curb return profiles** option as shown in Figure 8–47. Accept the defaults for the **Lane Slope** and **Curb Return Profile** parameters and click **Next>**.

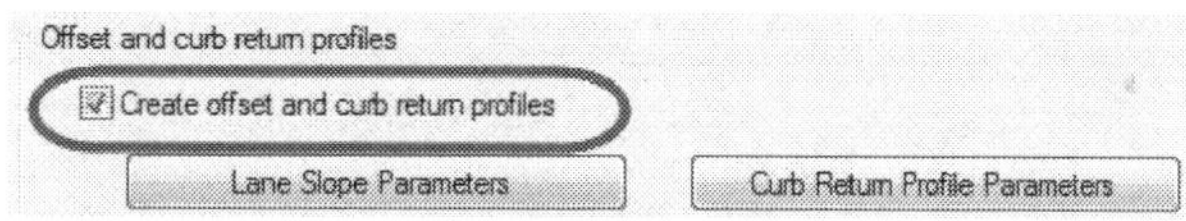

Figure 8–47

13. In the *Corridor Regions* page, you can create a new corridor or add this intersection to an existing corridor. Select the **Create corridors in the intersection area** option and select the **Create a new corridor** option, as shown in Figure 8–48.

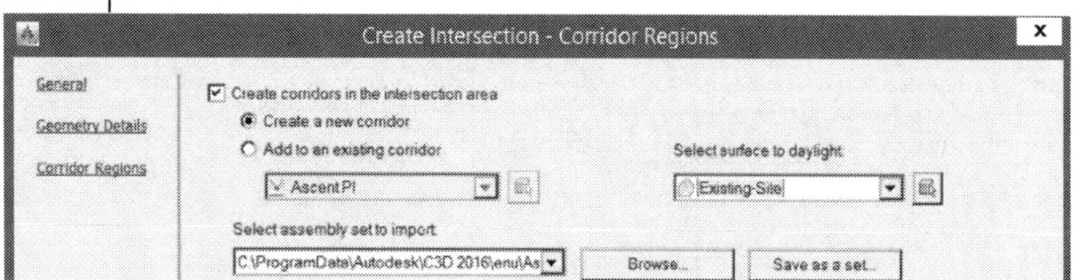

Figure 8–48

14. For the Curb Return Fillets, click on [...] and select the **Residential – Curb Return** assembly, as shown in Figure 8–49. Click **OK**.

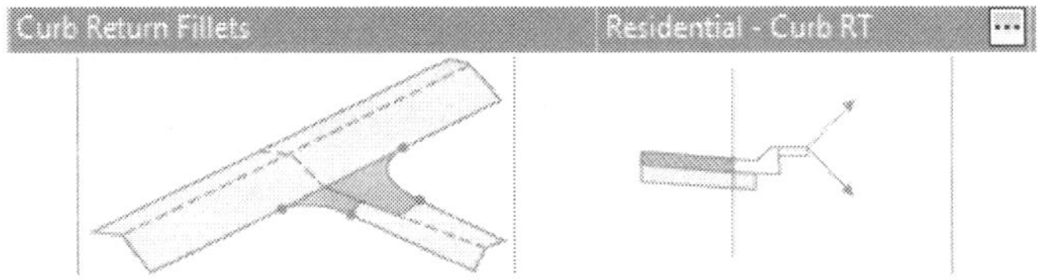

Figure 8–49

15. For the Primary Road Full Section, select the **Collector - Full** assembly, as shown in Figure 8–50.

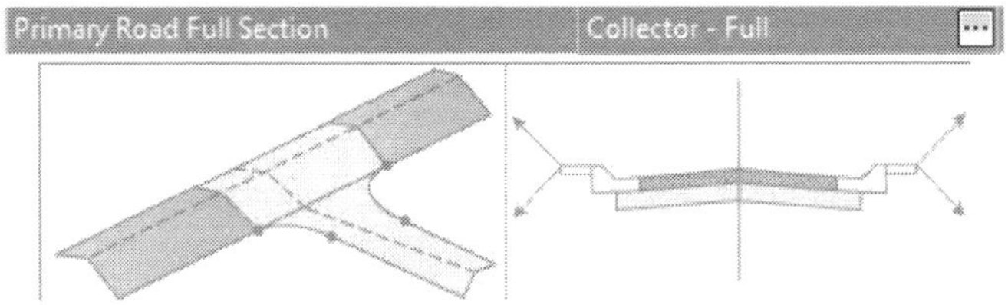

Figure 8–50

16. For the Primary Road Part Section – Daylight Left, accept the default value as shown in Figure 8–51, as this is not applicable to your intersection.

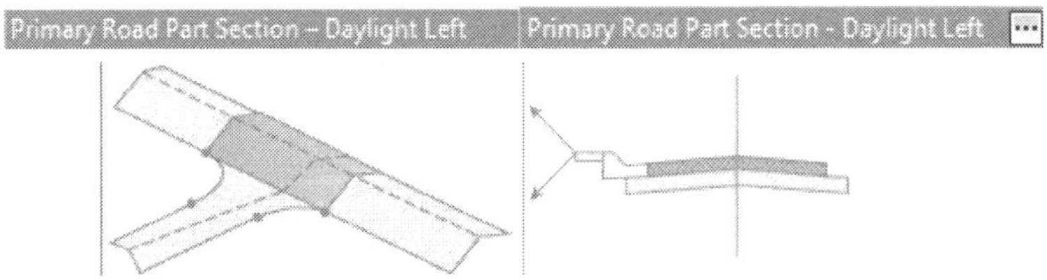

Figure 8–51

17. For the Primary Road Part Section – Daylight Right, select the **Collector – Part Curb RT** assembly, as shown in Figure 8–52.

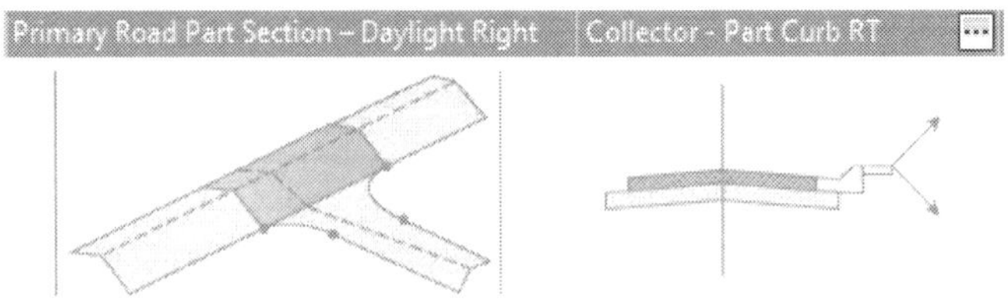

Figure 8–52

18. For the Secondary Road Full Section, select the **Residential – Full** assembly, as shown in Figure 8–53.

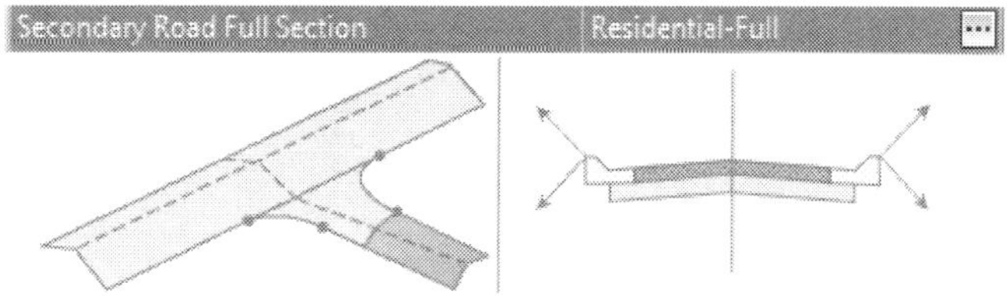

Figure 8–53

19. For the Secondary Road Half Section – Daylight Left, select the **Residential - Half Curb LT** assembly, as shown in Figure 8–54.

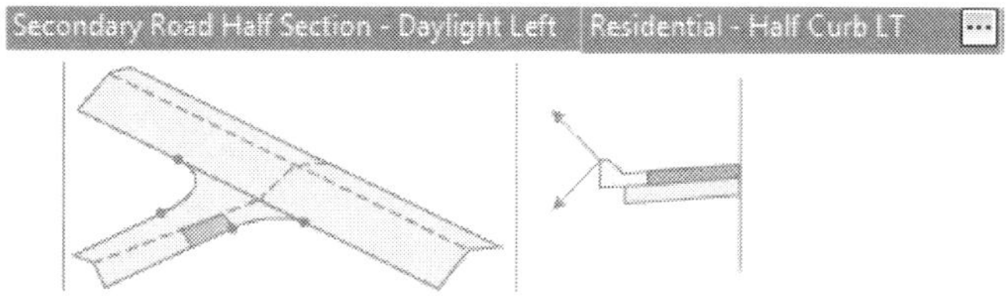

Figure 8–54

20. For the Secondary Road Half Section – Daylight Right, select the **Residential - Half Curb RT** assembly, as shown in Figure 8–55.

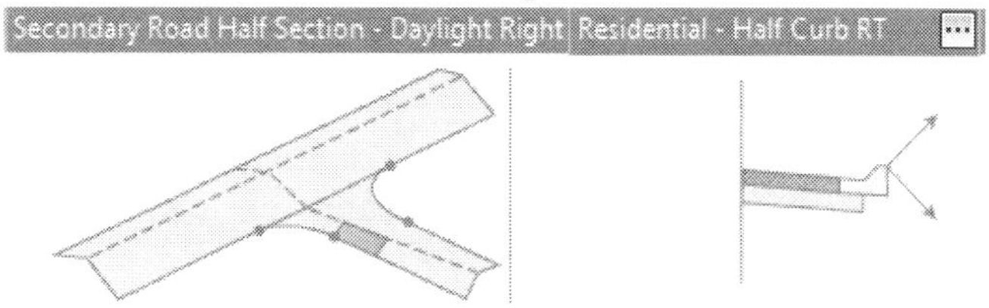

Figure 8–55

21. When finished, click **Create Intersection**. You might need to perform a **REGEN** to display the newly created Intersection Corridor.

22. In the Events Viewer, expand Action, and select **Clear All Events**, as shown in Figure 8–56. Click the **X** to close the Events Viewer.

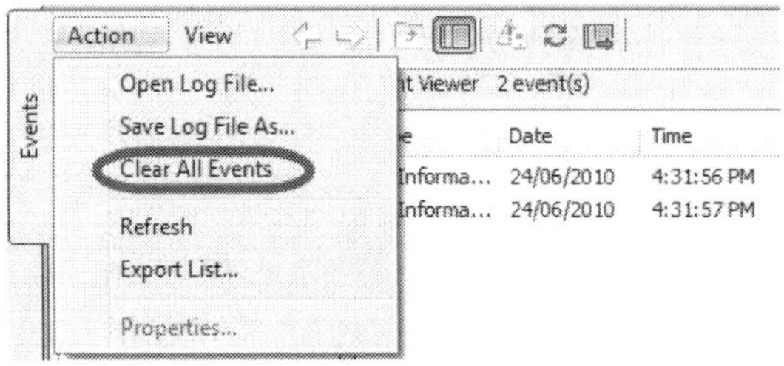

Figure 8–56

23. Save the drawing.

Practice 8e

Working with Corridors Part III

Estimated time for completion: 10 minutes

Practice Objective

- Create a finished ground surface from the design corridor.

Task 1 - Create corridor surfaces.

1. Continue working with the drawing from the previous practice or open **COR1-E1-Corridor.dwg**.
2. In the AutoCAD Model Space window, select the **Ascent Pl corridor** and click (Corridor Properties) on the contextual *Corridor* tab > Modify Corridor panel.
3. In the *Surfaces* tab, do the following, as shown in Figure 8–57.
   - Click (Create a Corridor Surface).
   - The surface displays in the dialog box with the default name **Ascent PL Surface - (1)**. Rename the surface to **Road 1** by clicking on the surface name.
   - The default surface style **Contours 2' and 10' (Design)** works well for this task, so leave it as the active surface style.
   - In the *Add Data* area, verify that the *Data type* is set to **Links** and the *code* is set to **Top**. Click (Add Surface Item)

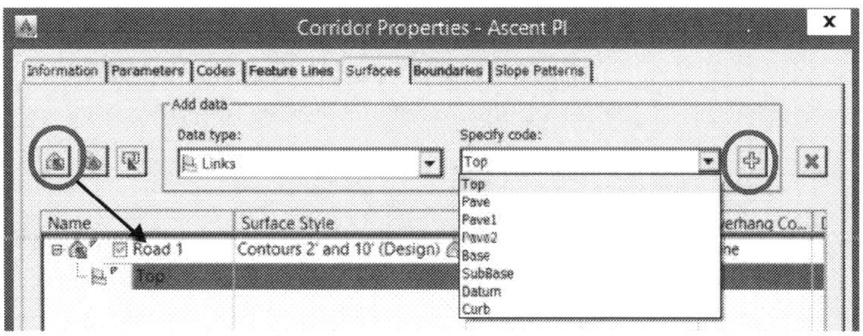

Figure 8–57

4. Select the *Boundaries* tab. Right-click on the corridor surface name and select **Corridor extents as outer boundary**, as shown in Figure 8–58.

This automatically adds a boundary that follows the corridor extents (in most cases, the daylight lines) on both sides.

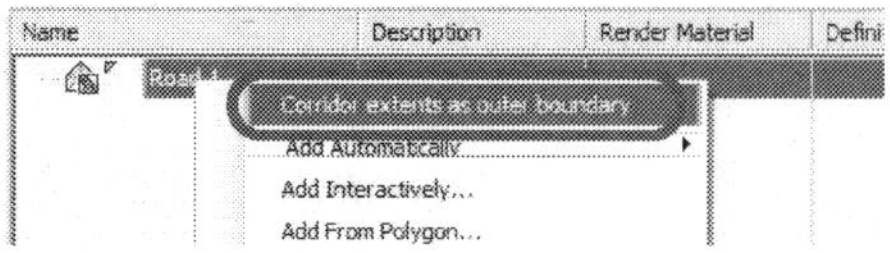

Figure 8–58

5. Click **OK** to close the Corridor Properties dialog box. If prompted, select **Rebuild the Corridor**. The corridor surface has been created and is displayed using contours.

Chapter 9

Sections and Section Views

This chapter includes instructional content to assist in your preparation for the following topic and objective for the AutoCAD® Civil® 3D 2016 Certified Professional exam.

Autodesk Certification Exam Objectives in this Chapter

Exam Topic	Exam Objective	Section
Sections and Section Views	• Create and analyze sections and section views	• 9.1

9.1 Create and Analyze Sections and Section Views

Corridor Sections

Creating complex corridors can be greatly simplified using (Corridor Section Editor). It is accessed through the shortcut menu or contextual ribbon after selecting a corridor, as shown in Figure 9–1.

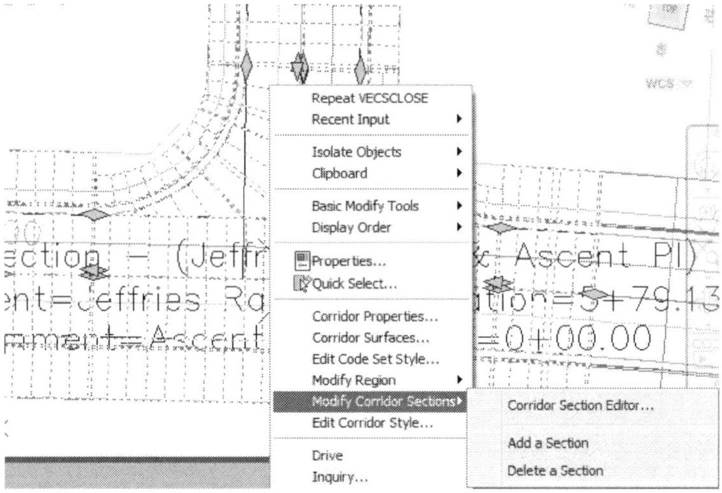

Figure 9–1

This command launches the *Section Editor* contextual tab, which enables you to review and edit sections interactively using the appropriate panels. The **Parameter Editor**, as shown in Figure 9–2, enables you to review and change most subassembly parameters.

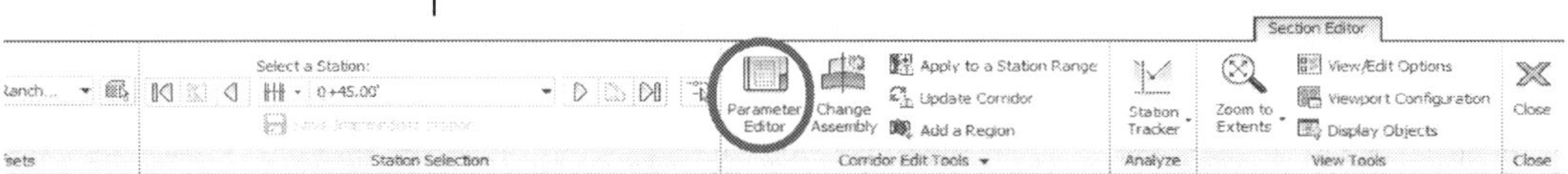

Figure 9–2

The editor enables you to modify those sections that need special attention, such as different daylight slopes. The editor also enables you to add and remove some subassemblies or links directly to and from a section. These parameter changes, additions, and deletions can be done for a single section or for a range of sections. An example is shown in Figure 9–3.

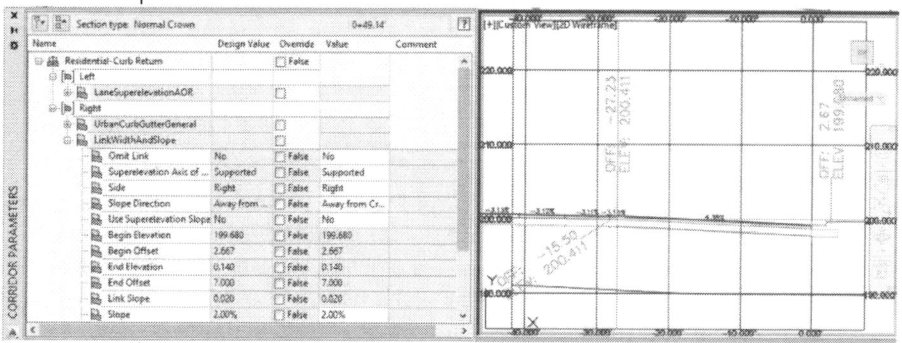

Figure 9–3

To more easily display the modifications in the corridor section, you can work in three different zoom modes in the **View/Edit Corridor Section** command:

- **Zoom To Extents:** Ensures that the full assembly is in view when you navigate to another station after zooming in.
- **Zoom to a Subassembly:** Ensures that a selected subassembly remains at the center of the view when you navigate to another station. The zoom level is also maintained.
- **Zoom to an Offset and Elevation:** Ensures that the current zoom level is maintained when you navigate to another station after a zoom.
- Before launching the **Corridor Section Editor** command, you can set up multiple viewports using (Edit Viewport Configuration) for viewing the plan, profile, and section during the **Section Edit** command. Then, while in the **Corridor Section Editor** command, a Station Tracker indicates the current section (with a vertical line), in both the plan view and any associated profile views.

Analyze Sections

Two types of quantity takeoffs can be calculated based on sections: earthwork volumes and material volumes. Earthwork volumes represent the amount of cut (existing material above the vertical design) or fill (the vertical design above the existing material). Material volumes are the amount of materials needed to build the road. Materials include asphalt pavement, concrete curbing, sub-base materials, and other materials.

Earthwork Volumes

Earthwork volumes represent an amount of displaced surface materials. The displacement represents the excavation of high areas or filling of low areas in the existing ground surface, relative to the vertical road design.

One goal road designers strive for is to balance the amount of excavated material (called cut) and the amount of material to be added (called fill). On any site, not all of the excavated material (cut) is reusable. For example, the spoil materials could be from a bog, a type of material that does not compact well, or rock debris. The reuse of cut material can be a percentage of the overall cut value and affects the overall earthwork calculation. An example is shown in Figure 9–4.

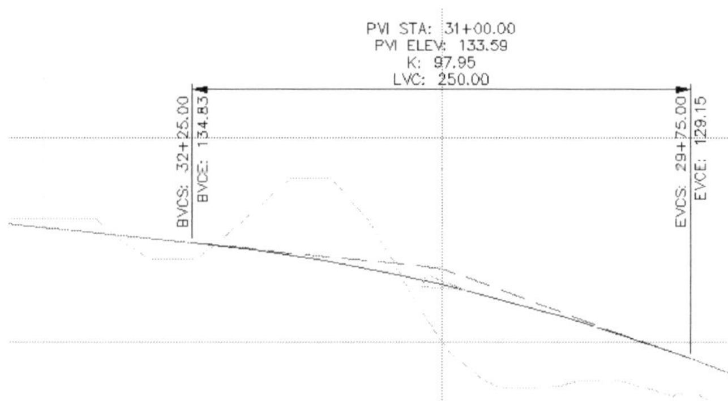

Figure 9–4

The earthworks calculations are applied between the existing ground surface and the datum surface of an assembly. The datum surface represents the roadbed on which the sub-base gravel, asphalt, and concrete materials lie. Earthwork volumes affect the revisions that occur to a roadway design. For example, excessive cut material (material needing excavation) could lead to raising the vertical design or, if possible, moving the horizontal alignment to create less cut.

Mass Haul

A mass haul diagram can be generated and used as a visual representation of the cumulative cut and fill material volumes along a corridor. Contractors use mass haul diagrams as a primary tool in determining and balancing haulage costs when bidding on an earthwork job. Mass haul is the volume of excavated material multiplied by the distance it is required to be moved. When the mass haul line is above the balance line, it indicates how much cut there is going to be at that station. When the mass haul line is below the balance line, it indicates the volume to be filled. To generate a mass haul diagram, you need an alignment, a sample line group, and a materials list. The mass haul diagram calculates and displays the following:

- The distance over which cut and fill volumes balance.
- Free haul and overhaul volumes.
- Volumes offset by borrow pits and dump sites.

Construction costs can be reduced by enabling the designer to compare alternative designs, add dump sites, and borrow pits at key locations in the free haul distance, thus eliminating a portion of the overhaul volume. An example of a mass haul diagram is shown in Figure 9–5.

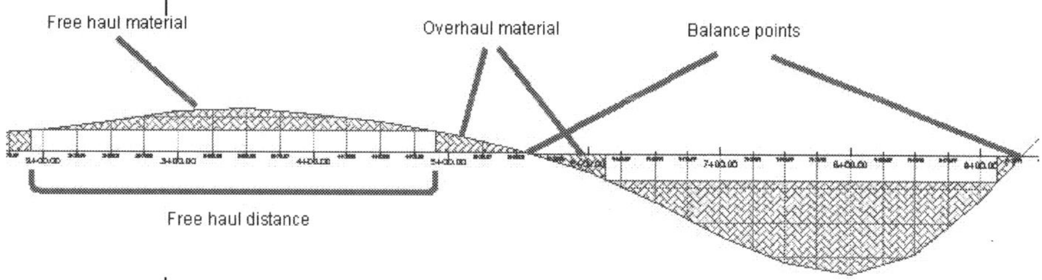

Figure 9–5

Material Volumes

Subassembly shapes represent the materials available for quantity takeoffs. These quantities come from the subassembly shapes (e.g., curb, pave, shoulder, sidewalk, etc.).

Quantity Takeoff Criteria

The Quantity Takeoff Criteria defines the surfaces and materials to be analyzed. Takeoff criteria can identify two surfaces for earthwork calculations and/or a list of shapes for material volumes.

The criteria style entries are generic because they are intended to be used on multiple corridors, which might contain different subassembly components. When computing section calculations, you are prompted to identify which entries correspond to the corridor shapes. The Quantity Takeoff Criteria dialog box is shown in Figure 9–6.

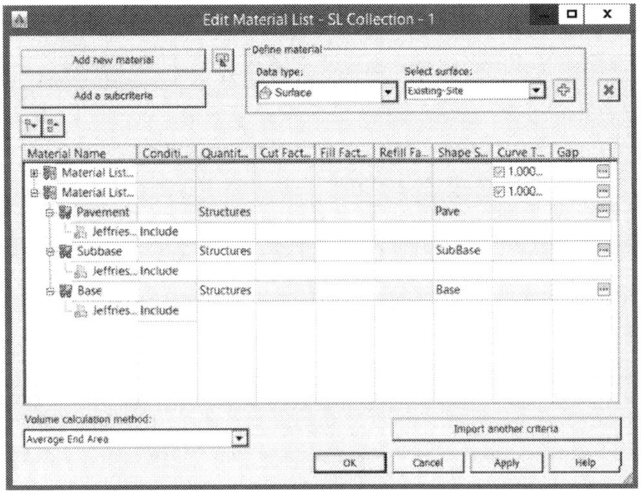

Figure 9–6

Define Materials

After defining the volume criteria, you create data from the criteria settings. In the *Analyze* tab>Volumes and Materials panel, click (Compute Materials) to set the alignment and a sample line group to use for data extraction. The command is shown in Figure 9–7.

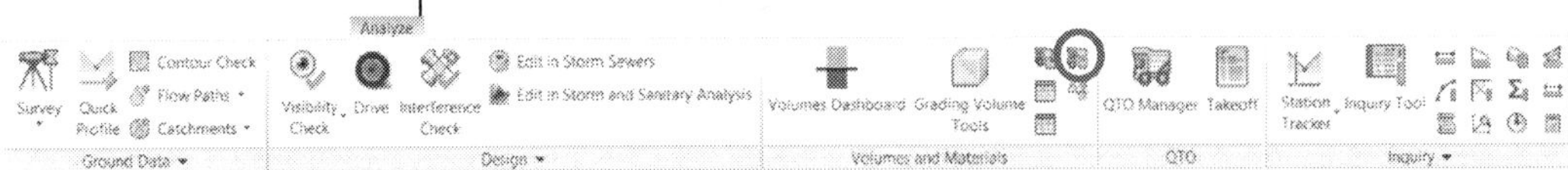

Figure 9–7

When the Edit Material List dialog box opens, you can associate surfaces and/or structures (subassembly shapes) to the appropriate entries. Click **OK** to exit. The AutoCAD Civil 3D software then calculates the required report data.

Section Views

A section view can display sampled surface sections, corridor assemblies, and any pipes or structures. Similar to profiles, sections use a section view to annotate their elevations and center line offsets. Styles affect the look of a section view.

Section views can annotate an assembly's offsets, elevations, and grades. The All Codes style assigned to the assembly in the sample line group makes all of the points and links available for labeling. The Section Label styles do not interact with the assembly, only with the corridor surfaces.

- As with Profile views, Section views can be moved and retain the correct information.
- Section views can be created individually or in groups.

Section View Wizard

In the *Home* tab, the Profile & Section Views panel enables you to create a single section view, multiple sections organized into columns and rows, and project objects to a section view. The **Single** and **Multiple View** commands open the Section View wizard, which guides you through the process of creating Section views. There are six tasks in the Section View wizard, as shown in Figure 9–8.

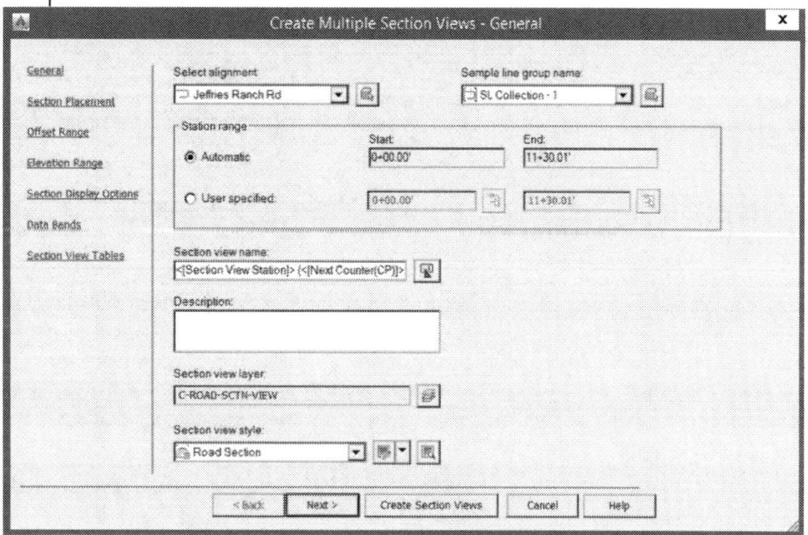

Figure 9–8

- **General:** Specifies basic information about the Section view, including which alignment to use, the sample group and line, and the view template. If creating multiple views, the Group Plot Style method specifies how to create multiple section views (**All** or **Page**). You can define page styles that define sheet sizes and plottable areas (sheet size minus margins and border).

- **Section Placement:** Only displays when you are creating multiple views. It enables you to set the Group Plot Style to use for setting the row and column settings for placing multiple section views.
- **Offset Range:** Enables you to set the width of the view.
- **Elevation Range:** Enables you to set the height of the view.
- **Section Display Options:** Enables you to select what gets drawn in the view and the section style.
- **Data Bands:** Enables you to specify one or more band set styles for the sections and their positions in the view.
- **Section View Tables:** Enables you to add and modify volume tables calculated using the Section view (a material list must be created from the sample line group for this option to be available).

Section View Styles

A Section view style defines the vertical and horizontal grid and its annotation. The horizontal lines represent the elevations and the vertical lines represent the center line offset.

Section View Band Styles

A band style defines the offset and elevation annotation at the bottom of a Section view. The style affects the annotation's format and the information that displays in the band. Using the band styles provided in the sample templates, set your existing ground surface as **Surface 1**, and the proposed surface (such as a Corridor Top surface) as **Surface 2**.

Section Styles and Section Label Styles

A section style assigns a layer and other layer properties to a surface section. The section label styles annotate grade breaks, slopes, and offsets.

Multi-Purpose Styles

In Multi-Purpose styles, the All Codes style assigns object and label styles for corridor assemblies. This is the most important style for section labeling.

The All Codes style defines object styles for points, links, or shapes. It specifies which labels display in a Section view.

- All link styles annotate a grade or slope.
- All point styles annotate an offset and elevation.

Page Styles

A page style defines the plottable area of a sheet size. The plottable area is what remains after removing the non-printing margins and border from the sheet size. The page style also defines a sheet grid. The Plot Group styles use the grid to space sections on a sheet.

Practice 9a Quantity Take Off Part I

Estimated time for completion: 20 minutes

Practice Objective

- List the various types of projects that are going to use alignments and profiles in their designs.

Task 1 - Generate Earthworks Quantities.

In this task you will compute the site cut and fill required to create the datum surface below the corridor. You will then calculate the construction materials that will be placed above the datum (asphalt, gravel, etc.).

1. Open **QTO1-B1-Sections.dwg** from the *C:\Civil 3D Projects\Civil3D-Training\QTO-Sections* folder.

2. In the *Analyze* tab>Volumes and Materials panel, click  (Compute Materials), as shown in Figure 9–9.

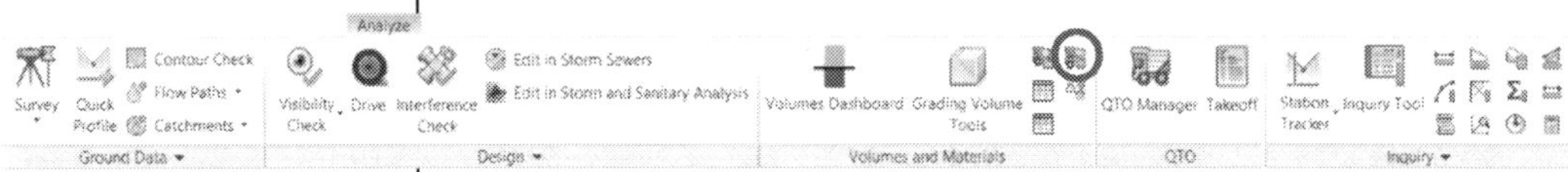

Figure 9–9

3. In the Select Sample Line Group dialog box, accept the default alignment **Jeffries Rand Rd** and sample line group **SL Collection - 1**, as shown in Figure 9–10. Click **OK**.

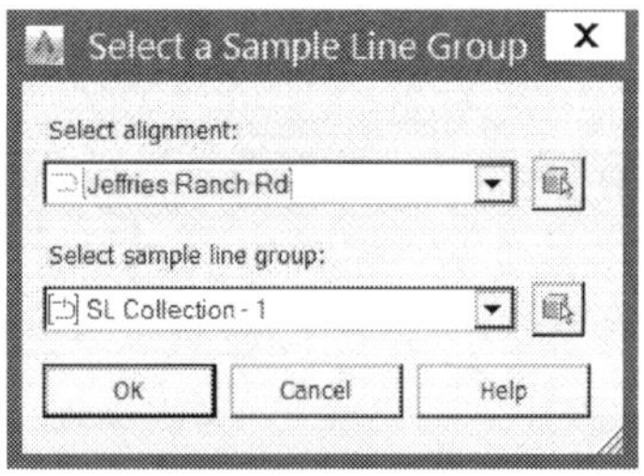

Figure 9–10

4. In the Compute Materials dialog box, select **Existing-Site** for the *EG* and **Finish Ground** for the *DATUM*, as shown in Figure 9–11. Click **OK** when done.

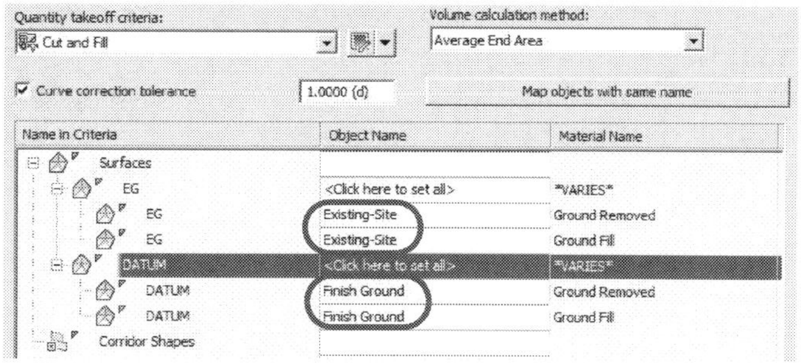

Figure 9–11

5. Generate a volume report. In the *Analyze* tab>Volumes and Materials panel, click  (Volume Report).

6. In the Report Quantities dialog box, ensure that you select the correct XSL file. Click  next to the *Select a style sheet* field, as shown on the left in Figure 9–12. Browse to and select **earthwork.xsl**, as shown on the right, and open it. Click **OK** to close the Report Quantities dialog box.

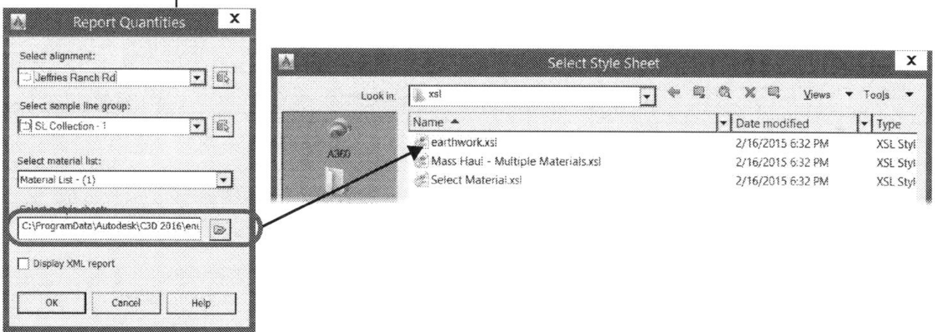

Figure 9–12

7. Internet Explorer will open when the HTML format report is created. Depending on your Internet Explorer security settings, you might be prompted to permit the script to run. Click **Yes** if this prompt displays. Your report will display, as shown in Figure 9–13.

Volume Report

'roject: C:\Users\mrasmussen.RATC\appdata\local\temp\QTO1-B2-ections_1_1_2060.svS
.lignment: Jeffries Ranch Rd
ample Line Group: SL Collection - 1
tart Sta: 1+50.000
nd Sta: 10+00.000

Station	Cut Area (Sq.ft.)	Cut Volume (Cu.yd.)	Reusable Volume (Cu.yd.)	Fill Area (Sq.ft.)	Fill Volume (Cu.yd.)	Cum. Cut Vol. (Cu.yd.)	Cum. Reusable Vol. (Cu.yd.)	Cum. Fill Vol. (Cu.yd.)	Cum. Net Vol. (Cu.yd.)
1+50.000	49.90	0.00	0.00	31.27	0.00	0.00	0.00	0.00	0.00
2+00.000	119.48	156.83	156.83	16.14	43.89	156.83	156.83	43.89	112.94
2+50.000	1188.74	1125.38	1125.38	5.01	18.77	1282.22	1282.22	62.67	1219.55
3+00.000	1334.45	2336.28	2336.28	49.59	50.56	3618.50	3618.50	113.22	3505.28
3+50.000	1262.57	2404.64	2404.64	231.87	260.62	6023.14	6023.14	373.84	5649.30
4+00.000	749.74	1863.25	1863.25	541.58	716.16	7886.40	7886.40	1090.00	6796.40
4+50.000	0.00	694.21	694.21	701.47	1150.97	8580.60	8580.60	2240.96	6339.64
5+00.000	0.00	0.00	0.00	808.42	1398.05	8580.61	8580.61	3639.01	4941.59

Figure 9–13

8. Close the HTML report.

9. Create an AutoCAD table listing earthwork volumes. In the *Analyze* tab>Volumes and Materials panel, select **Total Volume Table**, as shown in Figure 9–14.

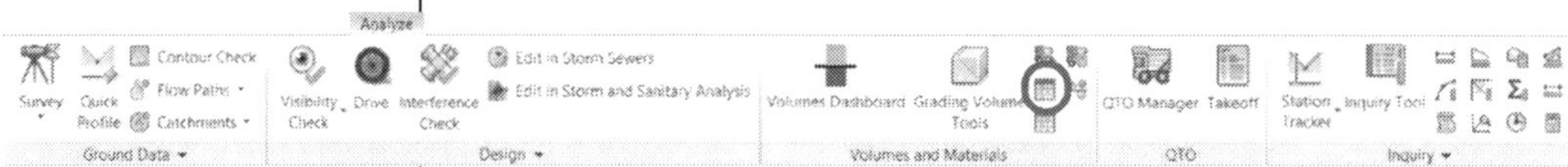

Figure 9–14

10. Accept the defaults in the Create Table dialog box, as shown in Figure 9–15, and click **OK**. When prompted, click in empty space to create the table.

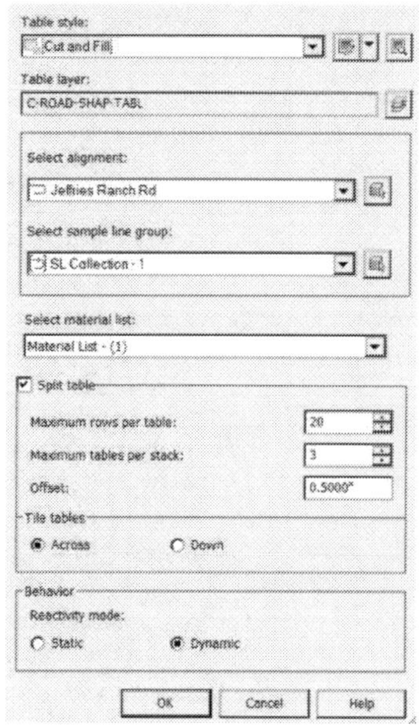

Figure 9–15

11. Select a point in Model Space to insert the table, as shown in Figure 9–16. Note that the top left of the table is the reference point.

Total Volume Table						
Station	Fill Area	Cut Area	Fill Volume	Cut Volume	Cumulative Fill Vol	Cumulative Cut Vol
1+50.00	31.27	49.90	0.00	0.00	0.00	0.00
2+00.00	18.14	119.48	43.89	156.83	43.89	156.83
2+50.00	5.01	1188.74	18.77	1125.38	62.67	1282.22
3+00.00	49.59	1334.45	50.56	2336.28	113.22	3618.50

Figure 9–16

12. Save the drawing.

Task 2 - Calculate Material Quantities.

Your assemblies include five defined shapes: Pave1 and Pave2 (the top two courses), Base, Sub-base, and Curb. The default Material List only includes one material for Pavement so you will need to adjust it. You will not calculate curb volume at this time.

1. Continue working with the drawing from the previous task or open **QTO1-B2-Sections.dwg**.
2. In the *Analyze* tab>Volumes and Materials panel, click (Compute Materials).
3. In the Select Sample Line Group dialog box, accept the default alignment **Jeffries Ranch Rd** and sample line group **SL Collection - 1**, and click **OK**.
4. In the Edit Material List dialog box, click the **Import another criteria** button.
5. In the Select a Quantity Takeoff Criteria, select **Material List** and click **OK**.
6. In the Compute Materials dialog box, for the Pavement Material, select **Jeffries Ranch Rd Pave1**, for the SubBase Material, select **Jeffries Ranch Rd SubBase** and for the Base Material, select **Jeffries Ranch Rd Base**, as shown in Figure 9–17. Click **OK**.

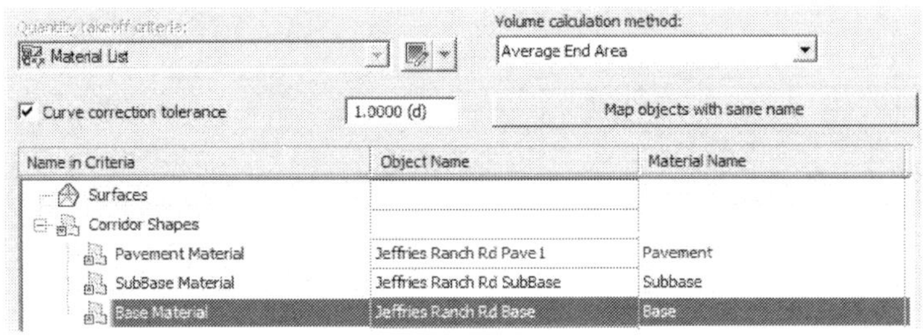

Figure 9–17

7. Click **OK** to close the dialog box and calculate the material.
8. Generate a volume report. In the *Analyze* tab>Volumes and Materials panel, select **Volume Report**.
9. In the Report Quantities dialog box, select **Material List - (2)** and ensure that you select the correct XSL file in the Select a style sheet drop-down list. Click next to the drop-down list. Browse to and select **Select Material.xsl** and open it. Click **OK** to close the Report Quantities dialog box.

10. Internet Explorer will open as the AutoCAD Civil 3D software creates an HTML format report. Depending on your Internet Explorer security settings, you might be prompted to permit the script to run. Click **Yes** if this prompt displays. The report will display with the volume of Pavement 1 from your corridor, as shown in Figure 9–18.

Material Report

Project: C:\Civil 3D Projects\Civil3D-Training\QTO-Sections\QTO1-C1-Sections.dwg

Alignment: Jeffries Ranch Rd
Sample Line Group: SL Collection - 1
Start Sta: 1+50.000
End Sta: 10+00.000

	Area Type	Area	Inc.Vol.	Cum.Vol.
		Sq.ft.	Cu.yd.	Cu.yd.
Station: 1+50.000				
	Pavement	2.57	0.00	0.00
	Subbase	37.79	0.00	0.00
	Base	10.32	0.00	0.00
Station: 2+00.000				
	Pavement	2.57	4.76	4.76
	Subbase	37.79	69.98	69.98
	Base	10.32	19.12	19.12

Figure 9–18

11. Close the HTML report.

The road design, specifically the corridor assembly, has a second shape called Pave 2. This is also Pavement, but might be based on a different composition than Pave 1. You can quantify this value as a separate amount, but for demonstration purposes, you will create a total volume for Pavement.

12. In the *Analyze* tab>Volumes and Materials panel, click (Compute Materials).

13. In the Select Sample Line Group dialog box, accept the defaults and click **OK**.

14. In the Edit Material List dialog box, do the following:

- Select **Pavement** in the *Name* column. Click (Delete).
- Click the **Add new material** button.
- Click on the new material name and rename it **Pavement**.
- In the *Quantity Type* column, select **Structures**.
- Select **Corridor Shape** in the Data type drop-down list.
- Select **Jeffries Ranch Rd Pave 12** in the Select corridor shape drop-down list, as shown in Figure 9–19. Click to add **Jeffries Ranch Rd Pave 1** to the *Pavement* collection. (Repeat these steps for Pave 2)

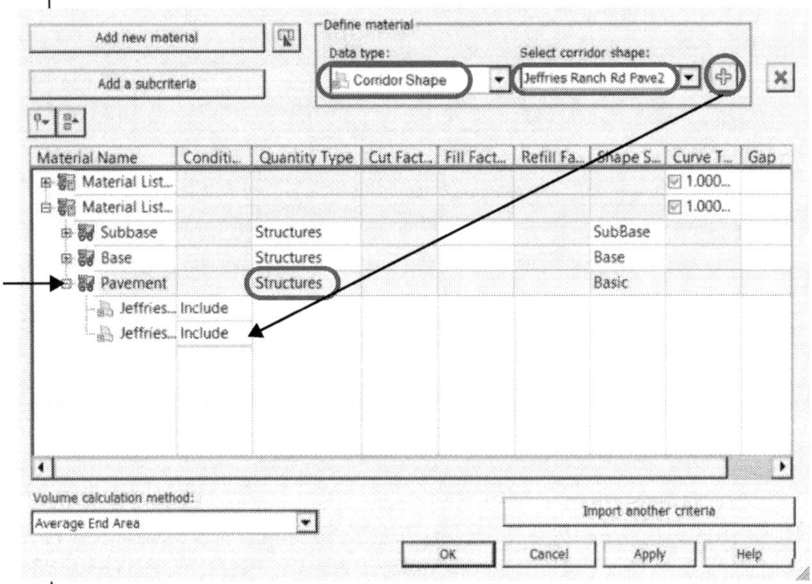

Figure 9–19

15. Click **OK** to apply the changes and close the dialog box.

16. As in Steps 8 to 10, generate a volume report. In the *Analyze* tab>Volumes and Materials panel, select **Volume Report**.

- In the Report Quantities dialog box, ensure that you select the correct XSL file in the Select a style sheet drop-down list. Click next to the drop-down list. Browse to and select **Select Material.xsl** and open it. Click **OK** to close the Report Quantities dialog box.

- Internet Explorer will open as the AutoCAD Civil 3D software creates an HTML format report. Depending on your Internet Explorer security settings, you might be prompted to permit the script to run. Click **Yes** if this prompt displays. Your report will display, as shown in Figure 9–20.

Material Report

Project: C:\Users\mrasmussen.RATC\appdata\local\temp\QTO1-C1-Sections_1_1_0567.svS
Alignment: Jeffries Ranch Rd
Sample Line Group: SL Collection - 1
Start Sta: 1+50.000
End Sta: 10+00.000

	Area Type	Area	Inc.Vol.	Cum.Vol.
		Sq.ft.	Cu.yd.	Cu.yd.
Station: 1+50.000				
	Pavement	5.15	0.00	0.00
	SubBase	37.79	0.00	0.00
	Base	10.32	0.00	0.00
Station: 2+00.000				
	Pavement	5.15	9.53	9.53
	SubBase	37.79	69.98	69.98
	Base	10.32	19.12	19.12

Figure 9–20

17. Save the drawing.

You can also create drawing tables displaying this information using the **Material Volume Table** command in the Volumes and Materials panel.

Practice 9b

Creating Sections Part II

Practice Objective

- Show what is happening with existing and proposed surface data at predefined intervals along an alignment using section views.

Estimated time for completion: 10 minutes

Task 1 - Create a single Section view.

1. Open **QTO1-D1-Sections.dwg** from the *C:\Civil 3D Projects\Civil3D-Training\QTO-Sections* folder.

2. In the *Home* tab>Profile & Section Views panel, expand Section Views and click  (Create Section View), as shown in Figure 9–21. The Create Section View wizard opens.

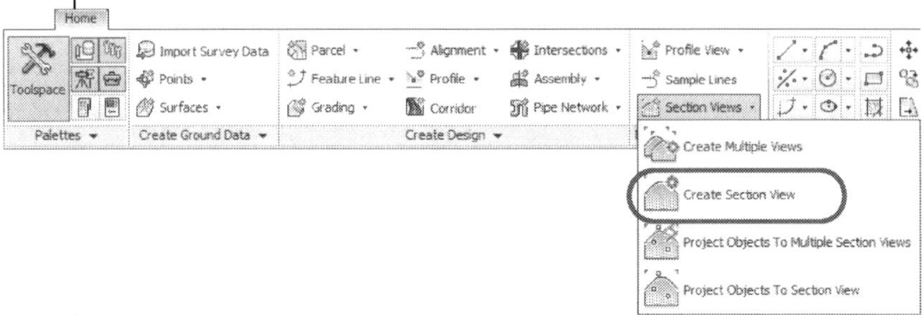

Figure 9–21

3. In the *General* page, in the *Sample Line* field, select **4+50.00** as shown in Figure 9–22. Set the *Section view style* to **Road Section** and click **Next>**.

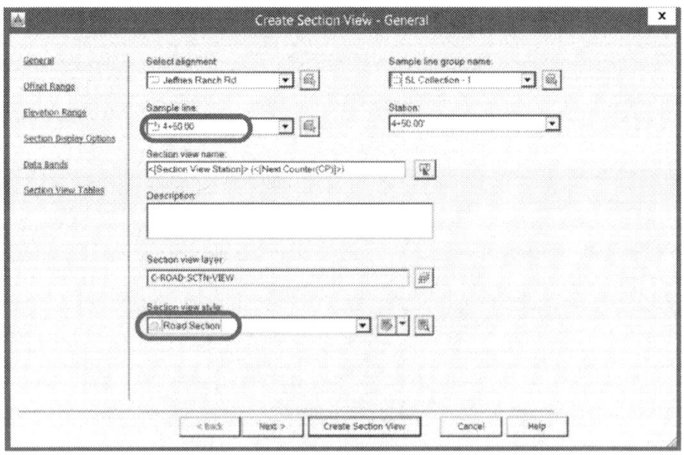

Figure 9–22

4. In the *Offset Range* and *Elevation Range* pages, accept the defaults and click **Next>**.

5. In the *Section Display Options* page, do the following:

   - Set the *Style* to **Existing Ground** for Existing-Site.
   - **View-Edit with Shading** for the *Jeffries Ranch Rd and Corridor - (1)* sections.
   - **Finished Ground** for the *Jeffries Ranch Rd and Corridor - (1) Surfaces*.
   - Assign the label options and styles to **_No Labels** for all, as shown in Figure 9–23 and click **Next>**.

Note that the quantity take offs only display if the material quantities are calculated before the section views are created.

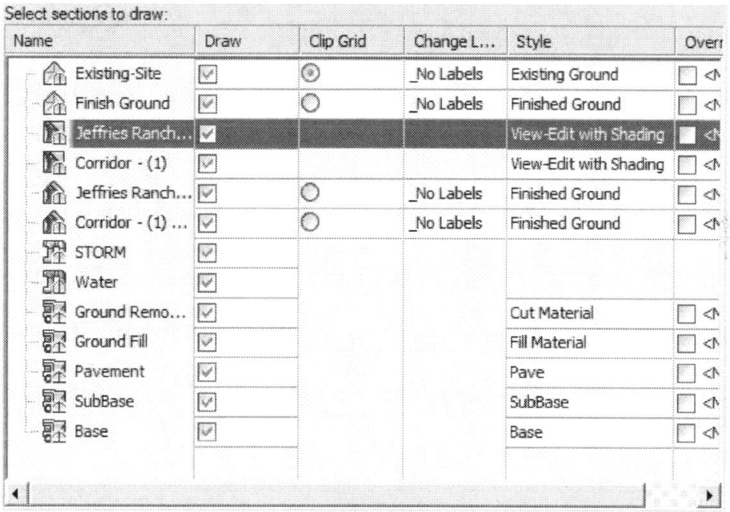

Figure 9–23

6. On the left, click the **Section View Tables** button to skip setting the Data Bands because **No_Labels** was selected in Step 5.

7. In the ***X Offset*** field, type **0.5** and click the **Add>>** button to add the Total Volume Table to the list. Then expand the Type drop-down list and select **Material**. Click **Add>>** again to include the material table in the section view, as shown in Figure 9–24.

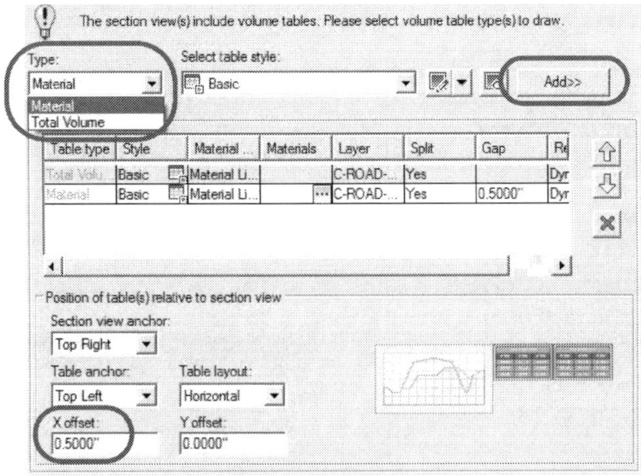

Figure 9–24

8. Click **Create Section View**. At the *Identify section view origin* prompt, click in empty space in Model Space, north of the surface to locate this section in the drawing.

9. Pan and zoom to display the section close-up. The labels are provided by the default AutoCAD Civil 3D template.

10. Adjust the section by dragging or deleting unwanted labels. (Hold <Ctrl> when selecting.) The drawing is shown in Figure 9–25.

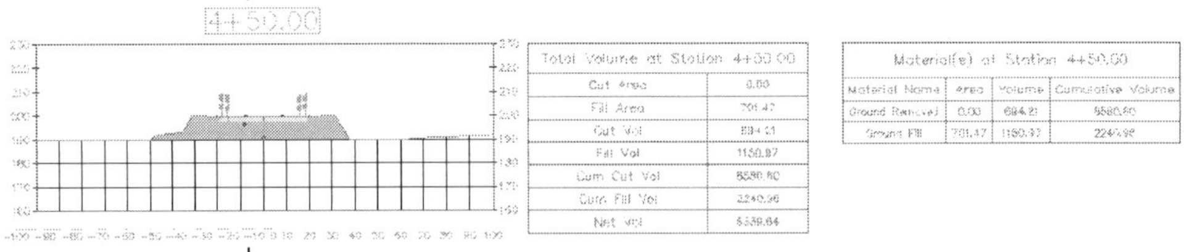

Figure 9–25

Task 2 - Create a Multiple Section view.

1. Continue working with the drawing from the previous task or open **QTO1-D2-Sections.dwg**.
2. In the *Home* tab>Profile & Section Views panel, expand Section Views and click  (Create Multiple Section Views).
3. In the Create Multiple Section Views dialog box, click **Create Section View**. Click in empty space in Model Space next to the previous single section view to insert all of the sections, as shown in Figure 9–26.

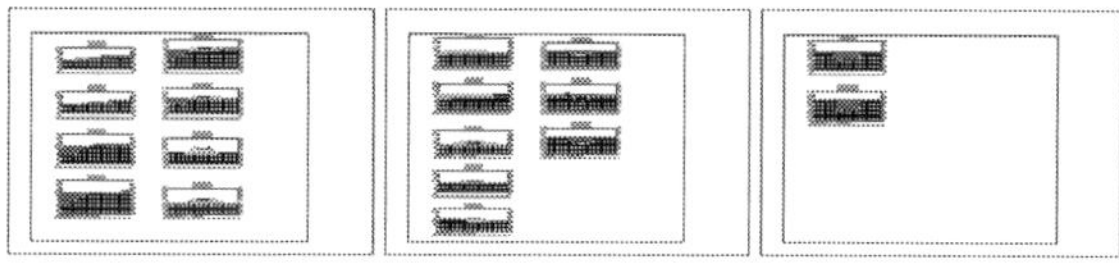

Figure 9–26

4. Save the drawing.

Pipe Networks

This chapter includes instructional content to assist in your preparation for the following topic and objective for the AutoCAD® Civil® 3D 2016 Certified Professional exam.

Autodesk Certification Exam Objectives in this Chapter

Exam Topic	Exam Objective	Section
Pipe Networks	• Design and create a pipe network	• 13.1

10.1 Design and Create a Pipe Network

Create Networks from Objects

In addition to creating networks by layout, a pipe network can be created from a 2D or 3D object, including a polyline or feature line. In the *Home* tab>Pipe Network panel, and click (Create Pipe Network from Object) to start the creation of a pipe network. Next you are prompted to select the object or type **X** and press <Enter> to select objects from an external reference file. Once selected, a flow arrow displays along the pipe network. The flow is set to the direction in which you drew the original entity but you can reverse the direction by selecting **Reverse**. To leave the flow directions set as is, press <Enter> or select **OK**. A Create Pipe Network dialog box opens enabling you to:

- Name the network
- Set the parts list
- Select the default pipe and structure to use
- Set the surface and alignment to reference
- You can also clean up the drawing as you create the network by selecting the **Erasing existing entity** option, as shown in Figure 10–1.

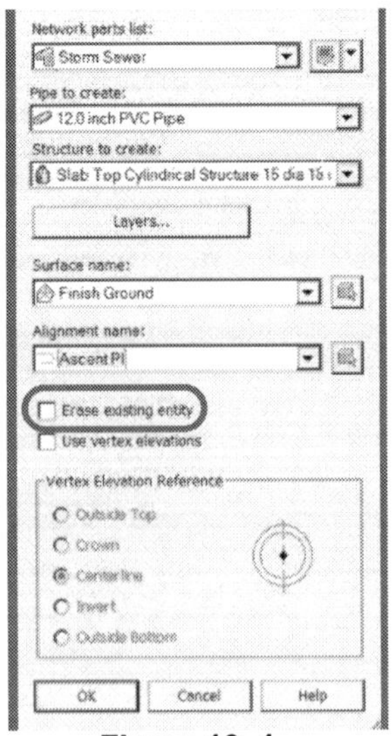

Figure 10–1

The Network Layout Toolbar

The Network Layout Tools toolbar contains commands for creating pipe networks by layout (interactively, similar to creating an alignment by layout) and for editing them after creation. This toolbar is opened by selecting *Home* tab>Pipe Network panel, and clicking (Pipe Network Creation Tools) or selecting *Modify* tab>Pipe Network panel, and clicking (Edit Pipe Network).

> **Hint: Editing Pipes**
>
> If you want to modify or add to a pipe network that you have already defined, use (Edit Network) instead of Pipe Network> (Create Pipe Network by Layout), as this creates a new network.

The toolbar commands are shown in Figure 10–2.

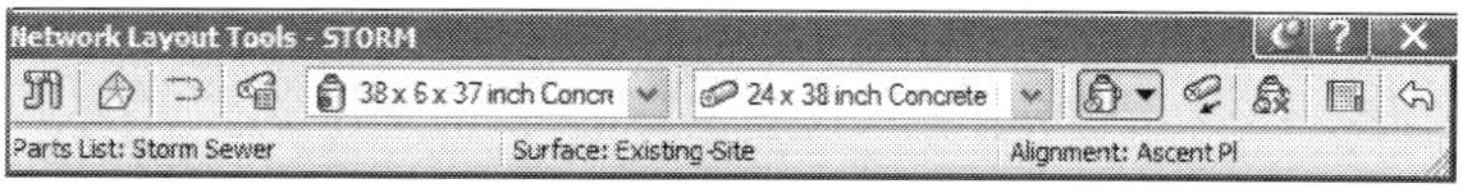

Figure 10–2

- **(Pipe Network Properties):** Enables you to review and edit the properties of a pipe network. These include the default labeling, layers, and default parts list to be used.
- **(Select Surface):** Enables you to select a surface model to calculate rim elevations and pipe invert elevations. This can be changed while laying out pipes and structures.
- **(Select Alignment):** Enables you to specify an alignment to lay out components by station and offset. The selected alignment can be changed while laying out pipes and structures.
- **(Parts List):** Enables you to change the current parts list, even in the middle of a layout.
- 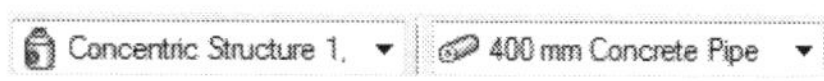

(Structure and Pipe drop-down lists): Enables you to select the next type of structure or pipe to add.

-  **(Create flyout):** Enables you to select whether you want to lay out pipes only, structures only, or both pipes and structures. When laying out pipes, you graphically select the location of the next structure (or pipe end point if laying out pipes only).

-  **(Toggle Upslope/Downslope):** Controls the direction of the next pipe to be laid out in gravity flow networks.

-  **(Delete Pipe Network Object):** Enables you to delete a pipe or structure from the network.

-  **(Pipe Network Vistas):** Opens a grid view where pipes and structures can be reviewed and have their properties edited. Here you can assign meaningful names to pipes and structures (such as **DMH-1**), which can be included in labels.

-  **(Undo):** Enables you to undo the last pipe network edit.

Connecting Pipes and Structures

When creating or editing networks with the Network Layout Tools toolbar, you can connect new pipes to previously created structures (in the same network) by hovering the cursor over that structure until the tool tip image displays, as shown in Figure 10–3. When displayed, click to connect the new pipe to the structure.

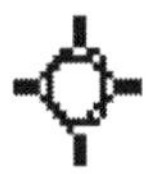

Figure 10–3

New pipes and structures can also be used to divide an existing pipe into two pipes. To do so, hover the cursor over the connection point until the tool tip image displays, as shown in Figure 10–4.

Figure 10–4

Pressure Pipe Networks

Pressure Pipe Networks are available for designing and laying out pressurized systems, such as water networks. There are three types of pressure pipe network objects: Pipes, Fittings, and Appurtenances.

Pressure Pipes can be created from existing objects (lines, arcs, 2D and 3D polylines, splines, feature lines, alignments, and survey figures) or created by layout.

Pressure Pipes

To start the Pressure Pipe Layout command, in the *Home* tab> Create Design panel, expand Pipe Networks and click

 (Pressure Network Creation Tools). This opens the Create Pressure Pipe Network dialog box, as shown in Figure 10–5. In it, you can type a name and description, set the parts list to use, and the surface and alignment to reference. You can also set label styles for pipes, fittings, and appurtenances so that they receive labels as you layout the pressure network.

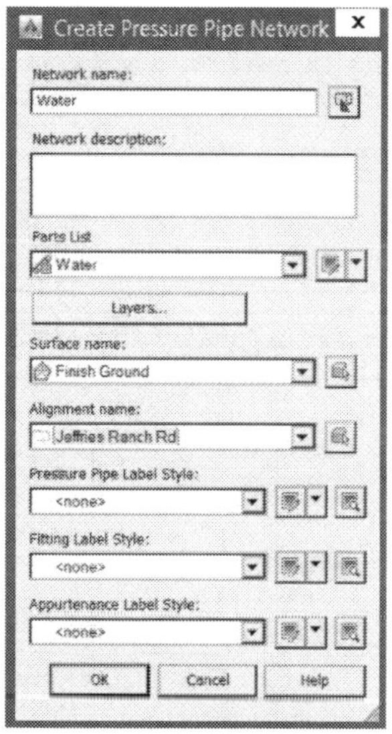

Figure 10–5

Once in the command, the *Pressure Network Plan Layout* contextual tab displays, as shown in Figure 10–6.

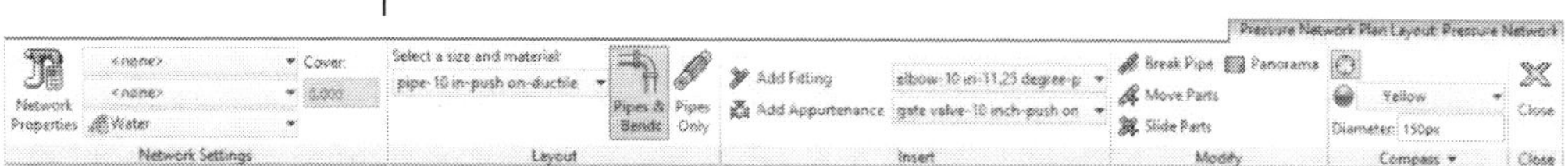

Figure 10–6

The reference surface and alignment that were set up during creation are displayed in the Network Settings panel along with the current parts list. The Cover setting is also found in the Network settings panel and specifies the minimum depth the network should be below the selected surface. Ideally, you would select a finished ground surface. In the Layout panel, you can select the pipe material to use. Pressure pipes can be laid out by themselves or with bends. When you lay a pipe out by itself using (Pipes Only), you can set the deflection angle with a compass glyph at pipe to pipe match locations (vertices), as shown on the left in Figure 10–7. Note that the ticks only permit a slight bend in the pipe when a fitting is not used. Using the (Pipes & Bends) in the *Layout* tab automatically places fittings with many more bend options in the compass glyph (up to 90 degree bends), as shown on the right in Figure 10–7.

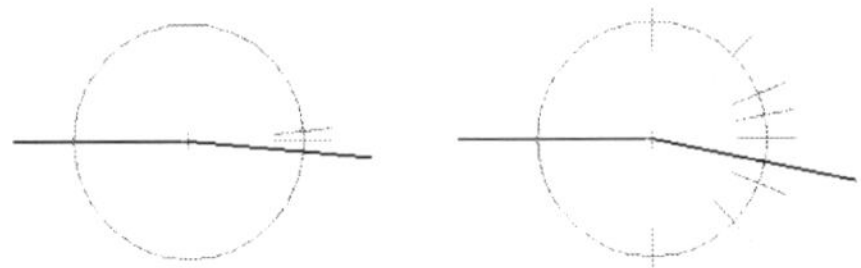

Figure 10–7

Fittings

Fittings enable you to specify the T's and other bends to layout a pressurized utility network. Additional fittings can be added to the AutoCAD Civil 3D software using the parts catalog. To add additional fittings to a network in the drawing click (Add Fitting) in the *Pressure Network Plan Layout* tab>Insert panel.

Appurtenances

Appurtenances are valves, which can be added in the same manner as fittings. Click (Add Appurtenance) in the *Pressure Network Plan Layout* tab>Insert panel.

Practice 10a Creating Pipe Networks by Objects

Estimated time for completion: 5 minutes

Practice Objective

- Create a pipe network from objects already in the drawing or external reference file.

Task 1 - Create a Pipe Network by Object.

In a production environment, the line assignment for utilities is often based on the offsets from the Right -Of-Ways boundary. Based on the tools available in the Network Layout Tools toolbar, it is easier to use the AutoCAD tools to lay out the utility line assignments and then convert it to a pipe network. In this task, you will review the process of converting a line assignment to a pipe network.

1. Continue working with the drawing from the previous practice or open **PIP1-B1-PipeWorks.dwg** from the *C:\Civil 3D Projects\Civil3D-Training\PipeNetworks* folder.
2. Select the preset view **Pipe-Create**. You might need to type **Regen** in the Command Line.
3. In the *Home* tab>Create Design panel, expand Pipe Network, and click (Create Pipe Network from Object).
4. When prompted to select the object or XREF type, type **X** at the Command Line and press <Enter>. When prompted to select the XREF object, select the storm line (the red line at the center of the road), as shown in Figure 10–8.

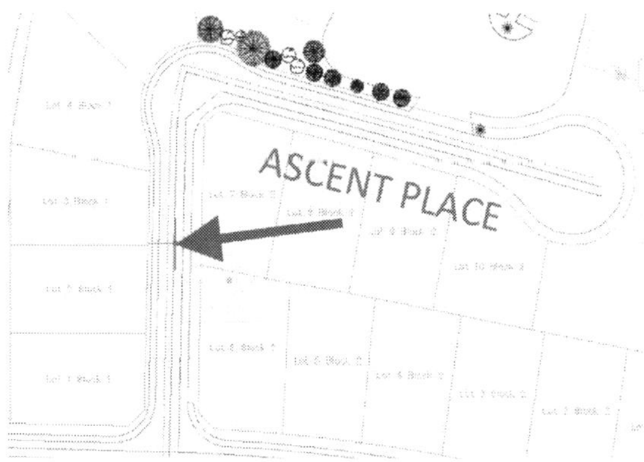

Figure 10–8

5. To ensure that the pipe slopes from the cul-de-sac to the intersection to the south, select **Reverse** to reverse the default flow direction. Press <Enter> to continue. In the Create Pipe Network from Object dialog box set the following, as shown in Figure 10–9.

    - For *Network name*, type **STORM**.
    - In the *Network parts list*, select **Storm Sewer**.
    - For *Pipe to create*, select **12in PVC Pipe**.
    - For *Structure to create*, in the Cylindrical Structure Slab Top Circular Frame structure family.
    - Select **Slab Top Cylindrical Structure 15 in dia** (in the Cylindrical Structure Slab Top Rectangular Frame family).
    - For *Surface name*, select **Finish Ground**.
    - For *Alignment name*, select **Ascent PI**.
    - Clear the **Use vertex elevations** option.
    - Click **OK** to accept the selection and close the dialog box.

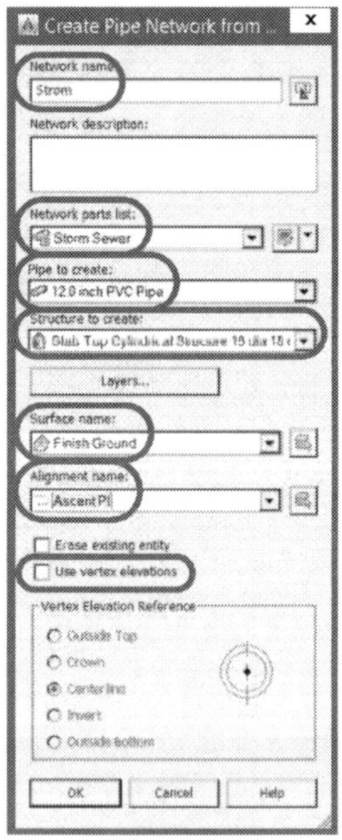

Figure 10–9

The AutoCAD Civil 3D software has created a Pipe network based on the rules and values entered in the Create Pipe Network from Objects dialog box. After you have completed building the network, you will go back and make adjustments to the design inverts, slopes, and part sizes.

6. Save the drawing.

Practice 10b Creating Pipe Networks by Layout

Practice Objective

- Create a gravity fed pipe network by layout.

Estimated time for completion: 15 minutes

Task 1 - Create a Pipe Network by Layout.

In this task, you will continue adding to the network using AutoCAD Civil 3D's **Pipe Network** creation tool.

1. Continue working with the drawing from the previous task or open **PIP1-C1-PipeWorks.dwg** from the *C:\Civil 3D Projects\Civil3D-Training\PipeNetworks* folder.

2. Select the preset view **Pipe-Create**.

3. In Model Space, select a part in the STORM network. In the contextual tab>Modify panel, click (Edit Pipe Network), as shown in Figure 10–10.

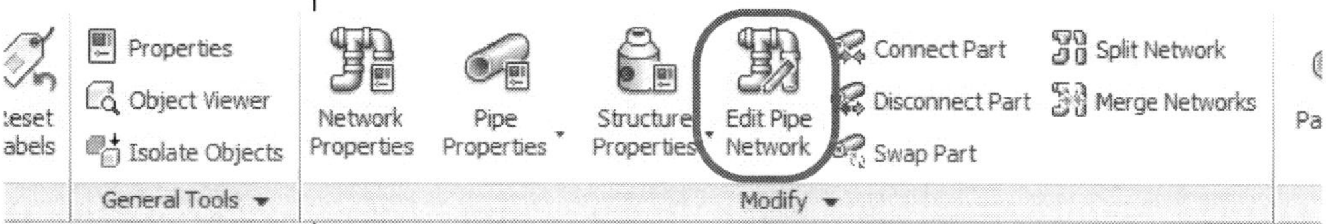

Figure 10–10

4. To change the referenced alignment, in the Network Layout Tools - STORM toolbar:

   - Click (Alignment) and select **Jefferies Ranch Rd**.
   - Select **68 x 6 x 57 inch Concrete Rectangular Headwall** for the manhole structure.
   - Select **12 in PVC Pipe** for the Pipe part.

- Toggle the slope to **Upslope**, as shown in Figure 10–11.
- Click (Draw Pipe and Structure).

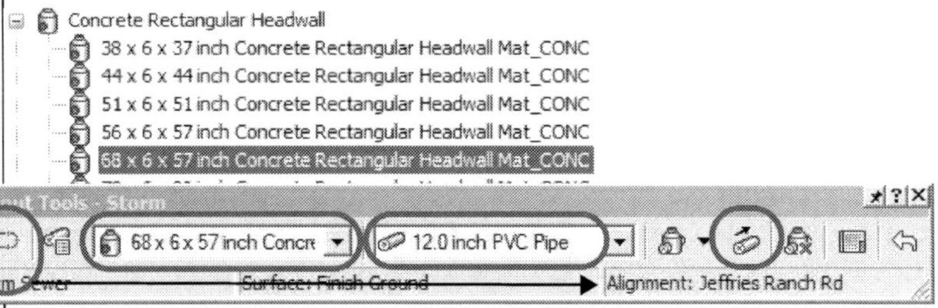

Figure 10–11

5. The AutoCAD Civil 3D software prompts you for the locations of the structures. Select end point **pt1** and then select an approximate location near point **pt2** for the next structure location, as shown in Figure 10–12.

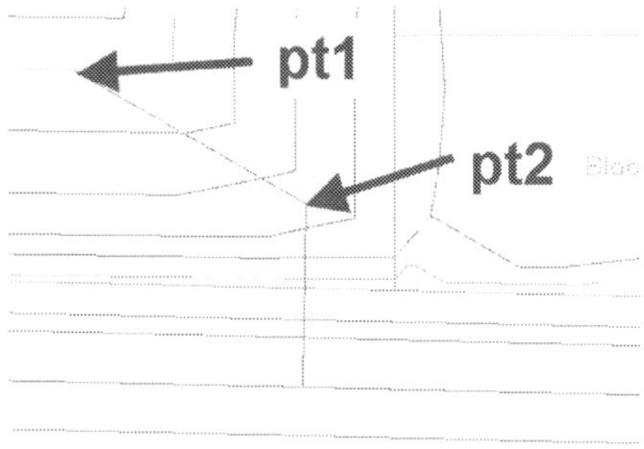

Figure 10–12

6. In the Network Layout Tools - STORM toolbar, select **Slab Top Cylindrical Structure 15 dia 18 dia Frm 4FrHt 4 Slab 3 Wall 4 Floor** for the manhole structure and toggle the slope to **Downslope**, as shown in Figure 10–13.

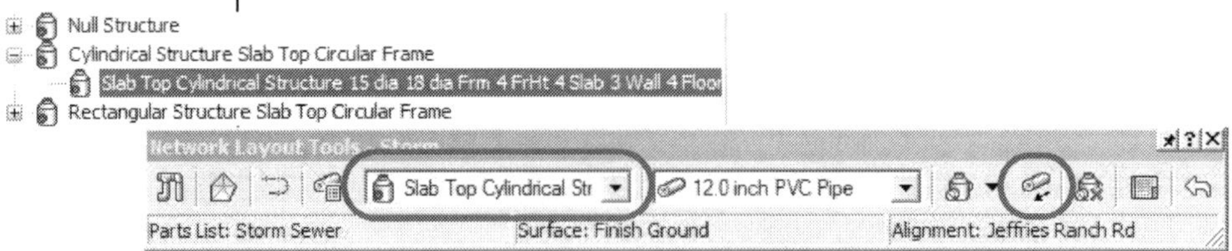

Figure 10–13

7. In the Command Line, you should still be prompted for a structure insertion point. Type **S** and press <Enter> for a start point.

You will insert manholes based on Figure 10–14. The first structure, **pt1**, is located at station 11+00 of Jeffries Ranch Rd. The next structure, **pt2**, is located at the beginning of the curve, **pt3** is at the intersection of Jeffries Ranch Rd and Ascent Pl, and **pt4** is at a station of 3+24' along the Jeffries Ranch Rd alignment. Use the information shown in Figure 10–14 as a guide as you complete the following steps.

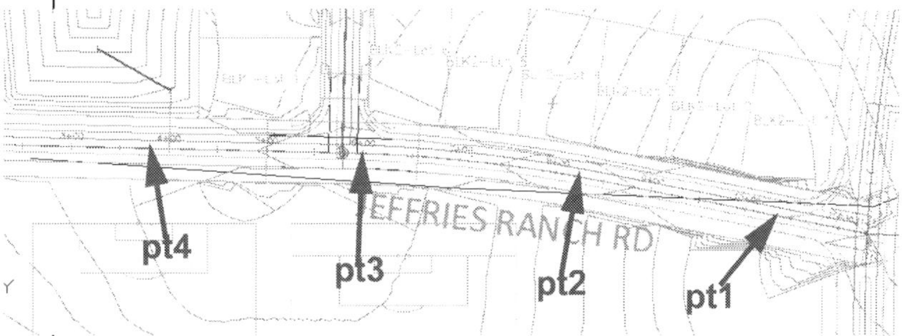

Figure 10–14

8. The AutoCAD Civil 3D software prompts you for the locations of the structures. Click  (Station offset), as shown in Figure 10–15.

Figure 10–15

9. When prompted for an alignment, select the **Jeffries Ranch Rd** alignment (select an alignment label if it is difficult to select the alignment centerline). Type **1100'** for the station and type **0** for the offset. Press <Esc> to exit the **Transparent** command while remaining in the **Pipe Layout** command.

10. Select the **end point pt2** for the next structure.

11. When prompted for the next structure, type **C** and press <Enter> to draw a curved pipe. When prompted for the end of curve, select the manhole structure at the intersection of Jeffries Ranch Rd and Ascent Pl. A symbol should display indicating that you are tying into a manhole, as shown in Figure 10–16.

Figure 10–16

You now want to use a different pipe size.

12. In the Network Layout Tools - STORM toolbar, expand the drop-down list and select **18in PVC Pipe**, as shown in Figure 10–17.

Figure 10–17

13. At the prompt for the end of curve, type **L** and press <Enter> to draw a line. When prompted to select the next structure location, click  (Station offset), as shown in Figure 10–18.

Figure 10–18

14. When prompted for an alignment, select the **Jeffries Ranch Rd** alignment (select an alignment label if it is difficult to select the alignment centerline). Type **324'** for the station, and type **0** for the offset. Press <Esc> to exit the command and press <Enter> to exit the prompt for the insertion point of a structure.

You have made a design change and decided to insert a manhole east of the original intended location, as shown in Figure 10–19. This requires you to make further adjustments to the network.

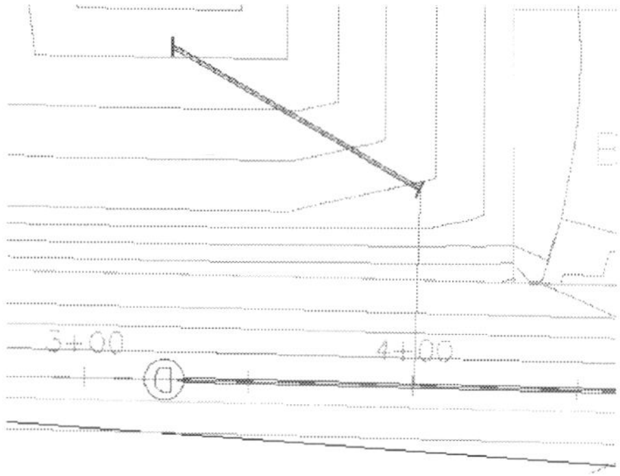

Figure 10–19

15. Close the Network Layout Tools toolbar by clicking the **X**.

16. Save the drawing.

Task 2 - View Pipe network in profile view.

1. Continue working with the drawing from the previous task or open **PIP1-C2-PipeWorks.dwg**.

2. Draw a window from left to right around the pipes to select the last three pipes and four structures that you created in the last task, as shown in Figure 10–20.

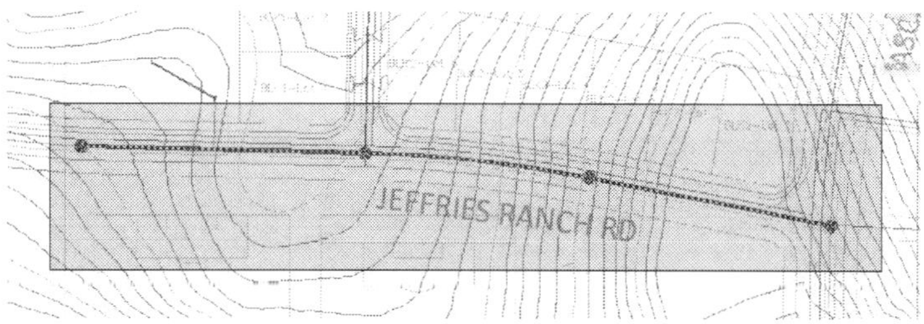

Figure 10–20

3. In the *Pipe Networks* contextual tab>Network Tools panel, click (Draw Parts in Profile).

4. When prompted to select the Profile view, select the Jeffries Ranch Road profile view to the right of the site plan. Press <Esc> to release the selected pipe network parts.

5. Because you only selected certain network parts to be added to the profile, you will now review the parts that are relevant to this profile view. Select the Profile view and in the contextual tab>Modify Views panel, click (Profile View Properties), as shown in Figure 10–21.

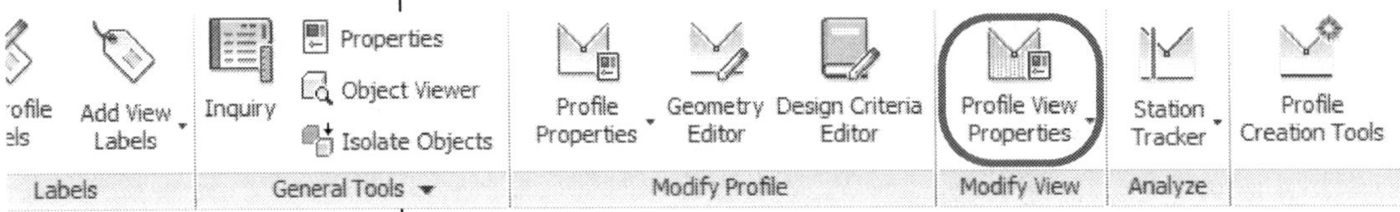

Figure 10–21

6. In the Profile View Properties - Jeffries Ranch Rd dialog box, in the *Pipe Networks* tab, ensure that only the following parts are enabled, as shown in Figure 10–22: **Pipe - 5, 6,** and **7**, and **Structure - 4**, **7**, **8**, and **9**. Click **OK** to close the dialog box and apply the changes.

Note that your numbers might be slightly different. The key is that not all pipes and structures will be checked.

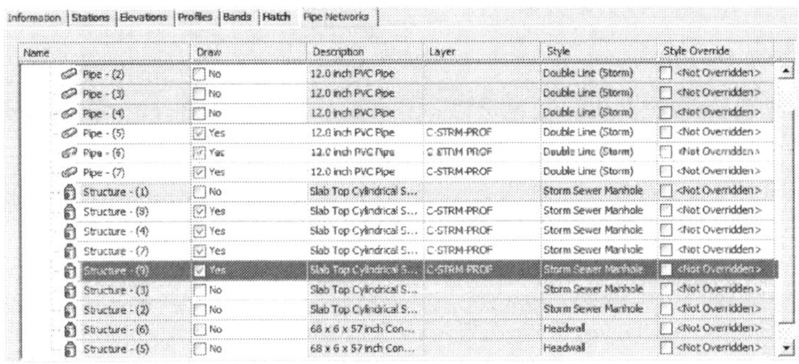

Figure 10–22

7. Save the drawing.

Practice 10c Create a Pressure Pipe Network

Estimated time for completion: 15 minutes

Practice Objective

- Create and edit a pressure pipe network.

Task 1 - Create a Pressure Pipe Network.

In this task, you will create a water network using the **Pressure Pipe Network** commands.

1. Continue working with the drawing from the previous practice or open **PIP1-F1-PipeWorks.dwg** from the *C:\Civil 3D Projects\Civil3D-Training\PipeNetworks* folder.
2. Select the preset view **Pipe-Create**.
3. In the *Home* tab>Layers panel, click (Layer Off). Select any Storm Sewer pipe network label and then press <Enter> to end the command. In the *Home* tab>Create Design panel, expand Pipe Networks and click (Pressure Network Creation Tools).
4. Name the pressure network **Water**, select the **Water** parts list, select **Finish Ground** for the reference surface, and select **Jeffries Ranch Rd** as the reference alignment, as shown in Figure 10–23. Click **OK** to accept the selection and close the dialog box.

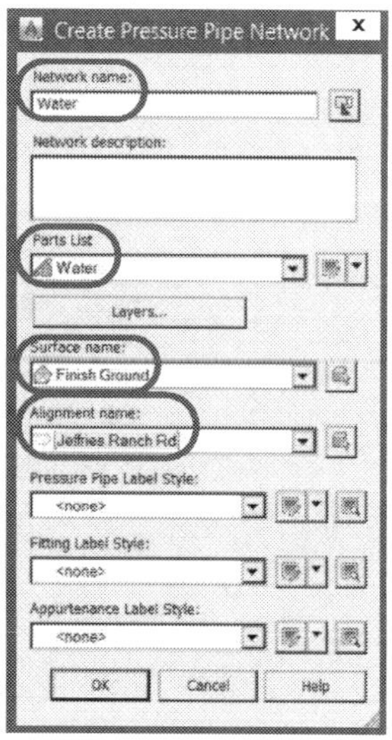

Figure 10–23

5. In the *Pressure Network Plan Layout* contextual tab> Network Settings panel, verify that the cover is set to **3'**, as shown in Figure 10–24.

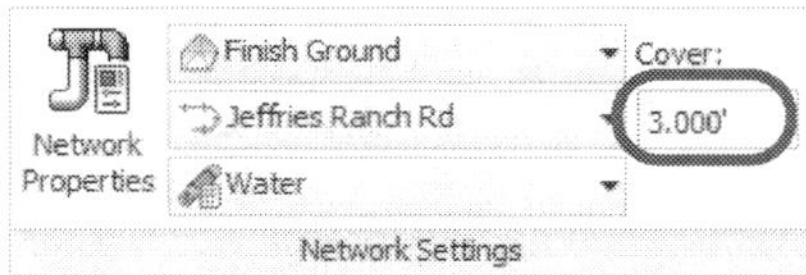

Figure 10–24

6. In the *Pressure Network Plan Layout* contextual tab> Layout panel, click (Pipes Only) and set the pipe size and material to **pipe-12 in-push on-ductile iron**, as shown in Figure 10–25.

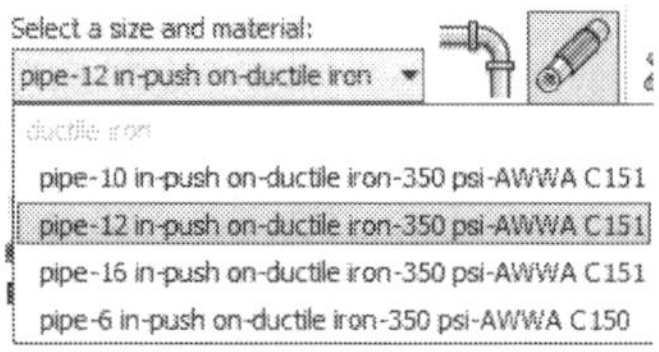

Figure 10–25

7. In the drawing, use the **Endpoint** object snap to help you select the points along the polyline north of the storm sewer, as shown in Figure 10–26.

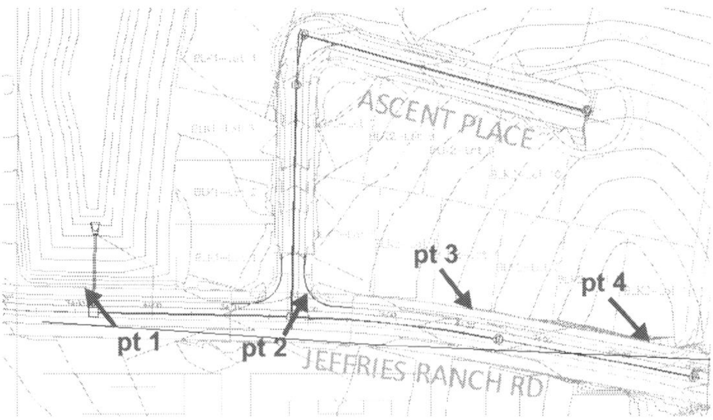

Figure 10–26

8. At the second point the pipe only glyph should be displayed, as shown in Figure 10–27. Rather than accept one of the deflection angles, type **C** and press <Enter> to start a curve.

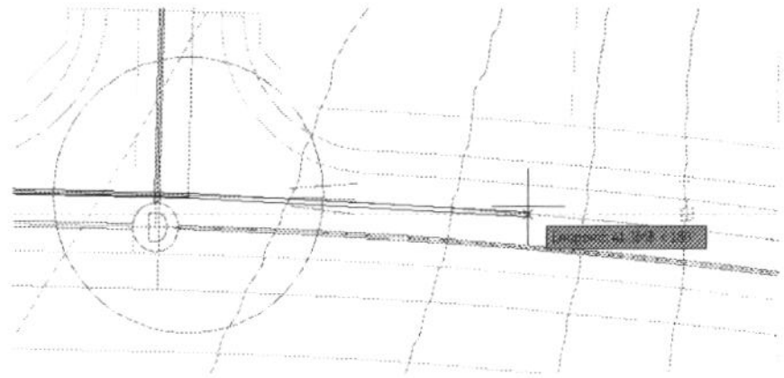

Figure 10–27

9. After the third point, type **S** and press <Enter> to make a straight pipe run.

10. Press <Enter> to end the command and save the drawing.

Task 2 - Place fittings and appurtenances

1. Continue working with the drawing from the previous task or open **PIP1-F2-PipeWorks.dwg**

2. In the *Pressure Network Plan Layout* contextual tab> Layout panel, click (Add Fitting) and set the fitting to **tee-12 in x 10 in on ductile iron**. Select the end point where you placed point 2 in the previous task, as shown in Figure 10–28. Press <Esc> to end the command.

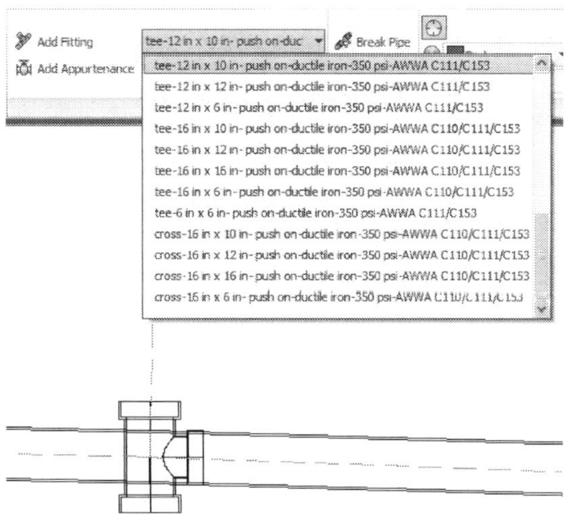

Figure 10–28

3. Note that the fitting is set in the wrong rotation. Select it and pick the circular grip. Hold <Ctrl> as you right-click, select **Nearest** in the object snap options, and pick the vertical water line going up Ascent Pl, as shown in Figure 10–29. Press <Esc> to release the fitting.

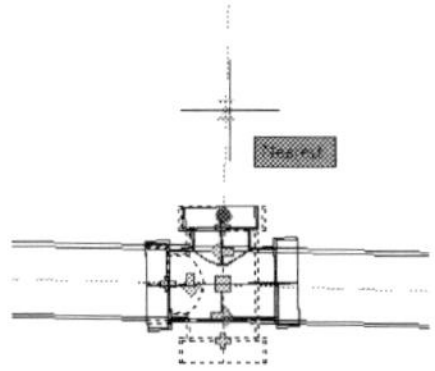

Figure 10–29

4. In the *Pressure Network Plan Layout* contextual tab> Layout panel, click (Pipes & Bends) and set the pipe size and material to **pipe-10 in-push on-ductile iron**. Hover over the tee fitting that you placed until the structure tool tip image displays, as shown in Figure 10–30. Click to accept the connection and start the new pipe.

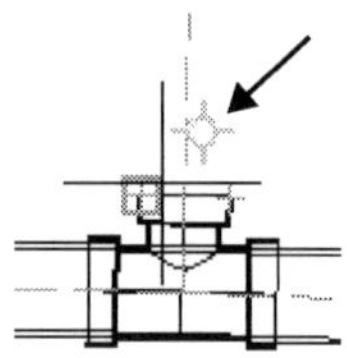

Figure 10–30

5. Use the **Endpoint** object snap to help you select the next point as shown in Figure 10–31.

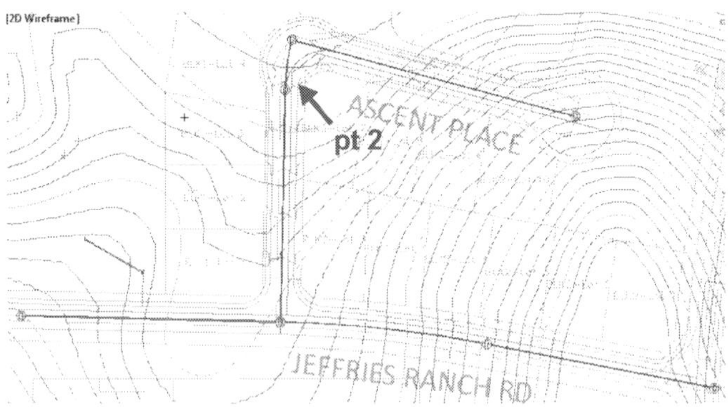

Figure 10–31

6. Note that the bend options available for the next pipe will require you to make a change in the original conceptual design, as shown in Figure 10–32. Hover the cursor over the intended pipe intersection and then move the cursor to the left along the projectory of the original pipe alignment. Click when the pre-programmed bend displays to intersect the intended route. Press <Esc> to end the command.

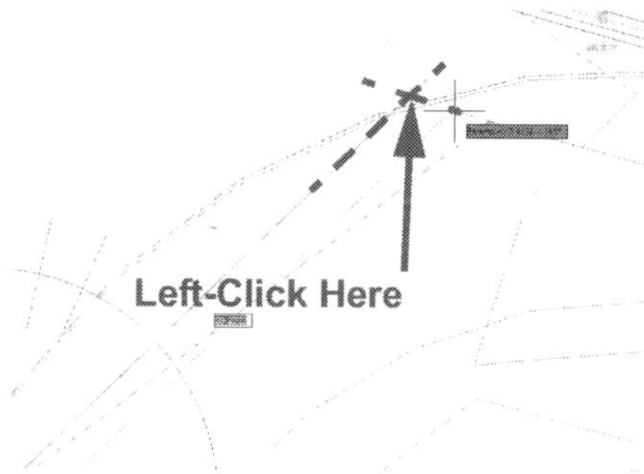

Figure 10–32

7. Save the drawing.

Task 3 - Draw pressure pipes in the profile view.

---

1. Continue working with the drawing from the previous task or open **PIP1-F3-PipeWorks.dwg**

2. Select the three water pipes running along Jeffries Ranch Rd. In the *Pressure Networks* contextual tab, click (Draw Parts in Profile).

3. When prompted, select the **Jeffries Ranch Rd** profile view.

4. Save the drawing.

Chapter 11

Grading

This chapter includes instructional content to assist in your preparation for the following topic and objectives for the AutoCAD® Civil® 3D 2016 Certified Professional exam.

Autodesk Certification Exam Objectives in this Chapter

Exam Topic	Exam Objective	Section
Grading	• Design and create a grading model	• 11.1
	• Create a grading model feature line	• 11.2

11.1 Design and Create a Grading Model

AutoCAD® Civil 3D® grading uses objects called *feature lines* and *grading groups*.

- Feature lines are complex, linear 3D objects that define a string of known elevations, such as the perimeter of a proposed pond. Feature lines can be created by converting AutoCAD® lines, arcs, or polylines. Grading feature lines can also be exported from Corridors by selecting the *Modify* tab> Corridor panel and launching the **Feature Lines from Corridor** command.
- Parcel lines double as feature lines, and can be edited directly using the Feature Line Elevation Editor. Parcel lines in the extents of a grading group are also automatically added to the surface, even if they are at elevation 0. (You can avoid this by locating feature lines and parcels in separate sites.)
- The feature lines can be created from an alignment. They can also be dynamically linked to the alignment or corridor model from which they were created.
- The AutoCAD Civil 3D software can calculate the position of one feature line based on another, such as a pond bottom calculated at a specific slope and elevation below the perimeter. Distance, slope, and surface parameters used in solutions are assigned using *grading criteria*.
- *Grading groups* are collections of these solutions that form a contiguous whole, such as the detention pond shown in Figure 11–1.

Figure 11–1

- Grading groups can be used to automatically generate AutoCAD Civil 3D surfaces. Tools are also available for calculating grading group volume, and adjusting grading groups to help balance cut and fill.
- Surfaces created from grading groups (as well as corridor surfaces) display in the *Prospector* and can be adjusted using normal surface editing tools, such as **Add** or **Delete Surface Point** or **Swap Edge**. These edits are maintained and dynamically reapplied if the grading group is modified.
- Feature lines and grading groups are organized by site, so that any feature lines added in the perimeter of a grading group (in the same site) are automatically added to the grading group.

Grading Creation Tools Toolbar

Grading groups are created and edited using the Grading Creation Tools toolbar (as shown in Figure 11–2), which is accessed in the *Grading* tab>Create Grading panel.

Figure 11–2

Some of the more commonly used tools include:

-  **(Set the Grading Group):** Enables you to consolidate grading objects into a single collection to generate a grading group surface for volume computations.
- 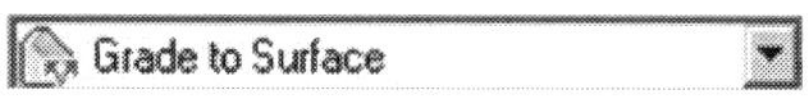

(Criteria drop-down list): Enables you to select specific criteria in a given criteria set.
-  **(Create Grading):** Generates a grading solution from the currently selected criteria.
-  **(Edit Grading):** Enables you to change the grading parameters after a solution has been generated.
-  **(Grading Volume Tools):** Opens the Grading Volume Tools toolbar, which provides cut and fill information about the grading group, and adjustment tools.

11.2 Create a Grading Model Feature Line

Feature Line Contextual Tab

The *Feature Line* contextual tab (shown in Figure 11–3), contains commands to edit and modify feature lines. These commands include tools to edit feature line elevations and feature line geometry, such as **Break**, **Trim**, **Extend**, and **Fillet** (which creates a true, 3D curve).

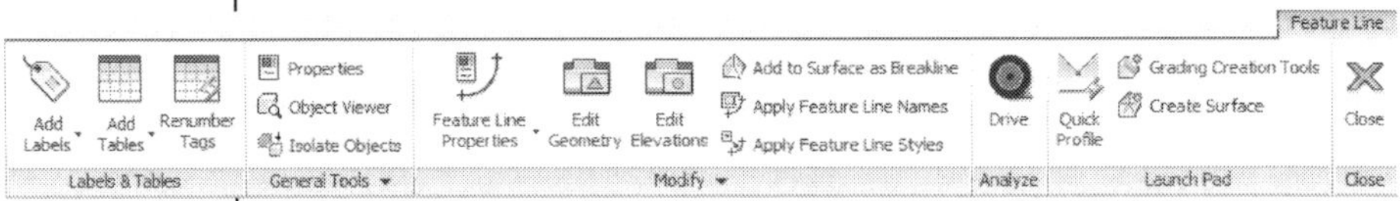

Figure 11–3

The **Create Feature Lines from Objects** command is available in the *Home* tab>Create Design panel, expanded Feature Line flyout, as shown in Figure 11–4.

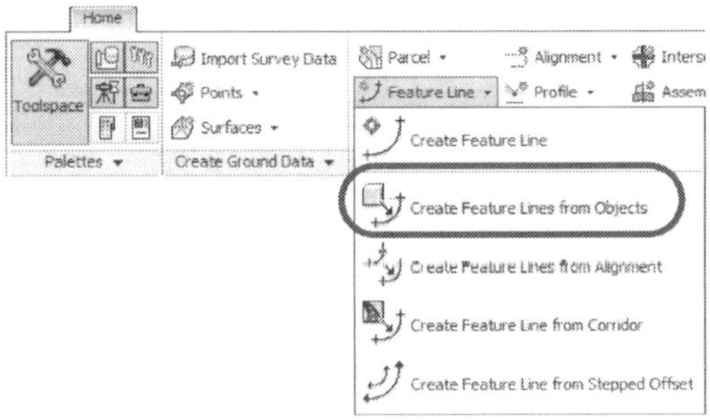

Figure 11–4

Elevation Editor

The Grading Elevation Editor vista (shown in Figure 11–5), enables you to add, modify, or vary the elevations of a feature line. The feature line data is organized into rows, where one row lists the data for a specific vertex.

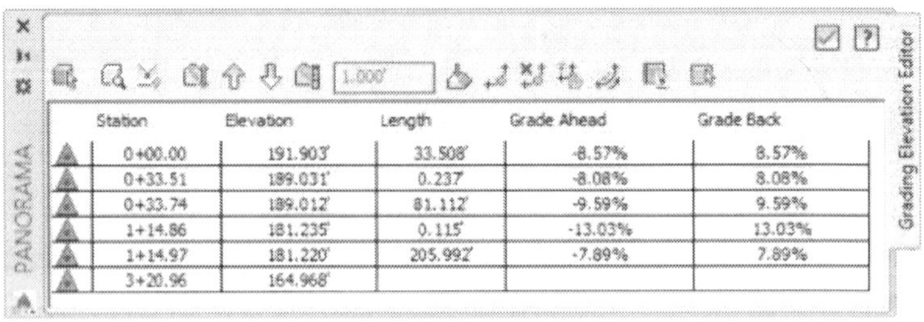

Figure 11–5

- **(Select a Feature Line Or Lot Line):** Enables you to change the feature line that you are editing.
- **(Zoom to):** Enables you to zoom in to a highlighted vertex.
- **(Quick Profile):** Creates a quick profile along the feature line.
- **(Raise/Lower):** Raises or lowers all of the feature line vertices by the elevation entered in the edit field on the right.
- **(Raise/Lower Incrementally):** Raises or lowers the elevations by the elevation increment entered (the default is 1).
- **(Set Increment):** Enables you to set the increment value.
- **(Flatten Grade or Elevations):** Enables you to flatten selected vertices to a specified grade or single elevation.
- **(Insert Elevation Point):** (Green) Adds an elevation control to the feature line. Elevation points provide an elevation control without creating a new vertex. These points are Z-controls without X- or Y-components.
- **(Delete Elevation Point):** (Red) Removes elevation points.
- **(Elevations from Surface):** Takes the elevations of all of the vertices from the surface if no rows are selected. If a row is selected, it only takes the surface elevation for that vertex.
- **(Reverse the direction):** Changes the direction of the feature line by reversing the order of its points.

- **(Show Grade breaks only):** Only displays rows for vertices where there is a change to grade.

- **(Unselect All Rows):** Clears any selected vertices. With no rows selected, the **Raise/Lower** commands apply to all of the rows.

You can edit the elevations of a feature or parcel line before or after it becomes part of a grading group.

Practice 11a Working with Feature Lines

Practice Objectives

- Create a feature line from objects.
- Create a feature line using design data.

Estimated time for completion: 15 minutes

The first step in grading is to establish existing site conditions. In this practice you will define feature lines for a parking lot and some ball fields.

Task 1 - Create a feature line from objects.

To establish a design control line for the parking lot, you will create a feature line that temporarily extracts elevations from the existing surface. You will then modify the feature line to follow a specific slope. A second feature line will be created using specific design parameters outlining the baseball field to ensure correct drainage.

1. Open **GRD1-A1-Grading.dwg** from the *C:\Civil 3D Projects\ Civil3D-Training\Grading* folder.

*You might need to type **Regen** in the Command Line to regenerate the graphics.*

2. Select the preset view **Grad-ParkingLot**. A red polyline should be displayed that runs north and south through the center of the parking lot.
3. In the *Home* tab>Create Design panel, expand Feature Line and select  (Create Feature Lines from Objects), as shown in Figure 11–6.

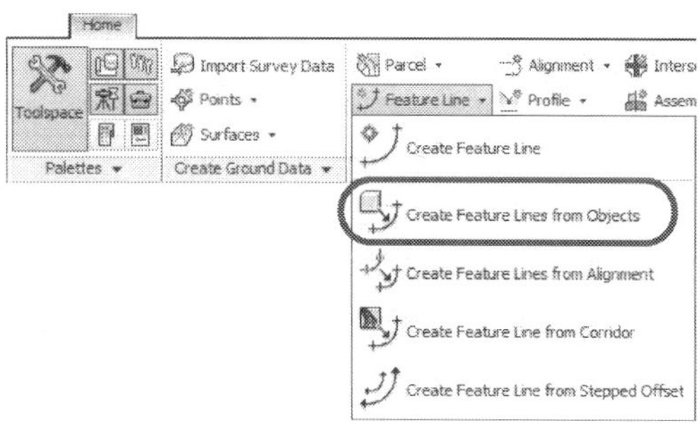

Figure 11–6

4. When prompted to *select the object*, type **X** for (XREF), select the red polyline, and press <Enter>.

5. In the Create Feature Lines dialog box, create a new site called **Site 1** for the site and select the **Assign elevations** options in the *Conversion options* area, as shown in Figure 11–7. Accept all other defaults and click **OK** when done.

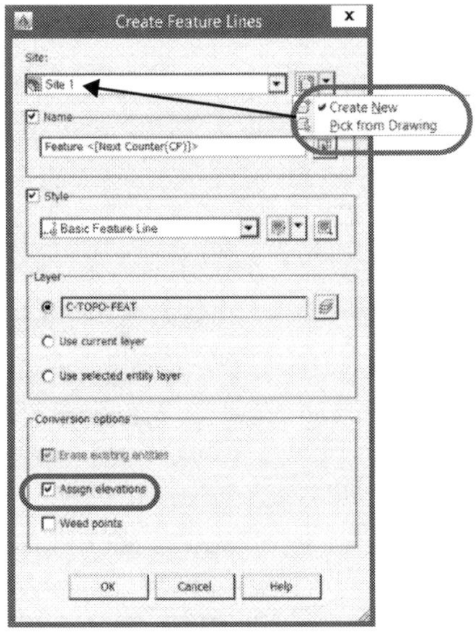

Figure 11–7

6. In the Assign Elevations dialog box, select the **From surface** option, expand the drop-down list, and select **Existing-Site.** Clear the **Insert intermediate grade break points** option as shown in Figure 11–8. Click **OK** to accept the changes and close the dialog box.

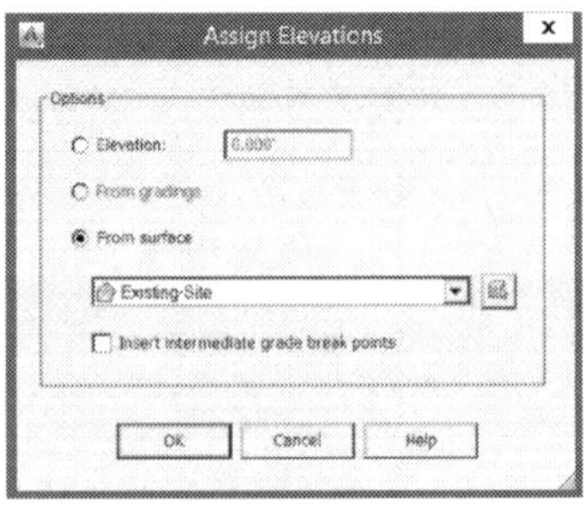

Figure 11–8

A feature line has been created for the center of the parking lot with elevations matching the existing ground surface. Ideally you will already have the corridors designed for Ascent PI and Mission Ave so that you can match the designed elevations from them.

7. Select the green feature line that you just created. In the *Feature Line* contextual tab, click (Edit Elevations).

If the Edit Elevations panel is not displayed.

Click (Elevation Editor) in the Feature Line contextual tab>Edit Elevations panel.

8. In the Grading Elevation Editor, place the cursor in the first row, hold <Shift> and pick in the last row to highlight all of the vertices. In the top row, type **-2** in the *Grade Ahead* column to change all of the grades to **-2%**, as shown in Figure 11–9.

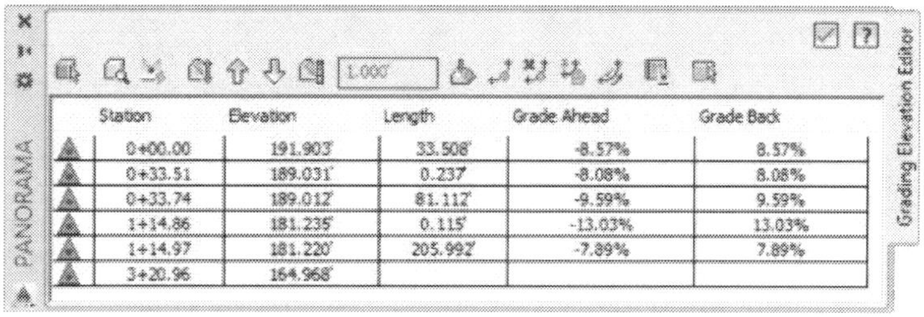

Station	Elevation	Length	Grade Ahead	Grade Back
0+00.00	191.903'	33.508'	-8.57%	8.57%
0+33.51	189.031'	0.237'	-8.08%	8.08%
0+33.74	189.012'	81.112'	-9.59%	9.59%
1+14.86	181.235'	0.115'	-13.03%	13.03%
1+14.97	181.220'	205.992'	-7.89%	7.89%
3+20.96	164.968'			

Figure 11–9

9. Save the drawing.

Task 2 - Create a feature based on design elevations.

In this task you will create a feature line for the baseball field whose elevations have been pre-calculated to ensure correct drainage. Based on the required drainage for the baseball field, the elevations have been roughly calculated, as shown in Figure 11–10. Use these elevations to create a feature line in the following steps.

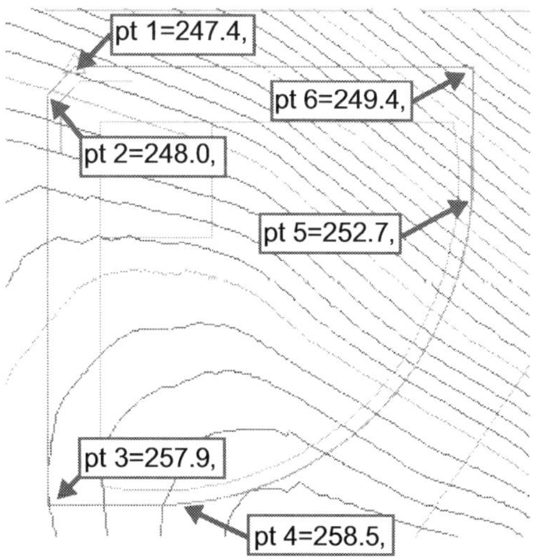

Figure 11–10

1. Continue working with the drawing from the previous task or open **GRD1-A2-Grading.dwg**.

2. Select the preset view **Grad-Baseball**.

3. In the *Home* tab>Create Design panel, expand Feature Line and select **Create Feature Line**, as shown in Figure 11–11.

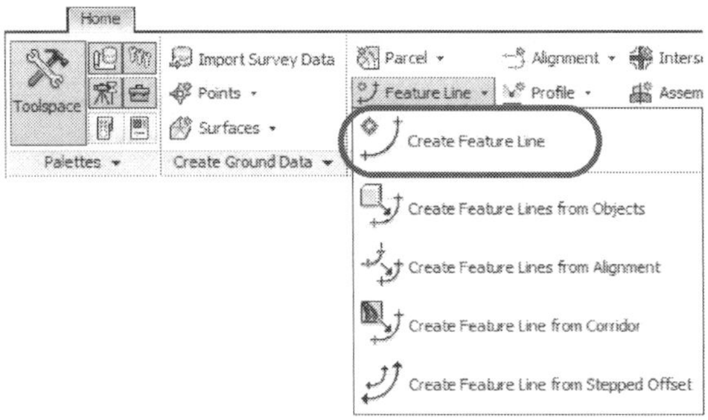

Figure 11–11

4. In the Create Feature Lines dialog box, select **Site 1** and accept all of the other defaults. Click **OK** to close the dialog box and start creating the feature line.

5. When prompted for the feature line points, select the end point **Pt1** (as shown in Figure 11–10). At the *Specify elevation or [surface]:* prompt, type **247.4** and press <Enter>.

6. When prompted for the next point, select end point **Pt2**, as shown in Figure 11–10.

7. You are prompted to *Specify grade or [SLope/Elevation/Difference/SUrface/Transition] <0.00>:*. If the option is not set to accept elevations, type **E** and press <Enter> to set the default as the elevation.

8. Once the option has been set to accept elevations, you are prompted to *Specify elevation or [Grade/SLope/Difference/SUrface/Transition]:*. Type **248** and press <Enter>. Continue selecting the end points and entering the elevations for all of points shown in Figure 11–10. After inputting the elevation for point 4, type **A** and press <Enter> to start an arc. After point 5, type **L** and press <Enter> to return to straight lines. When finished entering the elevation for the last point (pt6, **249.4**), type **C** to close the feature line and press <Enter> to exit the command.

9. In Model Space, select the feature line that you just created and in the contextual tab>Modify panel, select **Edit Elevations** to toggle on the Edit Elevations panel, and then select **Elevation Editor**, as shown in Figure 11–12.

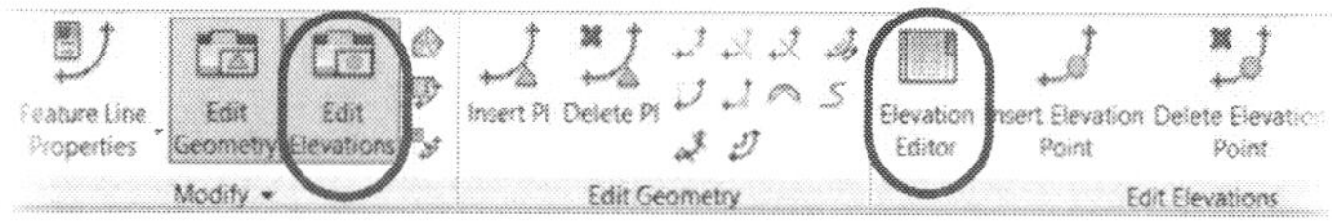

Figure 11–12

10. In the Grading Elevation Editor vista (shown in Figure 11–13), you can change the feature line design.

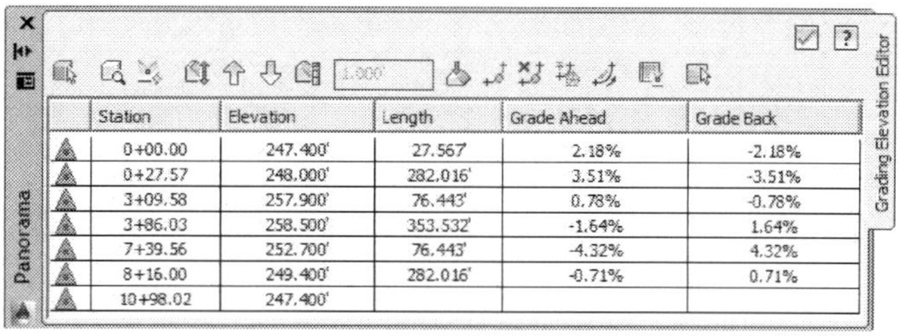

Figure 11–13

11. Save the drawing.

Practice 11b Create Grading Groups

Estimated time for completion: 15 minutes

Practice Objective

- Create grading objects to design the finish ground and display the finish ground contours.

Task 1 - Create a grading object that grades to a surface.

The baseball park will have a grade of 4% for 10 feet, and then grade to the existing site surface.

1. Open **GRD1-B1-Grading.dwg** from the *C:\Civil 3D Projects\Civil3D-Training\Grading* folder.
2. Select the preset view **Grad-Baseball**. The dark green feature line created in the last practice should be displayed.
3. In the *Home* tab>Create Design panel, expand Grading and select **Grading Creation Tools**, as shown in Figure 11–14.

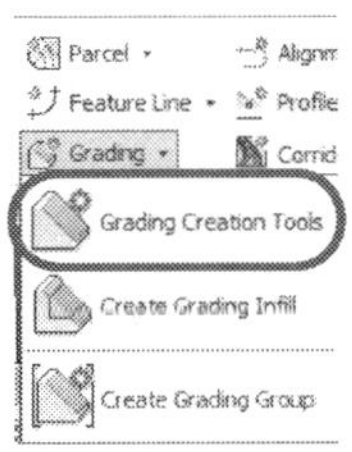

Figure 11–14

4. In the Grading Creation Tools, click (Set Grading Group), as shown in Figure 11–15.

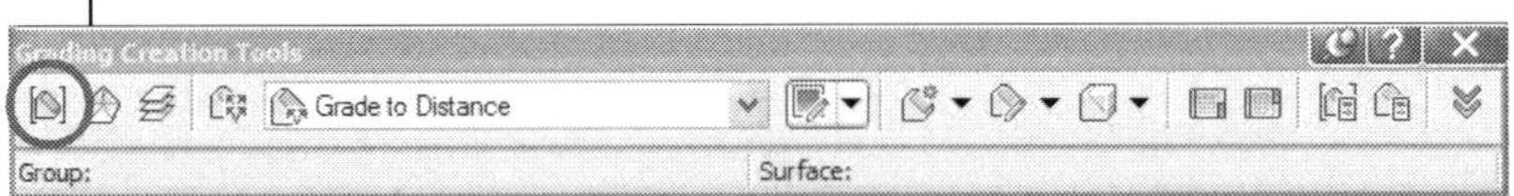

Figure 11–15

5. Select **Site 1** and click **OK**.

6. In the Create Grading Group, type **Baseball Field** as the name. Do not select the **Automatic surface creation** option, as shown in Figure 11–16. Click **OK**.

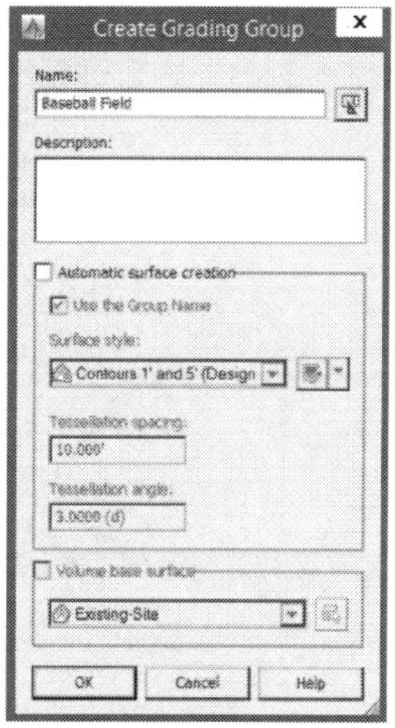

Figure 11–16

7. On the left in the Grading Creation Tools, click  (Set Target Surface), as shown in Figure 11–17. Select **Existing-Site** and click **OK**.

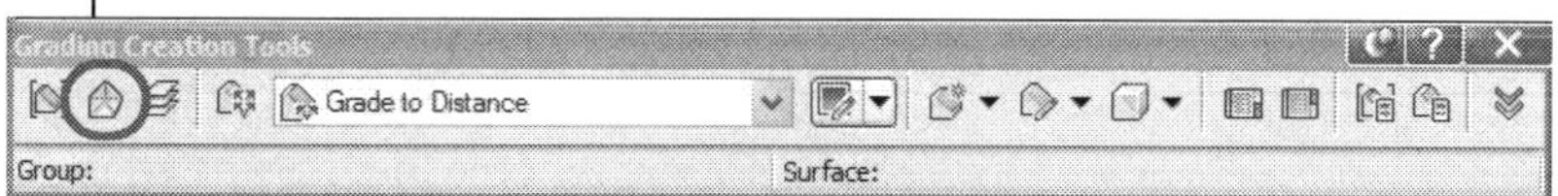

Figure 11–17

8. In the Grading Creation Tools, set the grading criteria to **Grade to Distance**, as shown in Figure 11–18.

Figure 11–18

9. In the Grading Creation Tools, click  (Create grading), as shown in Figure 11–19.

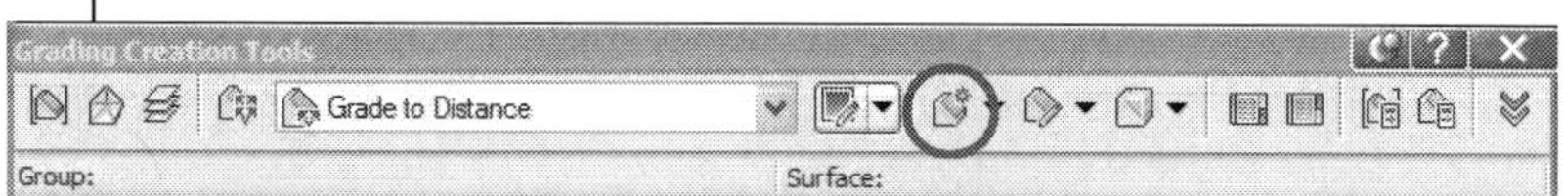

Figure 11–19

10. When prompted:

    - To *select the object*, select the dark green feature line outlining the baseball field.
    - Pick a point to the outside of the feature line for the side to grade.
    - Select **Yes** to apply it to the entire length.
    - Type **10** to specify the distance.
    - Select **Grade** to specify a format of grade.
    - Type **-4** to grade down 4% from the feature line.

11. In the Grading Creation Tools, set the grading criteria to **Grade to Surface**, as shown in Figure 11–20. Click  (Create grading).

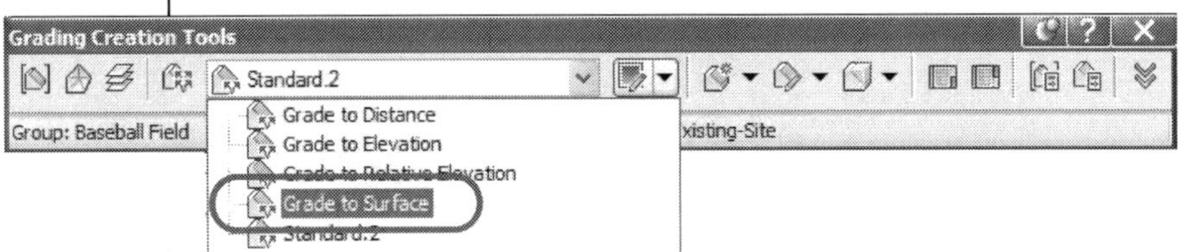

Figure 11–20

12. When prompted:

    - To *select the feature*, select the outer-most dark green feature line created with the last grading object.
    - Select **Yes** to apply it to the entire length.
    - Press <Enter> through the remaining prompts, accepting the defaults.
    - Close the Grading Creation toolbar.

13. Save the drawing

Task 2 - Create an infill.

Playing fields are graded for drainage. Grassed surfaces usually have a 1% to 2% minimum slope. The baseball field that you will be working on has a 2% slope across the field with a 4% slope surrounding it before turning into a 2:1 slope out to daylight.

1. Continue working with the drawing from the previous task or open **GRD1-B2-Grading.dwg**.

2. Select one of the grading objects that you created in Task 1. In the contextual *Grading* tab>Modify panel, click  (Grading Group Properties).

3. In the *Information* tab, select the **Automatic Surface Creation** option. Accept the defaults in the Create Surface dialog box and click **OK**. Select the **Volume Base Surface** option and select **Existing-Site** as the base surface, as shown in Figure 11–21. Click **OK**.

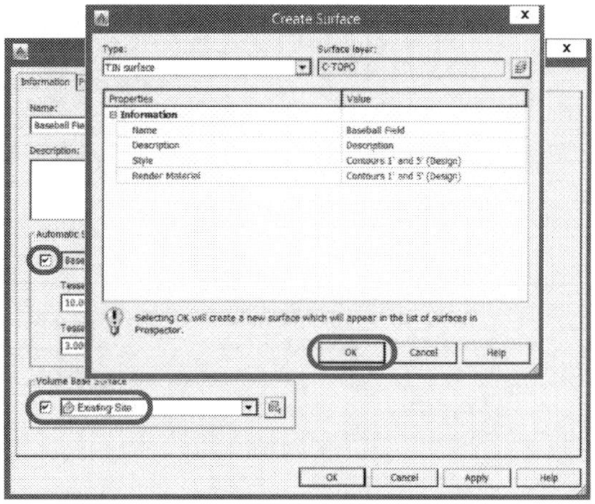

Figure 11–21

4. Select the baseball field surface. In the *Surface* contextual tab, click  (Object Viewer). Set the view direction to **SW Isometric** and the style to **Shades of Gray**. Note the hole in the surface, as shown in Figure 11–22. Press <Esc> twice to close the object viewer and release the surface.

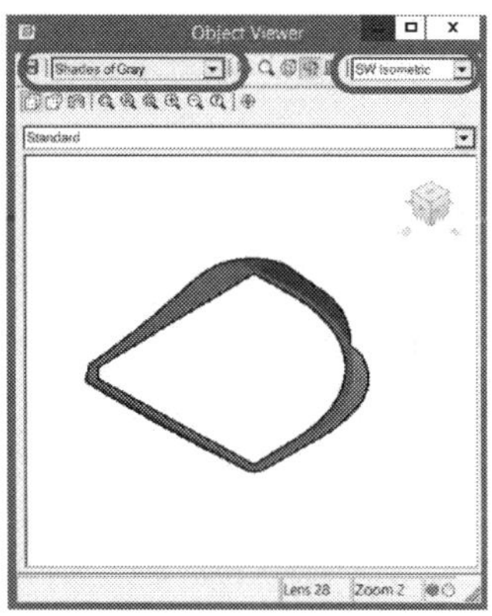

Figure 11–22

Alternatively, you can expand Grading, and click (Create Infill) in the Home tab>Create Design panel.

5. Expand **Grading Creation Tools**, and select **Create Infill**, as shown in Figure 11–23.

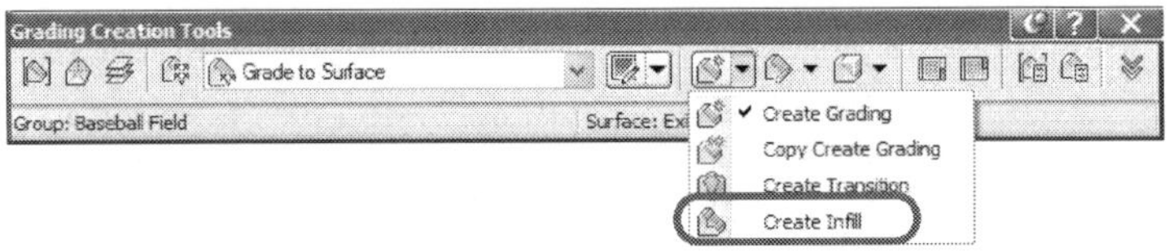

Figure 11–23

6. Pick a point in the middle of the baseball field grading object and press <Enter>. Contours should fill in the middle, as shown in Figure 11–24.

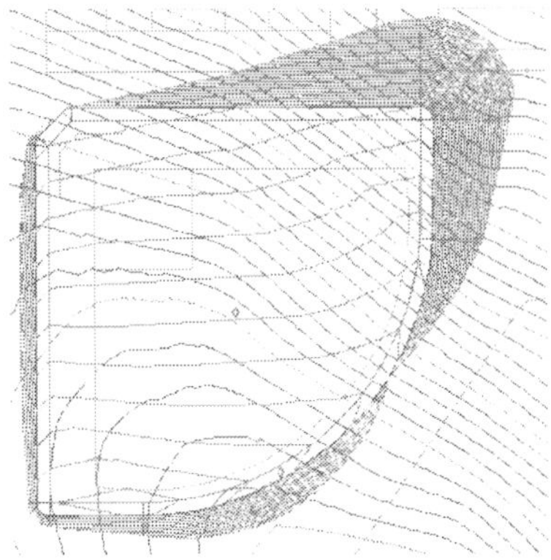

Figure 11–24

7. Save the drawing.

Chapter 12

Managing and Sharing Data

This chapter includes instructional content to assist in your preparation for the following topic and objective for the AutoCAD® Civil® 3D 2016 Certified Professional exam.

Autodesk Certification Exam Objectives in this Chapter

Exam Topic	Exam Objective	Section
Managing and Sharing Data	• Create a data sharing setup	• 12.1

12.1 Create a Data Sharing Setup

Data Shortcuts can be used to share design data between drawing files through the use of XML files. Using Data Shortcuts is similar to using the Autodesk Vault software, but does not provide the protection of your data or the tracking of versions the way the Autodesk Vault software does.

Data Shortcuts are managed using the *Prospector* tab of the Toolspace under the *Data Shortcuts* collection or in the *Manage* tab>Data Shortcuts panel, as shown in Figure 12–1. The shortcuts are stored in XML files in one or more working folders that you create. They can use the same folder structure as the Autodesk Vault software. This method simplifies the transition to using the Autodesk Vault software at a future time.

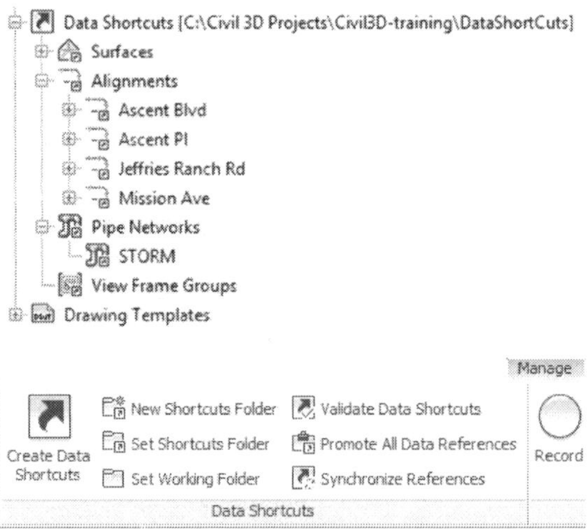

Figure 12–1

Whether using the Autodesk Vault software or Data Shortcuts, the intelligent AutoCAD Civil 3D object design data can be consumed and used on different levels. However, this referenced data only can be edited in the drawing that contains the original object. As referenced data can be assigned a different style than those in the source drawing, you can separate the design phase (where drawing presentation is not critical) from the drafting phase (where drawing presentation is paramount). Therefore, after the styles have been applied at the drafting phase, any changes to the design have minimal visual impact on the completed drawings.

Changing the name of a drawing file that provides Data Shortcuts or the shortcut XML file itself invalidates the shortcut. Although the Data Shortcuts Editor outside the AutoCAD Civil 3D software permits re-pathing if a source drawing moves, shortcuts might not resolve if the source drawing location has changed.

Update Notification

If the shortcut objects are modified and the source drawing is saved, any drawings that reference those objects are updated when opened. If the drawings consuming the data referenced in the shortcuts were open at the time of the edit, a message displays to warn you of the changes, as shown in Figure 12–2.

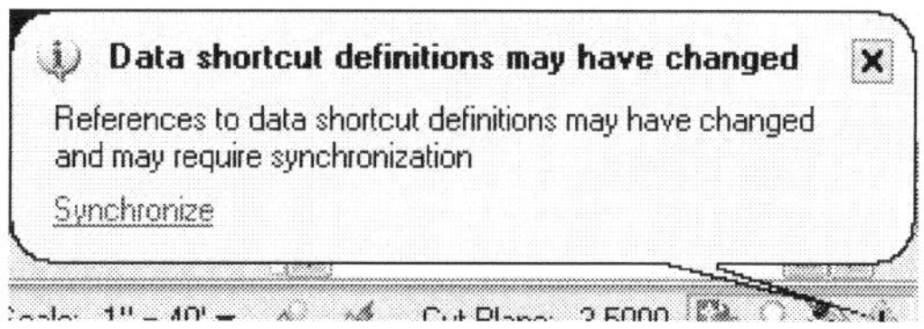

Figure 12–2

The following modifier icons help you to determine the state of many AutoCAD Civil 3D objects.

	The object is referenced by another object. In the *Settings* tab this also indicates that a style is in use in the current drawing.
	The object is being referenced from another drawing file (such as through a shortcut or Autodesk Vault reference).
	The object is out of date and needs to be rebuilt, or is violating specified design constraints.
	A project object (such as a point or surface) has been modified since it was included in the current drawing.
	You have modified a project object in your current drawing and those modifications have not yet been updated to the project.

Figure 12–3 shows how the modifier icons are used with an AutoCAD Civil 3D object as it displays in the *Prospector* tab.

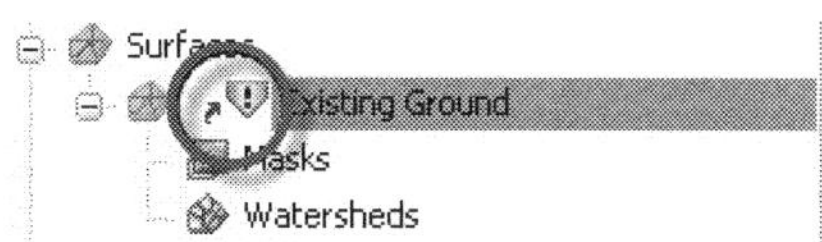

Figure 12–3

To update the shortcut data, select **Synchronize** in the balloon message or right-click on the object in the Prospector and select **Synchronize**.

Removing and Promoting Shortcuts

Shortcut data can be removed from the Shortcut tree in the Prospector by right-clicking on it and selecting **Remove**, but this does not remove the data from the drawing. To do so, right-click on the object in the Prospector and select **Delete**. This removes the shortcut data from the current list, so that the item is not included if a Data Shortcut XML file is exported from the current drawing.

You can also promote shortcuts, which converts the referenced shortcut into a local copy without any further connection to the original. You can promote objects by right-clicking on them in the Prospector and selecting **Promote**.

eTransmit Data References

Projects that use Data Shortcuts can be packaged and sent to reviewers, clients, and other consultants using the AutoCAD **eTransmit** command. With the **eTransmit** command, all of the related dependent files (such as XML files, XREFs, and text fonts) are automatically included in the package. This reduces the possibility of errors and ensures that the recipient can use the files you send them. A report file can be included in the package explaining what must be done with drawing-dependent files (e.g., XML, XREFs) so that they are usable with the included files. The Create Transmittal dialog box is shown in Figure 12–4.

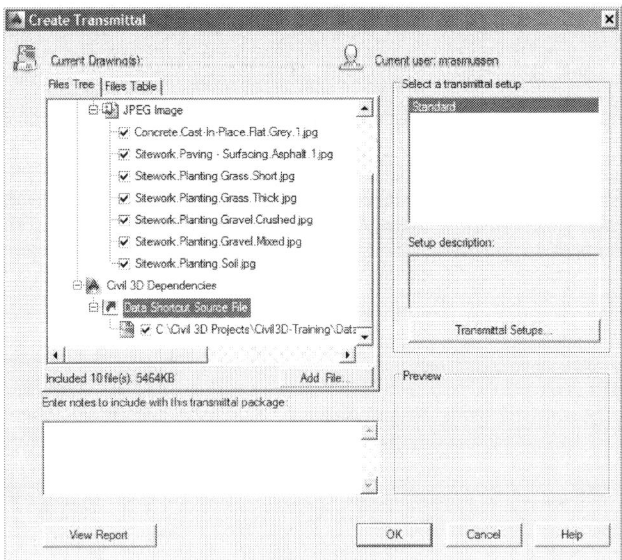

Figure 12–4

Data Shortcut Workflow

1. In the *Prospector* tab, right-click on Data Shortcuts and select **Set the Working Folder...**
2. In the *Prospector* tab, right-click on Data Shortcuts and select **New Data Shortcuts Folder...** to create a new project folder for all of your drawings.
3. Create or import the data that you want to share in the source drawing and save it in the current working folder under the correct project folder.
4. In the *Prospector* tab, right-click on Data Shortcuts and select **Associate Project to Current Drawing**.
5. In the *Prospector* tab, right-click on Data Shortcuts and select **Create Data Shortcuts**.
6. Select all of the items that you want to share, such as surfaces, alignments, or profiles, and click **OK**.
7. Save the source drawing (and close as required).
8. Open, create, and save the drawing to receive the shortcut data. Expand the *Data Shortcuts* collection and the relevant object trees (*Surfaces*, *Alignments*, *Pipe Networks*, or *View Frame Groups*).
9. Highlight an item to be referenced, right-click and select **Create Reference...** Repeat for all of the objects as required. You are prompted for the styles and other settings that are required to display the object in the current drawing.
10. You might also want to add an XREF to the source drawing if there is additional AutoCAD® line work that you want to display in the downstream drawing.
11. The AutoCAD Civil 3D tools for Data Shortcuts are located in the *Manage* tab (as shown in Figure 12–5), and in the *Prospector* tab.

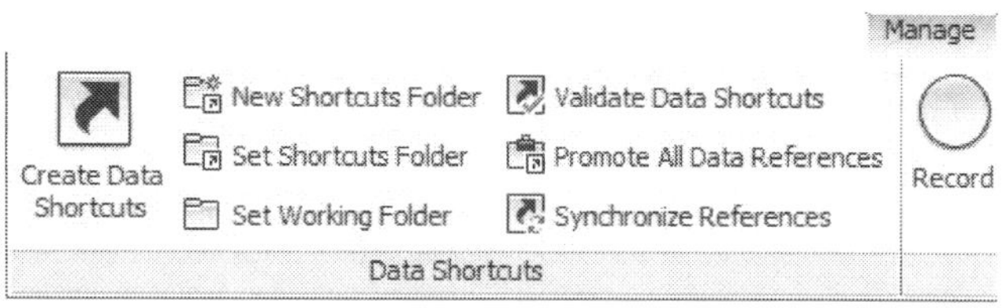

Figure 12–5

Workflow Details

- **Set Working Folder:** Sets a new working folder as the location in which to store the Data Shortcut project. The default working folder for Data Shortcut projects is *C:\Civil 3D Projects*. The default working folder is also used for Autodesk Vault projects and local (non-Vault) Survey projects. If you work with the Autodesk Vault software, local Survey, and Data Shortcut projects, you should have separate working folders for each project type for ease of management.

- **New Shortcuts Folder:** Creates a new folder for storing a set of related project drawings and Data Shortcuts.
- **Create Data Shortcuts:** Creates Data Shortcuts from the active drawing.

Data Shortcuts are stored in the *Shortcuts* folder for the active project and used to create data references to source objects in other drawings. Each Data Shortcut is stored in a separate XML file.

Advantages of Data Shortcuts

- Data Shortcuts provide a simple mechanism for sharing object data, without the added system administration needs of the Autodesk Vault software.
- Data Shortcuts offer access to an object's intelligent data while ensuring that this referenced data can only be changed in the source drawing.
- Referenced objects can have styles and labels that differ from the source drawing.
- When you open a drawing containing revised referenced data, the referenced objects are updated automatically.
- During a drawing session, if the referenced data has been revised, you are notified in the Communication Center and in the *Prospector* tab in Toolspace.

Limitations of Data Shortcuts

- Data Shortcuts cannot provide data versioning.
- Data Shortcuts do not provide security or data integrity controls.
- Unlike the Autodesk Vault software, Data Shortcuts do not provide a secure mechanism for sharing point data or survey data.

Maintaining links between references and their source objects requires fairly stable names. However, most broken references can easily be repaired using the tools in the AutoCAD Civil 3D software.

Practice 12a Starting a Project

Practice Objective

- Create a new data shortcut project with the correct working folder for the project being worked on.

Estimated time for completion: 15 minutes

In this practice you will walk through the steps of creating project-based Data Shortcuts folders.

Task 1 - Set the *Working* folder.

In this task, you will set up a new working folder as the location in which to store Data Shortcut projects. The default working folder for Data Shortcut projects is *C:\Civil 3D Projects*.

1. Open **DS-A1-Shortcuts.dwg** from the *C:\Civil 3D Projects\Civil3D-Training\DataShortcuts* folder.

2. In the *Manage* tab>Data Shortcuts panel, select **Set Working Folder**, as shown in Figure 12–6.

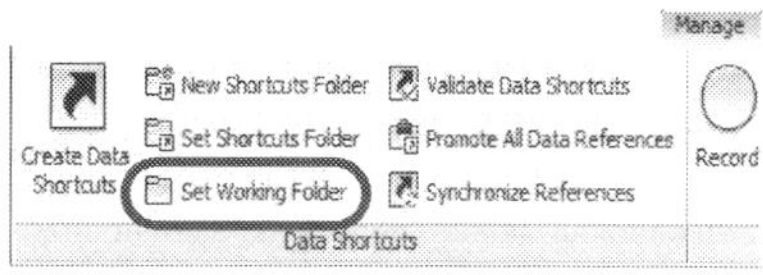

Figure 12–6

3. In the Browse For Folder dialog box, select the *Civil 3D Projects* folder and click **Make New Folder**, as shown on the left in Figure 12–7. Type **Learning Data Shortcuts** as the folder name and click **OK**, as shown on the right in Figure 12–7.

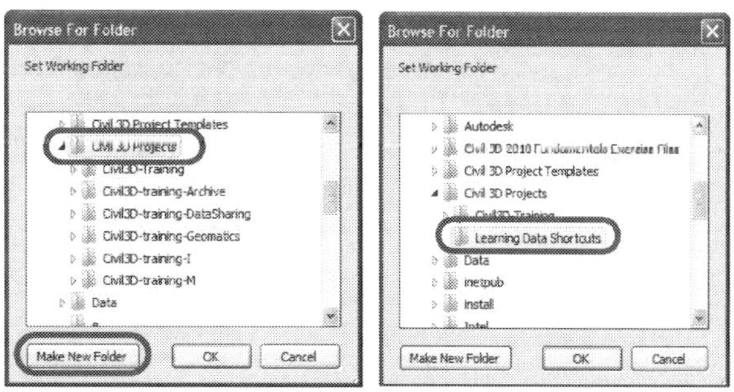

Figure 12–7

Task 2 - Create new *Shortcuts* folders.

In this task, you will create a new folder for storing a set of related project drawings and Data Shortcuts. A second project folder is created to help you understand how to change the project in which you are working.

1. Continue working with the drawing from the previous task.

2. In the *Manage* tab>Data Shortcuts panel, select **New Shortcuts Folder**, as shown in Figure 12–8.

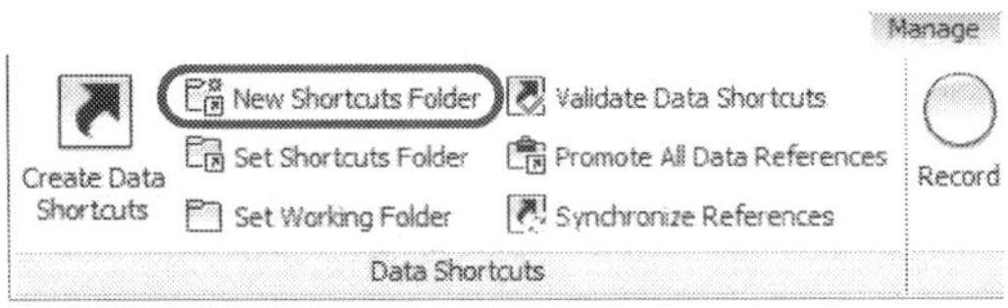

Figure 12–8

3. In the New Data Shortcut Folder dialog box, type **Ascent Phase 1** for the name and select the **Use project template** option. The template is found in the default folder *C:\Civil 3D Templates*, as shown in Figure 12–9. The AutoCAD Civil 3D software will replicate this template folder structure in the Data Shortcuts project folder. Click **OK** to close the dialog box.

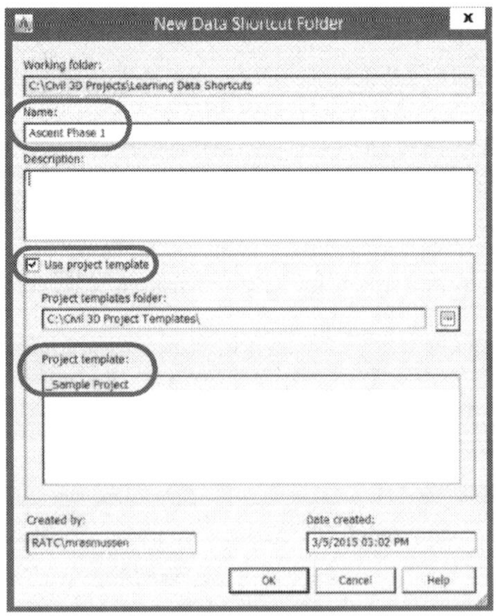

Figure 12–9

4. In the *Prospector* tab, a Data Shortcut folder should be displayed in *C:\Civil 3D Projects\Learning Data Shortcuts\Ascent Phase 1*. In Windows Explorer, verify that the *Civil 3D* folder structure was created for this project, as shown on the right in Figure 12–10.

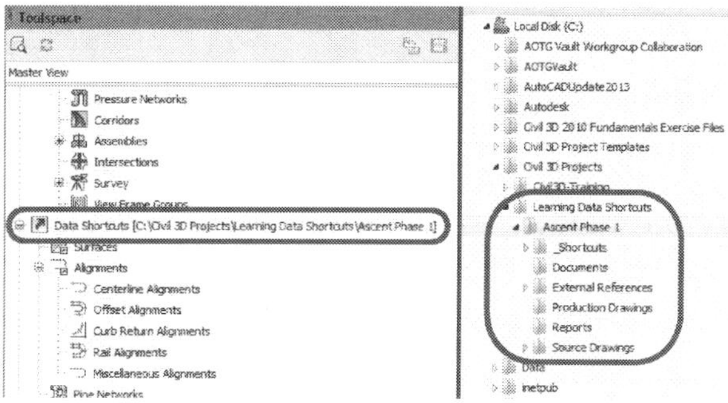

Figure 12–10

5. Create another new shortcuts folder. In the *Manage* tab>Data Shortcuts panel, select **New Shortcuts Folder**.

6. In the New Data Shortcut Folder dialog box, type **Ascent Phase 2** for the name and select the **Use project template** option. Click **OK** to close the dialog box.

   You now have two projects in the working folder: *Ascent Phase 1* and *Ascent Phase 2*, as shown in Figure 12–11.

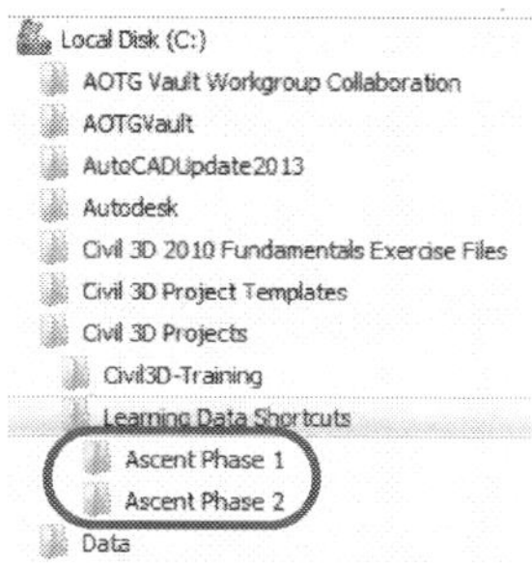

Figure 12–11

Task 3 - Set up *Shortcuts* folder.

Setting the shortcut folder specifies the project path for Data Shortcuts. The path to the current *Data Shortcuts* folder (also known as the project folder) is specified in the *Prospector* tab in the Toolspace, in the *Data Shortcuts* collection. The project folder typically contains both Data Shortcuts and source objects for data references.

1. Continue working with the drawing from the previous task.
2. In the *Manage* tab>Data Shortcuts panel, select **Set Shortcuts Folder**.
3. The current *Data Shortcut* folder is indicated by a green circle with a checkmark. Select **Ascent Phase 1** to make it current and click **OK**, as shown in Figure 12–12.

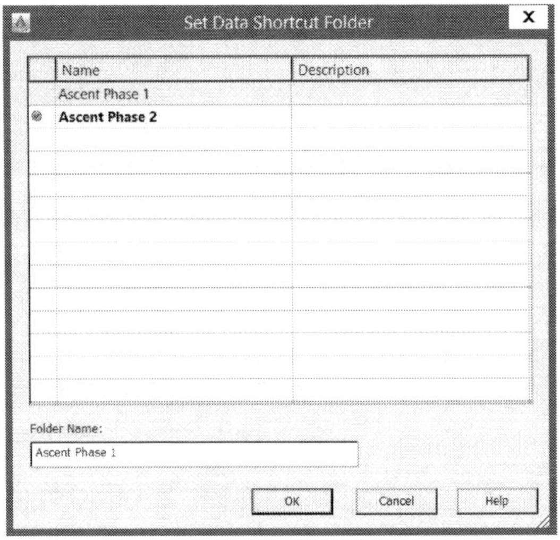

Figure 12–12

4. In the *Prospector* tab, right-click on Data Shortcuts and select **Associate Project to Current Drawing**, as shown in Figure 12–13.

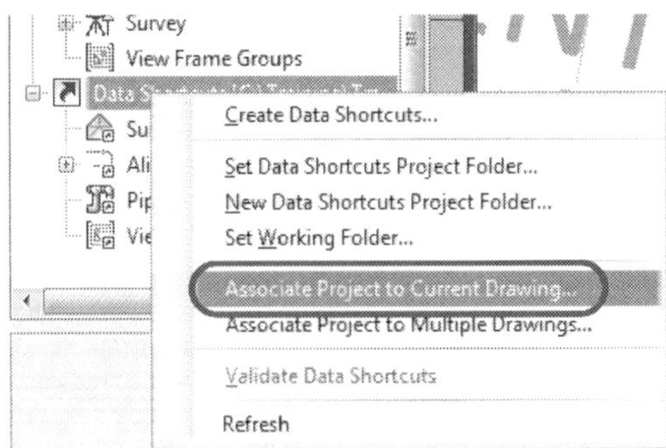

Figure 12–13

5. Verify that **Ascent Phase 1** is the selected project. Click **OK**.

Practice 12b Manage File Sizes with Data Shortcuts

Practice Objective

- Create Data Shortcuts from objects in a drawing to share with other team members.

Estimated time for completion: 20 minutes

In this practice you will walk through the steps of creating project-based *Data Shortcuts* folders. It simulates a situation in which some design work has been done and you now need to share elements of the design with team members.

Task 1 - Create Data Shortcuts.

1. Continue working with the drawing from the previous practice or open **DS-A1-Shortcuts.dwg**.
2. In the *Prospector* tab, verify that the Data Shortcuts points to the correct folder, as shown in Figure 12–14.

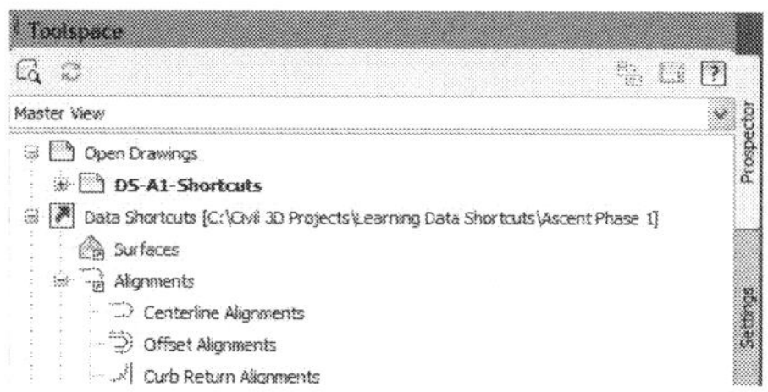

Figure 12–14

3. In the *Manage* tab>Data Shortcuts panel, click (Create Data Shortcuts).
4. If you receive a message that the drawing has not yet been saved, click **OK**. Save the drawing and start the **Create Data Shortcuts** command again.

5. In the Create Data Shortcuts dialog box, a list of all of the available objects for use in shortcuts is displayed. Select **Surfaces** and **Alignments**, as shown in Figure 12–15, and click **OK**.

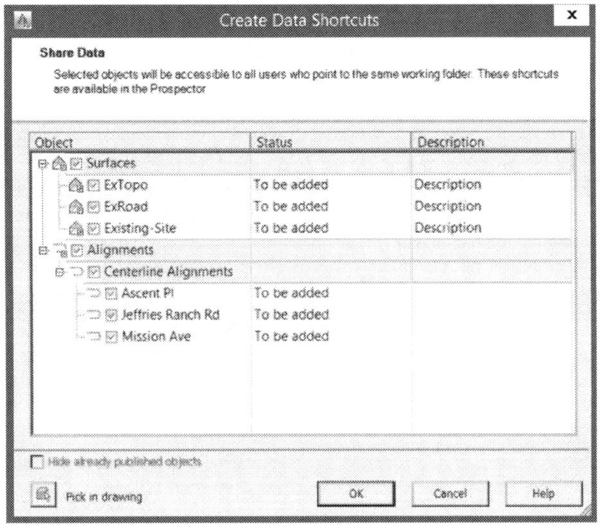

Figure 12–15

6. You have now created shortcuts for the surfaces and alignments. This means that if the shortcuts and drawings are in a shared network folder, anyone on the network has access to these AutoCAD Civil 3D objects.

Note that in the *Prospector* tab, under the *Data Shortcuts* and *Surfaces* collections, you can now access all of the surfaces. In the list view, the source filename and source path are displayed, as shown in Figure 12–16.

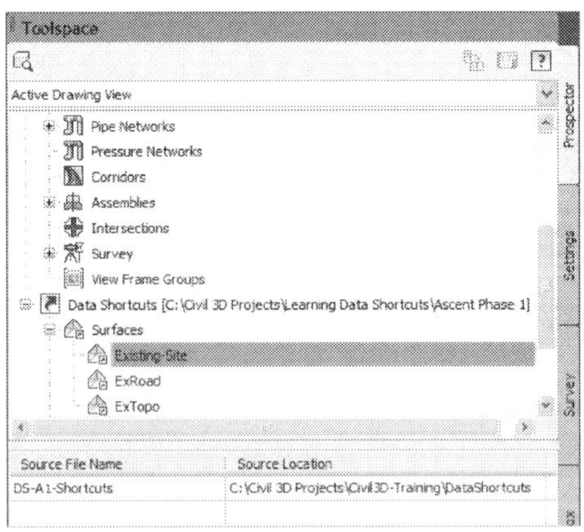

Figure 12–16

7. Save the drawing, but do not close it.

Task 2 - Data-reference Data Shortcuts.

1. Start a new drawing from **_AutoCAD Civil 3D (Imperial) NCS.dwt**. Save the file as **DS-B2-Shortcuts.dwg**.
2. In the *Prospector* tab, ensure that *Data Shortcuts* point to the *C:\Civil 3D Projects\Learning Data Shortcuts\Ascent Phase 1* folder.
3. In the *Prospector* tab, under the *Data Shortcuts* collection, expand the *Surfaces* collection (if not already expanded) and expand the *Alignments>Centerline Alignments* collection, as shown in Figure 12–17.

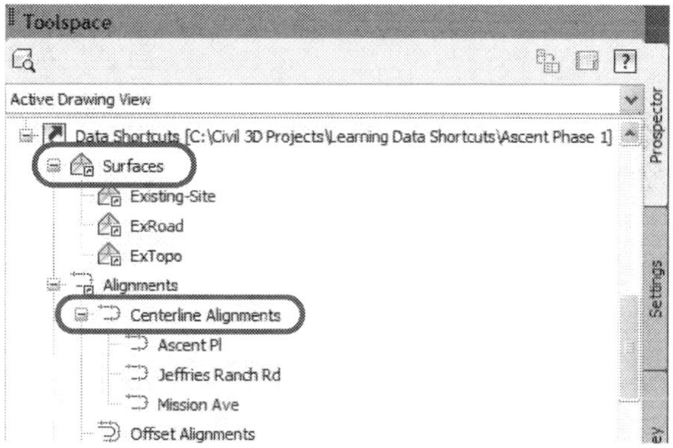

Figure 12–17

4. Under the *Surfaces* collection, select the surface **Existing-Site**, right-click, and select **Create Reference**, as shown in Figure 12–18.

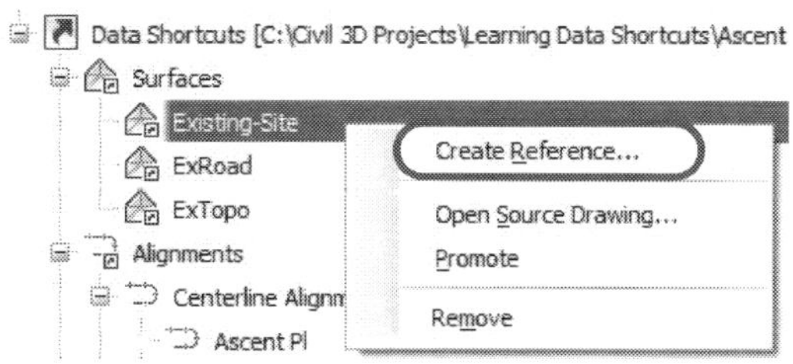

Figure 12–18

5. In the Create Surface Reference dialog box, do the following:
   - Type **ExSurface** for the *Name.*
   - Type **Data referenced surface** for the *Description.*

- Select **Contours 5' and 25' (Background)** for the *Style*, as shown in Figure 12–19.
- Click **OK** to close the dialog box.
- Type **ZE** and press <Enter> to display the surface reference.

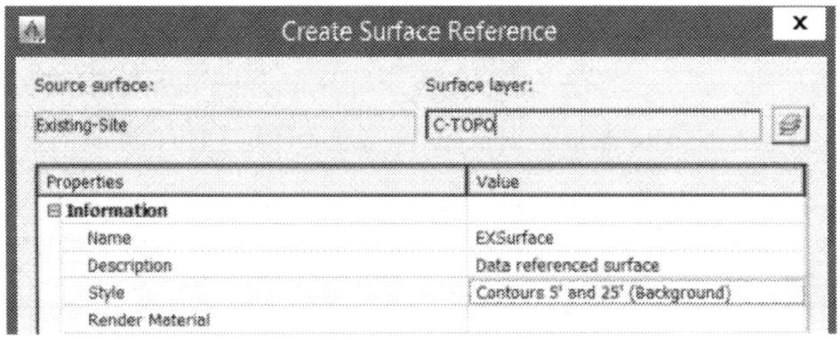

Figure 12–19

6. You will now create a data reference to the alignment. In the *Alignments* collection, right-click on **Ascent PI** and select **Create Reference**.

7. In the Create Alignment Reference dialog box, accept the default for the *Name*. Type **Data referenced alignment** for the *Description*. Set the *Alignment style* to **Layout** and set the *Alignment label set* to **Major and Minor only**. Click **OK** when done, as shown in Figure 12–20.

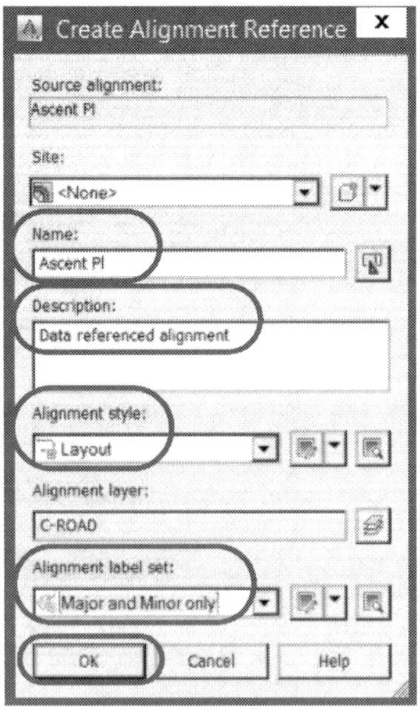

Figure 12–20

8. Zoom in to the end of the Ascent PI alignment, as shown in Figure 12–21.

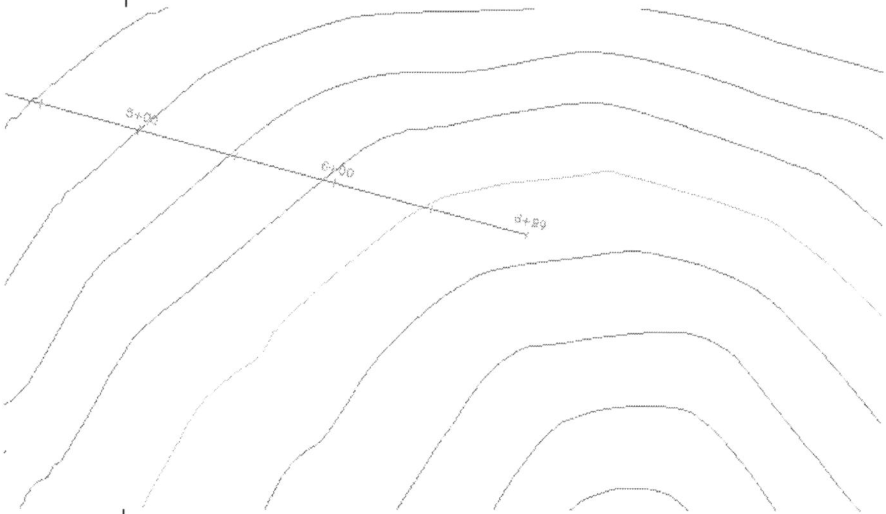

Figure 12–21

9. In Model Space, select the **Ascent PI** referenced alignment. Note that there are no grips and you cannot graphically redefine this alignment. However, you can add labels using the contextual tab.

10. In the contextual tab>Labels & Tables panel, expand Add Labels and select **Station/Offset - Fixed Point**, as shown in Figure 12–22.

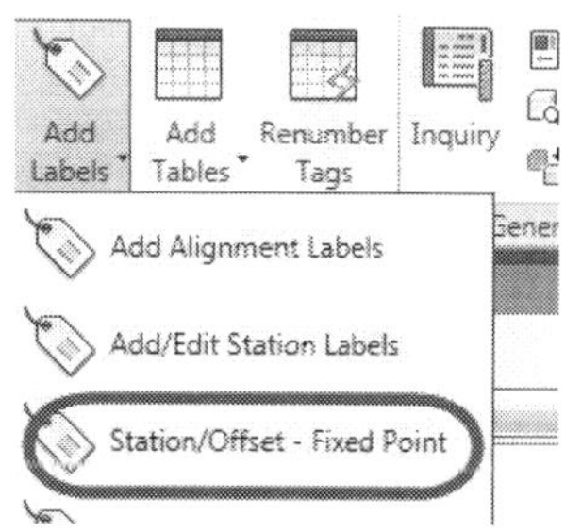

Figure 12–22

11. When prompted to select a point, select the end point of Ascent Pl, as shown on the left in Figure 12–23. Select the label and move its location so that it is easier to read, as shown on the right. Note that the station is 6+98.72.

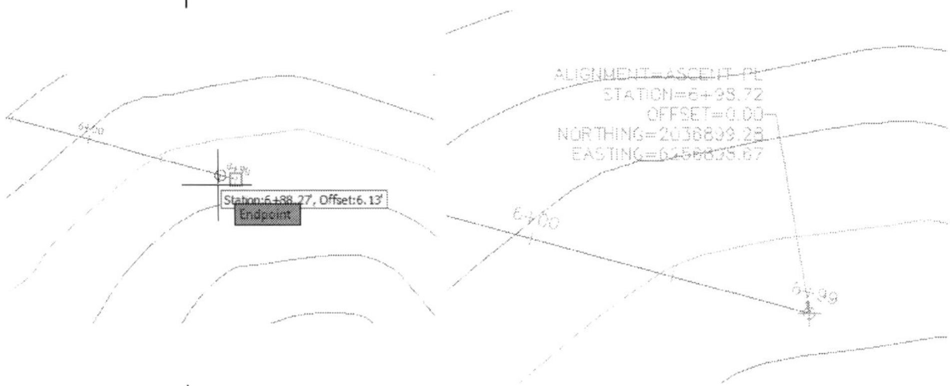

Figure 12–23

12. In the *Prospector* tab, expand the *Surfaces* and *ExSurface* collections, as shown on the left in Figure 12–24. Note that it does not contain the definition elements that might otherwise be displayed in a surface that is not data-referenced, as shown on the right. Therefore, you cannot edit or make design changes to a referenced surface.

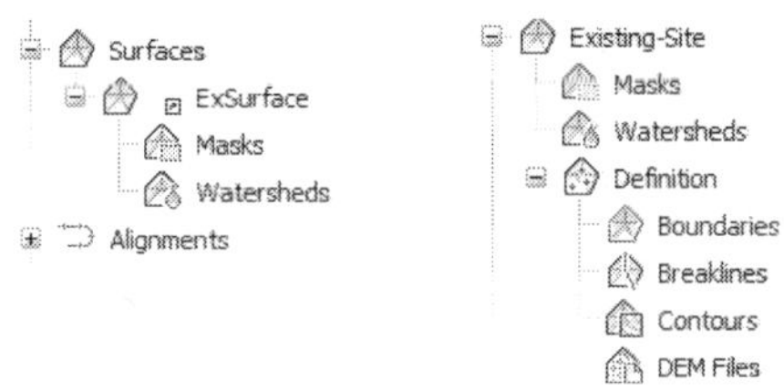

Figure 12–24

13. Save the drawing but do not close it.

Task 3 - Revise original referenced object.

1. In the *Prospector* tab, ensure that *Data Shortcuts* point to the *C:\Civil 3D Projects\Learning Data Shortcuts\Ascent Phase 1* folder.

2. Ensure that the **Master View** is enabled in Toolspace so that all of the drawings that are loaded are displayed. Select **DS-A1-Shortcuts**, right-click and select **Switch to**, as shown in Figure 12–25. **DS-A1-Shortcuts.dwg** is now the current drawing. However, if you had closed the drawing, you need to open **DS-A1-Shortcuts.dwg.**

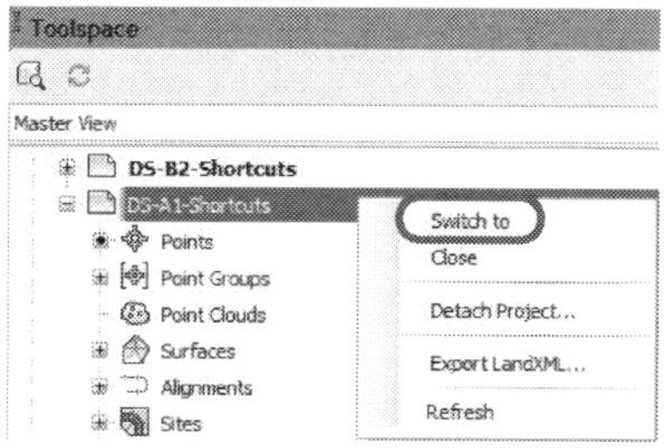

Figure 12–25

3. Zoom into the end of Ascent Pl to get a better view of the cul-de-sac.

4. You will now change the length of this alignment. In Model Space, select the alignment, select the grip that signifies the end of the alignment, and move it to the intersection where it crosses the cul-de-sac bulb, as shown in Figure 12–26.

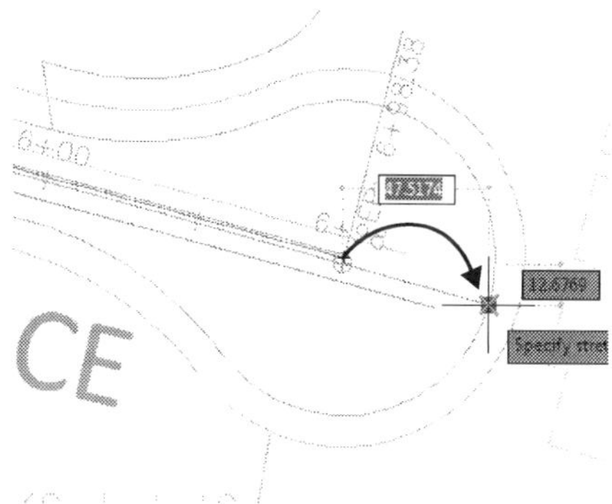

Figure 12–26

5. In the contextual tab>Modify panel, select **Alignment Properties**, as shown in Figure 12–27.

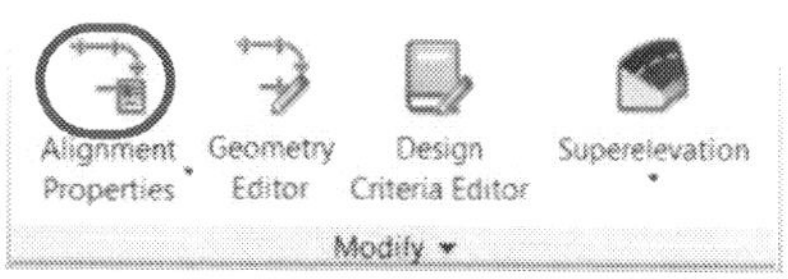

Figure 12–27

6. In the *Station Control* tab in the Alignment Properties - Ascent PI dialog box, set the reference point Station to **100**, as shown in Figure 12–28. A warning displays prompting you that changing the station will affect objects and data that have already been created. Click **OK** to dismiss the warning. Click **OK** to close the Alignment Properties dialog box.

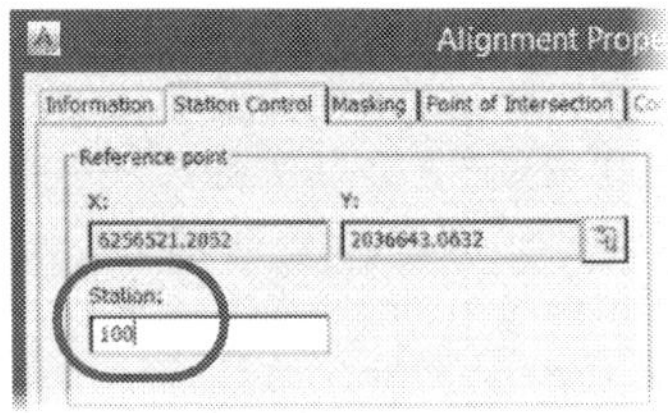

Figure 12–28

7. Save the drawing. This will cause the Data Shortcut to update.

8. If you are continuing with the drawing from the previous task, ensure that the Master view is enabled in the Toolspace so that you can see all of the drawings that are loaded. Select **DS-B2-Shortcuts**, right-click, and select **Switch to.** **DS-B2-Shortcuts.dwg** is now the current drawing.

9. If you closed the drawing in Step 8, open the drawing **DS-B2-Shortcuts.dwg** (move to Step 12).

10. In the Status Bar, you should see (Data Shortcut Reference), as shown on the left in Figure 12–29. To synchronize your current drawing, right-click on see (Data Shortcut Reference) and select **Synchronize**, as shown on the right in Figure 12–29.

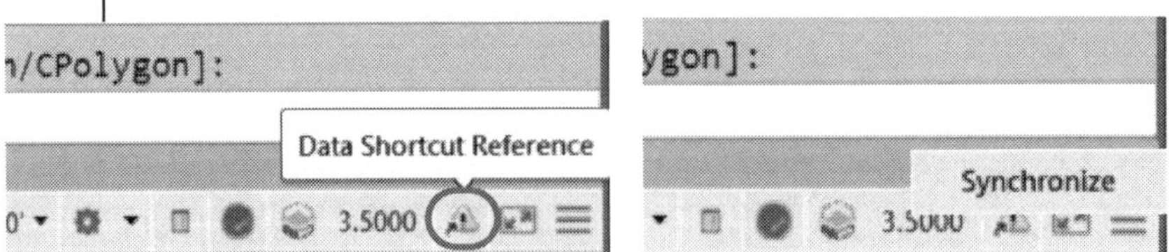

Figure 12–29

11. Alternatively, in the *Prospector* tab, select the alignment **Ascent Pl** in the *Alignments* collection. Right-click and select **Synchronize**, as shown in Figure 12–30.

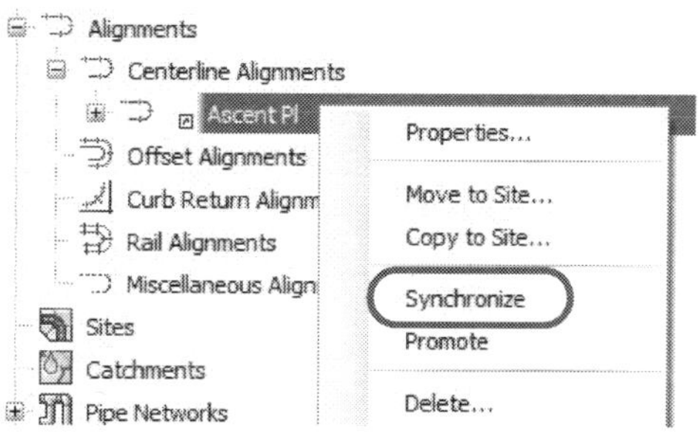

Figure 12–30

12. If **DS-B2-Shortcuts.dwg** was not previously created, open **DS-B3-Shortcuts.dwg**.

13. Note that the alignment has updated geographic information, as shown in Figure 12–31. The end of the alignment has been extended to intersect the cul-de-sac bulb, and the station label is updated to reflect the change to the original alignment design.

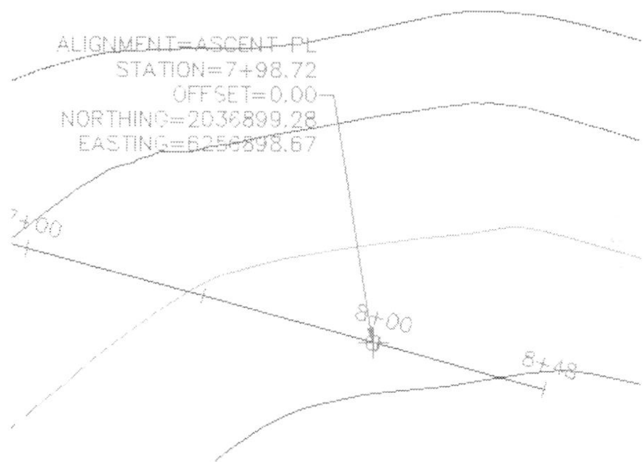

Figure 12–31

14. Save the drawing.

Practice 12c Share Projects with Team Members Outside the Office Network

Practice Objective

- Create a transmittal package to send to other design professionals on the project team, which includes all of the referenced object drawings, XREFs, and other required files.

Estimated time for completion: 5 minutes

1. Continue working with the previously opened drawing **DS-B2-Shortcuts.dwg**.

2. Expand (Application Menu), expand Publish, and select **eTransmit**, as shown in Figure 12–32. If a Warning dialog box opens stating that the current drawing is not saved, click **Yes** to save it.

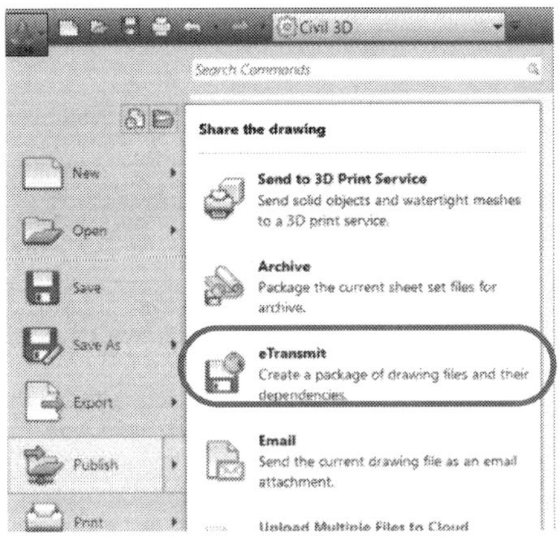

Figure 12–32

3. In the eTransmit dialog box, click **Transmittal Setups**, as shown in Figure 12–33.

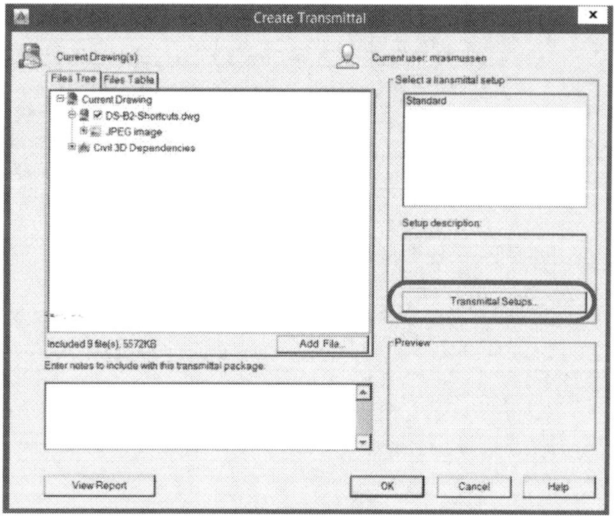

Figure 12–33

4. In the Transmittal Setups dialog box, select the **Standard** setup and click **Modify.**

5. In the Modify Transmittal Setup dialog box, accept the default for *Transmittal file folder*. Expand the Transmittal filename drop-down list and select **Prompt for a filename**. Select the **Keep files and folders as is** option. In the *Include options* area, select all of the options, as shown in Figure 12–34. Accept the remaining defaults and click **OK** to close the dialog box.

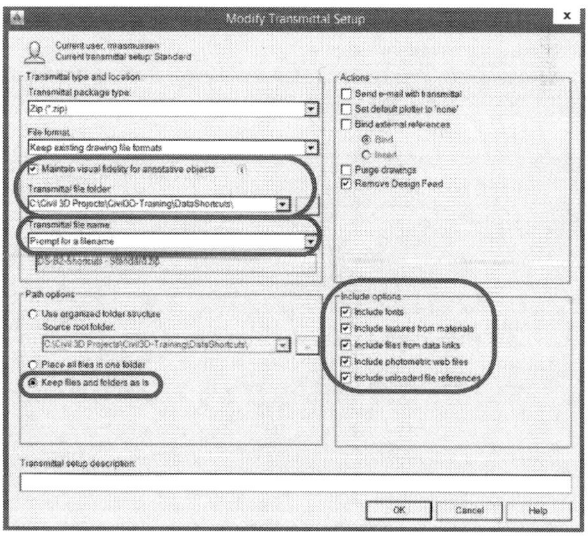

Figure 12–34

6. Close the Transmittal Setups dialog box.
7. Click **OK** to close the Create Transmittal dialog box and create the transmittal.
8. When prompted for the filename for the transmittal file, accept the default and save it. The AutoCAD Civil 3D software will create a compressed file of all of the relevant data.

Plan Production

This chapter includes instructional content to assist in your preparation for the following topic and objectives for the AutoCAD® Civil® 3D 2016 Certified Professional exam.

Autodesk Certification Exam Objectives in this Chapter

Exam Topic	Exam Objective	Section
Plan Production	• Create a sheet set	• 13.1
	• Use view frames	• 13.2

13.1 Create a Sheet Set

Once the Match Lines, View Frames, and associated View Frame Groups have been established, you can start the next phase of generating sheet sets.

The AutoCAD Civil 3D software includes a wizard that helps you create sheets from the View Frames. The flexibility of this wizard, in addition to the selection of styles, enables you to create sheets automatically that conform to many of your existing standards. The wizard is shown in Figure 13–1.

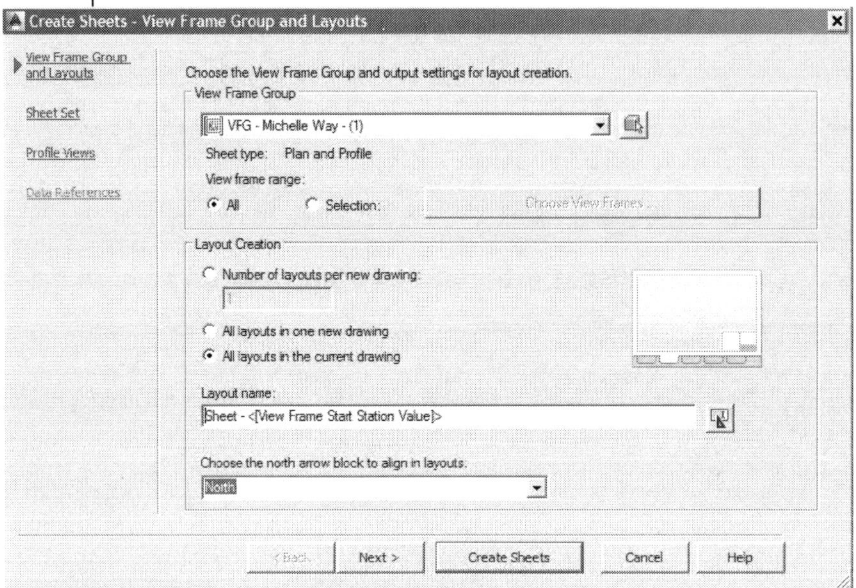

Figure 13–1

Since a dynamic link does not exist between the View Frames and the sheet, it is important that the required View Frames are established before creating the sheets. Changing or editing View Frames after the sheets are created has no effect on the sheets.

- In addition to using the wizard for creating sheets, this workflow also uses the AutoCAD Sheet Set Manager.

13.2 Use View Frames

The first step in using the Plan Production tools is to assemble all of the relevant data. This process is the same, whether you use the AutoCAD Civil 3D Plan Production tools or not. Some of the steps you might use in assembling this base plan involve external referencing pertinent data into your drawing to give the plan geographic reference (i.e., ROW lines, contours, survey data, aerial photographs, etc.). AutoCAD Civil 3D design objects are also data-referenced into the base plan.

The AutoCAD Civil 3D software provides a tool to help automate plan and production sheet creation: the Create View Frames wizard. It is the next step in plan production after the base plan has been created. Using this wizard, you can create View Frames, View Frame Groups, and Match Lines, all of which are plan production objects. The wizard is shown in Figure 13–2.

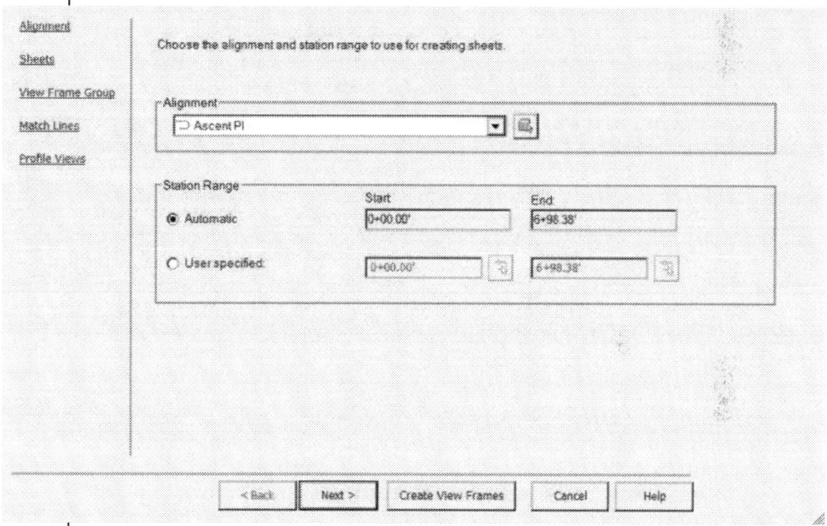

Figure 13–2

View Frames

View Frames are interactive, rectangular objects that are placed along a selected alignment. These rectangular shapes represent a view for each plan sheet that is created in the AutoCAD Civil 3D software. View Frames divide the alignment into segments. These segments are based on the base drawing scale and the viewport settings on the Layout tab from the drawing template that is used to define the views.

View Frame Groups

View Frame Groups are collections of the View Frames along a single alignment. View Frame Groups enable you to manage a group of views, including properties, such as styles and labeling.

Match Lines

A Match Line is a line that designates a location along an alignment that is used as a common reference point for two adjacent plans. If you create plan and profile or profile only sheets, the **Insert Match Lines** option is automatically selected and you cannot edit it.

Match Lines, as with all other AutoCAD Civil 3D objects, are style-driven. Typically, they have labels that can identify both adjacent plans, one plan, or no plans. You can also have these labels displayed at the top, bottom, or middle of the Match Line.

Practice 13a

Plan Production Tools I

Estimated time for completion: 20 minutes

Practice Objective

- Create and edit view frames to divide the alignment into printable areas.

For this practice, two alignments from the project have been combined into one alignment and profile to better demonstrate the full power of the plan production tools in the AutoCAD Civil 3D software when used with longer corridor projects. Combining alignments is not necessary or recommended for real projects.

Task 1 - Create View Frames.

1. Open **PPR1-A1-PlanProduction.dwg** from the *C:\Civil 3D Projects\Civil3D-Training\PlanProduction* folder.

2. You will create the plan - profile sheets at a scale of 1"=20'. The sheets will be created more consistently if the Model Space scale matches the final output scale. If not already done, set the *Annotation Scale* to **1"=20'**, as shown in Figure 13–3.

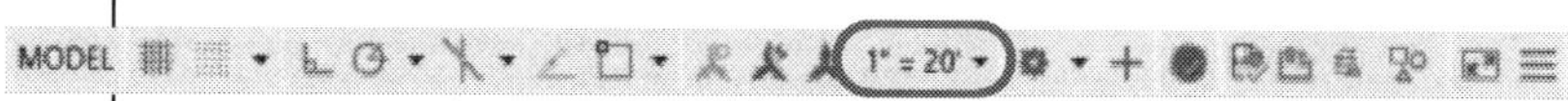

Figure 13–3

3. In the *Output* tab>Plan Production panel, click  (Create View Frames).

4. In the wizard, in the *Create View Frames - Alignment* page, select **Michelle Way** as the *Alignment* and select the **Automatic** option in the *Station Range* area, as shown in Figure 13–4. Click **Next>**.

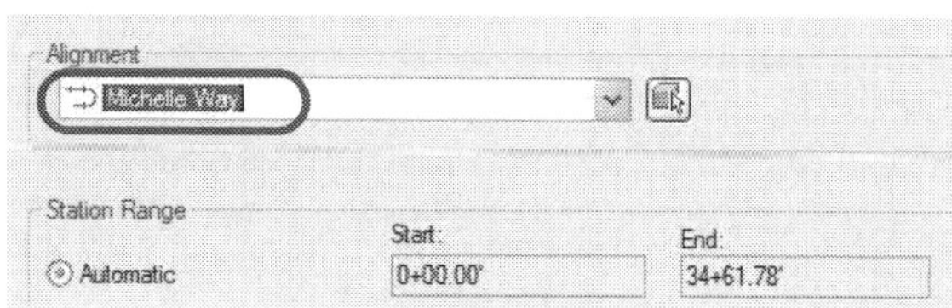

Figure 13–4

5. In the *Create View Frames - Sheets* page, in the sheet settings, select the **Plan and Profile** option. In the *Template for Plan and Profile sheet* area, click ... .

6. In the *Drawing template file name* field, click ... and browse to **C3D Training Plan and Profile.dwt**. This file is located in *C:\Civil 3D Projects\Civil3D-Training\PlanProduction*.

7. In the *Select a layout to create new sheets* area, expand the drop-down list and select **Arch D Plan and Profile 20 Scale**, as shown in Figure 13–5, and click **OK**.

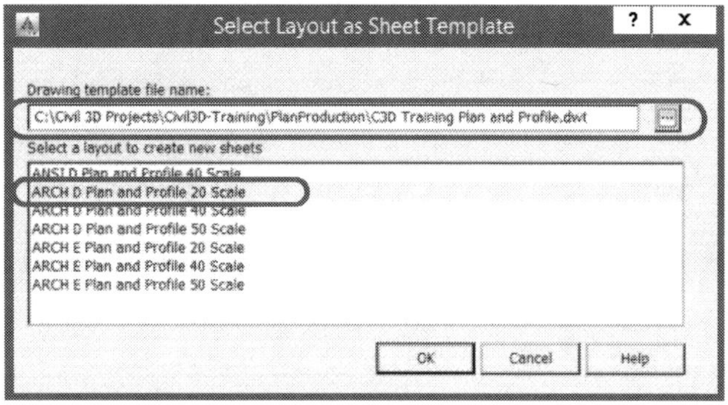

Figure 13–5

8. For the *View Frame Placement*, select the **Along alignment** option, as shown in Figure 13–6. Click **Next>**.

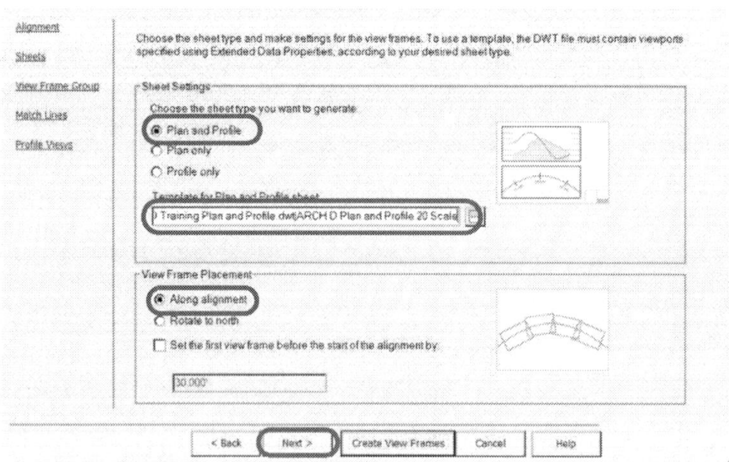

Figure 13–6

This will append the alignment name and a counter to the VFG.

9. In the *Create View Frames - View Frame Group* page, accept the default for the *Name*.

10. To name the View Frame with the starting station, click (Edit View Frame Name).

If these settings in the name template are standard, you can save them in the Setting tab in the master DWT file.

11. In the Name Template dialog box, type **VF - Sta** in the *Name* field. In the Property fields drop-down list, select **View Frame Start Raw Station** and click **Insert**, as shown in Figure 13–7. Click **OK** to close the dialog box.

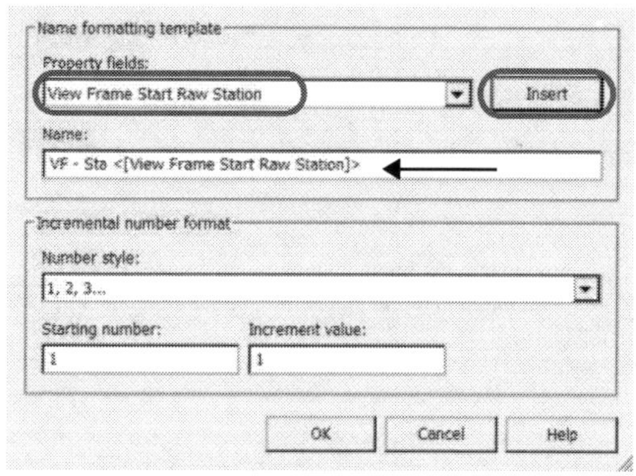

Figure 13–7

12. Accept the default Label and Label style. Accept the Label location of **Top left**, as shown in Figure 13–8, and click **Next>**.

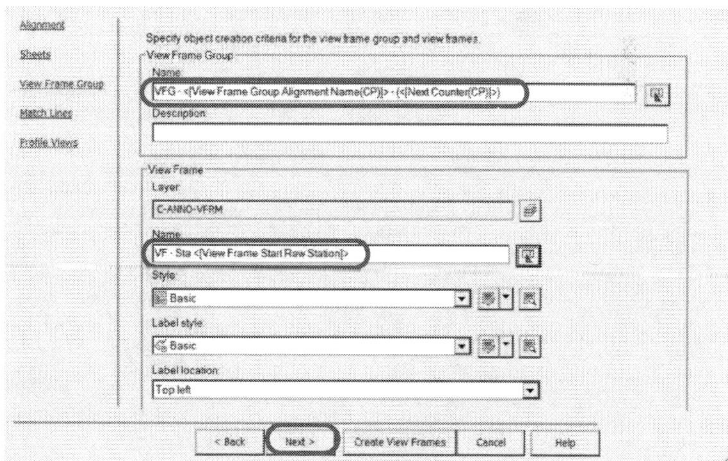

Figure 13–8

The procedure to do this is similar to Step 12.

13. In the *Create View Frames - Match Lines* page, select the **Allow additional distance for repositioning** option and change the *Match Line* name to **ML - <[Match Line Raw Station]>**, as shown in Figure 13–9. Accept all other defaults and click **Next>**.

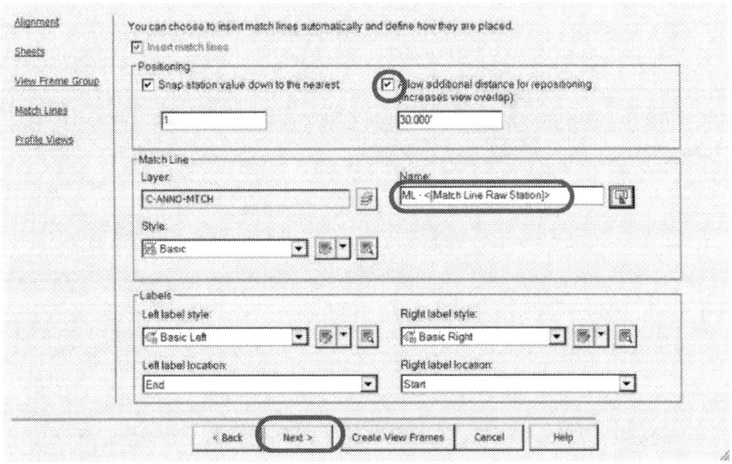

Figure 13–9

14. In the *Create View Frames - Profile Views* page, accept the default values for the *Profile View Style* and the *Band Set*. Click **Create View Frames**, as shown in Figure 13–10.

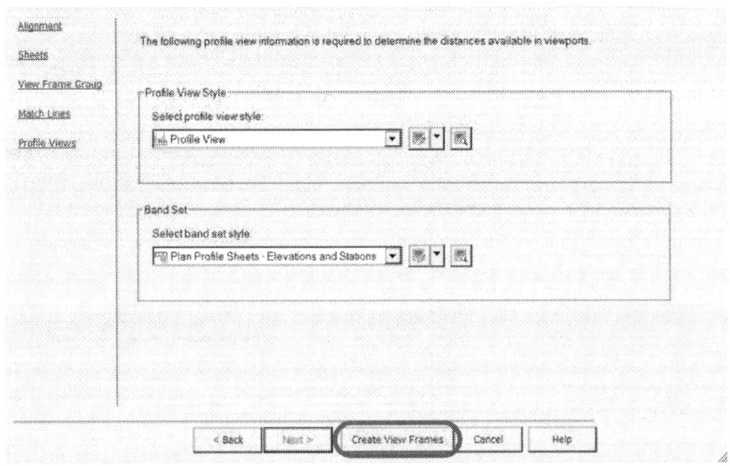

Figure 13–10

15. In the *Prospector* tab, expand the *View Frame Groups* collection, expand the *VFG - Michelle Way View* Frame Group, and then expand the *View Frames* collection and the *Match Lines* collection. Note that the Create View Frame wizard has created three Plan Production objects, two View Frames, and one Match Line, as shown in Figure 13–11.

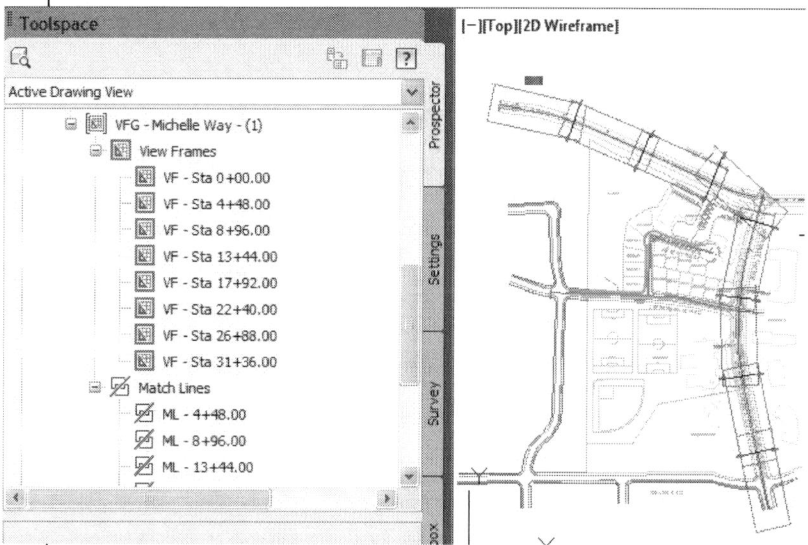

Figure 13–11

16. Save the drawing.

Practice 13b Plan Production Tools II

Practice Objective

- Create plan and profile sheets using the Plan Production tools and previously created View Frame objects.

Estimated time for completion: 10 minutes

Task 1 - Create sheet files and a new Sheet Set Manager file.

1. Open **PPR1-B1-PlanProduction.dwg** from the *C:\Civil 3D Projects\Civil3D-Training\PlanProduction* folder.
2. In the *Output* tab>Plan Production panel, click (Create Sheets).
3. In the wizard, in the *Create Sheet - View Frame Group and Layouts* page, ensure that the *View Frame Group* is **VFG - Michelle Way**, and the *View frame range* is set to **All**. In the *Layout Creation* area, set the *Layout* creation to **All layouts in the current drawing**.

If these settings to the name template are standard, it is recommended that you save them in the Setting tab in the master DWT file.

4. For the *Layout name*, click (Edit Layout Name). In the *Name* field, delete the current name and type **Sheet -**. Expand the Property fields drop-down list, select **View Frame Start Station Value** and click **Insert**. The AutoCAD Civil 3D software will append the data string **<[View Frame Start Station Value]>** to the text **Sheet -**, as shown in Figure 13–12. Click **OK** to close this dialog box.

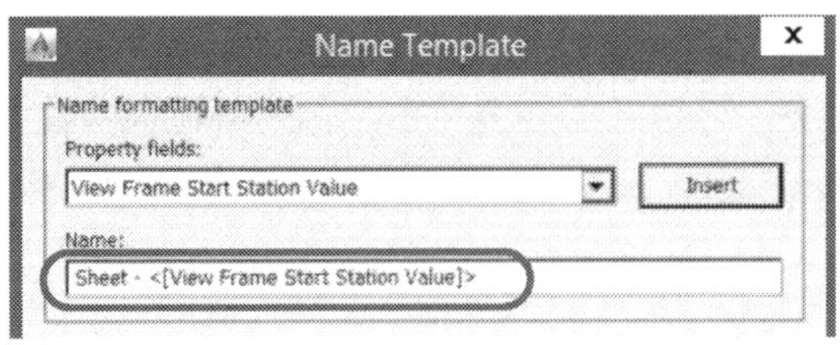

Figure 13–12

5. Expand the Choose the north arrow block to align in layouts drop-down list and select the **North** block, as shown in Figure 13–13. Once this is complete, click **Next>**.

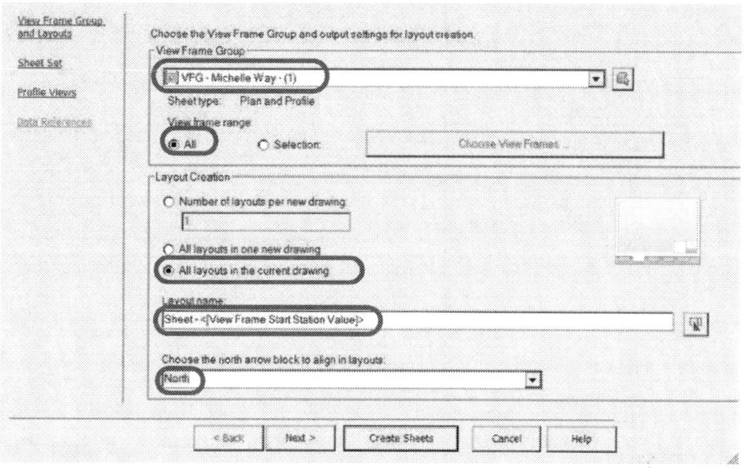

Figure 13–13

6. In the *Create Sheets - Sheet Set* page, set the following:

   - Select the **New sheet set** option, and type **Ascent Phase1** in the *Sheet Set name* field. Leave the *Sheet set file (.DST) storage location* field set to the default, as shown in Figure 13–14. Click **Next>**.

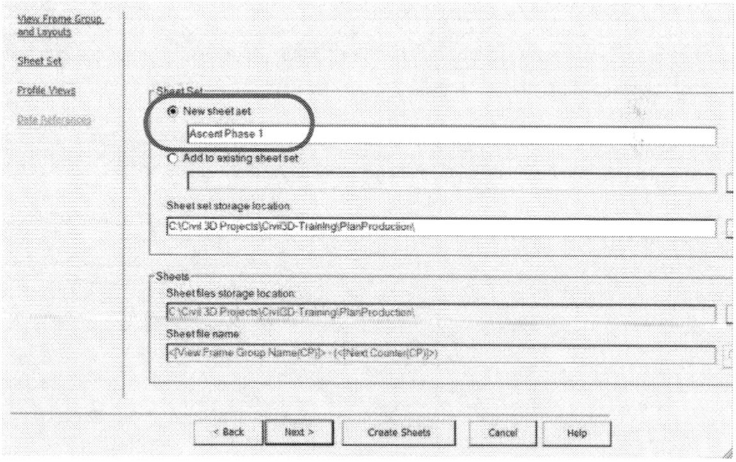

Figure 13–14

7. In the *Create Sheets - Profile Views* page, accept the defaults, as shown in Figure 13–15, and click **Create Sheets**.

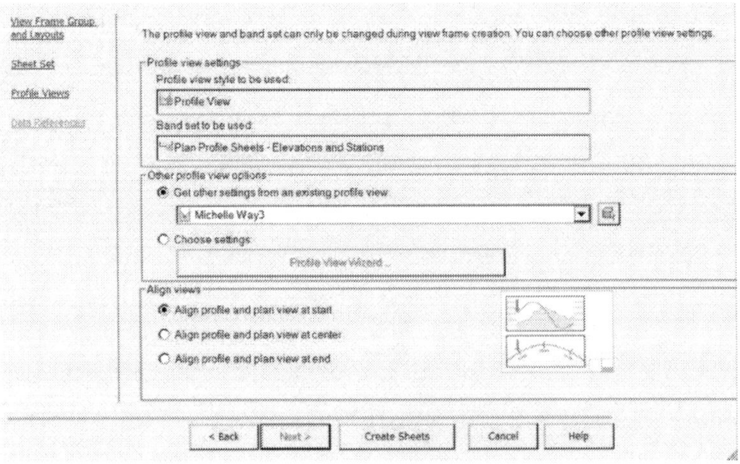

Figure 13–15

8. The wizard prompts you that the drawing will be saved before creating the new sheets. Click **OK** to accept this.

9. When prompted for the location of the profile, select a blank space in your drawing, as shown in Figure 13–16. The AutoCAD Civil 3D software will use this location to insert a profile of your alignment. Note that this profile is inserted in the newly created sheet and not in the current drawing.

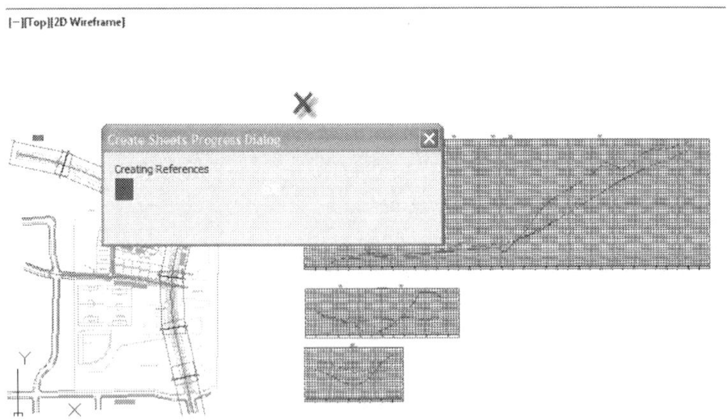

Figure 13–16

10. The AutoCAD Civil 3D software creates the sheets and the Sheet Set Manager files. The Sheet Set Manager opens, as shown in Figure 13–17.

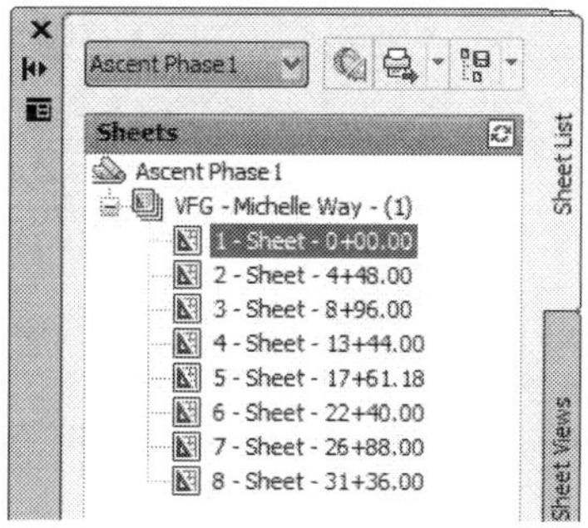

Figure 13–17

11. Hover the cursor over the filename in the Sheet Set Manager to display all of the properties of the sheet, including the name and location of the drawing file, as shown in Figure 13–18.

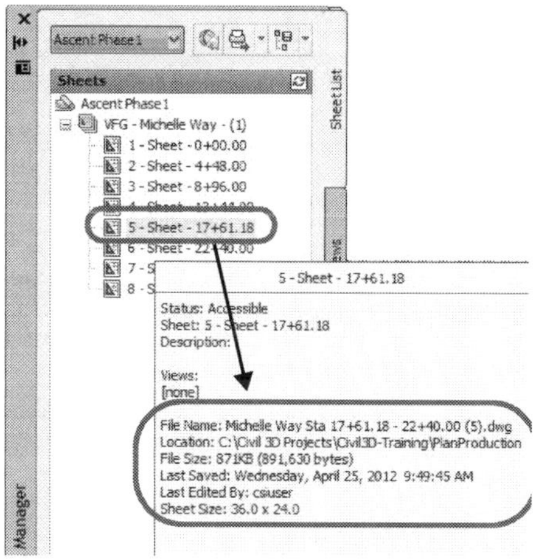

Figure 13–18

12. Save the drawing.

Chapter 14

Survey

This chapter includes instructional content to assist in your preparation for the following topic and objectives for the AutoCAD® Civil® 3D 2016 Certified Professional exam.

Autodesk Certification Exam Objectives in this Chapter

Exam Topic	Exam Objective	Section
Survey	• Identify key characteristics of survey data	• 14.1
	• Use description keys to control the display of points created from survey data	• 14.2
	• Create a boundary drawing from field data	• 14.3

14.1 Identify Key Characteristics of Survey Data

Survey figures consist of linework generated by coding and placed in a file that is imported into the Survey Database. A figure represents linear features (edge-of-pavement, toe-of-slopes, etc.)

A figure has many functions, which include:

- Acting as linework in a drawing.
- Acting as breaklines for a surface definition.
- Acting as parcel lines.
- Acting as a pipe run.
- Acting as targets for *Width* or *Offset Targets* in a Corridor.
- Acting as targets for *Slope* or *Elevation Targets* in a Corridor (e.g., limits of construction for a road rehab project might be to the face of walk, which exists in the drawing as a Survey Figure, hence a target).

The Figure Prefix database should be set up before importing any survey data to obtain the required entities in a drawing. As point and label styles and the Description Key Set need to exist before importing points, figure styles and entries in the Figure Prefix database need to exist before importing survey data.

Figure Prefix Database

The Figure Prefix database (found in the *Survey* tab of the Toolspace) assigns the figure a style, a layer, and defines whether the figure is a surface breakline or lot line (parcel segment). If you did not define any figure styles, you should at least assign a layer to correctly place the figure in the drawing. Toggling on the *Breakline* property, as shown in Figure 14–1, enables you select all of the tagged survey figures and assign them to a surface without having to insert or select from a drawing. Toggling on the *Lot Line* property creates a parcel segment from the figure in the drawing and, if there is a closed polygon, assigns a parcel label and an entry in the survey site.

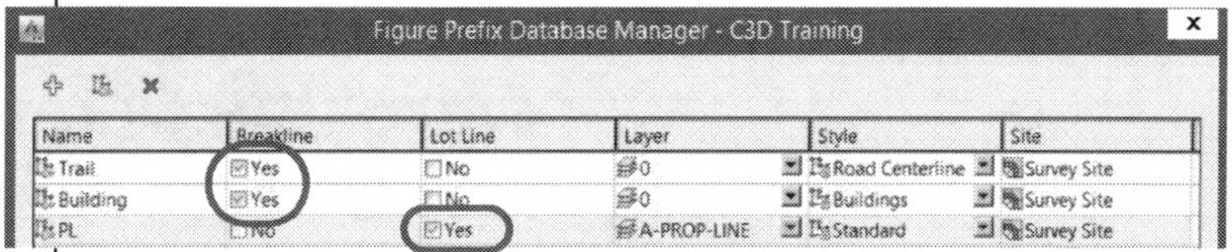

Figure 14–1

If the *Name* is **PL** (as shown in Figure 14–1), any figure starting with PL uses these settings. This is similar to using a Description Key Set, except that the entry in the Figure Prefix database does not need an asterisk (*). The entry GUT matches PL1 through PL100. When inserting survey figures in the drawing, Survey checks the Figure Prefix database for style or layer values.

14.2 Use Description Keys to Control the Display of Points Created from Survey Data

Description Keys categorize points by their field descriptions (raw description). If a point matches a Description Key entry, the point is assigned a point and label style, and a full description (a translation of the raw description). Description Key Sets can also scale and rotate points.

The Description Key's first five columns are the most used entries, as shown in Figure 14–2.

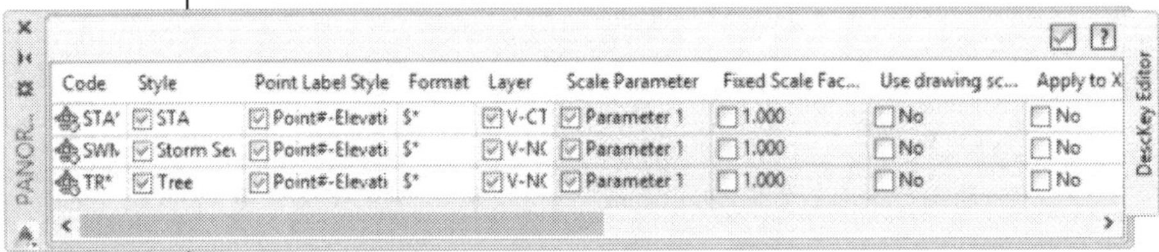

Figure 14–2

- To create a new Description Key row, select an existing code, right-click, and select **New**. To edit a code, double-click in the cell.

Code, Point, and Label Style

Description code is a significant part of data collection. Code assigned to a raw description triggers action by the Description Key Set. Each entry in the set represents all of the possible descriptions that a field crew would use while surveying a job. When a raw description matches a code entry, the Key Set assigns all of the row's values to the matching point, including point style, label style, translates the raw description, and possibly assigns a layer. Codes are case-sensitive and must match the field collector's entered raw description.

A code might contain wild cards to match raw descriptions that contain numbering or additional material beyond the point's description. For example, MH* would match MH1, MH2, etc. and UP* would match UP 2245 14.4Kv Verizon. Common wild keys are described as follows:

# (pound)	Matches any single numeric digit. (T# matches T1 through T9.)
@ (at)	Matches any alphabetic character. (1@ matches 1A through 1Z.)
. (period)	Matches any non-alphanumeric character. (T. matches T- or T+.)
*** (asterisk)**	Matches any string of characters. (T* matches TREE, TR-Aspen, Topo, or Trench.)
? (question mark)	Matches any single character. (?BC matches TBC or 3BC.)

Matching a Key Set entry for the code assigns a Point Style at the point's coordinates. If the *Point Style* is set to **Default**, the *Settings* tab's Point feature *Point Style* is used (set in the Edit Feature Settings dialog box), as shown in Figure 14–3.

Matching a Key Set entry for the code assigns a point label style to annotate important point values. This is usually a number, elevation, and description. If the *Point Style* is set to **Default**, the *Settings* tab's Point feature *Point Label Style* is used (set in the Edit Feature Settings dialog box), as shown in Figure 14–3.

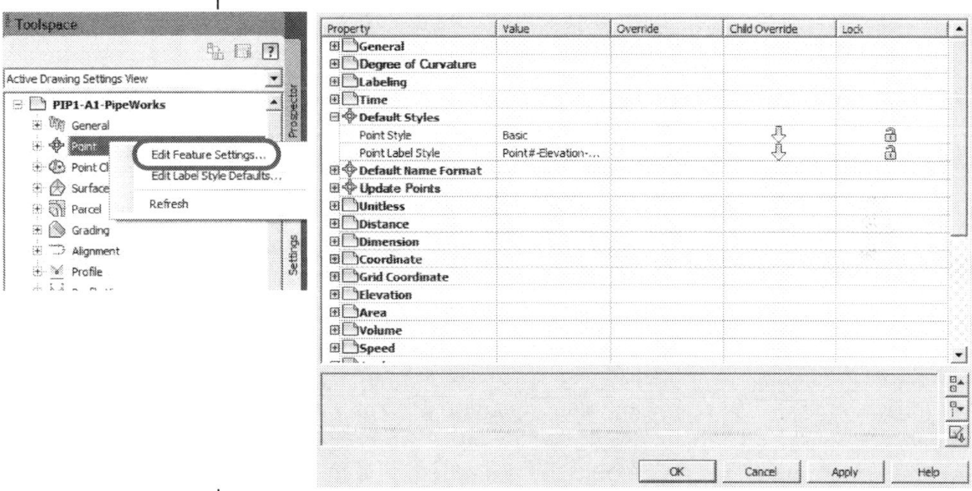

Figure 14–3

Format

The *Format* column translates the raw description (what the surveyor typed) into a full description (what you want it to read). When including spaces in a raw description, the AutoCAD Civil 3D software assigns parameter numbers to each description element. Parameters are represented by a $ sign followed by a number. For example, the description *PINE 6* has two elements: PINE and 6, with PINE as parameter 0 ($0) and 6 as parameter 1 ($1). When the *Format* column contains $*, it indicates that the software should use the raw description as the full description. The *Format* column can reorder the parameters and add characters to create a full description. For example, the raw description *PINE 6* can be translated to 6" PINE by entering **$1" $0**.

A complex raw description is as follows:

TREE D MAPLE 3

For the raw description to match the Description Key Set entry, the entry **TREE** must have an asterisk (*) after TREE (as shown in Figure 14–4). The raw description elements and their parameters are TREE ($0), D ($1), Maple ($2), and 3 ($3). The *Format* column entry of **$3" $2 $0** creates a full description of **3" MAPLE TREE**.

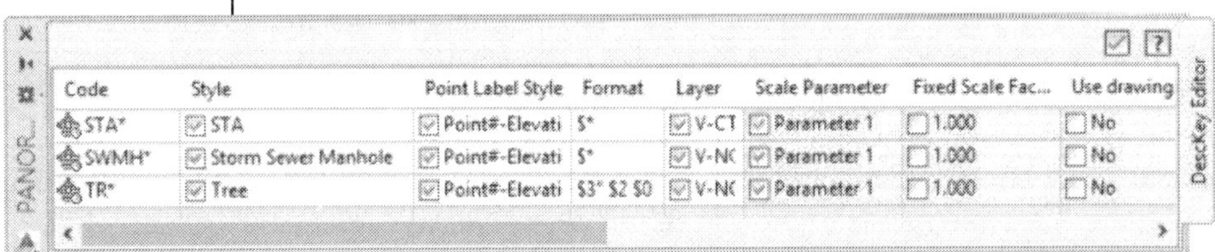

Figure 14–4

If a point does not match any Description Key Set entry, it receives the default styles assigned by the _All Points group.

The *Layer* column assigns a layer to the matching point. If the Point Style already has a marker and label layer, this entry should be toggled off. The Description Key Set also contains the *Scale* and *Rotate Parameter* columns. In the example in Figure 14–4, the 3 for the trunk diameter can also be a tree symbol scaling factor when applied to the symbol's X-Y.

14.3 Create a Boundary Drawing from Field Data

The AutoCAD Civil 3D software has methods to import point data from ASCII text files, AutoCAD Land Desktop point databases, and Autodesk LandXML files, as well as methods to convert AutoCAD Land Desktop points to AutoCAD Civil 3D points. The *Survey* tab also inserts points from a survey to a drawing.

Import Points and Figures Using the Survey Database

After collecting and coding the data, and then downloading and converting it, the next step in Survey is to import the survey data, review it, and place the survey points and figures into a drawing. A working folder defines where the local Survey Database is located. The preferred location is a network folder, in which you place the local Survey Databases. The Survey User Settings dialog box sets the defaults for all new Survey Databases. You should set these before starting Survey. The Survey Working Folder is the location for all of the Survey Databases and can be local or on the network. The default working folder is *C:\Civil 3D Projects*.

How To: Set the Working Folder for the Survey Database

1. In the *Survey* tab, select **Survey Databases**.
2. Right-click and select **Set working folder...** as shown in Figure 14–5.

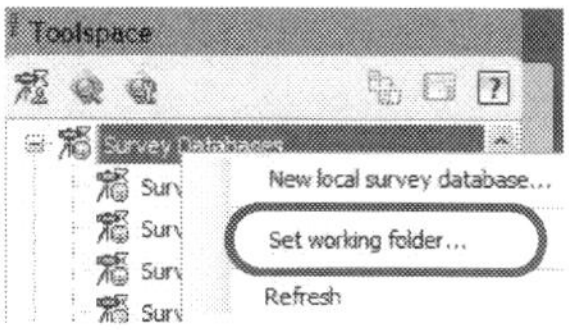

Figure 14–5

Survey Database

Survey Database Folders cannot be deleted in AutoCAD Civil 3D Survey. If you want to delete the working folder, this process must be done manually, external to the AutoCAD Civil 3D software.

A Survey Database is a subfolder in the working folder. The Survey Working Folder contains the Survey's settings and observation database. This database contains the Survey's Networks, Figures, and Survey Points.

To import a field book, you use the Survey's *Import Events* collection. *Import Events* provides access to an Import wizard, which guides you through the steps of importing a file. To open the Import wizard, select **Import Events** in the Survey, right-click, and select **Import survey data...**

The Specify Database page is shown in Figure 14–6. It sets the survey, creates a new survey, and edits the Survey's settings.

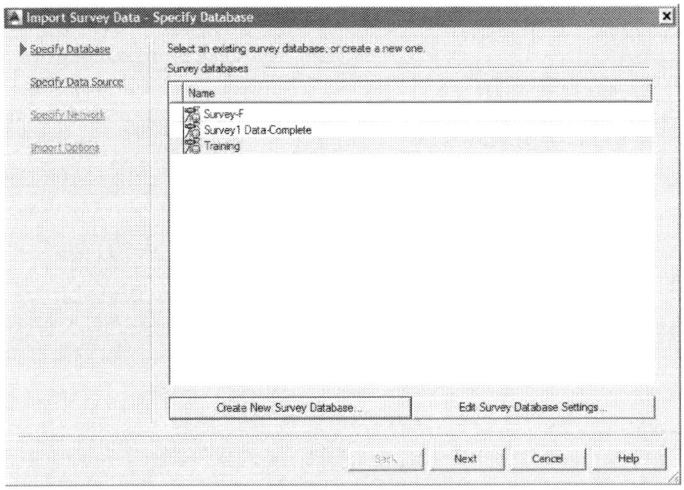

Figure 14–6

Click **Next**. The *Specify Data Source* page (shown in Figure 14–7), defines the file import type, the file's path, and its format (if it is a coordinate file).

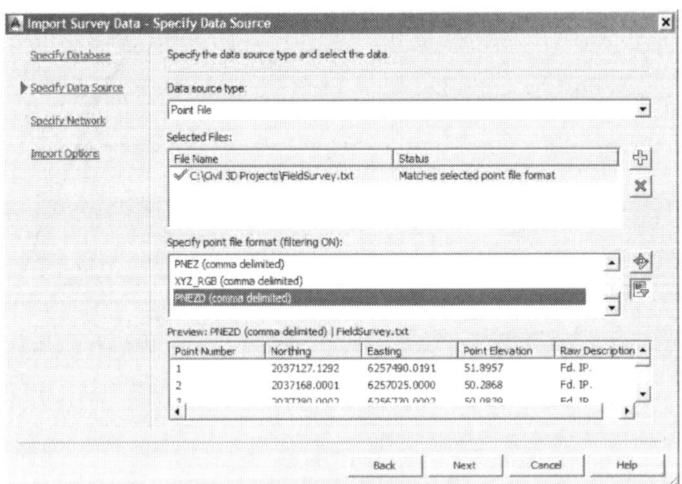

Figure 14–7

Click **Next**. The *Specify Network* page (shown in Figure 14–8), enables you to change the network or create a new survey network.

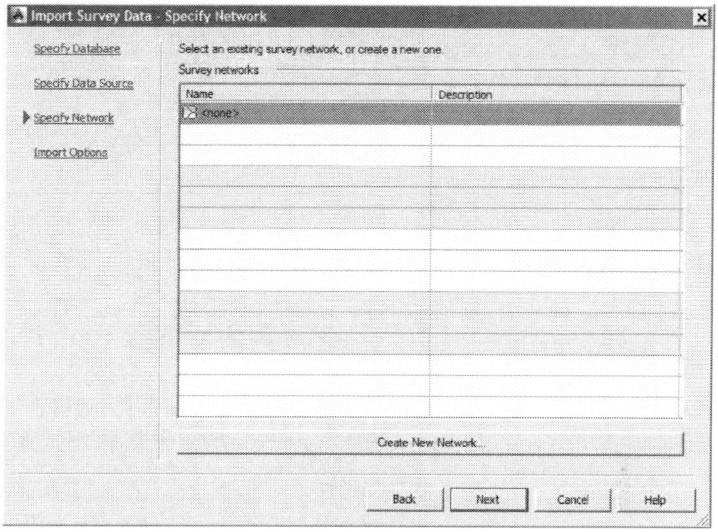

Figure 14–8

Click **Next**. The *Import Options* page (shown in Figure 14–9), sets the values for the import. These settings affect what the import does and which support files it uses.

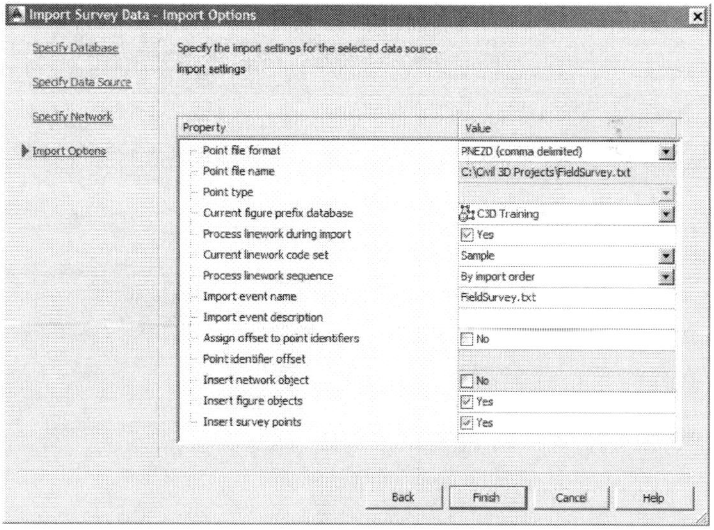

Figure 14–9

If the field book has figure coding from a conversion, you do not need to toggle on the *Process linework during import* property. This is for ASCII files other than field books that have ***Linework Code Set*** commands included in the point's description.

Inserting figures requires entries to be in the Figure Prefix database and figure styles to be in the drawing. This is required to point the figure and linework to the correct layers in the drawing and to specify whether the figure is also a breakline in a surface.

When inserting points, it is necessary to have a Description Key Set defined to assign points, point label styles, and layers, and to translate raw descriptions to full descriptions.

Open a Survey Database for Editing

Only one Survey Database can be edited at a time. When opened for editing, this prepares the survey for reading and writing.

There are options to set the path or location for the Survey Database project files, and for all of the settings. When you create a new Survey Database, a Windows folder is created with the same name. If you close a drawing with a survey open, the Survey Database closes automatically. You must start a new drawing and then open the required Survey Database. You can only have one Survey Database open at a time.

How To: Open a Survey Database

1. Expand the Survey Database branch.
2. Select the survey database that you want to open, right-click, and select **Open for edit** or **Open for read-only**, depending your requirements, as shown in Figure 14–10.

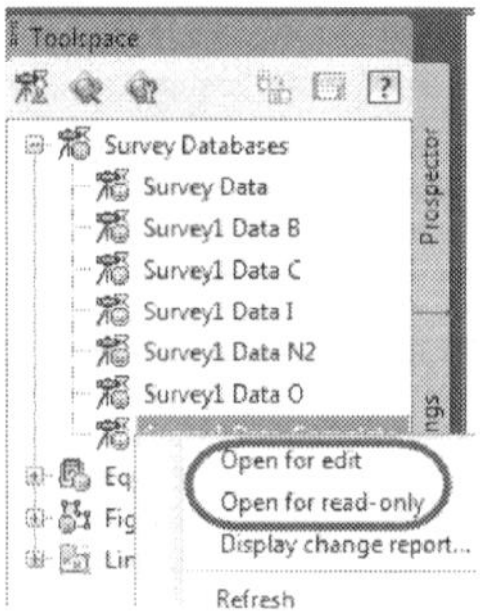

Figure 14–10

Practice 14a Creating a Description Key Set

Practice Objective

- Assign point symbols, labels, layers, etc., on importing by setting up Description Key Sets.

Estimated time for completion: 25 minutes

In this practice you will learn to create a new Description Key Set entry and apply it to an existing point. In addition you will update the Description Key Set to use parameters.

Task 1 - Create a new Description Key Set entry.

1. Continue working with the drawing from the previous practice, or open **SUV1-D1-Survey.dwg**.
2. In the Toolspace>*Settings* tab, expand the *Point* collection until the *Description Key Set* collection and its list are displayed.
3. Select **Civil 3D**, right-click, and select **Edit Keys...**
4. Right-click in any *Code* cell and select **New...**, as shown in Figure 14–11.

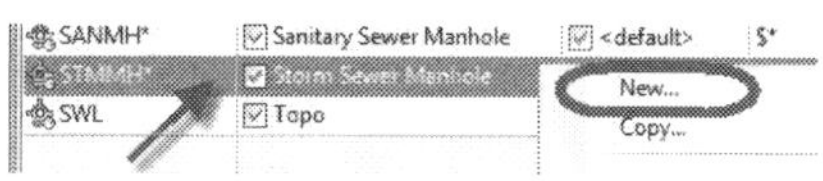

Figure 14–11

5. Double-click in the *Code* cell in the newly created row and type **HYD**, as shown in Figure 14–12.

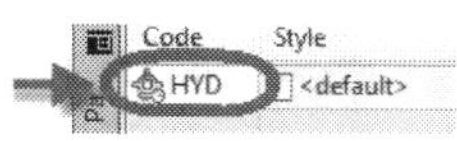

Figure 14–12

6. In the *Style* cell, toggle on the Point Style and select the **Style** cell to open the Point Style dialog box, as shown in Figure 14–13. Select **Hydrant (existing)** in the drop-down list and click **OK** to assign the style to the code.

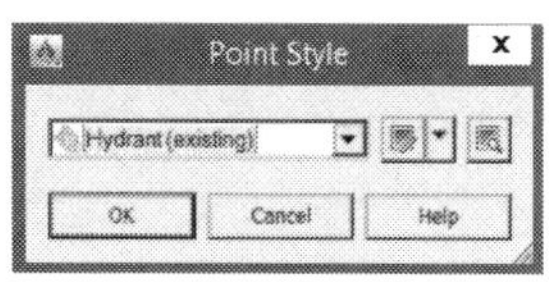

Figure 14–13

7. Leave **<default>** selected as the *Point Label Style* and **$*** as the *Format*. This means the label will be the same as the one entered by the surveyor.

8. Leave the check box toggled off in the *Layer* column.

You do not have a scale parameter and will not be using a fixed scale.

9. Select the **Yes** option in the *Use drawing scale* column, and clear the check box for the **Scale Parameter**, as shown in Figure 14–14.

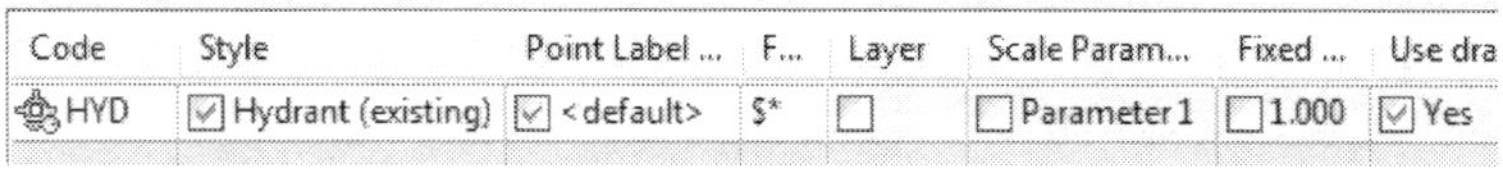

Figure 14–14

10. Close the DescKey Editor vista by clicking [icon] in the top right corner of the palette, as shown in Figure 14–15.

Figure 14–15

Task 2 - Apply the new Description Key Set to an existing point.

1. Continue working with the drawing from the previous task or open **SUV1-D2-Survey.dwg**.

2. Zoom in to the hydrant and note the changes to the hydrant symbol when you apply the updates. In the Transparent Command toolbar, click [icon] (Zoom to Point), type **260**.

3. In the *Prospector* tab, select the **_All Points** group, right-click, and select **Apply Description Keys**, as shown in Figure 14–16.

The point updates to display the Hydrant symbol and its new description

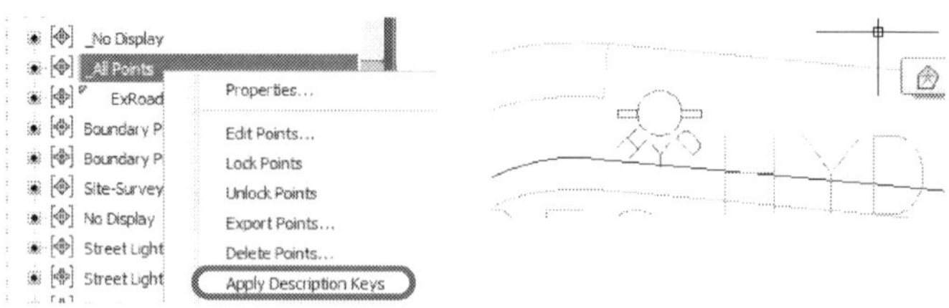

Figure 14–16

4. Save the drawing.

Task 3 - Update the Description Key Set to use parameters.

In this task you will use the Parameters feature to control the display properties of symbols in your drawings. The most common parameter is the **Scale** parameter. With this parameter, a surveyor will enter the size of a tree as part of the description and the description key file will insert a symbol scaled to the value provided by the surveyor. In this case, you want the pumpers on the hydrant to display correctly (i.e., running parallel to the road).

1. Continue working with the drawing from the previous task or open **SUV1-D3-Survey.dwg**

2. In the *Settings* tab, expand *Point>Description Key Sets*. Select **Civil 3D**, right-click, and select **Edit Keys...**, as shown in Figure 14–17.

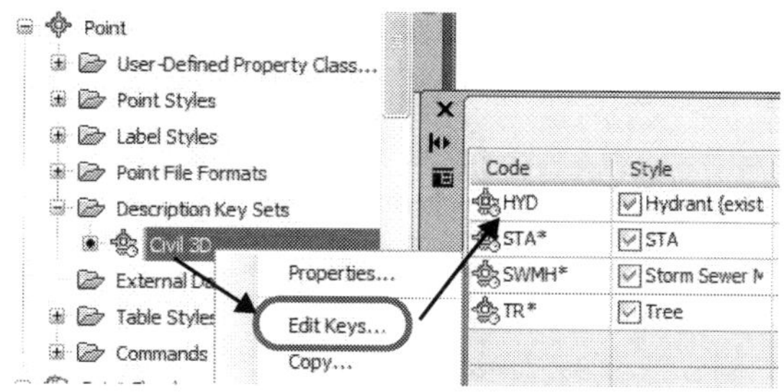

Figure 14–17

In this example, -5 is Parameter1, which you will enter in Step 6.

3. In the HYD row, *Code* column, type **HYD***. The asterisk symbolizes a wildcard, (i.e., any character after the letters HYD).

4. In the HYD row, select the check box in the *Marker Rotate* column, select the cell, and then select **Parameter1** in the drop-down list. The selected parameter is shown in Figure 14–18.

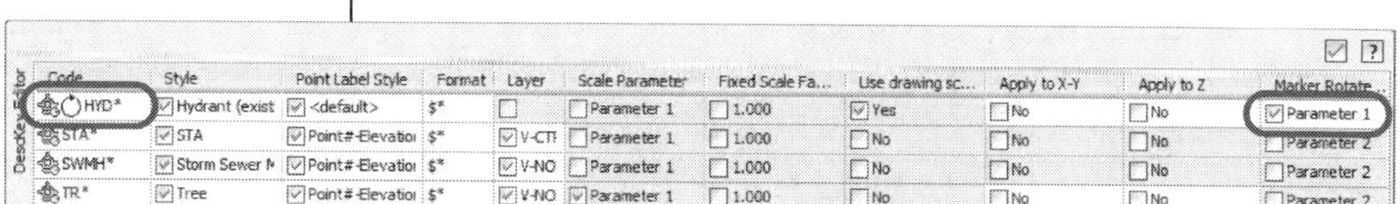

Figure 14–18

5. Click in the top right corner of the dialog box to close the Panorama view.

6. In Model Space, select the Hydrant point object, right-click, and select **Edit Points**.

The -5 indicates the required rotation.

7. Set the *Raw Description* from HYD to **HYD -5**.

8. Select the row, right-click, and select **Apply Description Keys**, as shown in Figure 14–19.

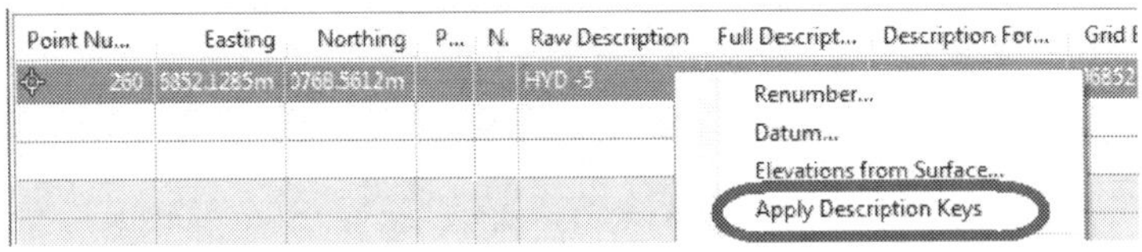

Figure 14–19

9. Click in the top right corner of the dialog box to close the Panorama view.

   The hydrant has now been rotated to display the hydrant pumpers following the rotation of the road, as shown in Figure 14–20.

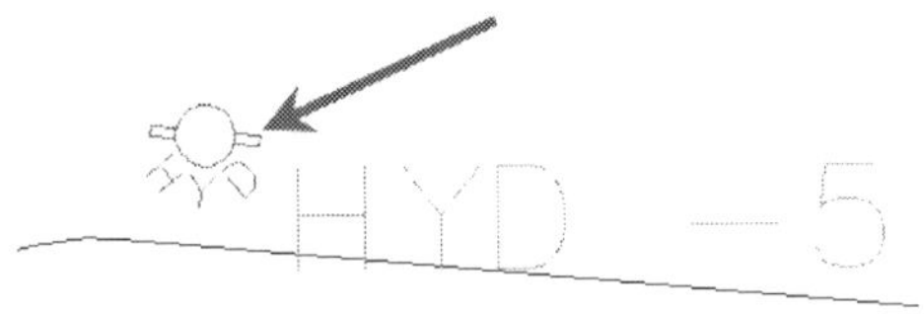

Figure 14–20

10. The label also displays the rotation angle text -5, which you do not want. In the *Settings* tab, expand the *Point* collection and expand the *Description Key Sets* collection. Select **Civil 3D**, right-click, and select **Edit Keys...**

11. In the HYD row, change the *Format* from $* to **Hydrant**, as shown in Figure 14–21.

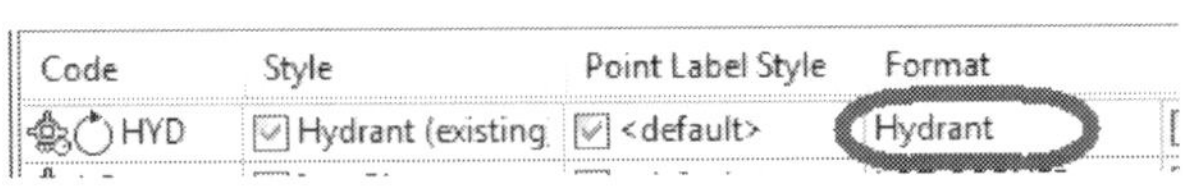

Figure 14–21

12. Click in the top right corner of the dialog box to close the Panorama view.

13. In Model Space, select the Hydrant point object, right-click, and select **Apply Description Keys**. The changes are now applied, as shown in Figure 14–22.

Figure 14–22

14. Save the drawing.

Practice 14b Creating Figure Prefixes

Practice Objective

- Create a figure database for automatically stylizing linework on importing field book or ASCII files.

Estimated time for completion: 5 minutes

1. Open **SUV1-A1-Survey.dwg**, from the *C:\Civil 3D Projects\Civil3D-Training\Survey* folder.

2. You might have to change the draw order of the image to be able to view other objects. In Model Space, select the image, right-click, expand Display Order, and select **Send to Back**.

3. In the Toolspace, select the *Survey* tab. Right-click on Figure Prefix Databases, and select **New...** Type **C3D Training** for the name.

4. Right-click on the newly created C3D Training Figure Prefix database, and select **Make Current**.

5. Right-click on the C3D Training Figure Prefix database again, and select **Manage Figure Prefix Database....**

6. Click to create a new Figure definition. The AutoCAD Civil 3D software creates a default Figure. Change the *Name* to **Trail**, and set the *Breakline* to **Yes** and the *Style* to **Road Centerline**, as shown in Figure 14–23. Any figure starting with **Trail** will now be selectable for a surface breakline and will use the style **Road Centerline**. As noted earlier, unlike the Description Key Set, an asterisk (*) is not necessary to match Trail1, Trail2, etc.

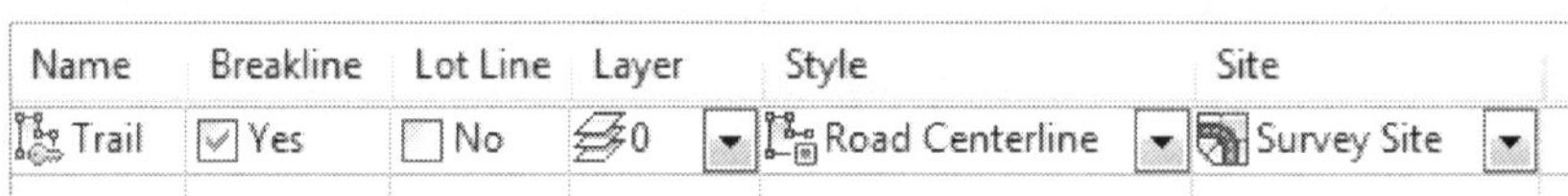

Figure 14–23

7. Click to create a new Figure definition. Change the name to **Building**, and set the *Breakline* to **No** and the *Style* to **Buildings**. Click **OK** to exit the dialog box.

8. Save the drawing.

Practice 14c Importing Survey Data

Practice Objective

- Import points from and export points to ASCII files created from the field survey.

Estimated time for completion: 25 minutes

In this practice you will import an ASCII file created in the field.

Task 1 - Import an ASCII file.

1. Continue working with the drawing from the previous practice or open **SUV1-E1-Survey.dwg** from the *C:\Civil 3D Projects\Civil3D-Training\Survey* folder.
2. In the *Home* tab>Create Ground Data panel, click (Import Survey Data).
3. On the Specify Database page, click **Create New Survey Database...**, as shown in Figure 14–24.

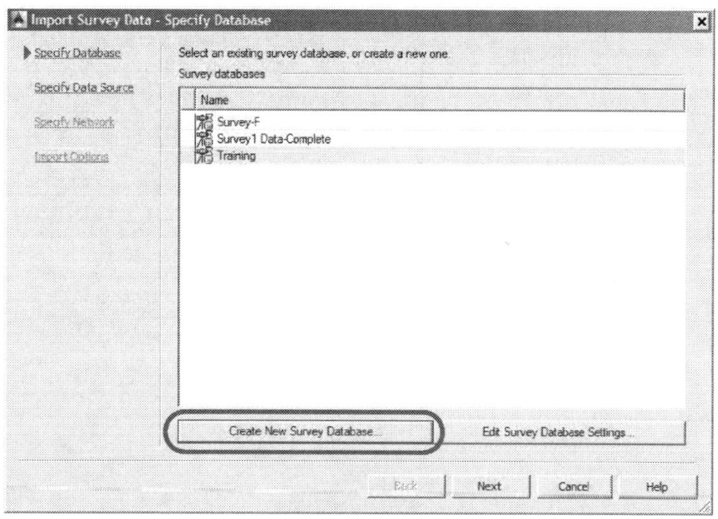

Figure 14–24

4. Type **Training** for the name and click **OK**.

5. Click **Edit Survey Database Settings...** as shown in Figure 14–25.

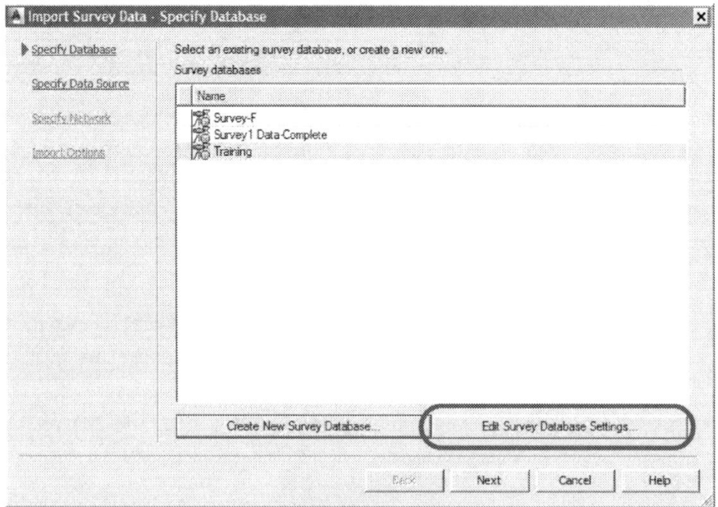

Figure 14–25

6. Under *Units* in the Survey Database Settings dialog box, for the *Coordinate Zone*, click the **Browse** icon. In the Select Coordinate Zone dialog box, select **NAD83 California State Planes, Zone VI, US Foot** (as shown in Figure 14–26). Click **OK** twice and then click **Next**.

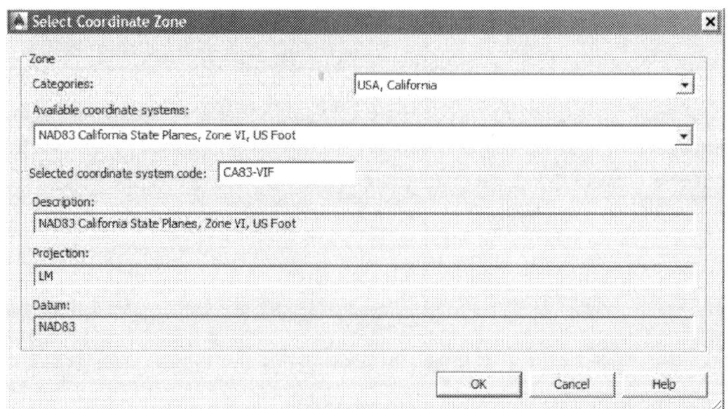

Figure 14–26

7. On the Specify Data Sources page, expand the Data source type drop-down list and select **Point File**, as shown in Figure 14–27. Click (Add file) and browse to *C:\Civil 3D Projects\Civil3D-Training\Survey*. Select **Field Survey.txt** and open it. Finally, for the file format, select **PNEZD (comma delimited)**. Click **Next**.

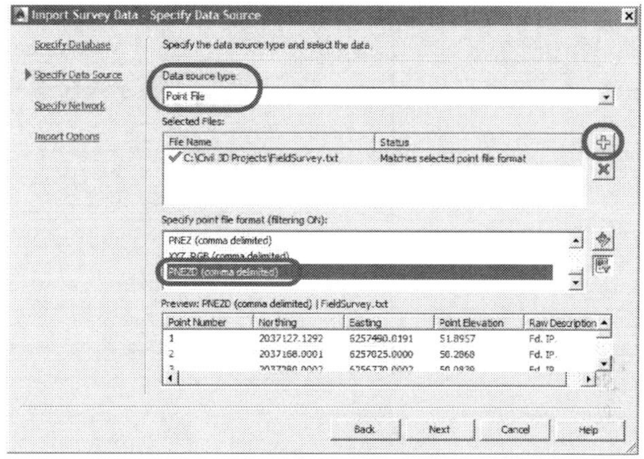

Figure 14–27

8. On the Survey Network page, click **Next**.

9. On the Import Options page, select **Process linework during import**, **Insert figure objects**, and **Insert survey points**, as shown in Figure 14–28. Click **Finish**.

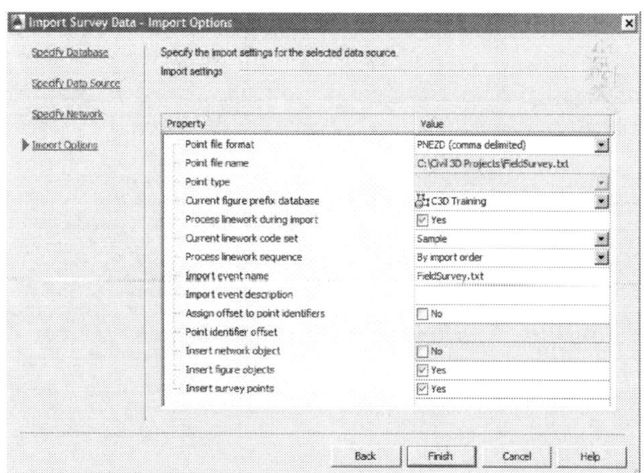

Figure 14–28

10. Save the drawing.

Appendix A

Review Questions

The following review questions are provided to help you to self-evaluate your understanding and retention of the topics presented in *AutoCAD® Civil® 3D 2016: Review for Certification*. They are not intended to represent the types of questions found in the AutoCAD Civil 3D 2016 Certified Professional exam.

Answers are provided at the end of each topic.

Styles

1. Which tab in the Point Label Style Composer dialog box controls the appearance of a point label when the point label grip is selected in the drawing and moved away from the point itself?
   a. *General* tab
   b. *Layout* tab
   c. *Dragged State* tab
   d. *Summary* tab
2. Styles cannot be shared between drawing files.
   a. True
   b. False
3. Where do you set the layer for various components of object styles?
   a. The *Information* tab.
   b. The *Summery* tab.
   c. The *Display* tab.
   d. The *Layer* tab.

Answers: 1c, 2b, 3c

Lines and Curves

1. How do you draw a parcel boundary from a legal description in the most efficient way possible?
   a. Calculate the Cartesian coordinate angle for each bearing or azimuth within the legal description and type (distance)<(angle) for each line or curve.
   b. Calculate the cartesian coordinate angle for each bearing or azimuth within the legal description, place your cursor in that direction, and type the distance.
   c. Use the extended **Lines** and **Curves** options in the *Home* tab>Draw panel or **Transparent** commands in the **Line** or **Polyline** command.
   d. There is no fast way to do this.

2. Which Lines and Curves options would you use to create a curve if you are starting from an existing curve and have been given the chord or curve that goes in the opposite direction to the last curve?
   a. **Create Reverse or Compound Curve**
   b. **Create Multiple Curves**
   c. **Create Curve from End of Object**
   d. **Curve Calculator**
3. Which transparent command would you use to create a line when you know the distance and direction of the line (given as a bearing)?
   a. **Angle Distance**
   b. **Azimuth Distance**
   c. **Direction Distance**
   d. **Bearing Distance**

Answers: 1c, 2a, 3d

Points

1. If you need linework, which method should you use to import survey data?
   a. Import survey data using the Survey Database.
   b. Import survey data using the **Import Points** command.
   c. Import survey data using the Map Explorer.
   d. Create points using the *Prospector* tab in the Toolspace.
2. How do you control the next point number to be used in a drawing?
   a. The **Point Identity** parameters located in the expanded area in the Create Points toolbar.
   b. Under Label Styles in the *Settings* tab in the Toolspace.
   c. In the *Survey* tab, right-click on Survey Points.
   d. In the *Prospector* tab, right-click on Survey Points.
3. Can the _**All Points** point group be deleted?
   a. Yes
   b. No

4. Can a point group be made out of point groups?
    a. Yes
    b. No

Answers: 1a, 2a, 3b, 4a

Surfaces

1. Put the following steps in the order suggested for building a surface...
    a. Add Breaklines, assign more data, modify the data, or edit the surface as needed.
    b. Assign data to a surface.
    c. Accumulate data.
    d. Evaluate the resulting surface.
2. What controls how an AutoCAD Civil 3D surface displays (whether it displays contours, TIN lines, or an analysis)?
    a. Surface Style
    b. Surface Definition
    c. AutoCAD Layers
    d. Surface Boundary
3. Where would you set the lowest and highest acceptable elevations for a surface?
    a. In the Create Surface dialog box when you are first creating the surface.
    b. In the *Definition* tab in the Surface Properties dialog box.
    c. In the *Analysis* tab in the Surface Properties dialog box.
    d. Under Edits within the surface definition.
4. Select which type of breakline this statement defines: *This type of breakline is a 3D polyline or Feature Line. It does not need a point object at each vertex because each has its own elevation.*
    a. Non-Destructive
    b. Proximity
    c. Wall
    d. Standard

5. What are the types of edits that can be done to a surface? (Select all that apply.)
    a. Line Edits
    b. Point Edits
    c. Simplify Surface
    d. Grip Edit
6. How do you remove an edit from a surface? (Select all that apply.)
    a. Clear it in the Operations Type list in the Surface Properties in the *Definition* tab.
    b. Remove it from the Edits list in the Prospector's Preview.
    c. Select it and press <Delete>.
    d. Delete it from the Operations Type list of the Surface Properties in the *Definition* tab.
7. Which type of boundary can be added before anything else without being ignored if you add information later, which falls outside of the boundary?
    a. Hide
    b. Show
    c. Data Clip
    d. Outer
8. Which of the following is not a surface label that is available out of the box in the AutoCAD Civil 3D software?
    a. Contour Labels
    b. Spot Elevation Labels
    c. Slope Labels
    d. Cut/Fill Labels
9. How do you calculate the volume between two surfaces within a specific parcel?
    a. Bounded Volumes
    b. Grid Volume Surface
    c. TIN Volume Surface
    d. Show Cut/Fill Labels in a grid pattern

10. Which of the following is not a surface analysis that you can run within the AutoCAD Civil 3D software?
    a. Slope Analysis
    b. Visibility Check
    c. Runoff Coefficient Analysis
    d. Water Drop

Answers: 1c,b,d,a, 2a, 3b, 4d, 5a,b,c, 6a,b, 7c, 8d, 9a, 10c

Parcels

1. Where are parcels listed?
    a. Under the Survey tree in the *Prospector* tab.
    b. In a site under the Sites tree in the *Prospector* tab.
    c. Under the Figures Tree inside the Survey Database.
    d. In the Layers panel in the *Home* tab.
2. What does a parcel style assign in the *Display* tab?
    a. Layer to which parcel segments are assigned.
    b. How big the parcel can be.
    c. The label text that describes the line segments.
    d. The label text that describes the area and name of the parcel.
3. What is the default direction of a Mapcheck or Inverse report?
    a. Clockwise
    b. Counter-clockwise
    c. Always starts going north.
    d. Always starts going south.
4. How do you adjust parcel display order?
    a. Select the parcel segments, right-click and select **Draw Order**.
    b. Move the parcel up or down in the parcel preview list in the *Prospector* tab.
    c. Select the parcel area label, right-click and select **Draw Order**.
    d. Under Sites, right-click on Parcels and select **Properties**.

5. How do you draw a parcel boundary from a legal description in the most efficient way possible?
   a. Calculate the Cartesian coordinate angle for each bearing or azimuth within the legal description and type (distance)<(angle) for each line or curve.
   b. Calculate the cartesian coordinate angle for each bearing or azimuth within the legal description, place your cursor in that direction, and type the distance.
   c. Use the extended **Lines** and **Curves** options in the *Home* tab>Draw panel or **Transparent** commands in the **Line** or **Polyline** command.
   d. There is no fast way to do this.

6. How do you create or subdivide parcels interactively?
   a. Draw parcel segments at each location in which you want a parcel line.
   b. **Create** and **Edit** tools in the Parcel Layout toolbar.
   c. Select the parcel, right-click and select **Subdivide**.
   d. Used the AutoCAD **Measure** or **Divide** commands to help place lot lines and even intervals.

7. Which **Parcel Create** command enables you to hold a specified angle relative to the Right-Of-Way?
   a. Slide line-create
   b. Swing line-create
   c. Free Form create
   d. Use the **Add fixed line** command.

8. What are the types of AutoCAD Civil 3D Parcel labels that can be set up in the *Setting* tab? (Select all that apply.)
   a. Parcel Line
   b. Parcel Area
   c. Parcel Curve
   d. Parcel Perimeter

9. What does the Add Labels dialog box do?
   a. Creates label styles.
   b. Add or change labels interactively after parcel creation.
   c. Add or change labels during parcel creation.
   d. Creates static text describing what you want to label.

10. What are parcel tables an alternative to? (Select all that apply.)
    a. Drawing the parcels.
    b. Creating tags.
    c. Labeling parcel areas in an already crowded drawing.
    d. Labeling parcel segments in an already crowded drawing.

Answers: 1b, 2a, 3a, 4d, 5c, 6b, 7a, 8a,b,c, 9b, 10c,d

Alignments

1. When can an alignment subdivide parcels?
    a. When it is a design style.
    b. When the parcels are ROW parcels.
    c. When they are in the same drawing file.
    d. When they are in the same site.
2. How do you open the Alignment Layout toolbar for an existing alignment?
    a. Select the alignment in the drawing.
    b. Right-click on Alignments in the *Prospector* tab in Toolspace.
    c. In the *Home* tab>Create Design panel, select **Edit Alignments**.
    d. Select **Alignments** in the *Prospector* tab in Toolspace.
3. How do you select an individual alignment Station label for deletion?
    a. Click on it.
    b. Right-click on it.
    c. Hold <Ctrl> as you select it.
    d. Hold <Shift> as you select it.
4. To change minor stations in the alignment from 50 feet to 25 feet...
    a. Change the settings in the alignment.
    b. Change the minor increment in the label set to 25 feet.
    c. Change the station style.
    d. Change the alignment label style.

5. The Alignment Style controls the color of the major and minor tics.

   a. True

   b. False

Answers: 1d, 2a, 3c, 4b, 5b

Profiles & Profile Views

1. You can safely relocate profile views in the AutoCAD Civil 3D software using the AutoCAD **Move** command.

   a. True

   b. False

2. Which of the following is not a vertical curve option in the AutoCAD Civil 3D software?

   a. Circular

   b. Parabolic

   c. Spiral

   d. Asymmetric Parabolic

3. Which grip do you use to move the PVI to a new station and elevation at the same time?

   a. 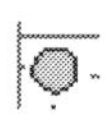 Circular

   b.  Center Triangle

   c.  Sideways Triangle

   d. 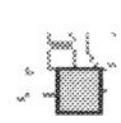 Square

4. What do Profiles 1 and 2 annotate in profile bands?

   a. Profile elevations of two different profiles from the same alignment.

   b. Alignment stations.

   c. Tangent Slopes.

   d. Vertical curve lengths.

5. Which of the following **Transparent** command tools helps you to design a finished ground profile?

   a. 

   b. 

   c. 

   d. 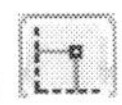

Answers: 1a, 2c, 3b, 4a, 5d

Corridors

1. Where would you find subassemblies to attach to an assembly?
   a. Tool Palettes
   b. *Home* tab>Create Design panel
   c. *Modify* tab>Design panel
   d. *Insert* tab>Block panel
2. How do you change the width of a lane within the corridor model? (Select all that apply.)
   a. Advanced Properties
   b. Assembly Properties
   c. Subassembly Properties
   d. Corridor Properties
3. Which of the following items must you have before you can create a corridor model? (Select all that apply.)
   a. Assembly
   b. Profile
   c. Survey Database
   d. Alignment
4. Which tab in the Create Intersection Wizard do you use to set the Curb Return Parameters?
   a. General
   b. Corridor Regions
   c. Geometry Details

5. Where would you go to create a surface representing the finished ground of a corridor model?
    a. *Prospector* tab in the Toolspace>Surfaces tree.
    b. *Home* tab>Create Ground Data panel.
    c. *Home* tab>Create Design panel.
    d. Corridor Properties
6. What does the Corridor Section Editor enable you to do?
    a. Review and edit each parameter of a subassembly.
    b. Adjust the existing ground grade at a specific station.
    c. Change the assembly being used at a specific station.
    d. Change the grid displayed behind a cross-section.

Answers: 1a, 2a,b,c, 3a,b,d, 4c, 5d, 6a

Sections and Section Views

1. What are sample line groups?
    a. Objects that sample corridor elements for cross-sections.
    b. Groups of lines where the surveyor sampled the soil.
    c. Lines connecting corridor points.
    d. Groups of lines that connect corridor shapes.
2. What does the Create Section View dialog box do?
    a. Creates a model space viewport for viewing sections.
    b. Creates grid(s) with a cross-section and labeling of a corridor model inside it at specified stations.
    c. Creates a paper space viewport for viewing sections.
    d. Nothing, there is no such thing.
3. Which of these tools enable you to compute the volume of a corridor material?
    a. 
    b. 
    c. 
    d. 

Answers: 1a, 2b, 3b

Pipe Networks

1. What does the **Swap Part** command do? (Select all that apply.)
   a. Make a pipe a structure.
   b. Make a structure a pipe.
   c. Change a pipe for another pipe of another size or material.
   d. Change a structure for another structure type or size.
2. What type of structure CANNOT be used in a regular pipe network?
   a. Headwall
   b. Manhole
   c. Gate Valve
   d. Catch Basin
3. Pressure pipe networks can contain all of the following except...
   a. Manhole
   b. Appurtenances
   c. Pipes
   d. Fittings
4. To draw pipes and structures in a profile view you need to...
   a. Manually draw each pipe and structure with the profile creation tools.
   b. Click **Draw Parts in Profile View** on the Network Layout Tools toolbar.
   c. Select the profile view, right-click, and select **Draw Parts from Pipe Network**.
   d. Select the pipes and structures in the plan view, click **Draw in Profile View** on the *Pipe Network* contextual tab, and select the profile view in which you want to draw.
5. Pipe Networks can be created from feature lines.
   a. True
   b. False

Answers: 1c,d, 2c, 3a, 4d, 5a

Grading

1. When creating a feature line from objects, which of the following cannot be used to create a feature line?
   a. Lines or arcs
   b. Circles
   c. Polylines or 3D polylines
   d. XREF

2. How do you ensure that you do not create a hole in the middle of your surface when using grading objects to create the finished ground contours?
   a. Grade to the inside.
   b. You cannot prevent holes in grading group surfaces.
   c. Create infill.
   d. Balance the Volumes.

3. What is the best method of editing a grading object without needing to go through each prompt?
   a. Grading Editor
   b. Edit Grading
   c. Delete the grading object and recreate it.
   d. Grip edit the resulting feature lines.

4. The grading object and the feature line have to be in the same site to be able to work together.
   a. True
   b. False

5. In the Grading Elevation Editor you can edit...
   a. Grading objects
   b. Finish Ground Profiles
   c. Pipe Structures
   d. Feature Lines

Answers: 1b, 2c, 3a, 4a, 5d

Managing and Sharing Data

1. In the AutoCAD Civil 3D workflow, what are the two main methods of project collaboration (or the sharing of intelligent AutoCAD Civil 3D design data)?
   a. Windows Explorer and X-refs.
   b. Data shortcuts and Vault references.
   c. X-refs and Data shortcuts.
   d. Vault references and X-refs.
2. Why would you want to use Vault references over Data Shortcuts?
   a. Added security and version control.
   b. Permit more people to have access.
   c. It works more like Land Desktop.
   d. It works better with multiple offices.
3. When sharing data in a project collaboration environment, what is the recommended number of levels into which the data should be broken?
   a. 1 level
   b. 2 levels
   c. 3 levels
   d. 4 levels
4. How can you edit an object referenced through Data Shortcuts?
   a. Open the source drawing.
   b. With grips.
   c. Using the Panorama view.
   d. You cannot.
5. What is the file format that Data Shortcuts use to share design data between drawing files?
   a. .SHP
   b. .DWT
   c. .DWG
   d. .XML

Answers: 1b, 2a, 3c, 4a, 5d

Plan Production

1. What are two of the steps needed to create plan and profile sheets using the Plan Production tools?
   a. Create layouts.
   b. Create View Frames.
   c. Create new drawings with references to data.
   d. Generate Sheets.
2. How can you integrate AutoCAD Civil 3D's Plan Production system layouts into an existing sheet set?
   a. When generating the sheets, select the option to **Add to existing sheet set** on the Sheet Set page in the Create Sheets wizard.
   b. Open the sheet set and manually import the sheets and views one by one.
   c. It is not possible, you have to have a separate sheet set for each alignment and profile.
   d. When generating the view frames, select the option to **Add to the existing sheet set** in the Sheets page.
3. How is the scale of the plan and profile sheet determined?
   a. Using the **Annotation Scale** tool in the Status Bar.
   b. Using the scale in the *Graph* tab in the Profile View Style dialog box.
   c. Using the template and layout selected during the View Frame creation process.
   d. Select the *Setting* tab, right-click on the current drawing, expand Edit Drawing Settings, and select the *Units and Zones* tab.
4. How do you ensure that the project name and number display on every sheet automatically?
   a. This cannot be automated.
   b. Set up the sheet template with project name and number fields, and then set the project name and number in the **Sheet Set Manager>Sheet Set Properties**.
   c. Set up the sheet template with project name and number fields, and then set the project name and number during the View Frame Creation process.
   d. When generating the sheets, select the option to add the project name and number to the sheets.

5. After creating the plan and profile sheets you can easily create additional sheets using the Sheet Set Manager.
   a. True
   b. False

Answers: 1b,d, 2a, 3c, 4b, 5a

Survey

1. If you need to analyze the field data using the analysis tools available in the Survey Database, you must use a field book file rather than a text file.
   a. True
   b. False
2. Which of these is not a function of a survey figure in the AutoCAD Civil 3D software?
   a. Automate linework creation from survey data.
   b. Make creating view frames easier.
   c. Make creating breaklines for a surface easier.
   d. Make creating parcel boundaries from survey data easier.
3. Which of these is NOT an option to define a survey figure?
   a. Import survey data using the Survey Database.
   b. In the *Survey* tab, right-click on Figures and select **Create figure from objects**.
   c. In the *Survey* tab, right-click on Figures and select **Create figure interactively**.
   d. In the Point Creation Tools toolbar, select the option to process linework to ensure that figures are created as you create points.

Answers: 1a, 2b, 3d

Index